Changing the Questions

Changing the Questions

Explorations in Christian Ethics

Margaret A. Farley

Edited and with an Introduction by Jamie L. Manson

ORBIS BOOKS
Maryknoll, New York 10545

Founded in 1970, Orbis Books endeavors to publish works that enlighten the mind, nourish the spirit, and challenge the conscience. The publishing arm of the Maryknoll Fathers and Brothers, Orbis seeks to explore the global dimensions of the Christian faith and mission, to invite dialogue with diverse cultures and religious traditions, and to serve the cause of reconciliation and peace. The books published reflect the views of their authors and do not represent the official position of the Maryknoll Society. To learn more about Maryknoll and Orbis Books, please visit our website at www.maryknollsociety.org.

Library of Congress Cataloging-in-Publication Data

Farley, Margaret A.
  [Essays. Selections]
  Changing the questions : explorations in Christian ethics / Margaret A. Farley.
    pages cm
  Includes bibliographical references and index.
  ISBN 978-1-62698-128-7
  1. Christian ethics. I. Title.
BJ1191.F37 2015
241—dc23
                                                                2014036912

To James M. Gustafson
Scholar, Ecumenist, Teacher, Colleague, Friend

Contents

Introduction

Jamie L. Manson

Margaret Farley's scholarship in the fields of bioethics, commitment, and sexual ethics has been well-established in academic circles for decades. One of today's most prominent Christian ethicists, Farley spent four decades as a professor of ethics at Yale University Divinity School, earning numerous accolades, including the John Courtney Murray Award for Excellence in Theology (1992), a Henry Luce III Fellowship in Theology (1996–97), and a U.S. Department of State Foreign Service Institute Award (2002) as well as over a dozen honorary doctorates.

Her 2006 book, *Just Love: A Framework for Christian Sexual Ethics*, earned her the prestigious 2008 Grawemeyer Award in religion for its clear and compelling framework for understanding what makes sexual and loving relationships just, and for guiding readers in understanding sexual ethics in the context of the Christian tradition. But *Just Love* would receive more worldwide attention after it was subjected to criticism from the Vatican's Congregation for the Doctrine of the Faith in June 2012. The episode brought Farley's work to an even broader audience and led to a demand for a revised version of her groundbreaking 1986 book, *Personal Commitments*.

For all of the impact that Farley's major works have made both in the academy and the church, the breadth of topics on which she has written remains relatively unknown to a wider readership. Many of her more than one hundred essays have appeared in journals or edited volumes with a limited circulation, and some of her most compelling lectures and sermons on ecclesiology, ethics, and spirituality have never been published.

The essays included in this collection offer fresh insight into Farley's exploration of major themes in theological ethics, such as freedom of choice, relationality, mutuality, respect for persons, love, hope, and justice. But this book also offers a portrait of Margaret Farley's distinct contributions to ethics not only as an academic discipline but as a moral and spiritual practice. Many of these works were also chosen to allow readers to appreciate the way in which Farley's core ideas, often expressed in original phrases such as "crucified love," "the cup of suffering," "the relaxation of heart," and "the discipline of nonfulfillment," have been interwoven not only in her writings on spirituality but also in her approach to theological ethics and moral discernment.

As readers encounter the richness of ideas behind these phrases, they may discover that, while her fundamental understandings of autonomy, relationality, respect, and freedom form the bedrock of Farley's ethical thinking, her concern for the practice of mercy continually grounds her approach to moral decision-making. This should be no surprise to those who know that Farley has been a member of the Sisters of Mercy for over fifty years. Founded in 1831 by Catherine McAuley, the order bases its charism on *misericordia*, a Latin term meaning "a suffering heart." For nearly two centuries, Mercy sisters have focused their work on responding to unmet needs, through both direct service and advocating for the change of unjust systems. Though Farley offers her fullest treatment of mercy in her 2002 book, *Compassionate Respect*, where she proposes an ethic of care that arises out of feminist ethics, women's experience, and the contributions of religious ethics, readers of this volume will surely notice the theme of *misericordia*, whether spoken or unspoken, evoked throughout these pages.

During the process of choosing the selections for this collection, a major goal has been to introduce a new generation of scholars as well as a general audience to Farley's work on issues that include ethical methodology, the contemporary church, feminism, death and dying, and new questions in the broader fields of bioethics. The selections are also intended to show the way in which Farley has applied her fundamental ideas to a spectrum of issues ranging from ecumenical intercommunion to divorce and remarriage, feminist theory and the HIV/AIDS pandemic, forgiveness, and the environment. The criteria for selection, of course, resulted in some overlapping of themes among the essays. These recurrences have not been removed, because ultimately they offer insight into the direction of her thought.

This book's title, *Changing the Questions*, emerged during the process of surveying essays for consideration in the collection. The phrase aptly captures Farley's approach to ethical inquiries throughout her scholarly career. As readers of this volume will come to realize, Farley's first response to any ethical challenge is to consider whether the right questions are being asked or whether the questions themselves have to change.

Readers will note in Farley's scholarly essays a rigorous academic who organizes her articles systematically to build her arguments with precision and clarity—and always with consideration for counterarguments. She takes pains to recount the history of a particular issue, often stretching back into early Christian and medieval thinkers like Augustine and Thomas Aquinas to establish the ground on which her own argument will be built.

Other essays exhibit Farley's distinct contribution as a moral philosopher, as she guides readers through some of the most complex and innovative theorists in the feminist and postmodern movements. Readers familiar with Farley's scholarship and those encountering her for the first time will undoubtedly recognize the spiritual dimension within some of her prose, particularly in her sermons. In these pieces, she not only uses her gift for homiletics to change the questions about the passion, death, and resurrection of Jesus, she does so with an emotional force and theological depth that will likely move even the closest readers of her academic work.

The works collected in this volume span over forty years, beginning with her first widely distributed scholarly article, "New Patterns of Relationship: Beginnings of a Moral Revolution," written in 1975 for the journal *Theological Studies*. Here Farley introduces themes in relationality and autonomy that will continue to be developed and refined over the course of her scholarship, particularly in "A Feminist Version of Respect for Persons," which appears later in this volume.

In "New Patterns of Relationship," she offers a theological and ethical case for why patterns of relationship, self-understanding, and gender roles ought to change. Readers will note her early application of the phrase "just love," in regard to the fundamental personal rights of women, women's rights to equal opportunity, and the relationship between men and women. At a time when the discussion of the ordination of women in the Catholic Church was nascent, Farley argued that hierarchical patterns of relationship are unjust "not only because they violate the reality of individual persons but because they inhibit or undermine the common good."

A second early piece, "Fragments for an Ethic of Commitment in Thomas Aquinas," also anticipates major developments in Farley's thought on the ethics of commitment, love, and free choice. The essay demonstrates her Aquinas scholarship and the ways in which she has used his work in her own thinking. As her generations of students will remember, one of Farley's most influential courses at Yale was a comparative study of the moral perspectives of Augustine, Aquinas, Martin Luther, and John Calvin. This essay exhibits Farley's method of employing the insights of a theologian from history to explore contemporary ethical issues.

This article is significant not only for the ideas she presents but for the context in which she originally presented them. Though published in 1978, the article is based on a paper Farley gave in the fall of 1974 at a conference in Chicago celebrating the medieval heritage, cosponsored by the University of Chicago, the Catholic Theological Union, and the Jesuit School of Theology in Chicago. Participants included some of the most distinguished theologians of the twentieth century: Karl Rahner, Paul Ricoeur, Bernard Lonergan, and Dom Hélder Câmara, among others. Farley was not only the most junior academic to be invited to present, she was also the only woman.

Farley has been as engaged in contemporary intellectual contexts as she has been with historical and ecclesiological ones. Two essays in particular showcase her treatment of literature beyond the theological field. In "Feminism and Universal Morality" (1993), she enters the broad (and largely secular) philosophical conversation on whether the construction of moral norms is beneficial to the feminist movement. Farley, writing as a moral philosopher, offers a map through the dense literature surrounding this issue, particularly the work of Alison Jaggar and Carol Gilligan. Although feminist theory has advanced beyond some of these considerations, these writings nonetheless offer an invaluable foundation to new generations of students who tend to be less familiar with some of the classical configurations of feminist theory. (Farley's own definition of feminism is best articulated in her later piece "Feminism and Hope" [2003], which is also included in this collection.)

Farley concludes "Feminism and Universal Morality" by offering two proposals. Using the pattern of autonomy and relationality that grounds both *Personal Commitments* and her *Just Love* framework, she suggests that feminist moral theory requires respect for the human capacity for both self-determination and relationship. Throughout history, women have learned that an emphasis on relationship without respect for autonomy can be as destructive as an emphasis on autonomy without affirmation of relationship.

In her second proposal, Farley questions Gilligan's argument that there are two gender-specific approaches to moral questions: the male ethic of "justice" and the female ethic of "care." Farley suggests that in the realm of moral decision-making, there is not an inevitable dichotomy between reason and care or justice and emotion. Rather, all human choices involve reason and emotions. In a passage that seems to herald *Just Love* (which would appear more than a dozen years later), Farley reminds readers that, in the most general sense, justice "means giving to each her or his 'due.' " The real problem for our moral lives, she writes, "is how to evaluate our care, our love, our relationships: according to what norms is care helpful and not harmful? The problem, one might say, is whether and how caring may be just."

Farley offers a similar road map through the complex terrain of postmodern thinking in "How Shall We Love in a Postmodern World?" (1994). Written at a time when issues related to postmodernity were affecting many disciplines in universities and public intellectual life, she transcends traditional boundaries of theological and philosophical ethics to discuss the themes of love and experience in a distinct intellectual context. Beginning her address with three stories—from film, art, and the personal narrative of an indigenous Venezuelan woman—she reminds readers that, even in a postmodern milieu, "questions of love ought not be abstracted from real persons who love and are loved, who are not loved and do not love, whose love is shaped by the groups to which they belong, who cry out sometimes across the centuries against the expectations of duty and love."

In using these three images to ground her argument, Farley illustrates that ethics must always pay attention to the concrete lives of individuals and groups, while also showing the value of nontraditional philosophical and theological sources to ethics. This essay and "Feminism and Universal Morality" demonstrate that Farley is far from a rigidly circumscribed moral theologian who only works within the literature and framework of that field.

Farley's insistence on the use of concrete human experience in examining questions of morality is perhaps best formulated in "The Role of Experience in Moral Discernment" (1996). Here she justifies the place of actual lived experience among the classic sources for Christian ethics, such as scripture, tradition, the physical and social sciences, and literature.

More importantly, she explores our understanding of authority itself, insisting that the authoritative quality of any source "is contingent on the 'truth' it offers and the 'justice' of its aims." Sources for ethical decision-making must give access to moral insight and motivation. In cases where one's experience seems to contradict other sources, that experience must be tested. If the experience continues to hold true, Farley explains, "to deny it would do violence to our very capacity for knowing." In such cases, experience can become a "hermeneutical key" that may allow traditional sources to be interpreted anew. Farley's justification of the authority of human experience provides the basis for what would become her unique and major contributions to the ethics of love, commitment, and just sexual relationships.

The theme of authority is expanded upon in "Moral Discourse in the Public Arena" (1987), an essay Farley wrote as part of the volume *Vatican Authority and American Catholic Dissent: The Curran Case and Its Consequences*. The book's title, of course, refers to Roman Catholic priest and ethicist Charles E. Curran's public battle with the Catholic University of America over the issue of academic freedom. Curran was dismissed from CUA in the late 1980s for publishing articles that debated theological views on issues related to divorce, contraception, and same-sex relations.

Farley's contribution argues that the "silencing" of theologians is neither effective nor ethical as a way to deal with a diversity of views in matters of Christian morality. She considers the negative effect that silencing has on the moral development of the church and demonstrates the value of encouraging and sustaining moral discourse in the public arena.

In making her claim, she takes an approach that can be seen in various essays throughout this volume: finding room within the tradition on which to stake her argument. Despite the tendency to centralize all teaching authority in the hierarchy, Catholic teaching offers an understanding of the exercise of authority that affirms a teaching role for others in the church and provides grounds for multiple voices in a process of ongoing discernment.

Farley reminds readers that Roman Catholic moral thinking is not known for absolute allegiance to divine command theory, but rather for affirming the "ultimate intelligibility of reality and the moral imperatives that emerge from reality." The irony is that though the Catholic tradition has never denied a central role for human reason in making sense of the moral life, it has nonetheless pushed toward hierarchical authority as the ultimate source of each person's moral understanding. Farley notes that a tradition that takes these sorts of considerations into account seriously runs a grave risk of inconsistency when it shuts down diverse avenues for making sense of reality. If Catholicism is a faith that claims to want to advance the moral growth of its adherents, it becomes difficult for the hierarchy to justify closing off the human search for truth.

At stake in all of this is our understanding of the moral life, Farley says, and efforts to somehow protect the faithful from hearing more than one side of a moral argument is a "soft paternalism" that fails to respect the moral agency of persons. "The search of reason for truth cannot be satisfied by an encounter only with institutional power," she writes, later adding that truth should never be "seen as so fragile, it cannot be trusted in the battles with possible falsehood."

Farley further developed these ideas in a 2002 collection, *A Call to Fidelity: On the Moral Theology of Charles E. Curran*, in her essay "Ethics, Ecclesiology, and the Grace of Self-Doubt." She begins by noting ironically that though ecclesiology and ethics share a common context—the church—the two seldom, if ever, interact. She explains that part of the Catholic tradition involves the belief that the Holy Spirit guides our efforts to discern whether our actions are faithful to God's plan for creation. One of the least recognized gifts of the Spirit is what she calls "the grace of self-doubt." Though the term "self-doubt" may have negative connotations, such as undermining one's capacity for discernment or compromising one's will to take action, Farley suggests that a "graced self-doubt" exists, particularly important for those in positions of power.

"If the greatest temptation of religious persons is self-righteousness, the second greatest is the grasping for certitude—fighting self-doubt in ways that shut the mind and sometimes close the heart," she explains. The grace of self-doubt allows for "epistemic humility," a basic condition for both individual and communal moral discernment. It is a grace that recognizes the contingencies of moral knowledge when we move from the theoretical sphere to the concrete realities of life. It allows us to listen to the experience of others, take seriously moral reasoning that is different from our own, and rethink our own last word. "The voice of the church is muted," Farley maintains, when "it does not represent the wisdom of a genuine discerning church."

Though Farley approaches the grace of self-doubt theme in the Roman Catholic context, her insight can be carried far beyond it, offering guidance to any office—religious, secular, or otherwise—that assumes some form of moral authority.

Both "Moral Discourse in the Public Arena," and "Ethics, Ecclesiology, and the Grace of Self-Doubt" clearly demonstrate the importance of the Catholic tradition as a source and context for Farley's theological and moral thinking. Nevertheless, bear in mind that she spent most of her academic career at Yale Divinity School; she has always been a theologian working in an ecumenical context. Her ecumenical approach to ecclesial and pastoral concerns is perhaps best on display in her original essay "No One Goes Away Hungry from the Table of the Lord: Eucharistic Sharing in Ecumenical Contexts" (1998).

The question of shared communion was raised continually over the decades of Farley's teaching at Yale Divinity School, where dozens of Christian denominations are represented among the student body. Each Friday the community celebrated the Eucharist, with a different denomination leading the liturgy. Often the Catholic students longed to lead a Friday service, but because the Roman Catholic tradition is especially strict in its doctrine of who receives the Eucharist, their desire typically created controversy and demanded communal and ecumenical dialogue.

Farley composed this essay not only to argue for the practice of intercommunion in divinity school settings but also to provide some reasoning for eucharistic sharing in the contexts of intermarriage and second marriages after divorce. In the course of the essay, Farley never reduces the meaning of the table to the "lowest common denominator." She maintains her belief in the real presence of Jesus Christ in the transformed bread and wine, and reaffirms her understanding of the Eucharist as the sharing of the very life of God.

At no point does Farley presume to judge those who do not agree with her position. Instead, she writes, her essay has the deeper goal of showing "the need for prudence, faithfulness, courage, and liberty of spirit on the way to Christian unity." Churches and individual believers never benefit from acting out of "unexamined experiences of power or fear." Taking her usual approach of finding room within the tradition for her argument, she locates a window in the Second Vatican Council's Decree on Ecumenism, which recognized that "the gaining of needed grace sometimes recommends" common worship.

In the Catholic tradition and other Christian traditions, Farley explains, there is a longing for fuller being, fuller love, and greater unity. In our practices as individuals and communities we actualize the potential for these kinds of graces. Often our rituals and actions affirm that some unity among Christians is unfolding in the present, and that this unity has a future. Even if we are fed at one another's tables, we will nonetheless go away from God's table hungry because we live in the "already/not yet of unity, transformation, of fullness of Life." That kind of hunger is holy, Farley believes, and it is both nourished and intensified in participation in the Eucharist.

To fully appreciate Farley's original ideas of crucified love, the cup of suffering, the already/not yet, and the discipline of nonfulfillment, one must read her sermons. Included in this volume are four different sermons written on the themes of Holy Week. In "Weep for Yourselves and for Your Children" and "Dignity and Humiliation," Farley considers details in the stories leading up to Jesus' passion. In "Weep for Your Yourselves," Farley suggests that one way to understand the sorrow of the daughters of Jerusalem is to understand that the suffering and death of Jesus reach down not only to their children but throughout all the centuries and into the present generation.

She further develops this theme in "Dignity and Humiliation," where she contemplates the paradox of Jesus' honorable entry into Jerusalem on Palm Sunday and the humiliation of his death on Good Friday. Palm Sunday helps us interpret the crucifixion, she explains: "Out of utter tragedy will emerge final hope; in death will be shown the ultimate power of life." The glory of God transforms what might otherwise appear only humiliating in our own lives: "a crucified dignity that remains eternally dignity, and a dignified 'humiliation' that is finally not humiliating."

In "The Cup of Suffering and of Love" she asks what it might mean to "drink the cup" that Jesus drinks. She considers the kind of suffering of which Jesus spoke, naming it "affliction" in the sense that Simone Weil used the word: a suffering that is both physical and spiritual. Jesus asks us whether we can enter into life even unto affliction. The cup of which he speaks is the cup of the sufferings of all persons.

But the cup is also a cup of love and commitment—a sign that God, too, drinks of human suffering in order to transform it. It is a sign that the relationship between God and Jesus, and between God and human persons, holds. The cup, therefore, is also a cup of life and, as such, should move us to yearn for justice and to do the deeds of love.

Crucified love is present where relationships are genuinely and profoundly sustained. It isn't a love that is destructive or that violates human dignity, but rather a love that survives, lives, and ultimately is stronger than death. Crucified love maintains its strength because it participates in the love of God made incarnate in Jesus. It bears all burdens and holds human suffering for the sake of transformation. It is crucified but never destroyed.

Farley continues the theme of "love that is stronger than death" in "Easter Rejoicing and the Discipline of Nonfulfillment," which offers a meditation on the meaning of the resurrection: that God is *still* with us, present everywhere, groaning with all of creation for fuller life and glory. Though Jesus still drinks the cup of suffering of each of us, and calls us to drink the cup of the suffering of all creation, we are also invited to share in his joy. This joy requires a "relaxation of heart," Farley writes, using one of her signature phrases, which she defines as "a melting of the heart that in turn makes it possible to receive both the mercy and the joy of God as well as one another."

Farley also introduces the phrase "the discipline of nonfulfillment," which readers may recall from *Personal Commitments*. The discipline is a strategy of the heart for receiving joy in circumstances in which our lives and loves are in a state of "presence but not full presence, presence but also absence, fulfillment but not complete fulfillment, being at home but still on a journey." She finds the discipline of nonfulfillment most vividly portrayed in the narrative of John's Gospel where Mary Magdalene first recognizes the gardener near the empty tomb as the risen Christ. "Do not cling to me," Jesus tells her. Her grief is turned into joy, but paradoxically she must also accept that the cross remains, even in this joy, and her relationship with Jesus will continue in an "already but not yet" existence.

The discipline of nonfulfillment keeps our longing for what we do not have from undermining the joy that we do have. Just as crucified love is a love that is not destroyed, the discipline of nonfulfillment is a crucified joy that nourishes our share in the life of Jesus, keeps alive our yearnings for justice and peace, and sustains our passions and our ability to faithfully keep our promises.

Some of the richest applications of her major themes of the discipline of nonfulfillment, the cup of suffering, and crucified love are evident in Farley's work on HIV/AIDS and on celibacy. Though Farley has written frequently on sexual ethics, marriage, family, and divorce, she has only addressed the issue of celibacy once, in an essay in the 2006 volume *Sexuality and the U.S. Catholic Church*. In "Celibacy under the Sign of the Cross," she briefly recounts the history of celibacy and then turns to contemporary problems that burden its concept and practice.

Rather than using this piece to address mandatory celibacy for Roman Catholic priests and women religious, she instead explores celibacy as revelatory of the meaning of sexuality for the Christian community as well as the wider society. Despite some of the aberrations in the past, she explains, "Celibacy has always held the potential of challenging existing power relations, liberating individuals for the unexpected, breaking the bonds of gender stereotypes, and resisting the social construction of sexual meanings in any era."

Celibacy is a radical commitment in that it embraces the decision to leave all things for the sake of the reign of God, which often means living without "a place to lay one's head." The choice makes sense only for the sake of a desire to love God with one's whole being, and to love and to be in full solidarity with one's neighbor. Like all great loves, Farley says, these are in a profound sense "crucified loves." In each of these loves, "There is fulfillment and nonfulfillment, rejoicing and waiting, in the mystery of the already/not yet." The celibate vocation, therefore, only makes sense "under the sign of the cross" because the cross is not a symbol of death, but rather a sign of life and a relationship that holds.

In "Prophetic Discourse in a Time of AIDS" (2009), Farley offers an analysis of the traditional role of the prophet, starting from biblical times, and weighs the value of using the term "prophetic" to describe advocacy on behalf of those suffering because of the HIV/AIDS pandemic. Prophetic discourse arises in contexts of massive needs and radical injustice, and few people of the world qualify as well as those who have suffered disproportionately in sub-Saharan Africa. Though prophets are typically associated with calls for repentance and social criticism, they succeed only when they also energize and offer hope. Prophets are called to safeguard their hearers from the despair that can result once we recognize the direness of a situation. Therefore, they must also offer concrete actions for groups to undertake.

Farley herself has heeded this advice in her own work on the pandemic. In 2002 she and fellow Mercy Sister Eileen Hogan founded the All Africa Conference: Sister to Sister (AACSS) to facilitate mutual empowerment among women religious in African countries hardest hit by HIV/AIDS. Women bear a disproportionate burden in the pandemic, and women religious often find themselves caring for the sick and orphaned, often with little education or resources. Although Farley had been touched personally by AIDS, having lost a beloved nephew to the disease years earlier, she hadn't previously taken it on as a global issue. AACSS offers one concrete way for these women to be educated on issues of sexuality and break the silence and taboos that still surround the disease.

Most importantly, AACSS has offered African women religious a place to tell their stories. Prophetic discourse can begin simply in articulating the grief of a suffering people. When Jesus asks in the Gospels, "Can you drink the cup that I will drink?" the cup is the suffering of all persons. "But at the heart of the image," Farley writes, "are the sufferings that are the consequence of injustice—the sufferings that do not have to be, the sufferings that cry out for an end not in death, but change."

Because their suffering is suffering that does not have to be, these narratives must give rise to social criticism. Farley concludes this essay offering her own prophetic criticism of the patriarchal influences and the ongoing morality of taboos that have led to a rejection of some means of HIV and AIDS prevention. "The sexual sphere of human life must be governed not by taboos but by considerations of justice," she writes, arguing that justice in the sexual sphere is importantly like justice in social, political, or economic aspects of human life. People who have read *Just Love* will recognize Farley's framework for just sexual relationships in the final pages of this essay, which she uses in this context to demonstrate that words of hope and deeds of love will only be effective when they are shaped by an accurate understanding of the situation of the pandemic and the claims of justice.

Like the global anguish wrought by the HIV/AIDS pandemic, the ongoing affliction of our ecosystem is also a suffering that does not have to be. "Religious Meanings for Nature and Humanity" is based on a presentation Farley offered at a Yale conference that examined the supposed divide between faith and reason, and sought a means for developing an environmental ethic that would help confront both global environmental destruction and an impoverished spirituality. Participants were asked to respond to the question, "Can religious and spiritual identity contribute to an understanding of humanity?" True to the title of the present volume, Farley changed the question, asking instead whether we can have religious beliefs that are relevant to our understanding of nature and humanity, and furthermore, whether spiritual practices emerge from or expand such beliefs?

She proceeds to offer a framework both for analysis and for constructive response to the crucial issue of ecological justice. Offering three critiques of Christianity's understanding of humanity, the natural world, and God, Farley demonstrates the ways in which some traditional beliefs (for example, in a distant God; a hierarchically ordered, static world; and a humanity ordained to master and subdue the earth) have contributed to our environmental crisis. Our new, unfolding understanding of the natural sciences demands that theology continue to undergo its own Copernican-like revolution.

Nevertheless, she also reaches back into early Christian texts, finding evidence that even Augustine, so often blamed for planting the seeds of Christian hierarchical structures, had a view of nature that challenges the notion of dominion over the earth. Citing a moving passage from the *Confessions*, she illustrates Augustine's belief that all beings are related to God and are of value in themselves. She later cites Aquinas's understanding that every being, because it is created by God and participates in the being of God, is of value in itself. "Such a theology yields what is sometimes called a sacramental view of the world," Farley writes. "God's presence is everywhere, and nothing falls outside God's embrace."

To move forward, Farley suggests a "new decentering" that involves finding "a center beyond ourselves in order to find a new center within ourselves." But our goal should not only be to consider what is good, beautiful, or awe-inspiring, but also to lament the evils of environmental degradation. Farley reminds readers that our assaults on nature are also assaults on other human beings, because the poor always suffer disproportionately from environmental destruction. One of the tasks of theology is to make the face of suffering and loss visible to us. Most urgently, our decentering, or conversion, should reach inside of us and awaken love in us, freeing us to turn away from our preoccupation with ourselves and to shift our gaze toward what is beyond us.

Farley's interests in scientific topics have never been limited to environmental concerns. For decades she has made distinct contributions to the field of bioethics. Three essays—"Death Be Not Proud," "Death Be Not Humble," and "Stem Cell Research: Religious Considerations"— offer readers access to Margaret Farley as a medical ethicist.

"Stem Cell Research" (2009) offers an invaluable overview of the perspectives of five of the world's major religious traditions on ethical questions surrounding the use of stem cells. The bulk of the essay is devoted to Christian and, later, specifically Roman Catholic viewpoints on this contentious issue. Farley makes it clear that particular religious groups are not necessarily univocal in their position: more than one view exists among Catholics, Muslims, and different strands of Judaism. She considers the moral status of embryos as well as moral assessments of what respect is due to embryos, whether they are viewed as individualized persons or not. She also asks broader questions of justice, such as whether gender and race discrimination will influence the research process and whether class will impact who will gain from advances in therapeutic advances.

In the "Death Be Not Proud" and "Death Be Not Humble" series, Farley probes the large questions surrounding human freedom in relation to death and to life, most specifically the choices that must be made about our dying. The titles, of course, are based on the poem by John Donne, published posthumously in 1633.

Developments in medical technology have made questions regarding death and dying increasingly complex. But rather than diving directly into an ethical consideration of choices for death in a medical context, Farley first turns to the question of the value of human physical life in this world. She begins "Death Be Not Proud" by considering the significance of free choice and the importance of death in determining the meaning of our life. "Freedom is not the power always to change our loves but to determine them, to decide what we really want, what it is for which we will live or die," she writes.

The meaning of death, she suggests, cannot be understood apart from the meaning of life, and the meaning of life is shaped by the meaning of death. She also offers some theological reflections on the hope that death will be an "act of communion with God," and, in cases where a choice can be made about death, that it will be "a surrender into the heart of God."

In "Death Be Not Humble," she focuses more specifically on the issue of ending lives that are afflicted by great suffering and enduring a prolonged dying process. She offers an in-depth consideration of the obligation to preserve human life, the distinction between actively taking life and passively allowing someone to die, and the difference between "ordinary" and "extraordinary" means of medical treatment. Farley's decades of service on the ethics committees of several hospitals becomes apparent in the detailed, practical applications of medical ethics to concrete situations. She makes her arguments about choices for death by raising a series of questions, which she asks "not to muffle but to intensify the deep experience of our call to cherish life and to hold back our hands from harming it."

The final essay in this volume, "Forgiveness in the Service of Justice and Love" (2014), offers the best representation of Farley's writing on forgiveness, which has become a significant theme in her most recent work. Here she expands on the idea of human decentering, which she likens to the traditional Christian notion of "other-centered love." Farley believes that forgiveness and love are intertwined, and that human and divine forgiveness ought both to be understood as forms of love. She wrote this essay, in part, as a response to a reawakening of interest in the theme of forgiveness—an interest that has arisen out of a "searing recognition of the lengths to which the inhumanity of humans against humans can go." Though the atrocities of war, poverty, greed, and exploitation are surely not unique to the twentieth and twenty-first century, technology, the Internet-based media, and globalization have made the conflict-driven nature of our world unavoidable. The interest in forgiveness, Farley writes, "may signal new energy for fashioning the 'conditions of possibility' for *recognition* and *respect* of one individual for another, one group toward others, one generation for all humanity."

But how does one forgive in situations where injustices continue to persist, rights continue to be violated, and oppression prevails? Here Farley introduces her original notion of "anticipatory forgiveness," which she defines as "a disposition of the heart required for forgiving and being forgiven" that also "resists the forces of evil until we can do no more." Farley is not suggesting "premature reconciliation" that covers over both large and small injustices or acts of violence; it is not passive acquiescence, silence, or failing to protect victims. "It is 'anticipatory' not because there is as yet no disposition for acceptance and love," she explains, "but because it cannot be fulfilled until the one who is forgiven (the perpetrator) acknowledges the injury and becomes able to recognize and accept, in turn, a forgiving embrace."

The grace of anticipatory forgiveness is as urgently needed in our church as it is in our world. Though Farley herself has never said it, her own difficult episode with the Vatican's condemnation of *Just Love* is surely an instance in which anticipatory forgiveness has sustained her peace and resolve. In her only public statement after the Congregation for the Doctrine of the Faith's criticism, Farley said that it was important to ask profound moral questions related to sexuality because people are suffering. As the editor of this volume, it has become clear to me that a concern for suffering is at the core of all of Farley's ethical inquiries. Whether the issue is love, feminism, silencing, AIDS, or death and dying, her first task is always to change the questions so that they are attentive to the concrete reality of the human person, in all of our longings and afflictions.

Those who read this collection will, I hope, come away with a deeper appreciation not only of Farley's contributions to ethical and theological thought but for breadth of ways in which she has applied her insights. Farley is not simply a Christian ethicist; she is a moral philosopher, medical ethicist, ecclesiologist, pastoral theologian, woman religious, and advocate for justice. Whether her inquiries are academic, ethical, or spiritual, her presence to suffering and her concern for mercy animate the questions.

We are grateful to Robert Ellsberg for his immediate and enduring enthusiasm for this project and to Jim Keane for his patience and thoughtfulness throughout the process of bringing this collection together.

CHAPTER 1

New Patterns of Relationship

Beginnings of a Moral Revolution

Patterns of relationship between women and men are changing. Why they are changing, and how rapidly, are matters of debate. It may be that the chief forces for change are, for example, economic. Industrialization and the accompanying trend toward smaller, independent families accounts in part for husbands having to share in domestic tasks that stand-in female members of large, extended families would have assumed. Technological development, which eliminates the requirement of physical strength for many occupations, accounts for the decrease in gender differentiation in portions of the workforce. Mass media make feminist ideas accessible to otherwise isolated women, facilitating an unprecedented broadening of the base of challenge from women no longer willing to live within past role definitions. Rising affluence eliminates the need for parents to choose to educate sons in preference to daughters.

It may also be, however, that much of the change in patterns of relationship between men and women is more apparent than real.

A version of this essay was published in *Theological Studies* 36, no. 4 (December 1975): 626–46. Published in this volume with permission. The substance of the essay provides, now, a kind of "voices from the past" regarding gendered relationships. Yet the philosophical and theological analyses of the issues involved remain contemporary, and they continue to "change the questions" regarding these relationships. Some sociological resources have been to some extent superseded, but they may still be useful. See studies such as Harriet Holter, "Sex Roles and Social Change," in *Family, Marriage, and the Struggle of the Sexes*, ed. Hans Peter Dreitzel (New York: Macmillan, 1972), 153–72; and Viola Klein, *The Feminine Character: History of an Ideology* (London: Routledge & Kegan Paul, 1971), 10.

Some researchers claim, for example, that despite the seeming loss of authority on the part of fathers, husbands still retain the preponderance of power in the family.[1] Feminist interpreters of life in society and the churches call attention to the fact that, since the 1920s, women have lost more ground than they have gained in their struggle to share in the public world.[2] Statistics show that, in the United States, women's growth numerically in the workforce has not significantly changed their economic status vis-à-vis men.[3]

Whatever the actual changes already realized in women's and men's social roles, there can be no doubt that an important change is occurring in persons' assessment of those roles. Gender roles have ceased to be unproblematic, accepted as a given. They are everywhere subject to critical appraisal—whether there is consensus on the critique or not. They have thus at least changed insofar as they have been raised to a level of reflective awareness. Often they have been changed in terms of legal rules, even if they have not yet really altered because of custom or attitude. In any case, for many persons profound conceptual and symbolic shifts have occurred in relation to gender differentiation and sex roles. Indeed, so profound are these changes and so far-reaching their consequences that one is tempted to say that they are to the moral life of persons what the Copernican revolution was to science or what the shift to the subject was to philosophy.

My concern in this essay, however, is less with what has already happened in interpersonal relationships than with what ought to happen. Patterns of relationship, self-understanding, and gender differentiations ought to change. They ought to change because overall they have been inadequate, based on inaccurate understandings of human persons, preventive of individual growth, inhibitive of the common good, conducive to social injustices, and in the Christian community not sufficiently informed by or faithful to the teachings of Jesus Christ.

The reasons for past inadequacies and inaccuracies in understand-

---

[1]See D. L. Gillespie, "Who Has the Power? The Marital Struggle," in Dreitzel, *Family*, 121–50.

[2]See, for example, Beverly Wildung Harrison, "Sexism and the Contemporary Church: When Evasion Becomes Complicity," in *Sexist Religion and Women in the Church: No More Silence!*, ed. Alice L. Hageman (New York: Association Press, 1974), 195–216.

[3]Figures in the U.S. Bureau of Census Report 1970 show that the median income of full-time employed women is half that of men. In 2014 the gap has been significantly lessened, at least in some fields of work, but not erased.

ings regarding the relations between men and women are many. It is important to try to understand those reasons, for they help to disclose the need for present and ongoing changes. We may, however, never be able finally to settle questions of, for example, whether the Jewish and Christian traditions in the past were ultimately responsible for sexism in religion and culture, or whether they only suffered along with other components of human history under limitations imposed by economic, cultural, or psychological factors.[4] More important now, given a kind of fullness of time in human history (however prepared for by economic exigencies, technological supports, or whatever else), is to understand the reasons why patterns of relation ought to change.

Role for Theology and Ethics: Filling the Hiatus

Christian theology and ethics have an important role to play in articulating reasons for changes in patterns of relationship and in clarifying what the changes should be. They also have an important role in translating reasons into motives, in providing a climate within which conceptualization and symbolization can facilitate experiences of moral obligation. It is, after all, incumbent upon the Christian community no less than any other group in society to consider what is right and just, loving and wise, and called for by the gospel regarding human interpersonal relationships. Christian theology is the effort of the Christian community to understand what it believes, and Christian ethics is the effort of the Christian community to understand how it should live what it believes. As such, Christian faith does have something to do with relationships between persons, and Christian theological and ethical traditions have offered insights and guidelines, even principles and rules, regarding these relationships. They have done so, in fact, with some degree of specificity regarding gender roles.

Hiatus in the Revolution

We are not now in a situation where Christian theology and ethics must simply provide a Christian commentary on general societal patterns that are questioned or, in fact, changing. We are rather in a situ-

---

[4]See Elizabeth Gould Davis, *The First Sex* (New York: Penguin, 1973).

ation where, precisely within the Christian community, for whatever reasons, many persons' ideas about sexual identity and gender roles have already changed. To understand the present task of theology, we need to look at the hiatus between past assumptions regarding fundamentally hierarchical patterns for relationship between men and women and today's growing acceptance of egalitarian patterns of relationship.

The "old order" was clearly one in which women were considered inferior to men and in which women's roles were subordinate, carefully circumscribed, and supplementary. Numerous studies have documented the tendency of Christian theology to undergird this old order by identifying women with evil, by refusing to ascribe to women the fullness of the *imago dei*, and by defining women as derivative from and wholly complementary to men.[5] Beyond this, Christian theological ethics offered theories of justice that systematically excluded the possibility of criticizing sexism. Given the interpretations of women's "nature" as inferior, there was no question of violating the principle of giving "to each her due" when women were placed in subordinate positions or denied rights that were accorded to men. Subordination *was* her "due." And given a concept of "order" in which one person should hold authority over others, justice was served precisely by the maintenance of a hierarchy—in family, church, or society—in which a male person stood at the head.[6]

The "new order," however, is based upon a view of women as autonomous human persons, as claimants of the rights that belong to all persons, as capable of filling roles of leadership in both the public and private spheres, as called to equality and full mutuality in relation to both men and women. It is difficult to exaggerate the radical nature of the shift in the perception of the reality of women and the consequent potential changes in relationships between persons (between men and women, but also between women and women and between men and men). Rainer Maria Rilke spoke of a time when women "will have stripped off the conventions of mere femininity in

---

[5]See, for example, such key studies as Mary Daly, *The Church and the Second Sex* (New York: Harper and Row, 1975); and Rosemary Radford Ruether, ed., *Religion and Sexism* (New York: Simon and Schuster, 1974).

[6]For Aquinas's position in this regard, see, for example, *Summa Theologiae* I.9.1; 93.4; 96.3; *On Kingship* 2.17–20. It is almost superfluous to note here that so-called pedestalism, whereby women were in some sense exalted as paragons of virtue, etc., served only to finally reinforce their subordination to a woman's "place."

the mutations of her outward status," when "there will be girls and women whose name will no longer signify merely an opposite of the masculine, but something in itself, something that makes one think, not of any complement and limit, but only of life and existence: the feminine human being."[7] The new order is characterized by the belief that such a time has at least begun to be.

The hiatus between the old and the new moral orders is first of all one of understanding. For some Christians, the process has been one of awakening, of unfolding, of conversion of thought if not of heart. For others, there has been no process at all. The new order of understanding is tacitly accepted, or at least not actively denied; but its implications are not all seen. The new order cannot, however, either in logic or in persons' lives, simply be spliced to the old order as if it were another frame in an unwinding film. If there is to be growing clarity regarding social roles and individual identity, Henri Bergson's "between" of process is as important as the beginning and the end. What is at stake is not only a Copernican revolution, where insight may be achieved in the flash of an eye, but a moral revolution wherein the Christian community's first obligation is to try to discern the claims of persons qua persons and the true common good of all persons.

The hiatus is also, of course, a hiatus between thought and reality and a hiatus between persons who behold a new order and those who do not. The gap in these senses is characterized differently in the different Christian traditions, so I shall limit my generalizations to the Roman Catholic tradition.[8] Here new understandings of the nature and role of women have not yet penetrated the pastoral teachings of the church.[9] Unlike most other Christian traditions, even formal legal barriers to women's fuller participation in the life of the church still remain. And obviously not all persons in the church share the new understandings of social roles and interpersonal relationships or the new experiences of moral thought that are grounded in these understandings. Even those who do readily share in these understanding

---

[7]Rainer Maria Rilke, *Letters to a Young Poet*, trans. M. D. H. Norton (New York: W. W. Norton, 1962), 59.

[8]Thus far, more efforts have been made to analyze such situations in the Protestant churches than in the Roman Catholic; see Harrison, "Sexism and the Contemporary Church."

[9]This was eminently visible in the 1975 statements of Paul VI regarding the International Women's Year. It is a point of view that remains largely unreformed among the Catholic hierarchy.

admit that new patterns of relationship are not fully clear and that achievement of new self-understandings has not finally been realized.

Filling the Hiatus

The task of theology obviously has something to do with bridging the gap. Nowhere is the hiatus more visible, in fact, than in theology itself. The work of transition from old to new understandings has hardly begun, and the revolution in thought that it entails cannot come full circle until the meaning and consequences of the new order are more adequately probed. What is needed, therefore, is not simply a further promulgation of new understandings, or a move by the theological community from tacit to spoken acceptance of new models of interpersonal and social relationships, or even exhortations of the community by theologians and ethicists. The task of theology is to engage precisely as theology and as theological ethics in the process whereby new understandings are born and develop.

The most obvious beginning work for theology in this regard is the self-critical work of disclosing past inaccuracies and distortions in theological interpretations of, for example, the "reality" of women and the role of sexuality in human life (a work well begun primarily by some few feminist theologians).[10] But theology has also a reconstructive task that will entail, for example, efforts at a resymbolization of evil and a further probing of the doctrine of the *imago dei*. The reconstructive task of Christian ethics is derivative from and dependent upon the fruits of theological reflection, but it will inevitably involve new efforts to discern the moral imperatives rising from new understandings of the indicative regarding relations between persons. It is still the principles of Christian love and justice that must illuminate and regulate these relationships. There are, however, crucial considerations to be taken into account in the elaboration of these principles if they are to be faithful to Christian revelation as it is received in the concrete experience of the contemporary Christian community. What I should like to do in the remainder of this essay is to suggest key ways in which further considerations precisely of Christian love and justice can aid the process from old to new understandings of patterns of relationship between women and men and can thereby inform and give impetus to

---

[10]See references in n. 5 above.

the moral revolution that now promises to touch and reshape these relationships from the ground up.

Ethical Reconstruction:
New Patterns of Relationship:
The Relevance of Christian Love

At first glance it seems a simple matter to apply the norms of Christian agape to patterns of relationship between persons. If agape means equal regard for all persons, then it requires that women be affirmed no less than men. If agape means a love that is self-sacrificing, then men as well as women are to yield one to the other, to know the meaning of sacrifice and surrender at the heart of their love for God and for human persons. If agape includes mutuality—as the gift it receives, if not the reward it seeks—then some form of equality is assumed in every Christian love.

Yet in the context of male-female relations, there have appeared throughout the centuries countless ambiguities regarding the form of agape when it is for a person precisely as man-person or as woman-person. Among other things, the very notions of equal regard, self-sacrifice, and mutuality become problematic. When agape has been understood as a graced love called forth and measured by the reality of the one loved (as it has been largely in the Roman Catholic tradition), then affirmation of a lesser share in life and in being for women than for men has been justified on the grounds that women are simply inferior to men.[11] When agape has been understood as indifferent to the reality of the one loved, coming forth "unmotivated" from the graced power of the one loving (as it has been in many of the Protestant traditions), then inequality in what is affirmed for women in relation to men has been justified by making love for women as women a "preferential" love, not under the norm of agape.[12] And while Christian love in all persons has indeed always included the notion of self-sacrifice, there have been ways of attributing that element of love especially to women—reinforcing, on the one hand, a sense of subservience in women, and leading, on the other hand, to such strange conclusions as that

---

[11]*Summa Theologiae* 1.92.1, ad 1 and 2.

[12]Such is the conclusion that can be drawn from, for example, the theories of Søren Kierkegaard or Anders Nygren.

the woman is the "heart" of the family and the man is the "mind."[13] Finally, the mutuality of love envisioned between men and women has seldom in theory included the full mutuality that is possible only in a relation marked by equality. It has, more often than not, found its analogues in the mutuality of relationships between parent and child, ruler and subject, master and servant.[14]

Many aspects of Christian love could be examined in an effort to reconstruct a Christian ethic that would aid the process toward new patterns of relationship between women and men. The notions of equal regard, self-sacrifice, and mutuality offer particularly relevant areas for consideration, however, and in these areas I would like to raise and to consider representative issues.

Equal Regard and Equality of Opportunity

The notion of equal regard as a component of Christian agape has generally meant that all persons are to be loved with Christian love, regardless of their individual differences or their individual merit. They are to be loved, so the Roman Catholic tradition generally holds, because they are lovable precisely as persons (all beloved by God, all objects of the command to love them as we love ourselves).[15] Equal regard has not had sufficient content in the past, however, to save agapeic ethics from sexism; for, as we have seen, it is possible to affirm all persons as persons in a way that maintains a gradation among persons. All are loved as equal before God but not necessarily as equal before one another. When the norm of the objective reality of the person loved is added to the notion of equal regard, then the affirmation of persons as equals depends on the perception of their reality. Now, at this point, Christian ethics has suffered from an inadequate theology of the human person, for as long as the reality of women is considered

---

[13]Pius XI wrote in *Casti connubii*, no. 27 (Washington, DC: National Catholic Welfare Conference, 1931): "As he occupies the chief place in ruling, so she may and ought to claim for herself the chief place in love."

[14]These analogous polarities must not be thought to appear only in the Roman Catholic tradition. Reformation views of relationships between men and women did not revolutionize the pattern of hierarchy and subordination. See, for example, Martin Luther, *Commentary on Galatians* 1535 (WA 40.543); *Commentary on Genesis* 1535–45 (WA 44.704).

[15]For a general analysis of the meaning of "equal regard," see the original work (including coinage of the term) of Gene Outka, *Agape: An Ethical Analysis* (New Haven, CT: Yale University Press: 1972), chap. 1.

to be essentially lesser in being than the reality of men, women can be affirmed as personal but as essentially subordinate to men (in much the same way as children can be loved as persons without love demanding that they be affirmed in all the ways that adults are affirmed).

No one would argue that there are no differences between individual persons or that there are no differences between men and women. The question, of course, for a right love of women as human persons is whether the differences between men and women are relevant in a way that justifies differentiating gender roles and consequent inequality of opportunity for women to participate in the public sphere or to determine the mode of their participation in the private sphere.

The primary method that theology used in the past to come to conclusions regarding the differences between women and men was a method of extrapolation from biological and sociopsychological data.[16] If theology is today consistent in its method in this regard, it has no choice but to reject its earlier position regarding the nature of "woman." Evidence from the biological and behavioral sciences, from history and current practice, is overwhelmingly in contradiction to old claims regarding the intellectual superiority of men, the innate suitableness of women and men for gender-specific social roles, the physiologically determined psychological patterns of women and men, and so forth.[17] The differences between women and men are not differences that justify gender-specific variations in a right to education, work, access to occupational spheres, participation in political life, just wages, or an equitable share in the burdens and responsibilities of family, society, and church. History clearly shows that efforts to restrict social roles on the basis of sex inevitably lead to inequities, to circumscription of persons in a way that limits the possibilities of growth in human and Christian life. A love that abstracts from the fundamental potentialities and needs of persons qua persons (in the name of attending to specific differences among persons) cannot finally be a Christian love that is a love of equal regard.

---

[16]This is not to deny that scriptural exegesis of, for example, the story of creation has played an important part in theological reflection on the "nature" of women. I would argue, however, that such exegesis served until recently to proof-text conclusions drawn largely from other sources.

[17]It is, I hope, superfluous to document such an assertion, but it may be helpful to point to such studies as Margaret Mead, *Male and Female* (New York: William Morrow, 1949); and Jean Strouse, ed., *Women and Analysis* (New York: Grossman, 1974).

Self-Sacrifice and Active Receptivity

Self-sacrifice and servanthood go together as important concepts in a Christian understanding of a life of Christian love. In general, there is no difficulty in seeing them as part of the call of every Christian to a love that is like the love of Christ. Yet women have become conscious of the potential falsification of these concepts when they are tied to a pattern of submissiveness to men. As members of the contemporary Christian community, women have thus experienced grave difficulty in sharing the new enthusiasm of men for an understanding of Christian life and ministry in terms of servanthood and surrender. Women have long known their ministry (in home, society, or church) as a ministry of service, but they are painfully aware that for too long they have been primarily the servants of men, subject to the regulations of men, and surrendered to the limitations imposed upon them by men. Thus, for women, theological reflection on servanthood has come to focus newly on the revelation of service as a form of divine help, a role of privilege and responsibility, never "an indication of inferiority or subordination."[18]

Such clarifications would seem sufficient to restore a needed balance in patterns of relationship and ministry, preserving the fundamental elements of a surrendered and effective, free and whole love. But the ambiguities of sexual identity and culturally conditioned gender roles are not so easily removed from actual efforts to live lives of Christian love. The process toward a new order calls for more careful analysis of the problems and opportunities in integrating sexual identity with agapeic love.

At the root of the difficulty in correcting false emphases in both women's and men's understandings of self-sacrifice, surrender, and servanthood in Christian love are false notions of receptivity. An implicit but direct connection exists between historical theological interpretations of women as passive and historical difficulties in interpreting agape as active. In both cases, receptivity constitutes a stumbling block.

It is, of course, a favorite theme in traditional interpretations of male-female relations to consider the feminine as passive and the

---

[18]Letty M. Russell, "Women and Ministry," in Hageman, *Sexist Religion and Women in the Church*, 54–55.

masculine as active, the woman as receptacle and the man as fulfiller, the woman as ground and the man as seed. No other interpretation of the polarity between the sexes has had so long and deep-seated an influence on both men's and women's self-understanding. The source of this interpretation was primarily reflection on the reproductive structures of men and women. These structures served not only as symbols of male and female nature and roles but determined the meaning of the reality they symbolized. A perception of the function of bodily organs molded the consciousness of men and women for centuries. And there was no question that he who was considered an active principle was somehow greater in being than she who could be only a principle of passivity.[19]

In the history of Christian conceptualizations of agape, two trends are apparent. On the one hand, there has been a tendency to describe agape as wholly passively received in the human person from God and wholly actively given by the human person to his or her neighbor.[20] The primacy of the active principle is maintained in such a way that in the relation between God and the human person, only God can be active, and in the relation between the Christian and his or her neighbor, Christian agape must be wholly active.[21]

On the other hand, where there has been a theology of grace that allows for secondary causality and freedom, both activity and receptivity are allowed in the response of Christian agape to God and to neighbor. That is to say, love of God is receptive not only in the sense that the power and the act of love are received from God as grace but in the sense that love for God is awakened by the received revelation of God's lovableness and responds in active affirmation; and love of neighbor is likewise awakened by the lovableness of the neighbor, and only when it is so awakened (when it has so received the beauty

---

[19]Were there space here, it would be interesting to speculate on the reasons for some variations on this theme. Thus, why did the seventeenth century sustain the myth of female passivity, yet give rise to a belief that women's sexuality was insatiable?

[20]See, for example, Anders Nygren, *Agape and Eros*, trans. Philip S. Watson (New York: Harper and Row, 1969), 75–80, 92–95, 127; Outka, *Agape*, 49–52; Norman Snaith, *The Distinctive Ideas of the Old Testament* (New York: Schocken Books, 1969), 174–75.

[21]The major difficulties that this position sees with allowing agape to be active vis-à-vis God and receptive vis-à-vis one's neighbor are the difficulties of preserving total divine causality in grace and the difficulties of the emergence of egocentricity in "preferential" love.

of the neighbor) is it an actively affirming response.[22] An important irony, however, is that those theological traditions which have tended to allow both receptivity and activity in the integral reality of Christian love have also tended to identify woman with love and man with active mind.[23]

The fact that receptivity has been a stumbling block both in the self-understanding of women and some theologies of Christian love is readily apparent. We can see it first in the effort of women to transcend old-order understandings of themselves. A major part of this effort has been the struggle of women to reject identification in terms of bodily structures. Voices raised in the women's movement years ago were more often than not stressing the unacceptability of the "anatomy is destiny" dictum. They had come to see the inadequacies of traditional interpretations of the structure of the human self that tied sexual identity and social roles too closely to biological givens. A certain kind of identification with the body had to be transcended if women were to achieve the personal identity that had so long eluded them. A body objectified by the other had become objectified for the self, and too simple interpretations of bodily structures led to conclusions about women's identity that were in contradiction to women's own experience. The old understandings of body and woman and receptivity had to be left behind.

Similarly, flight from receptivity in modern theologies of Christian love parallels a general fear of receptivity in a modern age when for Sartrean man "to receive is incompatible with being free,"[24] and for "protean man" everywhere there is a "suspicion of counterfeit nurturance."[25] But such fears are the result of an experience and an interpretation of receptivity that is oppressive, deceiving in its illusory offer of meaning and happiness, destructive in its enforced passivity. It is not only women but all persons who can sense that certain forms of receptivity, of passivity and submission, are not appropriate for the human person and never truly constitutive of Christian love.

---

[22]This view of agape is found most representatively in the Roman Catholic tradition of a theology of Christian love.

[23]See n. 13 above.

[24]Gabriel Marcel puts these words in the mouth of the early Sartre; see Gabriel Marcel, *The Philosophy of Existentialism*, trans. M. Harari (New York: Citadel Press, 1965), 82.

[25]Robert Jay Lifton, "Protean Man," in *The Religious Situation: 1969*, ed. D. Cutler (Boston: Beacon Press, 1969), 824.

New light can be shed, however, on the meaning of receptivity for all persons. Women have found important access to that light, paradoxically, by returning to considerations of bodily structures. Their move to transcend reference to bodily structures and processes was never complete; at the same time that women were rejecting anatomical determinism, they were also taking more seriously their relation to their own bodies, seeking a way to integrate embodiment with personal selfhood and womanhood. The very forcefulness of the negation of the body as sole determinant of identity and social function allowed an undercurrent of interest in a feminist rediscovery of the body to emerge dialectically as a major theme for today's voices in the women's movement.

In their efforts to reclaim their bodies, women finally took seriously the scientific discoveries of the nineteenth and twentieth centuries that showed, for example, that even at the physiological level the female body is never only a receptacle for male sperm. Knowledge about the ovum, and the necessity of two entities (sperm and ovum) meeting in order to form a new reality, forever ruled out the analogy of the earth receiving a seed that was whole in itself and only in need of nourishment to grow.[26] Suddenly enwombing took on a different meaning, and inseeding had to be conceptualized in a different way. Even the passivity of the waiting womb had to be reinterpreted in the face of discoveries of its active role in aiding the passage of the sperm. Receptivity and activity began to coincide.

There are dangers, of course, in women's new efforts to understand and to live their embodiment. First, if only women take seriously human existence as embodied, they may simply reinforce past stereotypes that identify woman with body and man with mind. Second, if women fall into the trap that Freud did—that is, by taking account of the body in only some of its manifestations and not the body as a whole—distortions will once again be introduced into the self-understanding of both men and women. Thus, for example, to fail to see all the ways in

---

[26]While the ovum was discovered only in the nineteenth century, Hippocrates had taught that woman's participation in reproduction includes a positive contribution. This was taken up into philosophy and theology by the Franciscan school in the Middle Ages, but there was as yet no acknowledgment of equal contributions from male and female principles. The male contribution was considered "efficient cause," and the female contribution still "material cause." See Bonaventure, *In Sent.* 2, d. 20, q. 2.

which, even at a physical level, men's bodies receive, encircle, embrace, and all the ways women's bodies are active, giving, penetrating, is to undermine from the start any possibility of growing insight into patterns of mutuality in relationships between persons.[27] Finally, there is the danger of forgetting that bodily structures and processes, whether in themselves or as symbolic of something beyond themselves, cannot provide the key to the whole of personal identity. They do, after all, demand to be transcended, so that we come to recognize all the possibilities of activity and receptivity that belong to both men and women, not as masculine and feminine poles of their beings, but as full possibilities precisely as feminine or precisely as masculine.

But if insight can be gained into active receptivity and receptive activity at the level of human embodiment, there is also a way to further insight in the experience of Christian agape. Receptivity is indeed at the heart of Christian love, and it does indeed lead finally to receptive surrender and to a life of active and receptive self-sacrifice. But it may be that we can grasp the meaning of receptivity in Christian agape only by seeing it in the broader context of Christian faith. Theological interpretations of Christian beliefs have pointed to a mystery of receptivity in the life of God's own self; in the incarnation of the Son, his life, death, resurrection, and return to the Father; in the dwelling of the Spirit in the church; in the life of grace that is the sharing of human persons in the life of the triune God. "The Father, who is the source of life, has made the Son the source of life" (John 5:26). "I can do nothing by myself. . . . My aim is to do not my own will but the will of Him who sent me" (John 5:30). "God gives the Spirit without reserve. The Father loves the Son and has entrusted everything to him" (John 3:34–35). The Son's incarnate existence as God-human is an existence of receiving, of utter openness to the Father, of finally receptive surrendering unto death, and in death beyond death into life, and into new assumption into the life of the Godhead.[28] The church is alive with that same life only because and insofar as it receives the Spirit of Christ, the Spirit of God (John 4:14; 6:37; 14:15–19; 15:5–5). Human

---

[27]This, I take it, constitutes a morally significant factor in understanding homosexuality as well as heterosexual relations. There is not the opportunity here to pursue this topic, but it is of utmost importance to juxtapose these insights with the testimony of the contemporary gay community that the "new generation" of homosexuals does not reject their given sexual identity even though their sexual preference is for persons of the same sex.

[28]For a brief but excellent summary of the element of receptivity in the life of Jesus, see Hans Urs von Balthasar, *A Theology of History* (San Francisco: Ignatius Press, 1994), 25–30.

persons, subsistent receptors of their very being, awaken into life and consciousness, into love and communion, even into the love of God and communion with God and all persons in God, only through the mystery of their capacity to receive, their possibility of utter openness to the creative and created word of God.

Christian love, no less and indeed radically more so than other forms of human love,[29] is essentially receptive in relation to both God and neighbor. It is God's self-communication that enables Christian love, and that self-communication includes the manifestation of God's lovableness for the conscious reception in and response of Christian love. And Christian love of neighbor is radical love, not in that it involves no reception of the one loved, but because the one loved is received according to his or her deepest reality (her existence in God in Christ Jesus) and responded to with an active affirmation that reaches to that reality.

But all this receptivity at the heart of Christian existence is not in any way only passivity. "To receive," as Gabriel Marcel has noted, can mean anything from passive undergoing to a receiving that is an active giving, as when a host "receives" a guest.[30] The receiving that is the Son's in relation to the Father is an infinitely active receiving. The receiving that is each human person's from God, and from one another within a life shared in God, is an active participation in the active receptivity of Christ, awakening, growing, reaching to the coincidence of peak receptivity with peak activity. Theologians who worry that if agape is active in relation to God, God's power will not be preserved, or theologians who worry that if agape is receptive of neighbor, it will inevitably be a self-centered love, fail to understand that receiving can be self-emptying, and giving can be self-fulfilling. They fail to see the meeting between lover and beloved (whether God or a human person) that is utterly receptive but utterly active, a communion in which the beloved is received and affirmed, in which receiving and giving are but two sides of one reality, which is other-centered love. Theologians or any persons who persist in identifying women with love and men with knowledge, or who neglect to find in self-sacrificial love the coincidence of opposites (giving and receiving),

---

[29]See Jules J. Toner, *The Experience of Love* (Washington, DC: Corpus Books, 1968), 95.
[30]See Marcel, *Creative Fidelity*, trans. R. Rosenthal (New York: Farrar, Straus and Company, 1964), 89–91.

fail to understand the reality of either man or woman and fail to see the absurdity of withholding the possibilities of great Christian love from the heart of all persons.

Mutuality on a Trinitarian Model

We can take a further step in trying to understand the reality of women and men, the nature of the love that can be between them, and the model of interpersonal relationship that is offered to them in Christian revelation. That step is to the doctrine of God. It is suggested by the fact that Christian theology has failed to grant equality to women precisely insofar as it has failed to attribute to women the fullness of the image of God. All persons, it is said, are created in the image and likeness of God, but men participate in the *imago dei* primarily and fully, while women have long been thought to participate in it secondarily and partially. It is not surprising, then, that the only way to move beyond a long-standing inability to conceptualize and actualize patterns of relationship that do not depend upon a hierarchical model is to see whether sexual and gendered identity does indeed give graded shares in the *imago dei*. At the same time we may see whether God's own self-revelation includes a revelation of a model of interpersonal love that is based upon equality and infinite mutuality.

If we are to pursue the question of whether women as women can be understood to be in the image of God, we must ask whether God can be imaged in feminine as well as masculine terms.[31] The Christian community has traditionally tried to articulate its understanding of the inner life of God in the doctrine of the Trinity, and here we might expect to find also the fullest meaning for the *imago dei*. Certain cautions, however, are in order. First, the Christian doctrine of God has never ceased to affirm that God is a transcendent God whose reality is beyond all of our images and who cannot be understood to be either masculine or feminine. Nonetheless, we do use images to help our un-

---

[31]This does not eliminate the need to consider women as persons participating in the *imago dei*. To go to this without considering also women as women participating in the *imago dei* does not, however, meet the historical problem of identifying men as the primary sharers in the image of God. My use of the terms and metaphors for God's life in the Trinity (that is, "Father," "Son," and "Spirit") can be replaced by other descriptive terms and metaphors (as, for example, "First Person," "Second Person," and "Third Person," or Creator, Redeemer, Sanctifer). No matter what, terms and metaphors need to alternate sufficiently, or be changed sufficiently, to yield an overall inclusive language.

derstanding of God; and since God holds all the fullness of being, it is as legitimate to say that the perfections of masculinity and femininity are in God as to say that they are not in God. There will, of course, be radical limitations to any use of masculine or feminine images of God, but there are radical limitations to the use of any images—including those of fatherhood and sonship, or those of word and wisdom, or those of memory, understanding, and will.

It is important for us to bear in mind, however, two special limitations of masculine and feminine (or male and female) imagery. (1) Given no history of careful delimitation of the imagery (such as we do have for the images of fatherhood and sonship), constant care must be taken to place it within a clear affirmation of the unity of God.[32] (2) Any use of masculine or feminine imagery, whether in relation to God or not, runs the risk of being caught once again in reifying notions of the masculine and the feminine. I shall say more about this second concern later.

There are, I suggest, in traditional Roman Catholic Trinitarian theology,[33] grounds for naming each of the persons in the Trinity feminine as well as masculine. "Fatherhood" is the image traditionally used for the First Person of the Trinity. In the first two centuries of Christian thought, it connoted primarily the Godhead as the creator and author of all things,[34] but it soon began to signify the unoriginated "begetting" by the First Person of the Second Person. The exclusive appropriateness of the image of fatherhood is beyond question in an age when the sole active principle in human generativity was thought to be male. No absolute necessity remains for limiting the image to that of masculine generativity, however, when it becomes clear (as it has in our own day) that the feminine principle of generativity is also active and self-contributing. There is, in other words, no reason why the First Person of the Trinity cannot be named "Mother" as well as "Father," no reason why creation cannot be imaged as coming forth from the ultimate womb, from the ultimate maternal principle. Neither image is sufficient (since in the human analogue neither male nor female

---

[32]In other words, not only must modalism be eschewed, but "social" theories of the Godhead as well; see Claude Welch, *In This Name: The Doctrine of the Trinity in Contemporary Theology* (New York: Scribner, 1952), 29–34, 133–51, 252–72.

[33]These same reflections could be applied to the Trinitarian theology of, for example, Karl Barth.

[34]See J. N. D. Kelly, *Early Christian Doctrines* (New York: Harper, 1958), 83–95.

principle can be the whole source of life), but either is appropriate; and perhaps only with both do we begin to return the power to images that they had in a simpler day.

"Sonship" is the image traditionally used for the Second Person of the Trinity. Once again, the appropriateness of this image is unquestionable in an age when human sons were the always desired human offspring, and when relationships between fathers and sons could often be marked with greater equality and mutuality than could those between husband and wife.[35] But there is, again, no absolute reason why the Second Person cannot be named "Daughter" as well as "Son." There is, on the contrary, good reason to suggest that the Second Person is better imaged when both the images of sonship and daughterhood are used.[36]

However, another way exists in which feminine imagery may be ascribed to the Second Person of the Trinity. A large part of the history of the doctrine of the Trinity is a history of attempts to express the relationship between the First and Second Persons in a way that avoids subordinationism. From the Apologists to the Council of Nicaea, the attempts were unsuccessful. Nicaea affirmed the equality and the unity of the two Persons, but the images still faltered.[37] "Fatherhood" and "sonship" (even when elaborated upon in terms of Father and Logos or light, and so forth) were simply not capable of bearing the whole burden of the reality to be imaged.

With Augustine, new images were introduced (being, knowing, willing; mind, self-knowledge, self-love; memory, understanding, will) that described a triune life in which all that the Father is communicated to the Son, and all that the Son receives is returned to the Father, and the life of utter mutuality, communion, which they share, is the Spirit.[38] This life—imaged by analogues from the human mind—is still attributed, however, to Persons whose primary names are thought to be "Father" and "Son" (and "Spirit"). The further elaboration of

---

[35]I am passing over here the question of the influence of reflection on the incarnation on these views; see ibid., chaps. 4–5.

[36]Some theologians suggest the view that the Holy Spirit be considered as imaging "daughterhood" in the Trinity. This does not, it seems to me, adequately account for the theology of "spiration," and it still risks subordinationism.

[37]Athanasius, for example, still needed to draw upon such images as "stream" and "source" to try to express the relation of Father and Son. The Cappadocians still referred to the Father as cause and the Son as caused.

[38]Augustine, *De trinitate* 5.12; 5.15–17; 8.1; 15.5, 10; *In Ioan tract.* 99.6.

this same basic description is to be found in the rest of the history of the theology of the Trinity in the Western church and in the official teachings of the church.[39]

Given this articulation of the life of the Trinity, however, is it not possible to introduce images of masculinity and femininity that are no longer those of parent and child? Does not a feminine principle of creative union, a spousal principle, express as well as sonship the relation of the Second Person to the First? Is not the Second Person revealed as infinite receptor, in whom peak receptivity is identical with peak activity? Is it not possible on this account to describe the First Person as masculine and the Second Person as feminine, and the bond that is the infinite communion between them (the Spirit of both) as necessarily both masculine and feminine? Do we not have here revealed a relationship in which both the First Person and the Second Person are infinitely active and infinitely receptive, infinitely giving and infinitely receiving, holding in infinite mutuality and reciprocity a totally shared life? Do we not have here, in any case, a model of relationship that is not hierarchical, that is marked by total equality, and that is offered to us in Christian revelation as the model for relationship with Christ and for our relationships in the church with one another?

But let me return here to the caution I noted earlier, namely, that to use the images of masculinity and femininity to represent the Godhead runs the risk of sealing yet more irrevocably the archetypes of the eternal masculine and the eternal feminine. The God of Christianity is a transcendent God, one who breaks all archetypes and who can continually call us beyond their limitations in our own lives. It is surely the case that we do not want to find yet one more way to imprison women or men in what are finally falsifying notions of gender identity. We began these considerations, however, as part of a process—a process that may in fact lead necessarily beyond all sexual imagery to notions only of transcendence. What is important is that there be room in the process for women to know themselves as images of God, as able to be representatives of God as well as lovers of God. In addition, we cannot dismiss out of hand the possibility of finding in God's self-revelation grounds for understanding femininity in a way that begins to shatter

---

[39]For a concise summary of the official doctrine of the Catholic Church regarding the Trinity, see Karl Rahner, *The Trinity*, trans. Joseph Donceel (New York: Herder and Herder, 1970), 58–79.

its previous conceptual limitations, and that begins even to revolutionize archetypes. Finally, both the struggle of Trinitarian theology through the centuries to deny any subordination of the Second Person to the First, and the struggle of women and men to achieve equality and mutuality in more and more patterns of relationship, may well be served by adding the image of masculine-feminine polarity to past images of fatherhood and sonship.

New Patterns of Relationship: Relevance of Christian Justice

The Good of the Individual

There is a sense in which, once we have considered the norms of Christian love vis-à-vis patterns of relationship between women and men, we have already also considered the norms of Christian justice. At least in the theory of Christian justice to which I would subscribe, justice is itself the norm of love. What is required of Christians is a just love, a love that does indeed correspond to the reality of those loved. Thus, in a strict sense, justice requires that we affirm for persons, both women and men, what they reasonably need in order to live out their lives as full human persons and, within the Christian community, what they need in order to grow in their life of faith. It is therefore clear that to refuse to persons, on the basis of their sex, their rightful claim to life, bodily security, health, freedom of self-determination, religious worship, education, and so forth, is to violate the norms of a just love. Any pattern of relationship, in home, church, or civil society, that does not respect persons in these needs and claims is thereby an unjust pattern of relationship.

We have already seen the demand that a just love then makes for rejecting institutionalized gender differentiations and for affirming equality of opportunity for all persons regardless of their sex. Feminists have sometimes gone beyond an egalitarian ethic, however, to a "liberation" ethic in their delineation of the norms of justice for society and the churches.[40] The liberation ethic, in this sense, asserts that equal access to institutional roles is not sufficient to secure justice,

---

[40]See analysis in Jo Freeman, "The Women's Liberation Movement: Its Origins, Structures, and Ideas," in Dreitzel, *Family*, 213–16.

since institutions and roles are themselves at present oppressive to persons. The reality of both men and women is such that "the social institutions which oppress women as women also oppress people as people"[41] and must be altered to make a more humane existence for all. While the goal of a liberation ethic is ultimately the common good, it nonetheless asserts important claims for a just love in terms of the reality of individuals who are loved.

The Common Good

If traditional principles of justice are to be brought to bear in forming new patterns of relationship, then it is not only the good of individuals that must be taken into account but the common good of all. It is precisely here that moral discourse often breaks down when arguments are advanced for basic egalitarian patterns of relationship between men and women. At least three important areas of consideration suggest themselves if we are to discern seriously the moral imperatives in this regard.

1. From the standpoint of the Roman Catholic ethical tradition, it is a mistake to pit individual good against the good of the community, when what is at stake is the fundamental dignity of the individual. If the reality of women is such that a just love of them demands that they be accorded fundamental personal rights, including equality of opportunity in the public world, then to deny them those rights is inevitably to harm the common good. "The origin and primary scope of social life is the conservation, development and perfection of the human person. A social teaching or reconstruction program . . . when it disregards the respect due the human person and to the life which is proper to that person, and gives no thought to it in its organization, in legislation and executive activity, then instead of serving society, it harms it."[42] On the basis of such a view of the common good, all arguments for refusing women equality of opportunity for the sake

---

[41]Ibid., 214. This is the argument given by some women against ordination of women in the Roman Catholic Church. That is, although ordination should be open to women, the organizational structures in the church need to be modified before women are caught in untenable systems.

[42]Pius XI, Christmas Address, 1942, in Vincent A. Yzermans, ed., *The Major Addresses of Pope Pius XII*, vol. 2 (St. Paul: North Central Publishing, 1961), 54.

of safeguarding the "order" of society, church, or family must fall.

2. In the old order, as we have seen, it was argued that the common good (which consisted primarily in some form of unity) could best be achieved by placing one person at the head of any community. Strong utilitarian rebuttals can now be offered against this view of the nature of authority.[43] The tradition from which it comes has itself shifted, through the adoption of the principle of subsidiarity, from a hierarchical to an egalitarian model of social organization in contexts of civil society.[44] To extend the shift to include relationships between men and women, it is necessary to argue that in fact the good of the family, church, and society is better served by a model of leadership that includes at least some degree of collaboration between equals.

Thus, for example, it can be argued that past familial structures that give major responsibility for the rearing of children always and wholly to the mother do not, after all, provide the greatest good for children.[45] Or familial structures that entail a sharp split between the public and private worlds entail also strains on marital commitment[46] and a dichotomy between public and private morality.[47] Similarly, ecclesiastical structures that reserve leadership roles to men do not provide the needed context for all persons to grow in the life of faith. Within the confines of such structures, God is not represented in the fullness of triune life, and the vacuum that ensues is filled by false forms of chauvinism in the clergy and religiosity in the congregations. On the basis of this form of argument, hierarchical patterns of relationship are judged unjust not only because they violate the reality of individual persons but because they inhibit or undermine the common good.

3. If the ultimate normative model for relationships between persons is the very life of the Trinitarian God, then a strong eschatological ethic suggests itself as a context for Christian justice. That is to say, interpersonal communion characterized by equality, mutuality, and

---

[43]Other forms of rebuttal, on deontological grounds, can be offered as well. These may be inferred, however, from our discussion thus far.

[44]See the historical analysis of this shift in David Hollenbach, *The Right to Procreate and Its Social Limitations: A Systematic Study of Value Conflict in Roman Catholic Ethics* (unpubl. diss., Yale University, 1975), chap. 3.

[45]See Alice S. Rossi, "Equality between the Sexes; An Immodest Proposal," in Robert J. Lifton, ed., *The Woman in America* (Boston: Beacon Press, 1964), 105–15.

[46]See Martha Baum, "Love, Marriage, and the Division of Labor," in Dreitzel, *Family*, 83–106.

[47]See Beverly Wildung Harrison, "Ethical Issues in the Women's Movement," address given to the American Society of Christian Ethics, 1974.

reciprocity may serve not only as a norm against which every pattern of relationship may be measured but as a goal to which every pattern of relationship is ordered. Minimal justice, then, may have equality as its norm and full mutuality as its goal. Justice will be maximal as it approaches the ultimate goal of communion for each person with all persons and with God. Such a goal does not merely beckon from the future; it continually impinges upon the present, demanding and promising that every relationship between women and men, and between women and women and men and men, be at least turned in the direction of equality and opened to the possibility of communion.

The kinds of changes that are needed in the patterns of relationship between women and men are changes that are finally constituted in and by a moral revolution. It is difficult to imagine how such changes can be effected without a continuing process of conversion of thought and of love in the individual and in the community. I began this essay by suggesting that theology and ethics have an important role to play in such a process. Theological and moral insight do not come easily, however, in areas where centuries of thought and behavior have skilled us in selective vision. Surely some structures will have to change before minds and hearts can change. Surely laws and structures can begin to change without filling the hiatus between old and new understandings. We are talking, however, about a revolution that must occur in the most intimate relations as well as the most public. Without continuing changes in understanding and love, I doubt that we shall be able to effect sufficiently radical structural changes in the public sphere or structural changes at all in the world of our private lives. "We may sometimes decide to act abstractly by rule . . . and we may find that as a result both energy and vision are unexpectedly given . . . but if we do leap ahead of what we know we still have to try to catch up. Will cannot run very far ahead of knowledge, and attention is our daily bread."[48]

---

[48]Iris Murdoch, *The Sovereignty of Good* (New York: Schocken Books, 1971), 44.

CHAPTER 2

Fragments for an Ethic of Commitment in Thomas Aquinas

The questions that have arisen with such urgency in our time regarding the meaning of commitment, the possibility and wisdom of commitment, the obligations of commitment, are not the questions of Thomas Aquinas. In fact, of all the problems in relation to which we might try to assess the significance of Aquinas's teachings for contemporary ethics, the problem of commitment seems the least likely. In the works of Thomas we find no detailed treatment of interpersonal commitment, no theory of prereflective commitments, no careful delineation of social contract theory, only passing references to promise-keeping, and only minimal concern for the role of commitment in marriage and in friendship. Even where Aquinas gives attention to the instance of commitment that is the religious vow, there is little to satisfy a quest for a full and adequate ethic of commitment.

Nonetheless, precisely the questions that are raised today about commitment that may serve to test the continuing fruitfulness of the ethical theory of many philosophers and theologians of the past and, perhaps, especially of Thomas Aquinas. To open the question of commitment is to find ourselves in the midst of the traditional ethical and

A version of this essay was delivered at the University of Chicago in 1974 as part of a colloquy on medieval religious thought. It was later published in the *Journal of Religion* vol. 58 (Supplement, 1978): S135–S155. This particular study of commitment was in part motivated by Farley's earlier work, *A Study in the Ethics of Commitment within the Context of Theories of Human Love and Temporality* (dissertation, Yale University; Ann Arbor, MI: University Microfilms, 1974). Following both of these studies, her work on commitment continued in various of her publications, the most recent being *Personal Commitments: Beginning, Keeping, Changing*, rev. ed. (Maryknoll, NY: Orbis Books, 2013). Used with permission.

metaethical questions of freedom, obligation, interpersonal love, moral goodness, human temporality, and human destiny. It is, moreover, to find these questions situated within continuing questions about the nature of the human person, the validity of social institutions, the adequacy of theological formulations regarding the relations among human persons and between human persons and God. It has become commonplace, for example, to ask whether commitment constitutes an unwise limitation to human freedom, whether it functions to undermine and to stifle human love rather than to foster it and help it to be true, whether it must always be provisional at least in its incarnation in patterns and structures of life. At stake is not only the anguished cry of individual persons in the face of lost lives in waning commitments or driven lives in overcommitment. Fundamental human understandings of the worthiness of any reality for commitment, the sheer capacity of freedom for commitment, the ways of creation or destruction through commitment, are also at stake. It is not unfair, I think, to read the question of commitment back into a moral theory such as that of Thomas Aquinas.

At the same time that commitment has become problematic, it has also become more important, more necessary, to the fabric of ordinary human life. Aquinas's political theory could afford to ignore consent theory, or to relegate it to a subordinate position in an overall conception of society that grounded political obligation in natural inclinations and a created order. It is not possible to ignore it in a day when pluralism both demands and offers the opportunity for a social order whose base is voluntarily contracted mutuality. Aquinas's theory of familial institutions had minimal need to emphasize free covenanting between persons, since whole structural networks could serve simply to hold and to order what was already given in human tendencies and gracefully perceived obligations. Such covenanting must come to the foreground, however, in a time when supportive institutional structures no longer bear the burden of ensuring continuity of lives and when newly recognized equality between men and women makes free commitment both more necessary and more meaningful. Aquinas's analysis of vocation had less occasion to probe the complexities of freely chosen obligations than does an analysis that must take into account cultural factors that provide a multitude of possibilities for every individual's choice. No similar analysis can be indifferent to these complexities of commitment today. Fidelity in friendship was of no little importance for Aquinas, but even it could be taken for granted in a way no longer possible given accumulating insight into the psychological intricacies of the human person. It is not superfluous, I think, to assess the contemporary significance of Aquinas's moral theory by attempting to read out of it whatever light it may still have for contemporary questions of commitment.

There is a reason for asking questions about commitment of Thomas Aquinas that goes beyond merely testing the continuing relevance of his theory, however. It is, simply, that such questions still appeal for insight from whatever source. Language analysis has shed important light on the nature of obligation entailed by promise-making, but neither theories of promising as a practice nor theories of promising as a performative have been able to uncover, as A. I. Melden has noted, the nature of obligation to a person as distinguished from obligation to an act.[1] Phenomenology has probed the relation of persons in order to understand the possibilities of commitment, but where it has worked hardest on commitment questions (that is, in the hands of Jean-Paul Sartre), it has been brought up short against structures of interpersonal violence.[2] New efforts at social contract theory (such as that of John Rawls) are still under fire for a failure finally to ground political obligation.[3] Voluntaristic philosophies and theologies have sometimes found themselves with little to say to the agony of persons' disillusionment or confusion at the experience of loss of inner life in commitment.[4] Whatever the importance of the work of Marcel, Royce, or Ricoeur, and however significant the analyses of Erickson, Lifton, or Keniston, and however helpful the contributions of Polanyi, Whitehead, or Bergson, and however inspiring the interpretations of Barth, Rahner, or von Balthasar, no one would deny that they remain partial efforts at both clarifying questions and searching for answers regarding commitment. Something may yet be gained by an exploration that opens to philosophical anthropology, ontology, and theology in the way that Aquinas's moral theory does.

---

[1] A. I. Melden, "Utility and Moral Reasoning," in *Ethics and Society*, ed. Richard T. De George (Garden City, NY: Anchor Books, 1966), 182.

[2] I am referring here to Sartre's treatment of the "Oath" in *Critique de la raison dialectique* (Paris: NRF Librairie Gallimard, 1960), tome 1.

[3] See John Rawls, *A Theory of Justice* (Cambridge, MA: Harvard University Press, Belknap Press, 1971).

[4] I am thinking here of command theories of obligation—whether philosophical or theological.

In a thorough search for fragments for an ethic of commitment in Thomas Aquinas, we could identify an implicit theory of commitments to truths, values, future actions, and persons. It will not be helpful in this short essay, however, to try to work with these kinds of differentiations (and, in any case, it can be argued that these are not, finally, mutually exclusive categories of commitment).[5] To give realistic limits to this search, I focus primarily on the form of commitment that is commitment to persons and, within this, commitment to interpersonal love. It is, after all, interpersonal commitment that offers a prime case—both in Thomas Aquinas and elsewhere—for reflection on commitment as such. Contemporary questions of commitment and freedom, commitment and the growth of love, commitment and the possibilities of self-process, become most acute when they arise in relation to commitment between persons.

Where, then, shall we look in Aquinas's writings for assistance in developing an ethic of interpersonal commitment? We already know that we will not find a full-blown theory of commitment, and there is not the opportunity here and now to ask carefully of Thomas's theology all of the questions that might allow us to educe such a theory. What we can do, however, is to locate areas of Aquinas's thought where we are likely to find clues for our questions of commitment.

While Thomas pays relatively little attention to interpersonal commitments (especially explicit, expressed commitments), this means, primarily, that he does not often stop to ponder them directly; he spends almost no time in developing either a descriptive or normative theory about them. It does not mean that they never play an important role in his theory of relationships between human persons and between human persons and God. There is no question that implicit, unexpressed commitments (which, for example, characterize the assumption of roles within family, church, and society) abound in Thomas's theory.[6] But so, also, can explicit, expressed commitments be found functioning, for example, in human communication as a guarantee for truth tell-

---

[5]Thus, for example, all commitments imply some form of commitment to action (whether commitment to believe some truth, to continue affirming some value, or to perform some external action). Also, since commitment entails some kind of affective involvement, a commitment to truth is also a commitment to values, and so forth.

[6]See, for example, *Summa Theologiae* I-II.58.4; or *Summa contra gentiles* III.123; or *De regimine principum* 1.7–11 (hereafter cited as *S.T.*, *SCG*, and *De reg*, respectively).

ing[7] or in human society as a means to assure justice.[8] While Aquinas's social order rests on a more fundamental ground than social contract, nonetheless there is room within it for contractual relations.[9] At the center of his conception of human and Christian life, moreover, lies the commitment that is intrinsic to love and to charity. This sometimes seems for Thomas to be implicit and unexpressed, but it can also appear in explicit forms—as in the pledges of human love or vows instrumental of love of God.[10] It is not by studying directly any or all of these instances of interpersonal commitment, however, that we shall gain any great insight for an ethic of commitment. Thomas always presupposes more than he says about commitment, and the areas of his thought where we may engage him more sharply for our purposes are the larger contexts in which these instances of commitment appear. As a beginning, three locations suggest themselves in relation to three particularly critical ongoing problems for an ethic of commitment.

1. To make a commitment is to undertake an obligation, to yield a claim over oneself regarding whatever is pledged. To make a commitment to love is, then, to make love an obligation; it is, in some way, to give a law to one's love. But law, according to some contemporary views, is opposed to love; to make of love a duty is to contradict the very nature of love, to bind it without regard for its essential spontaneity. "Who would be content with a love given as pure loyalty to a sworn oath? Who would be satisfied with the words, 'I love you because I have freely engaged myself to love you and because I do not wish to go back on my word'?"[11] To love because of law, so it seems then, is to make of love hypocrisy and to refuse it the freedom that alone will allow it to stay alive and to grow. This problem of love and commitment is not Aquinas's problem. There are reasons why it is not so, and, whatever the validity of these reasons, they can at least be of interest to those who would struggle with this problem. One location for dialogue with Aquinas on commitment, then, is his overall conception of law in relation to love.

---

[7]*S.T.* II-II.109.3; II-II.88.3.

[8]*S.T.* II-II.57.2

[9]See *S.T.* II-II.90.3; II-II.42.2; II-II.61.3; *De reg* 1.6. See also Thomas Gilby, *The Political Thought of Thomas Aquinas* (Chicago: University of Chicago Press, 1958), 214.

[10]*S.T.* II-II.88; II-II.188; *SCG* III.138.

[11]Jean-Paul Sartre, *Being and Nothingness*, trans. Hazel E. Barnes (New York: Washington Square Press, 1953), 479.

2. Contemporary difficulties with commitment have something very important to do with the concepts of receptivity, of dependence, of surrender. To be called to commitment is to be awakened by the appeal of someone or something, and to yield in commitment is to allow oneself to be claimed in the future, to be done unto as well as to do. For some, however, "To receive is incompatible with being free; indeed, a being who is free is bound to deny to himself that he has received anything." [12] And Kenneth Keniston has observed, "A primary obstacle to the formation of a unitary sense of self among the alienated is their judgment that *commitment is submission.*" [13] Disillusionment with past commitments has led to widespread (and not unfounded) "suspicion of counterfeit nurturance." [14] Whether it should have been or not, the problem of commitment and dependence is also not Aquinas's problem. There may, nonetheless, be clues for an ethic of commitment in what might overall be called Aquinas's conception of "active receptivity."

3. Ours is an age of process. Never before has the sense of nonprocess been so intolerable in human experience, and never before the concern for self-process so clear and so urgent. Commitments have been experienced as a halting of process, a foreclosure on the future, a choking off of the as yet unknown possibilities for human life. Freedom, it seems, gathers up its future and binds it to another at the price of its own betrayal. On the other hand, commitments have been experienced as failing to halt processes that seem always to escape the power of freedom, or failing to ensure world-historical and personal processes that will not be held by freedom's choice. Past commitments may be impotent in the face of present desires. Freedom simply cannot stretch to the future in a way that finally makes the self be as it chooses to be. Aquinas has long ago been left behind in philosophical struggles to understand the human self and its possibilities for self-determination in a life lived out in time. Nonetheless, aspects of his thought may yet offer grist for the mills that labor over questions of commitment, freedom, and process.

Let me turn, then, to explore in some detail each of these three loca-

---

[12] Gabriel Marcel says this of Sartre in *The Philosophy of Existentialism*, trans. Manya Harari (New York: Citadel Press, 1964), 82.

[13] Kenneth Keniston, *The Uncommitted* (New York: Harcourt Brace, 1960), 185.

[14] See Robert Jay Lifton, "Protean Man," in *The Religious Situation: 1969*, ed. Donald Cutler (Boston: Beacon Press, 1969), 824.

tions—law and love, active receptivity, and freedom and process—to see whether they do indeed offer the possibility of fruitful dialogue with Thomas Aquinas regarding questions of interpersonal commitment.

The Law of Commitment and the Law of Love

Thomas worries very little about the kind of legalism that overwhelms love. Had he worried more about it, in fact, some of his followers might have been less easily seduced by it. There is, however, in Aquinas a view of law that sees it as primarily a liberating and not a restrictive force for love. The spontaneity of love is not seen as threatened by law because law is essentially a law for spontaneity, not against it.[15] But what can this mean in the context of commitment to interpersonal love?

Perhaps the chief reason why Thomas spends so little time on questions of commitment to love is that for him love already always has a law, already is obligated. The fundamental command of both the natural law and revealed divine law is the command to love God and to love human persons.[16] This means that the law of love comes not as an alien force to human persons, but as the appeal, demand, and guide for the continuing unfolding of the tendencies that rise from their own being. Natural law for Aquinas is a law of reason, but it is so precisely insofar as it is through reason that the very being of the person breaks through at a conscious level and speaks to itself a moral imperative. From the "is" does indeed come an "ought"—fundamentally an "ought to be." But the being of persons (as all being) is dynamic at its core, so what breaks through into the heard and spoken law of their being is the dynamic orientation of the person toward his or her end.[17] But the end, and the way to the end, are not other than what is pointed to by the tendencies of the person's being. This is why Thomas can assert that the fundamental inclinations of persons provide the material content of the natural law.[18] But this is why the New Law of graced human persons is also not, in Aquinas's view, alien to those who receive it. It,

---

[15]See *SCG* III.128.8.

[16]The central texts relevant here are *S.T.* I.60.5; I-II.99, 1 ad 2 and 2c; 100.3 ad 1; *SCG* III.116 and 117.

[17]See, for example, *S.T.* I-II.92.1.

[18]*S.T.* I-II.94.2. If one considers these first principles to be simply the first that human persons could be expected to become aware of, then the perhaps logically first principles— the law of love of God, neighbor, self—are no less directed to an end.

too, is the very being of persons, transformed by grace, hearing the law within itself and revealed from beyond itself.[19] Persons under the New Law hear the command to charity in a way in which they are "inclined of themselves . . . not as to something foreign, but as to something of their own."[20] This does not, of course, mean that Aquinas recognizes no chaos or contradictions or distortions in human inclinations. Nor does it mean that the task of discerning the law of human being or hearing with clarity the law of love is an easy one. For Aquinas, as for others, law functions as a restraint upon some human inclinations. It does so, however, for the purpose of releasing those inclinations that are most fundamental and that constitute the movement of the human person to the goal of interpersonal love. Law does not ignore or oppose or limit the spontaneity of love. It seeks, rather, to remove the limits that keep essential spontaneity from being truthful and whole.

If law serves love, for Aquinas, we need still to explore the implications of this for a commitment to love. Why should a love that is already dynamically oriented toward fuller love ever want to commit itself? Why should a love that already stands under a law seek to give itself yet another kind of law? If the movement in love toward wholeness were so determined that it could not fail, there would be no need for commitment. If a love standing under a command to love could fulfill its command all at once, there would be no need for commitment. But even Thomas Aquinas understands the vulnerability of human love, the possibility of its failure, the struggles it has with forgetfulness and distraction. And Aquinas knows of the kind of desire that can rise out of love itself to gather its life stretched out in time and yield itself all at once in affirmation of and union with the one loved.[21] And, finally, Aquinas recognizes the significance of freedom's finding a way to give itself a law whereby it can strengthen its chosen intention to love by giving to the one loved a claim over it for the future.

It is possible to reject Aquinas's general theory of law and love and nonetheless affirm an analogous theory for a law of commitment to love. If love can indeed give rise to a desire to endure and to be wholly for the beloved, then it can want to seal itself in relation to the beloved. Freedom cannot once and for all determine its future affirmation of

---

[19]*S.T.* I-II.106.1.
[20]*S.T.* I-II.107.1 ad 2. See also 106.1 and *De caritate* 9c (hereafter cited as *De car*).
[21]See *S.T.* II-II.88.5 and 6; 186.6 and 7.

love, but it can initiate in the present a new relation that will endure into the future (endure whether in the form of fidelity or betrayal). To commit oneself to another, to give one's word, is to place oneself in the other in a new way, to yield to the other a claim over one's future free choices. Freedom can thus give to itself a law—a law that corresponds to the love it seeks to commit and hence to preserve and which rises in response to the spontaneity of that love. Such a law is not understood as a binding from without, but as a being-for from within. The power and claim that are given to the one loved are the power to claim from the one who makes the commitment what he or she most deeply wants to have claimed, what one most profoundly asks of oneself.

It is, of course, true that even this law can prove to be a law that is experienced as over against the love it binds. Love can, after all, cease to want its own law. The law of commitment can become, then, a burden to love, a structure of fear and violence in relation to love, and hence a destroyer of love. Some commitments may be well served by obligation that is based in fear of the sanctions for breaking the commitment. A commitment precisely to love, as Thomas sees, cannot be so.[22] It may be the case, however, that the law of commitment is experienced as over against love in the sense that every human love needs at times to be coerced, or at least persuaded, to be faithful. Love, in this instance, can still welcome its obligation.[23] It is thereby called again and again to the spontaneity that is its fullness; it is held in relation so that it is not lost through the caprices of its accompanying or qualifying feelings and so that even they can finally also be integrated into a wholeness of response.[24] When love is for another (which it is in its highest forms of both natural love and charity), it is greater as it is more present in and to the other. Commitment is love's way of being wholly in the other even before it is whole in itself. Thus, even a coercive call can be, for Aquinas, a freeing and "happy necessity."[25]

If what I have been saying is at all faithful to Thomas Aquinas's thought, it means that for him the law of commitment partakes of the very dynamism of a person's being. Being, love, obligation, are all tendential, and what they tend toward is fuller being, fuller love.

---

[22]*SCG* III.116.2.
[23]*SCG* III.138.2; *S.T.* II-II.88.4c.
[24]*S.T.* II-II.27.2.
[25]*S.T.* II-II.189.2 ad 2.

Were there the opportunity here to unfold all of the implications of this for Aquinas, we should need to speak of the nature of love as he describes it, of the difference for commitment when love is for oneself or for another, of the ways in which commitment can be a means to love and an expression of love. Were there opportunity to do more than locate a place in Aquinas's thought for continuing reflection on commitment, we should need to chart the deficiencies in his theory for those who find commitment still a static form for love and for those who find human inclinations in need of a law but never directive of law. We should do well, moreover, to relate Aquinas's theory of love and law to still other theories of the "uses" of the law. The fruitfulness of this location for questions of commitment will depend upon what engagement of questioners can ensue.

Commitment and Active Receptivity

There are at least two reasons why it is important for an ethic of commitment to attend to the aspect of commitment that is receptivity. First of all, as we have seen, key objections to commitment are made precisely because it entails receptivity and a form of surrender. But, second, it may be that fidelity to commitment is dependent in some way upon the understanding one has of receptivity.

Objections to receptivity arise for more than one reason. If freedom is understood to be active and alive only when it is wholly independent of anything other than itself, then one who desires to be free may think it necessary to refuse any influence offered to freedom. If love is understood to be inevitably egocentric when it is motivated by the gift of the lovableness of the beloved, then one who wishes to love unselfishly may have to deny any importance to such a gift. If one understands commitment to entail a surrender that is a fundamental loss of self, then such a one may hesitate or refuse to make a commitment. And, finally, if one has learned over and over again that objects of commitment disappoint, then one will be suspicious of any future appeals for commitment.

How shall such difficulties be met? It will be justifiable for freedom to commit itself only if it cannot be wholly active without receiving something from beyond itself. Unselfish love can attend to the beauty of the beloved only if it can thereby be truly faithful. It will be important for our understanding of the self-surrender of commitment if we discover that such a surrender is paradoxically an action and a self-possession. And surely the question of the worthiness of any object for commitment can be answered only by discerning, or believing in, or trusting in, or finding, an object that is worthy. Where shall we look in Aquinas for light on such hypotheses?

Aquinas's theology is veritably shot through with a notion of receptivity that is, when it appears in personal dimensions of being, an active receptivity. When receptivity is discovered in the nature of human affectivity, or the nature of human knowledge, or the doctrines of creation, of providence, of grace, or in the life of God himself, it is inevitably discovered by Aquinas to be not a pure passivity but an active receptivity. When activity is examined in created existents, it inevitably turns out to be a receptive or at least a received activity.

Of central importance to us here is Aquinas's description of love. Human love, whether natural love or the love of charity, is clearly for Aquinas first of all a receiving. It is a *passio* (in every instance, and not only when it is a sensible "passion") precisely because it is caused by the good that is its object.[26] Love receives the lovableness of its object, and only so is it awakened as love. Love is, therefore, essentially in the first instance a response.[27] Aquinas would not be persuaded by the arguments of those who insist that at least *agape* must be wholly active (though it is received as a power and as an act).[28] He has not the problem of thinking love to be always finally self-centered if it arises as a response to the beauty and lovableness of the beloved. On the contrary, love, or charity, always is tapped into life by the revelation of

---

[26]*S. T.* I-II.26.2; 27.1; *De Veritate* 26.1 (hereafter cited as *De ver*); *De car* 7 ad 6; 4 ad 4.

[27]Frederick E. Crowe's essays in 1959 ("Complacency and Concern in the Thought of St. Thomas," *Theological Studies* 20 [1959]: 1–39, 198–230, 343–95) have had a great influence on discussions of an active and a passive element in Thomas's conception of love. Crowe, however, misses something very important when he makes complacency wholly passive (see pp. 3, 13, 18) and then identifies the active element in love as tendency. There is, of course, some ambiguity in his description of passivity. Words such as "acceptance, consent, concord" sound quite active. Then, too, since he places both *agape* and *eros* in the category of tendency, there is some doubt that the active aspect of love is, after all, only tendency. He makes the same mistake that Gilleman makes by interpreting *agape* as tendency (though his insistence on complacency as an element in love differentiates him from Gilleman). See Gerald Gilleman, *The Primacy of Charity in Moral Theology*, trans. W. F. Ryan and A. Vachon (Westminster, MD: Newman Press, 1959).

[28]This places Thomas Aquinas in opposition to, for example, Anders Nygren, Norman Snaith, Victor Furnish. It also differentiates him from someone like Karl Barth, who, though he wants to affirm a grateful responding love, names the first reception of grace "faith." For some of the issues involved in the dual terminology, see Gene Outka, *Agape: An Ethical Analysis* (New Haven, CT: Yale University Press, 1972), 49–52.

the goodness, the lovableness, of the one loved. Other-centered love is called into being for the beloved precisely because the beloved is lovable for his or her own sake.[29] It is motivated as love for another by the lovableness of the other. God's love is a totally creative love, making be in the object loved whatever there is of lovableness, of goodness, of beauty. But no human person's love is creative *ex nihilo* in this way.[30]

But if love is a receiving of the beloved, it is not a purely passive receiving. The reception that love is is an active reception, one that entails a willing of the beloved, a being with and a being for the beloved.[31] There is no created love that is not awakened by receiving the beloved; but there is no receiving of the beloved as beloved that is not the active receiving that is loving. Receptivity and activity are not here two separable realities; they are two aspects of one and the same love; they coalesce into the reality that is the loving.

The notion of active receptivity appears not only in Aquinas's description of love, however. There are some grounds for saying that Aquinas finds it in the very life of the Godhead itself, where all that the Father is is given to the Son, so that "the Father has power as giving . . . , but the Son has power as receiving," and this receiving is an infinitely active receiving.[32] Though Aquinas's theology of the *Verbum* can be interpreted as a theory of emanation such that it is improper to speak of anyone "receiving," he struggles with the mystery of the Trinitarian life, and he is willing to say such things as "what is gen-

---

[29]*De car* 2; 3 ad 13; 8 ad 16; 11 ad 6.

[30]*S.T.* I-II.110.1c. Here Aquinas asserts that a human person's love does not wholly cause the good of a thing, but presupposes it. This presupposition is at work wherever he insists that what is better should be loved more. See, for example, *S.T.* II-II.26.7.

[31]See *De car* 4 ad 4. Here Aquinas seems to indicate that the object loved touches affectivity directly, though it is mediated by knowledge. If this is so, there are important consequences for current debates about Aquinas's ethics. It may well be argued that, for Aquinas, reception and action are both present in loving, but they are not two sides of one and the same act. I myself think there is some ambiguity here. Aquinas surely speaks of both receptivity (since love is a response to good) and action (since love is willing the good of the beloved, and this is not only and always to be understood as a *passio*). Whether these are two different acts or two stages of one act or two sides of one act, the point must still be made that there is active receptivity in Aquinas. Texts of love as indwelling must be brought to bear on this question as well. See *S.T.* I-II.26.4; 28.2; II-II.27.2. It should be added that Aquinas would be more helpful here were he clearer on these two aspects of love. The only clear description I have seen of them is in the phenomenological analysis of the experience of love offered by Jules Toner, *The Experience of Love* (Washington, DC: Corpus Books, 1968). Aquinas would have gained by a more systematic phenomenological method.

[32]*S.T.* I.42.6 ad 2.

erated in God receives being from the generator, not as though that being were received in matter or into a subject . . . but [as] He Who receives divine being from another, not, however, as if He were other from the divine nature."[33]

Creation, for Aquinas, entails the gift of being, so that creatures are, as it were, subsistent receivers.[34] Whatever receives the act of being receives all that it has of being. Divine causality reaches down to being, to activity, to graced being and graced activity, even to freedom.[35] But if the gift of being includes the gift of acting (as it does according to Thomas), then the receptivity that marks created being can be an active receptivity. In personal beings it is active receptivity at the level of being, of knowledge, of love, of freedom.

The love that we saw to be actively receptive can even be a love whose receptive activity is free. The relation between God and human persons is finally a relation in which two liberties meet—God's and the human person's. Aquinas's is not a theology of an active God and a passive creation, nor of an active savior and a passive people. His is not a theology in which the concern to preserve the power of God necessitates a restriction of the freedom of human persons. Indeed, the power of God is more manifest as it can cause even the effect of freedom of choice in his creatures.[36] And this is as true at the level of grace as it is at the level of nature. Charity is itself an enabling grace, so that it does not only pass through the human person who receives it, but it becomes intrinsic to the person's own self. Paradoxically, the receptive awakening by and the active willing of the beloved that is the nature of charity rises truly from the human person as agent, and even as free agent.[37] What is gift must apparently, for Aquinas, be received in its fullness as gift by the kind of active receptivity that alone can be fully gifted.

---

[33]*S.T.* I.27.2 ad 3. See also I.27.1; 28.3 ad 1; 34.1 ad 3; and texts on the procession of the Holy Spirit: I.38.1 ad 3; 43.3. For insight into some aspects of this reality, see Bernard Lonergan, *Verbum: Word and Idea in Aquinas*, ed. David Burrell (South Bend, IN: University of Notre Dame Press, 1967), 207–10.

[34]*S.T.* I.44.1–2; 45.1.

[35]There is, of course, a long line of debate on these matters. It is, perhaps, necessary to caution that the notion of receiving being is a special notion in that there is no prior subject.

[36]*S.T.* I.83.1 ad 3; I-II.109.1; SCG III.94. Lonergan, following Lottin, traces Aquinas's overcoming of the Aristotelian doctrine that the will is a passive potency. See Lonergan, *Grace and Freedom*, ed. J. P. Burns (New York: Herder and Herder, 1971), 95–97.

[37]*De car* 1; 12 ad 24; *S.T.* II-II.23.2. See also *De ver* 28.3c; *S.T.* II-II.6.1 ad 3; I-II.112.2; 113.3 and 7.

Human love can be not only receptively active as spontaneous love, and reflexively free as a gift to the beloved, but it can be yielded across time in a free commitment. Charity is, for Aquinas, always implicitly a committed love.[38] This means that a new dimension of receptivity as well as activity is introduced into love. For a freely chosen commitment of love testifies to the reception of the beloved in the life of the one loving, and by commitment the one who loves yields to the beloved a new claim on his or her love. Such a "yielding" is indeed a surrender, at once eminently active and yet passive. By it one places oneself by one's own action into a relationship whereby one will be acted upon as well as act. One will be claimed, called, at the disposal of another. But the call of the other is always to the freedom of the one who has made the commitment. Freedom gives to another a claim on itself, but if it can respond to the claim only as freedom, then its new being-bound is not a foreclosure on freedom but a new call to continuing self-transcendence.

Finally, if Aquinas's analysis of love and being makes any sense at all, then it provides a clue for fidelity, for the faithful fulfillment of commitment to the end. That is, if love is awakened by the object that is loved, then at least one way for freedom to keep alive the spontaneity of love is to turn it continually to behold the beloved. Fidelity has something very important to do with attention, with rendering the self in its powers of affective and cognitive receptivity present to the beloved again and again—remembering the revelation of lovableness once received, waiting for the revelation still to be given, contemplating what is presently revealed.[39]

If one looks for anguish in Thomas Aquinas over the making of commitments to love, it is not to be found. There is wounding, for the lovableness of the beloved can pierce the heart of the one who loves.[40] There is need for hope, for love yearns and longs for wholeness and union with the beloved.[41] There is fear, for love takes a long time in receiving the peace-giving presence of the beloved.[42] Overall, however, the strongest notes that Thomas strikes are the notes of healing, of hopefulness, of trust. He may do so too easily for contemporary minds

---

[38]*De car* 12 ad 3.
[39]*S.T.* II-II.82.3c; 180.7.
[40]*S.T.* I-II.28.5.
[41]*S.T.* I-II.28.1; see also I.20.1 ad 3.
[42]*S.T.* II-II.19.7 and 8.

and hearts. He may pass too readily over the dread of loss of self, over the weakness and seeming impossibility of faithfulness on the part of human persons, over the uncertainty and doubt that can appear at the heart of even the greatest of committed loves. But his continuing assertion is simply that there is indeed something worthy to be loved, something calling to commitment; that human persons stand under a loving glance, finally, and not under a suspicious stare; that surrender of self is the way to life; that fidelity is, after all, possible; that forgiveness for infidelity is available.

Such assertions depend upon a comprehensive view of reality that sees all things as lovable because they come forth from the love and share in the lovableness of God, that sees human persons called to sealed friendship with God and all other persons in God. Those who find Aquinas's view of reality convincing may want still to challenge the need for commitment, for a pledged love, in the ongoing lives of human persons. Or they may want to clarify the different kinds of love called forth by different kinds of being and to justify the special forms of commitment and even the changes in commitment that some loves entail.[43] Those who find Aquinas's view of reality not persuasive may yet locate in his description of actively receptive human love a place for pondering the opportunities and difficulties of commitment.

Freedom and Process

The heightened experience of change that marks contemporary experience of nearly every aspect of human life has led, on the one hand, to an unwillingness to make commitments and, on the other hand, to a compelling desire to make commitments. If commitments are seen as the introduction of inertia and sterility into human life, as cutting off possibilities for newness in the future, they are eschewed. If they are seen as ways to escape the insecurity and fragmentation of too much change, they are embraced. These kinds of avoidance of commitment and impulsion to commitment are not always unrelated. Experience of the consequences of the latter has confirmed for many the importance of the former. Both, however, point clearly to the fact that an ethic of commitment must take into account the fundamental

---

[43]Aquinas does treat some questions regarding when and how a commitment may be changed or broken. See, for example, *S.T.* II-II.88.3 ad 2; 88.10; 89.9 ad 2; 110.3 ad 5.

element of temporality in human life. Does commitment allow self-process or hinder it? If an individual's life or the life of a community is to be at once open to the future, capable of process, free for the novelty that is entailed in true growth, how is it also to be integral, capable of continuity, free for wholeness? The answer to these questions is going to depend largely on one's notion of the human self and one's understanding of freedom and temporality as constitutive of the self.

The obvious places to turn in Thomas Aquinas with such questions are unfortunately fraught with difficulties for the contemporary mind and therefore likely to be more confusing than helpful—at least in as brief a study as this one. Substance and accident theories of change, for example, have become so obscured by centuries of reinterpretation and misinterpretation that they distract from rather than illuminate serious ethical dialogue about commitment.[44] Act and potency categories are also problematic for too many people to be of any more than minimal assistance for such dialogue, since they connote for contemporary philosophers too-limited notions of prepatterned change. Where we can turn, however, is to Aquinas's treatment of the "human act" and to his overall understanding of human virtue. In these aspects of his thought we shall find clues for discerning the role of freedom in human life and the possibilities for continuity, yet process, in the human self.

In order to sharpen the picture of what we are looking for in Aquinas, we need to digress for a moment to consider what elements are needed in a theory of the self that will provide both for freedom and true self-process. Thus, for example, a theory of the self that affirms process either because of wholly impelling tendencies rising from the person or wholly compelling objects calling forth response from the

---

[44]The substance and accident theory does indeed relate to the need to explain an enduring self that is nonetheless in process. Process philosophers such as Bergson and Whitehead have readily asserted that process entails duration—change with continuity. Insofar as any version of the theory of substance and accidents posits an unchanging, static substrate (or "substand"), it is incompatible with modern insights into process. In fact, however, the substance-accident theory was not, at its best, a theory of unchanging substrates. It was, rather, an attempt to explain how something can continue to exist and yet change profoundly in its mode of existing. It was a theory, at least for Aquinas, that explained how substance itself can change (not merely have extrinsic changes added on to it) and how it can change as a whole subsistent dynamic existent. See, for example, *De potentia* 7.3 ad 4; 9.1; 9.2 ad 6; *S.T.* I.3.5 ad 1; I.77.1 ad 5; *SCG* I.25.10; II.79; IV.49.13. What philosophers of process have so roundly rejected is the interpretation of the substance-accident theory that seventeenth-century empiricists reformulated and critiqued. Such a version of the theory confused, it seems to me, earlier distinctions between "first substance" and "second substance," collapsing the two into the latter.

person will manage to provide for self-process but not for freedom.[45]
On the other hand, a theory of the self that affirms freedom as wholly
unconditioned and undetermined by either forces rising from the
already existing self or objects appealing to the self for response will
manage to provide for freedom but not, in fact, for self-process. Since
the second of these theories has appeared most often in discussions of
commitment (the first renders free commitment an irrelevant issue),
examining it more carefully will be helpful.

An obvious example of a theory that affirms freedom as wholly
unqualifiable by other spontaneities in a person's being is, of course,
that of Jean-Paul Sartre. Sartre is no straw man in this regard, however,
for his whole effort is directed toward finding a way to hold together
the undetermined and the determined in the human self. Freedom is,
for him, fundamental spontaneity, and its impetus is always toward
unification with what it chooses—since that is the only way it can
finally be what it wants to be. All possibilities are open to freedom,
and it seeks to coincide with at least some of them, to objectify itself
in them. Its way of doing this while remaining spontaneous is to surge
forward continually, living out the synthesis between choosing and
being chosen by a temporal *ekstasis* that makes every choice a past as
soon as it is made and moves in the present to choose a new future.
Continuity in the self is attained only through commitment, for it is
by engagement in a fundamental project that freedom holds together a
future (by intention) and a past (as cause of the intention) in a present
(movement toward the end intended).[46]

Sartre, in trying to find a way to provide for continual process that
is free and that belongs to the self, overshoots his mark, however. Sartrean freedom by its very nature remains always capable of breaking
the process, of reversing a commitment. In an "instant" can come the

---

[45]It is interesting that some theories of the self as a social self and a responder have
fallen into the latter category. Thus, for example, George Herbert Mead's philosophy
has been criticized for failing to provide for freedom. Freedom is the "I" spasmodically
appearing almost as we shall see Sartre's for-itself appearing in the "instant." Even H.
Richard Niebuhr's "responsible self" is sometimes unclear about the room it provides for
freedom. See George Herbert Mead, *Mind, Self, and Society: From the Standpoint of a
Social Behaviorist* (Chicago: University of Chicago Press, 1962). See also Gibson Winter,
Elements for a Social Ethic: Scientific and Ethical Perspectives on Social Process (Chicago:
University of Chicago Press, 1960); H. Richard Niebuhr, *The Responsible Self* (New York:
Harper and Row, 1963).

[46]Sartre, *Being and Nothingness*, 563.

radical ending of one fundamental project and the radical beginning of another.[47] Freedom is never held, never bound, never qualified so that it cannot inject total discontinuity with its past. Is it not the case, then, that freedom itself is never changed? The fundamental spontaneity of the self[48] is never changed. Nothing, after all, ever happens in the deepest recesses of personal being. At heart, the person is finally nontemporal, not in process. Despite Sartre's effort to provide an alternative to the Cartesian and Kantian nontemporal self, it is difficult not to conceive of the Sartrean for-itself as finally an observer of the selves that it cannot grasp—a hungry, driving, plunging observer, it is true, but an observer nonetheless.[49] Self-creating, self-determining, self-processing freedom is finally, in Sartre, impotent. There is left, finally, only contradiction for a self-creating freedom that cannot create lest it destroy its possibility of creating.[50]

We begin to see that if a self is going to be in process precisely as free, then freedom must be able to determine itself, to change itself. As Merleau-Ponty asserts, "The very notion of freedom demands that our decision should plunge into the future, that something should have been *done* by it, that the subsequent instant should benefit from its predecessor and, though not necessitated, should be at least required by it."[51] If the whole self includes both freedom and other aspects such as affective spontaneities, then the whole self can be in process only if the relation between freedom and the rest of the self is more mutual than it is for Sartre. Thus, for example, freedom must be able to take

---

[47]At first glance Sartre's "instant" seems not other than the possibility of freedom as it comes through "fundamental option" theories. In fact, the latter include precisely the power for freedom finally to determine itself. Sartre radically eliminates this from freedom by the concept of the "instant."

[48]It is important, in order to avoid confusion, to note that Sartre equates "spontaneity" with freedom. I have been referring to it in relation to nonfree affectivities. The use of the term is equivocal, not analogous.

[49]In one sense it is unfair to Sartre to make of the for-itself a nontemporal observer. The for-itself as prepersonal in relation to the in-itself as the ego-self is Sartre's alternative to Kant's unification of consciousness. Even the characteristic of desire in the relation, however, does not keep consciousness from finally simply annihilating the in-itself as its own self.

[50]It is interesting to compare Lifton's description of the self-process of "protean man" with Sartre's theory here. Just as, in theory, Sartrean man seems finally unable to be in process because of Sartre's view of freedom, so "protean man" always seems to experience lack of process more clearly than process. This is as true for him between commitments as it is within commitments.

[51]Maurice Merleau-Ponty, *Phenomenology of Perception*, trans. Colin Smith (New York: Humanities Press, 1967), 437.

hold of spontaneities, but freedom itself must be finally qualified by them. If this is not to seem only the obvious point about freedom's limitations, then freedom must finally qualify, determine, itself through qualifying, determining, the spontaneities that it chooses. It is only a theory of the self that understands freedom in this way that can make sense of both freedom and self-process. If such a theory in turn makes sense of our experience, it will show us whether commitment is the friend or the enemy of creative self-process.

If we return, then, to Thomas Aquinas's philosophy, it is to look for a relation between free choice and other fundamental elements in the human self (especially spontaneous affectivity). We do not, I think, find a fully adequate description of freedom or of the self, but there are starting points, clues, that can be crucial for contemporary probing of these questions. One of these clues emerges from the obvious inconsistency between Aquinas's analysis of free choice of means within the human act[52] and his analysis of the will, in general, as willing ends spontaneously but without necessity.[53] When Aquinas is discussing free choice directly, he maintains with Aristotle that it can be choice only of means, not of ends—of useful goods, not goods that are good in themselves. Yet, when speaking of the spontaneous (that is, not free) response of the will to goods as ends, he insists that no ends move the will necessarily—that is, no ends short of God when he is encountered face to face in the Beatific Vision. This can mean simply that not all goods are able to awaken a spontaneous affective response on the part of human persons (goods are not always adequately revealed, and human capacities for perceiving goodness are sometimes deficient). But it means more than this for Thomas. Since spontaneous responses that human persons have toward goods are not absolutely necessitated, there is always the option of not thinking about, not attending to, a given good even if it has already awakened a spontaneous affective response.[54] There is, thus, according to Aquinas, not a freedom of "specification" regarding the will's response to ends (an end perceived as good will necessarily awaken a response), but there is a freedom of "exercise."[55] Now, this seems to imply some choice regarding ends.

---

[52]*S.T.* I-II.13. See also I.83.
[53]See *S.T.* I.82.2; I-II.10.2; *De ver* 24.7 ad 6.
[54]*S.T.* I.82.2.
[55]See Lonergan's interpretation of this in *Grace and Freedom*, 95ff.

Moreover, there is some indication in Aquinas that even when the will is spontaneously responding to an end (and does not cease to respond simply by not thinking about it), it can choose against it by choosing an opposing end (choosing to identify with one rather than the other, to place the means for, to attain or preserve, to implement one rather than the other).[56] Such choices of one end in opposition to another are surely some kind of specification of ends. If one were to argue that choices of ends in this way are really choices of ends that are for the sake of more ultimate ends (hence, ends that as objects of choice are really means), this would only push the problem further back. It is true that, for Thomas, the will necessarily wills happiness; but it is also true, apparently, that it can choose what, in fact, will constitute its happiness. This seems to be most accurately described as a choice of end.[57]

Let us take this line of thought in Aquinas and place it within the context of his description of the human act. As we have noted, here free choice is said to be choice only of means, not of ends. But the very possibility of free choice arises within the complex "human act" in which the will is first spontaneously moved in response to some good (volition) and, similarly, spontaneously moved to want to attain that good through some means (intention). Without the prior spontaneous inclinations of the will, no choice of means would be possible. That is, no action would constitute a possible object of choice (as means), unless it were perceived and desired as relating to some end that is also perceived and responded to with spontaneous affectivity. Is it not possible to say, then, that every choice of means is at least implicitly a ratification of the already existing spontaneous affection for an end? And if it is possible to choose the means to one end in opposition to another means to another end (a possibility suggested by the other line of thought we have noted in Aquinas), then is it not the case that free choice is a choice to ratify, identify with, one existing spontaneous affection and to refuse to ratify, identify with, another existing spontaneous affection?[58] Aquinas's theory cannot itself finally account for

---

[56]*De car* 12c.

[57]Given any validity to my interpretation of active receptivity in Aquinas's thought, this should not be taken to mean only an end to be attained in the sense that H. Richard Niebuhr interprets the ends of "man the maker."

[58]I am here, of necessity, oversimplifying the elements included in the self as chosen.

these conclusions, for he never sees the full consequences of his analysis of the human act, and he never adequately explains the seeming inconsistency between that analysis and his treatment of the nonnecessity of willing ends. His theory does, however, lay important groundwork for such conclusions, and, in fact, it may be said to demand a move to such conclusions beyond itself.

What are the implications of such a move? The first implication is that Aquinas's theory at least points to a theory of the self and freedom in which there is mutuality between freedom and spontaneity in the very act of choosing. Freedom is here not freedom in spite of spontaneous inclinations but, in fact, is dependent upon spontaneous inclinations. If the actions presented for choice are dependent upon prior inclinations rising out of the existing self, then free choice is possible only where there are such inclinations. On the other hand, spontaneous inclinations are also dependent upon freedom. When they arise in tension with opposing inclinations, they cannot issue in the action to which they incline until they are released by free choice. Further, even if they could issue in action without choice (the strongest inclination simply overwhelming any others—which is clearly sometimes the case), they are not wholly integrated into the human self until they are ratified by freedom.

The second implication of the move we have made based on but going beyond Aquinas's thought is that the mutuality between freedom and spontaneity accounts for self-process. This becomes clear if we look to Aquinas's theory of virtue. Whatever else this theory means, it includes the premise that free choices modify the being of the person who makes them. In our present context this can be clarified by saying that choices to ratify or not to ratify spontaneous inclinations to action (by allowing them to flow into action) modify the spontaneous inclinations. Over a period of time, the person changes; some spontaneous inclinations grow stronger and others weaker; fundamental loves out of which desires rise grow more or less intense, more or less integral with the whole of the person's being. Freedom does not have

---

Were there the opportunity to do a thorough analysis of this, I would need to include more than spontaneous affectivities (include, therefore, the self as knowing, the judgments the self makes, and so forth). It would also be necessary to distinguish more clearly than I have done here the spontaneous affective response that is fundamental love from spontaneous inclinations, tendencies, desires, which (as we have seen) arise from fundamental love. The necessary expansion of these ideas is included in my forthcoming work on the act of freedom and the nature of the self.

absolute control over such spontaneities, but it does affect them in some ways. Hence it is that the person through freedom determines himself or herself. But more than this, given the dependence of freedom upon these spontaneities, freedom itself is changed eventually by its own choices. The whole self, therefore, is in process—enduring yet changing, coming to be in the future yet in continuity with its own past.

Finally, it can be said that, if Aquinas offers a way to understand the mutuality of freedom and spontaneity in every free choice and in overall self-process, then there is also in his theory a way to understand freedom and process in relation to commitment to interpersonal love. First of all, in the mutuality between freedom and spontaneous response there is a self to give in commitment to another. This is simply not the case if there is only necessitated response and no freedom, or if there is an isolated freedom that can determine everything but its own self. But, second, if freedom can indeed gather itself and yield itself to the beloved so that it gives a claim over itself for the future, then we begin to see how it is that process continues but is changed. When a commitment is made, something happens in the present. That is to say, the person making the commitment steps into a new relationship with the one to whom the commitment is made. Two persons in process, two temporalities, meet in a way such that the one dwells in the other by reason of a yielded claim. The commitment event holds together the past (for the commitment could not have been chosen had there not already been a spontaneous love for the other and a desire rising out of that love to commit itself) and the future (for in yielding a claim to future free choices, freedom determines itself to be called now from the other). But the commitment event does so because it effects a commitment relation. It is the commitment relation that now moves into the future. Freedom yields itself to another and thereby gives itself a new law. The whole point of its new law is to call it to continual refinement of receptive activity and active receptivity so that the self may be ever more for the beloved, may dwell ever more wholly in and with the beloved. When the commitment is mutual, the process of each person is so qualified by the commitment relation that one may speak no longer only of virtue in each one but of the virtue of the relation. The names for virtue of relation are many, but one of them at least must be intimacy.

We have, however, gone beyond Thomas Aquinas. If our attention to his theories has been faithful, he has himself pointed to such going beyond. My contention throughout this exploration has been that the theology of Aquinas can indeed provide some prolegomena for an ethic of commitment. We miss in Aquinas a strong theology of covenant, a clearer recognition of mutuality between human persons, a closer view of temporality and process. Yet few theologies offer firmer grounds for understanding how even between God and human persons two liberties can meet. And few philosophies suggest so surely that there is indeed a self to give. And few theologies or philosophies point so profoundly to the graced hope of a committed love.

I have, in summary, tried to locate in the vast legacy of Thomas Aquinas those areas of his thought that can open to fruitful dialogue on pressing issues of commitment to interpersonal love. Law and love, active receptivity, freedom and process—they can only be fragments for an ethic of commitment. It is perhaps strange to take fragments when Aquinas's genius was for wholeness. When the pieces of contemporary questions of commitment have themselves settled into place, however, we shall perhaps be able to see in relation to Thomas Aquinas not the fragments of a whole but the wholeness in the fragments.

CHAPTER 3

The Role of Experience
in Moral Discernment

"Deliberation is an aspect of discernment, but discernment is more than deliberation."[1] The distinction is a readily recognized one between deliberation primarily as a rational process (which may include, for example, clarifying empirical data, weighing reasons, calculating consequences, determining priorities in the application of ethical principles) and discernment as a more complex (imaginative, affective, perhaps aesthetic and even religious) process of searching, illuminating, sifting, recognizing, comprehending, and judging options for moral action against and within a wide horizon of relevant factors. Experience plays an important role in both deliberating and discerning. This essay, while not ignoring the importance of experience for deliberation, nonetheless aims beyond it to explore the implications of experience for moral discernment as a whole.

In its broadest sense, experience is essential for every form of knowledge. Whether one holds that "all knowledge comes through the senses" or that ideas can be innate to our minds, human knowledge consists in some grasping of what is known in the experience of knowing. When a narrower meaning is sought for "experience," however, a multitude of usages emerge.[2] Many of them are theory-dependent, as when "ex-

A version of this essay was published in *Christian Ethics: Problems and Prospects*, ed. Lisa Sowle Cahill and James F. Childress (Cleveland: Pilgrim Press, 1996), 134–51. Used with permission.

[1]James M. Gustafson, "Afterword," in *James M. Gustafson's Theocentric Ethics: Interpretations and Assessments*, ed. Harlan R. Beckley and Charles M. Swezey (Macon, GA: Mercer University Press, 1988), 243.

[2]These meanings are selectively adapted from Karl Lehmann, "Experience," in *Sacra-*

periential" knowledge is contrasted with "objective" knowledge, or experience is contrasted with thought, or experience is limited to what is verifiable through the senses. Less theoretical or technical meanings of experience include the direct apprehension of an object, thought, or emotion, as in an "experience of a blizzard" or an "experience of hope"; the accumulation of knowledge or skills through repeated activities or encounters, as when one becomes "experienced with computers"; the development of an insight through participation in an event or the endurance of some influence, as when "experience teaches"; testing one's knowledge in some kind of experiment or trial, a meaning rooted in the Latin *experiri*, to test, confirm, find out.

The above meanings are familiar to most people, and they are not difficult to understand. When, however, we begin to ask about the role of experience in moral discernment and moral reasoning, its meaning becomes more elusive and its significance is frequently contested. Yet in theological ethics as in theology there was a kind of "turn to experience" in the twentieth century. The turn has been sufficiently remarkable to generate overviews of its emergence as well as historical and analytical studies of the sorts of appeals it represents.[3] Readiness for such a turn may be accounted for in a number of ways. Western philosophical traditions consistently have found a role for experience in the development of anthropologies, in a search for epistemological groundings, and in a concern for practical guides to action. Contemporary examples abound in which historical attention to human experience is brought forward into constructive proposals for ethical theory. The twentieth century also brought a new interest in Aristotelian "spheres of human experience" and their corresponding virtues.[4] Even when the term "experience" is not used, those who

mentum Mundi: An Encyclopedia of Theology, ed. Karl Rahner et al. (New York: Herder and Herder, 1968), 2:307–9; F. W. Dillistone, "Religious Experience," in *The Westminster Dictionary of Christian Theology*, ed. Alan Richardson and John Bowden (Philadelphia: Westminster Press, 1983), 204–7; Antony Flew, ed., *A Dictionary of Philosophy*, rev. 2nd ed. (New York: St. Martin's Press, 1984), 116–17; *The American Heritage Dictionary of the English Language*, 3rd ed. (Boston: Houghton Mifflin, 1992), 644.

   [3]See, e.g., George P. Schner, "The Appeal to Experience," *Theological Studies* 53 (March 1992): 40–59; Donald L. Gelpi, *The Turn to Experience in Contemporary Theology* (New York: Paulist Press, 1994); Susan L. Secker, "Human Experience and Women's Experience: Resources for Catholic Ethics," *The Annual: Society of Christian Ethics* (1991): 133–50.

   [4]See Martha Nussbaum, "Non-Relative Virtues: An Aristotelian Approach," in *The Quality of Life*, ed. Martha C. Nussbaum and Amartya Sen (Oxford: Clarendon Press, 1993), 242–76.

draw on Thomas Aquinas's theory of moral action are depending on descriptive analyses of human experience of complex choices.[5] Varieties of British empiricism and American pragmatism continue to make claims on ethical methodology and moral epistemology.[6] Edmund Husserl, Jean-Paul Sartre, and Maurice Merleau-Ponty cast shadows (however drastically altered) on phenomenological descriptions of the experience of moral obligation and affective moral response.[7]

What I shall mean by "experience" in this essay is the actual living of events and relationships, along with the sensations, feelings, images, emotions, insights, and understandings that are part of this lived reality. Experience in this sense is a given, something providing data to be interpreted; but it is also something that is already interpreted, its content shaped by previous understandings in a context of multiple influences. Moreover, experience, as I shall address it, can belong both to the self and to others; it can be both personal and social. Experience is private, individual, unique to the one who experiences; but there are shared experiences, communicated as well as formed within communities and societies. Experience in each of these senses—given but not primitive, immediate but not innocent of interpretation, personal but not isolated, unique but not without a social matrix—plays an important role in moral discernment. It is a source of moral insight, a factor in moral judgment, a test of the rightness, goodness, and wisdom of moral decision.

There are, of course, other sources for moral discernment. In Christian ethics, for example, experience commonly is identified as a source along with scripture, tradition (theological, pedagogical, devotional, communal), and secular disciplines (philosophy, the physical and social sciences, literature, and any other of reason's disciplined approaches to morally relevant understandings of human life and the world). Within the many strands of the Christian tradition, individuals and communities have made varying decisions about the relative significance of the different sources. Depending on the nature of these decisions, each of the sources can shape the content of the others and provide a perspective for their interpretation. All of the sources together can be

---

[5]See, e.g., Jean Porter, *Moral Action and Christian Ethics* (Cambridge: Cambridge University Press, 1995).

[6]See, e.g., Gelpi, *Turn to Experience.*

[7]See, e.g., Maurice Mandelbaum, *The Phenomenology of Moral Experience* (Baltimore: Johns Hopkins University Press, 1969); Jules J. Toner, *The Experience of Love* (Washington, DC: Corpus Books, 1968).

used dialectically in moral discernment. But whatever decisions are made about the use of sources, it seems fair to say that experience is never just one source among many. It is always an important part of the content of each of the other sources, and it is always a key factor in the interpretation of the others. Scripture, for example, is the record of some persons' experience of God; tradition represents a community's experience through time; humanistic and even scientific studies are shaped by the experience of those who engage in them.[8] Past experience, therefore, provides content for all of the sources, and present experience provides a necessary and inescapable vantage point for interpreting them.

Present experience also, in itself, offers a quasi-discrete (though not isolatable) source for knowledge, understanding, and moral discernment. It is experience in this sense—the contemporary actual living of events and relationships—whose role in moral deliberation and discernment is most frequently contested. It is beset by problems of access, authority, and the identification of criteria for governing its use. Deconstructive critiques have rendered knowledge of experience more and more unattainable and experience itself more and more suspect as a ground for self-knowledge or a guide for choice. Conflicts between appeals to experience and appeals to the Bible or to tradition have threatened to undermine the authority of experience or to place it over against the authority of at least other Christian sources for moral discernment. There are as yet no generally accepted criteria for determining what and whose experience counts as authoritative, especially when long-standing moral rules are challenged or when the experience of some is at odds with the experience of others.

It is not possible in an essay as limited as this one to address with any satisfaction all of the objections to a role for experience in moral discernment. Nonetheless, what I want to do is (1) explore, however briefly, the positive uses of experience in Christian ethics; (2) take account of some of the most telling weaknesses in these uses; and (3) advance, however modestly, a discussion of the ethical importance of experience in spite of its problems.

---

[8]See, e.g., Sandra Harding, *Whose Science? Whose Knowledge? Thinking from Women's Lives* (Ithaca, NY: Cornell University Press, 1991); Evelyn Fox Keller, *Reflections on Gender and Science* (New Haven, CT: Yale University Press, 1985).

An obvious way to examine the positive role of experience in moral discernment is to look to contemporary approaches to Christian ethics in which experience is given a central place. Two such approaches suggest themselves, unlikely in their overall pairing but alike in their insistence on a role for experience in more than one aspect of moral discernment. The two approaches are James M. Gustafson's in the development of his theocentric ethics and the approach taken by feminist theorists in their construction of a liberation ethics that is methodologically committed to beginning with the experience of women. In both of these efforts, experience has several significant roles. It is central for finding and establishing an overall framework for moral discernment; it is important for formulating and applying general ethical principles and specific ethical rules; and it plays a key role in developing theories of moral disposition.

Christian Ethics and Experience

Ethics and the Experience of God

No contemporary ethicist has addressed more consistently and systematically the question of the sources for Christian ethics than James Gustafson. For nearly five decades he has provided the field of Christian ethics with careful considerations of the methodological roles of scripture, theology, tradition, the sciences, philosophy, human experience, and countless variations on these in the development of theological ethics.[9] Each source is important in itself, but Gustafson's position has been all along that no one source is sufficient without the others. None of them alone constitutes an adequate court of appeal in determining moral obligation in a particular situation; no one of them by itself can provide all that we need to know about moral dispositions and the moral requirements of relationships. This said, there always has been, nonetheless, at least an implicit recognition in Gustafson's

---

[9]See, e.g., James M. Gustafson, *Christ and the Moral Life* (New York: Harper and Row, 1968), chap. 7; "The Place of Scripture in Christian Ethics: A Methodological Study," in *Theology and Christian Ethics* (Philadelphia: Pilgrim Press, 1974), 121–45; "The Relationship of Empirical Science to Moral Thought," in *Theology and Christian Ethics*, 215–28; "Theological Interpretation of the Significance of Circumstances," *Can Ethics Be Christian?* (Chicago: University of Chicago Press, 1975), 117–44.

work of what he explicitly identifies in *Ethics from a Theocentric Perspective* as the "priority of human experience."[10]

For Gustafson, experience is prior to other sources for Christian ethics at both the beginning and the end of moral discernment. It is chronologically and psychologically prior because it is what needs to be interpreted with the help of the other sources. And, in the end, it constitutes the final test of the accuracy and adequacy of the interpretation achieved.[11] There would be no Bible or any other form of revelation were there no human experience to be shaped and interpreted by it; there would be no work for practical reason were there no experience for reason to address and to employ; there would be no theology or ethics were there no religion and morality, aspects of experience whose meanings need to be understood and articulated. "Both revelation and reason are human reflections on human experiences."[12]

Criteria intrinsic to the formulations of both reason and revelation determine their general use in interpreting the moral significance of experience, and criteria governing the relationship between these resources and the experience to be interpreted determine their further usefulness for illuminating particular circumstances and events. In other words, there are tests to be met in the interpretive process, including the critical scrutiny of other interpreters.[13] But, in the end, the interpretation must "make sense" to the interpreter; it must make sense *of*, but also *to*, the interpreter's experience.[14]

The nature of experience insofar as it is relevant to Gustafson's moral theory is complex, and its content comes from multiple arenas, shaped by multiple forces. It is prior to reflection; yet like Aristotle's prime matter, it cannot exist without some form, some reflective elements that give it meaning from the start. Its arenas are nature, history, culture, society, the self, and the inevitable combinations of these. It involves more than one dimension of the self, for in it are commingled affectivity and cognition, imagination and the many forms of human activity. It can be predominantly aesthetic, intellectual, religious, or

---

[10]James M. Gustafson, *Ethics from a Theocentric Perspective*, 2 vols. (Chicago: University of Chicago Press, 1981–1984), 1:115 (hereafter *Ethics*).

[11]The terminology here is mine, but I believe it is a faithful rendering of Gustafson's position—not only in *Ethics*, but earlier in, e.g., *Christ and the Moral Life*, 57; *Can Ethics Be Christian?*, 143, 176.

[12]Gustafson, *Ethics*, 1:148.

[13]See Gustafson, *Can Ethics Be Christian?*, 130–43.

[14]Ibid., 176; *Christ and the Moral Life*, 57; *Ethics*, 2:144.

moral. It is profoundly social, rising out of the interaction between persons and events, generated in and by the historical and cultural matrix of meanings that make up the fabric of a community or society. "Its significance is explained and its meanings assessed in communities that share common objects of interest and attention and share some common concepts, symbols, and theories."[15] Socially conditioned, it also has universal human elements, as in the experience of "fault."[16]

If experience is always already structured (by previous experience previously interpreted), and if it is structured so that individually and socially we are predisposed to look for and find certain meanings, and if experience is itself the final judge of the interpretation it receives, then we appear to be faced, as Gustafson acknowledges, with an unavoidable circularity.[17] Moreover, insofar as moral theory depends on descriptive accounts importantly based in experience, "There is an inevitable circularity to moral theory."[18] But for Gustafson, the circles can be "large and nonvicious," drawn from different starting points, dependent not on naive intuition, subject to assessment and to change by the individual and the community. Perspective influences interpretation, but interpretations and their consequences can also influence perspective. Just as in modern science, a mutually corrective process can occur whereby "beliefs, metaphors, and theories presumed to be adequate to explain or interpret the meaning of what is experienced prove to be inadequate, and must be revised."[19] For Gustafson, then, there are "reality checks" for our interpretations of experience. These checks do not move us completely outside our experience but offer pragmatic tests within ongoing experience, social tests insofar as we share experiences, and even the tests endemic to experience itself because of its "objective pole": Grounded in experience of the self, it nonetheless has both content and sources that are "other than self."[20]

There are many ways in which James Gustafson appeals to experience, his own and others', in the development of his Christian ethic.

---

[15]Gustafson, *Ethics*, 1:115.
[16]See ibid., 1:194. The facets of "human fault" that Gustafson believes to be common to the experience of all human beings include misplaced trust, misplaced valuations of objects of desire, erroneous perceptions of the relations among things, unfulfilled obligations and duties.
[17]Ibid., 1:234.
[18]Ibid., 1:118.
[19]Ibid., 1:3.
[20]Ibid., 1:128.

Key to his theocentric ethic, however, is his initial description of the cultural and religious circumstances of the contemporary historical period. This description both motivates and provides direction for Gustafson's ethic. In an age of unprecedented scientific and social progress, Gustafson finds a sharpened experience of human limitation. In an era of massive efforts and achievements in the control of nature and the alleviation of human suffering, he discovers relentless experiences of threat from powers we are helpless to tame. In this context, religion has become a utility value, a source of assurance that all shall be well, a promise of benefits in this world if not in another.[21] The result in our moral lives is the fueling of desires and of fears that turn us in upon ourselves. Everything is measured in terms of human needs; the human species becomes the center of the universe; and human well-being, individual and social, becomes the central ethical concern.[22] All of this, unfortunately, is counterproductive, for we remain limited and under threat, human well-being is not finally served, and we are not even genuinely religiously consoled.

But there is another way. The fundamental elements in contemporary cultural experience can yield a different meaning. Paradoxes of possibility and limitation, mastery and helplessness, dependence and threat, admit of radically different interpretations from the ones currently favored in the culture. If one takes the experiences with utter seriousness, tests them with the resources of scientific reason, and consents to the appropriateness of religious symbols in discerning their meaning, one can understand the experiences differently and even transform them as experiences. This is what James Gustafson proposes in his development of a theocentric perspective for theology and ethics.

It is possible (though not inevitable), Gustafson argues, to experience the reality of God in all of the arenas and forms of human experience. We do so insofar as our awareness of objects (in nature, culture, ourselves) evokes affections that have religious meaning. Affections have religious meaning when they are responses to objects that are perceived to be related to an Ultimate Power.[23] The Ultimate Power is the Power that bears down on us but also sustains us, that sets an ordering of relationships within the cosmos and provides condi-

---

[21] Ibid., 1: chap. 1.
[22] Ibid.
[23] Ibid., 1:195–96, 225–35; 264.

tions of possibilities and a sense of direction for human activity. The experience of such a Power is still accessible in a culture where new desires for progress and control bring with them a heightened sense of limitation and vulnerability. For God can be met in our experiences of contingency and powerlessness just as in our experiences of beauty and order. And a genuine experience of God, of an Ultimate Power, makes possible in and for us a decentering of ourselves and the human community in our understanding of the universe and even in our desires for its good. From this experience emerges the radical possibility of a Christian ethic that relativizes human well-being not only before God but before reality as a whole.

Critics of Gustafson largely have focused on his doctrine of God—its agnosticism about divine agency, the unrelenting *via negativa* that disallows concepts of personhood or intelligence to be attributed to God, and Gustafson's acknowledged ambivalence regarding God's "friendship" or "enmity" toward humans. Charges are made regarding the importance given to science as a source for theology and ethics, the selection of symbols inappropriate to the biblical traditions, and the practical denial of Christian beliefs about God's self-revelation. It may be that all of these criticisms are finally rejections of Gustafson's interpretation of the experience of God and his use of that interpretation as the keystone for a theocentric ethic.

Yet Gustafson's theory about the role of experience (and in particular the experience of God) in moral discernment is carefully nuanced. It cannot be rejected wholesale, at least not without taking account of its parts. First of all, Gustafson does not argue from a necessary and humanly innate experience of God, but from a human experience of the world that is open to theological construal. Second, he affirms the pluralism even in Christian accounts of the experience of God. It is an experience that admits of many aspects, and some particular experiences may be marked by the predominance of one aspect over others.[24] Thus, for example, while an argument may be made from experience and the biblical witness for a more personal, promising, providential God than Gustafson's Ultimate Power, the stark and ambiguous evidence of a deity who is "in the details," not a guarantor of individual temporal well-being, is an important corrective to sentimental longings that reduce God to a safety net under life's mistakes

---

[24]Gustafson, *Can Ethics Be Christian?*, 138ff.

and disasters. In addition, Gustafson has theoretical room for the selective retrieval of traditional concepts and symbols as interpreters of present experience. He acknowledges that strands in the biblical and Christian traditions suggest purposes of God other than the ones he selects for his theocentric perspective.[25] Moreover, Gustafson's agnosticism regarding God's purposes and the well-being of humans does not rule out a divine intention for the genuine good of humans, precisely as participants in the *telos* of the whole of creation.[26] To hold that the dignity of the human individual is within the order of nature rather than in the grandeur of freedom is not to deny both dignity and grandeur that are both natural and free.[27]

However one adjudicates Gustafson's position in relation to the problems raised by his critics, the point here is the centrality of experience for the basic framework of a Christian ethic. More specifically, the point here is the centrality of an experience of God that provides a framework for Christian ethics, a determinant of general principles and specific rules, and a source for understanding the dispositions necessary for moral discernment. As the shaper of a framework, this experience of God makes possible a radical conversion from the self to the other and from a part to the whole.[28] In our experience of dependence and interdependence, we understand what we *are*[29] and we know that we are obligated.[30] Our general obligation is to relate to all things as they are related to God.[31] Moral discernment becomes an act of piety as we probe our experience in all of its details, and as we explore (with every resource that we have) God's ordering of a world full of value.[32] Searching for God's purposes, for what is "fitting" in our relationships and activities, we are not often privileged with absolute clarity and certainty. Specific moral norms are at best "almost universal" or "almost absolute."[33] Nonetheless, whether we are discerning population policies, the morality of abortion in particular cases, or our

---

[25]Ibid., chap. 5; Gustafson, *Ethics*, 1:111.

[26]Gustafson, *Ethics*, 1:91, 96, 112, 202, 271; *Can Ethics Be Christian?*, 159.

[27]Gustafson, *Ethics*, 1:96, 99.

[28]See summary profile of theocentric ethics in *Ethics*, 2: chap. 1.

[29]James M. Gustafson, "A Response to Critics," *Journal of Religious Ethics* 13 (Fall 1985): 191.

[30]Gustafson, *Ethics*, 1:131–32; *Can Ethics Be Christian?*, 173.

[31]Gustafson, *Ethics*, 1:131–32.

[32]Gustafson, in Beckley and Swezey, *Gustafson's Theocentric Ethics*, 243.

[33]Gustafson, *Ethics*, 1:113, 244; *Can Ethics Be Christian?*, 158.

obligation to those who choose suicide, we must examine the patterns of interdependence, hold ourselves accountable to one another and to the whole of which we are a part, and attempt to be faithful to the Power that is acting in it all. Dispositions of gratitude, of self-denial, of perseverance in attending to the objects of our experience are to be nurtured alongside dispositions of epistemic humility and courage.

Ethics and the Experience of Injustice

It is difficult enough in a short essay to attempt to present fairly the uses of experience in the ethics of an individual theologian. It is even more difficult to try to identify common features of a whole field within ethics. Contemporary feminist theological ethics has no one spokesperson and no one version upon which to draw. A shared enterprise, it has marked stages in its development and sharp disagreements among its participants. Still, some things can be said about it that will contribute to considerations of the role of experience in moral discernment.

Feminist uses of experience share much in common with James Gustafson's uses. In both there is a strong reliance on experience as a source of moral insight. Like Gustafson, feminists recognize the importance of other sources for Christian ethics, but the other sources can be tested by experience. Experience itself needs to be interpreted, but it also validates the interpretation it achieves. Experience is embedded in a social and cultural matrix, since "society is in us before we are in society."[34] A hermeneutical circle is unavoidable, but it need not be vicious. In fact, experience can "explode as a critical force,"[35] disrupting traditions even as it serves to sustain them.

If there are formal similarities between the role of experience in Gustafson's ethics and in feminist ethics, however, the content of the experience and the issues it raises are often different indeed. Contemporary feminist theory began with the experience of women, with the growing awareness among women of the dissonance between their

---

[34]The phrase is Beverly Harrison's. See "The Older Person's Worth in the Eyes of Society," in *Making the Connections: Essays in Feminist Social Ethics* (Boston: Beacon Press, 1985), 153.

[35]Rosemary Radford Ruether, "Feminist Interpretation: A Method of Correlation," in *Feminist Interpretation of the Bible*, ed. Letty M. Russell (Philadelphia: Westminster, 1985), 113.

interpretation of their own experience and the interpretations given to them by cultures and religious traditions whose experiential sources were almost solely those of men. Like other liberation theorists, feminists have pressed the question of whose experience counts when a community discerns its goals and actions and when it distributes its goods and its roles. Attention therefore turned to those whose voices of experience were largely absent from traditions, and the focus was on experiences of injustice and the efforts to change the systems and circumstances that caused the injustice. This is the experience that is necessary and primary, though not sufficient, for moral discernment.

Access to women's experience has been through individual reflection and group communication, but also through the gathering of new empirical data. The experiences of "ordinary people" as well as the "signs of the times" are raised up. Experiences of the past as well as of the present are retrieved and reinterpreted. What was hidden needs to be revealed, whether through biblical studies, literature, cultural analyses, or critical historical studies. In this process, the power of traditional religious symbols to explain women's experience has been weakened, so that reform efforts, reinterpretations of the symbols themselves, have become intrinsic to the task of feminist theology and ethics.

For women to claim their own interpretation of their experience is to claim a new identity. It is to claim gender equality, a capacity for mutuality, genuine agency, a right to bodily integrity, new valuations of sexuality, and gender justice in family and society. These claims are made as truth claims, the basis for ethical norms and for political strategies. To reach the beliefs that undergird such claims, feminists have not naively reflected on the experience of women but have engaged in a process of "unmasking" experience, deconstructing their own experience, resisting complicity in a generalized "false consciousness." This would not have been possible, at least not on a large scale, without some previous changes in experience, initiated by cultural shifts that allowed new possibilities for women. Access to experience has thus meant a dialectical process wherein the unthinkable becomes thinkable, experience influences experience, self-criticism yields cultural criticism, and a new consciousness develops.

Feminists who continue to stand in the Christian tradition have brought their experience to critical reformulations of doctrines of God and of creation, theological anthropology and ecclesiology. For many feminists, the problem with God has not been Gustafson's problem with utilitarian theological construals of a God too domesticated to be God; their problem has been whether God is an oppressor, one who uses women for men. For many feminists, the problem with traditional concepts of creation is not that women have been made the center of the universe, but that women, like nature, have been valued only instrumentally in relation to the human species and in relation to the goals of cosmic control. Feminist theologians have probed both experience and tradition, looking for intelligible and persuasive convergences, seeking theological meanings for the religious dimensions of experience. In doing so they have selected from the tradition symbols that they discerned to be appropriate to their experience. Through these symbols they can recognize the God of their tradition as both immanent and transcendent; they can expand on notions of *imago dei* and explore the possibilities of mutuality between God and the world; they can find theological models for justice and for judgment in human affairs; they are able to identify responsibility in relation to the universe; they find it possible to glimpse religious meaning even in human suffering.[36]

Critics of feminist theology frequently charge that the reformulation of symbols is unfaithful to the tradition. It offers a false god, the projection of selfish human desires. It gives human experience an unwarranted authority over God's self-revelation in the Bible and Christian tradition. Feminist ethics, it is said, imports both rationalism and romanticism into Christian understandings of relationship, eliminating rich concepts of gender complementarity and distorting the natural meaning of the human. Moreover, feminist theories of virtue trivialize traditional notions of self-sacrifice and miss the point of the sinfulness that pervades human nature. If liberation theologies generally are tempted to make of religion a utility value in the achievement of justice, critics maintain that feminist theologies go beyond even this when the justice they seek is distorted and false.

Yet feminists respond precisely that experience cannot be ignored and that religious traditions will be life-giving insofar as they help

---

[36]For examples of feminist theological and ethical efforts in these regards, see Rosemary Radford Ruether, *Sexism and God-Talk: Toward a Feminist Theology* (Boston: Beacon Press, 1983); Elizabeth A. Johnson, *She Who Is: The Mystery of God in Feminist Theological Discourse* (New York: Crossroad, 1992); Judith Plaskow, *Sex, Sin, and Grace: Women's Experience and the Theologies of Reinhold Niebuhr and Paul Tillich* (Washington, DC: University Press of America, 1980); Emilie M. Townes, ed., *A Troubling in My Soul: Womanist Perspectives on Evil and Suffering* (Maryknoll, NY: Orbis, 1993).

to explain it. The biblical witness claims to present insights that are healing, "hard sayings" that are ultimately freeing. It cannot do so if it contradicts the fundamental convictions that make sense in and to human experience. These convictions, whether we like it or not, constitute a negative test for any revelation of knowledge and a positive key to the workings of reason and the fullness of revelation. As such they do not triumph over, nor are they formed apart from, the witness of the biblical tradition; rather they help to liberate its historically accessible meaning. As for the category of gender, it is socially constructed, and a genealogy of its interpretations shows the caution that must be exercised in claiming too much for its meaning in nature. And if self-sacrifice refers to the conversion of mind and heart required to see and see again, to find a center in what is beyond the self yet within it, to love and to reverence all that is for what it is, then feminist theology acclaims its importance. But if self-sacrificial love means a requirement whereby women are expected to sacrifice more than men, where some groups are intrinsically suited to sacrifice more than others, then it needs conceptual revision. Finally, the God who would only be useful for the fulfillment of human wishes could not be the God of feminist theologies, for in that construal lies a theoretical contradiction and a practical impossibility.[37]

In spite of the emphasis on the role of experience in feminist moral discernment, or because of it, feminist theories have also argued that experience itself must be seriously problematized. This leads us, along with other persistent difficulties, to some of the weaknesses attached to experience as a source for Christian ethics.

The Problems of Experience as an Ethical Source

Of all the problems that beset experience in terms of access, authority, and methodological criteria for its use, I will focus on three. If formulated into questions, they can look like these: (1) What sort of evidence does experience actually offer? (2) What sort of univer-

---

[37]This is an assertion of principle, not a generalization of the doctrine of a divine entity as it appears in all feminist theological writings or religious traditions. A conclusion about agreement on the principle would have to take account of the vast differences between, for example, the feminist theology of Elizabeth Johnson, on the one hand, and Mary Daly on the other. See Johnson, *She Who Is*; and Mary Daly, *Beyond God the Father* (Boston: Beacon Press, 1973), and her subsequent works.

salization from experience is possible? (3) How is the authority of experience to be reconciled with the authority of the Bible, tradition, and systematized disciplines of reason?

The first of these questions is closely related to the hermeneutical circle acknowledged by James Gustafson and pressed by many feminist philosophers and theologians. As theories of language, social location, and power are developed, they threaten to make any appeal to experience vacuous. For example, what can an appeal to women's experience mean if that experience is shaped completely and ineluctably by normative expectations of a culture? What are we to make of an ethics of care based on women's experience of caring if we suspect its construction is attributable to the social pressures on women to take care of men? Thus Catherine MacKinnon cautions, "Women are said to value care. Perhaps women value care because men have valued women according to the care they give. Women are said to think in relational terms. Perhaps women think in relational terms because women's social existence is defined in relation to men."[38] The supposed bedrock of evidence that experience provides disappears in the endless circles of construction that threaten to eliminate moral agency as well as genuine moral discernment.

The second question is also one we have already met, but its urgency has grown as feminists have faced it in their movement and in their theory. Everyone recognizes that experience is particular precisely because it is concrete, but is there sufficient overlapping in the content of one person's experience and another's so that generalizations can be warranted? Or again, is experience so particular that it cannot be shared, so concrete that it cannot be rendered intelligible to others? If individuals can share experiences, can they be shared between groups as well?

Thus, for example, when women began to claim their own self-understandings based importantly in their own experience, they did so not only as individuals but as a group. Herein lay the power of their insights and the inspiration for their action. Soon, however, women were brought up short by the challenge of the diversity among them. Just as they had argued that the experience of men cannot be universalized to stand for the experience of all humans, so they had to

---

[38]Catherine A. MacKinnon, *Toward a Feminist Theory of the State* (Cambridge, MA: Harvard University Press, 1989), 51.

acknowledge that the experience of some women (in this case, white, middle-class, heterosexual, Western women) cannot be universalized to stand for the experience of all women. Women of color, lesbians, working-class women, women from across the world rejected the adequacy of too-narrowly drawn a delineation of women's experience. This, then, forced the question of whether women as women have anything in common and whether their experience can constitute a genuine source for theology and ethics. Beyond this, it forces the question of whether differences in experience make impossible any common morality even within communities of faith if their social and cultural diversities run deep.

The third question follows from the first and the second, but it, too, has been with us from the start. How can experience—elusive, socially constructed, diverse—be authoritative in the process of moral discernment? It may have confirmatory power (or, negatively, a veto power) at the end of a process, but it can do little work in the process itself. That is the point, so an argument may go, of our need not only for the disciplines of reason but for revelation. Experience is subject to the Bible and to faith traditions; if it helps us to understand them, it nonetheless does so only insofar as it does not at the same time usurp their authority. This is obviously not a problem for everyone, not even for everyone who does Christian ethics; but the question of how to relate the many sources for moral discernment is inescapable when experience is taken seriously as at least one of the sources.

Experience Revisited

To consider experience as a source for moral discernment probably gets closer to fundamental issues of moral epistemology than does a consideration of any other source. A major part of what is at stake is the nature of knowledge itself, its power and manner of access to reality, its cognitive and affective components, its communicability, and its consequences for those who come to know. These issues hover in the background of any responses to the questions I have raised regarding the validity, particularity, and authority of experience.

With this caution, let me nonetheless return to the first of my questions. What sort of evidence does experience actually offer? No one can argue that there is an uncontestable, foundational, direct, and immediate "deposit" of moral insights in a fund of experience. Yet some things are important for moral discernment that simply cannot be known without experience—things like the limitations and possibilities of ourselves as moral agents, the dimensions of suffering and diminishment, the ways to hope and to love, the parameters of intimacy, the multiple consequences of injury and injustice. Moreover, all of our morally relevant knowledge (from whatever source) is modified when it partakes of experience—whether this is our knowledge of disease or of the complexities of a moral situation or of God. And there are issues of specific moral rules (and their exceptions) that cannot be resolved without access to some persons' experience—for example, issues of sexuality, of discrimination, of fidelity to covenants. Finally, experience shapes who we are, our attitudes, our interests, and our capacities; "who we are" in turn influences our search for and appropriation of any of the knowledge that becomes part of our moral discernment.

This suggests that while the problems of learning from experience are serious, they are not intractable. Experience indeed may be socially constructed, lodged in a hermeneutical circle, layered with meanings never fully accessible, manipulated by forces never fully understood. But deconstructive methods yield more than an infinite regress. There *are* processes of discovery, of consciousness raising, of interpreting more accurately our experiences present and past, of making explicit what was previously implicit. Ambiguities in the evidence notwithstanding, critical uses of experience can be defended as both necessary and illuminating. James Gustafson's appeals to experiences of the divine and feminist theologians' appeals to experiences of injustice are cases in point.[39]

---

[39]There is not space here to provide other more specific cases in point. However, let me simply flag two issues regarding specific moral rules where experience appears to be an indispensable source. They are both issues in sexual ethics. The first is the issue of heterosexual marital intercourse when some form of "artificial contraception" is used. This issue is almost wholly unique today to the Roman Catholic tradition. One of the arguments currently offered in support of the continued official prohibition of artificial contraception is based on the supposed selfishness of married partners who use contraception. The claim is made that employing contraceptive technology to prevent pregnancy means that the love of the partners is intrinsically selfish, even exploitative (on the part of at least one of them). It takes little account, however, of the reported experience of married persons in this regard. The argument is difficult to sustain when this experience is taken seriously, for it offers the testimony of individuals who by their whole lives bear witness to unselfishness.

A second issue is that of same-sex relationships. Christian ethicists hold a number of positions on this issue, ranging from prohibition, to acceptance but as a lesser form of human relationship, to full acceptance as potentially conducive to human flourishing. Given the arguable inconclusiveness of testimony from scripture, tradition, and secular

Yet my second question remains: How much can be generalized from experience as a source? Diversity in experiences does constitute a significant obstacle to their use as an ethical source. The obstacle, however, is real but not absolute. First of all, there is evidence of some commonalities in morally relevant experiences despite differences in meaning. Across diverse experiences of race and class, gender and culture, for example, feminists affirm some form of right to bodily integrity. The experience of aging differs vastly from one historical period to another and one culture to another, yet it can be argued that there is something similar going on, requiring interpretation, wherever people grow old. There are marked variations from one time and society to another in the meaning of experiences of sexual desire, yet as Michel Foucault discovered, some commonalities seem to persist.[40] Experiences of mortality, bodily limitation, human affiliation, humor, and so forth, are *in some ways* culturally invariant, as Martha Nussbaum argues in defense of Aristotle's theory of virtue.[41] And though the experiences highlighted by James Gustafson are not the same as those central to feminist theological ethics, they converge significantly in their developments of an ethics of the environment.[42]

More importantly, what is different—even profoundly different—in human experience is not thereby completely isolated and unsharable. Experience affords privileged access to some moral insights, but what is experientially perspectival can be rendered at least partially intelligible to others who lack the experience. There are all kinds of evidences of this—in the cross-cultural power of literary classics, the sheer possibility of truly vicarious experience; in the emergence of friendships across seemingly impossible divides; in the learning through second languages of what is translatable and what is not.

Feminists were once brought up short by the claims of diversity. They have since recognized that difference need not preclude community. It is not difference but the ignoring of difference that constitutes an

---

disciplines, experience appears to be a determining resource on this issue. This implies, of course, criteria for the inclusion of experience and its use in discerning this issue.

[40] See Michel Foucault, *The History of Sexuality*, 3 vols., trans. Robert Hurley (New York: Pantheon Books, 1978; Vintage Books, 1988, 1990).

[41] Nussbaum, "Non-Relative Virtues," 260ff.

[42] Compare, for example, the ecological ethical imperatives of Gustafson, *A Sense of the Divine: The Natural Environment from a Theocentric Perspective* (Cleveland: Pilgrim, 1994); and Rosemary Radford Ruether, *Gaia and God: An Ecofeminist Theology of Earth Healing* (San Francisco: HarperSanFrancisco, 1992).

insurmountable barrier between women with disparate experiences. Attention to diversity disallows false universalization from limited experience, but it allows new ways to common moral insight. From it emerges a requirement for the study of the causes of difference[43] and the development of skills for interacting between "different worlds."[44] Therefore, feminist theory is required to incorporate the experience of women not only as gendered but as differentiated by race, by class, and by culture; and it is finally required to include the experience of all those—women, children, and men—who suffer injustice.

Still, there remains in regard to "difference" a problem that has been less adequately addressed and resolved. What if the experiences of one person or one group lead to an ethical perspective and even specific moral rules that are not only different from another's but mutually exclusive? What if different ethical conclusions are warranted by diversity in moral experiences? Suppose, for example, that Gustafson's interpretation of experiences of human vulnerability and pain are read as contradictory to feminist theologians' interpretation of women's experiences of powerlessness and oppression? The former thus warrants, so it appears, consent to a divine being "bearing down," while the latter grounds a protest against the changeable forces of evil. This aspect of the problem of diversity leads back to my third question: How shall we discern the authority of experiences for moral discernment?

Throughout this essay's considerations of the role of experience in moral discernment has been threaded the question of authority, but some answers to the question have also been threaded throughout. From Gustafson's "priority of human experience" to feminist theologies' experientially based method and insights, from my articulation of the weaknesses of experience as a source for moral discernment

---

[43]See Mary McClintock Fulkerson, *Changing the Subject: Women's Discourses and Feminist Theology* (Minneapolis: Fortress Press, 1994). Fulkerson's analysis of the need for feminist theory to account for differences (not just to acknowledge them) is important, and it can be accepted without agreeing with her overall argument about the loss of the subject. For another analysis of difference and the possibilities of interpretation, see Joan W. Scott, "The Evidence of Experience," *Critical Inquiry* 17 (Summer 1991): 773–97.

[44]Maria Lugones proposes a skill that she calls "'world'-traveling" in this regard. See Maria Lugones, "Playfulness, 'World'-Travelling, and Loving Perception," in *Making Face, Making Soul, Haciendo Caras: Creative and Critical Perspectives by Women of Color*, ed. Gloria Anzaldúa (San Francisco: Aunt Lute Foundation, 1990), 390–402. See also the discussion of this and other related matters in Janet R. Jakobsen, "Deconstructing the Paradox of Modernity: Feminism, Enlightenment, and Cross-Cultural Moral Interactions," *Journal of Religious Ethics* 23 (Fall 1995): 333–63.

yet defense of its role nonetheless, I have shown my own conviction that experience is authoritative. I do not thereby, any more than my conversation partners in this essay, maintain that only experience is authoritative or that it is ever sufficient for Christian moral discernment. I do not, any more than my conversation partners, adopt a fundamentalist view of the authority of experience. I am therefore not committed to agreeing with every conclusion that is drawn from experience—not committed, for example, to full agreement with Gustafson's understanding of God, or with every feminist theologian's interpretation of specific experiences of injustice, or even with all of my own interpretations from the past.

Decisions about whose experience and what interpretations of experience are to count in moral discernment are not without guiding criteria. Coherence of the conclusions of experience with general moral norms, intelligibility of accounts of experience in relation to fundamental beliefs, mutual illumination when measured with other sources of moral insight, manifest integrity in the testimony of the one who is experiencing, harmful or helpful consequences of interpretations of experience, confirmation in a community of discernment—all of these are tests for the validity and usefulness of given experiences in a process of moral discernment.[45] Yet experience may challenge its tests and assert an authority that modifies the prior norms that would order it. Something deeper is at stake.

Underlying all of these considerations is an understanding of authority itself. It is impossible, however, to separate the question of authority from the question of the intrinsic content or meaning of what is presented as authoritative. Hence, even if one accepts the authority of a source on some apparently extrinsic basis (for example, that it is God's word, or that the voice of the community is determinative), this very acceptance must have meaning, must "make sense" to the one who gives it. The moral authority of any source is contingent on our recognition of the "truth" it offers and the "justice" of its aims.[46] No source has real and living authority in relation to our moral attitudes and choices unless it can elicit from us a responding "recognition."

---

[45]The usefulness of these tests can be illustrated effectively in relation to the experiences I have cited in note 39 above.

[46]I use quotation marks for "truth" and "justice" to signal the complex issues surrounding their meaning. There is not the opportunity here to address these issues, nor, I think, the need.

When Christian ethicists consider scripture, tradition, secular disciplines, and contemporary experience as sources, it is precisely because they find in and through these resources access to moral insight and motivation.

The reason, then, why experience may challenge other sources and the measures of its own validity is precisely because moral truth must "make sense" to us. Truth from whatever source presents itself, to use the words of Paul Ricoeur, as a "nonviolent appeal."[47] It asks for something less like a submission of will and more like an opening of the imagination and of the whole mind and heart. It can be believed only insofar as it rings true in our capacity for knowing, our moral sensibilities, our affective capacity for the good. When a deeply held conviction, grounded in our experience, appears to be contradicted by information from other sources, it must be tested against them. But if it continues to persuade us, continues to hold "true" so that to deny it would do violence to our very capacity for knowing, then it must function as the measure against which the other sources are tested. It becomes a hermeneutical key that may relativize the other sources or allow them to be interpreted anew.

This does not leave us without recourse when disagreements about experience run deep. In fact, the nature of the disagreement itself suggests at least two remedies. On the one hand, disagreement is often not about differences in experience but about whether some persons' experiences should be allowed at all as a source for social or communal discernment.[48] The initial requirement here is to acknowledge the importance of experience, to admit the particular experience into ethical consideration, to test it and weigh it at least as a source among sources. As a remedy, this may not resolve disagreement, but it makes more responsible the process of discernment.

On the other hand, disagreements actually lodged in contradictory interpretations of experience are not without some possibilities of adjudication. Here the requirement is communication, and the potential is for enlargement of experience and expansion of its sources for interpretation.[49] It would be naive in the extreme to suggest that all

---

[47]See Paul Ricoeur, *Essays on Biblical Interpretation*, ed. Lewis S. Mudge (Philadelphia: Fortress Press, 1980), 95.

[48]See again the relevance of the examples in note 39 above.

[49]Proposals by feminist philosophers are particularly helpful in this regard. See, for example, Seyla Benhabib's case for a revised form of Jürgen Habermas's communicative

disagreements about experience are only apparent, and sufficient dialogue will in every case bring harmony. Nonetheless, what communication prevents is a premature acceptance of unbridgeable gaps. What it makes possible is the actual bringing together of diverse experiences in their concreteness and particularity. It prevents, for example, misleading interpretations of feminist ethics and of Gustafson's theocentric ethics that would conclude only to differences between dissent and consent, clarity of prophetic critique and ambiguities of moral experience, self-centered and other-centered grounds for moral obligation. It makes possible, for example, shared insights into systemic forces and individual responsibility, the relative value of particular social arrangements, the human part in a cosmic whole.[50]

But let me end where I began. Experience is essential to both moral discernment and deliberation. Its difficulties must be addressed because they cannot be allowed to vitiate its usefulness as a resource. Its significance is in its concreteness yet its potential for sharing. Its real fruitfulness depends not on the formal considerations I have offered but on its actual illumination of the matters for discernment and choice. Evidence of such illumination is available in the ongoing moral discernment of individuals and communities—and perhaps paradigmatically in the theocentric ethics of James Gustafson, the ethics of contemporary feminist theology, and the potential dialogue between them.

---

ethics, in *Situating the Self: Gender, Community, and Postmodernism in Contemporary Ethics* (New York: Routledge, 1992). See also feminist debates on this and other proposals in Seyla Benhabib et al., *Feminist Contentions: A Philosophical Exchange* (New York: Routledge, 1995).

[50]There is space here for me to be only suggestive and elliptical on these issues. Much of what I am pointing to refers comprehensively to whole theories, but interesting and less usual places to begin dialogue might be Gustafson's analysis of problems of population and nutrition or his reflective interpretations of his experiences in World War II. See *Ethics*, 2: esp. 219–21; and "August Seventh, 1945," *Christian Century* 112 (August 16–23, 1995): 779–81.

CHAPTER 4

Moral Discourse in the Public Arena

My focus in this essay is more specific than its general title might suggest. I do indeed intend to address the overall question of the possibilities and problems of public moral discourse, especially in the context of contemporary communications systems and media. But my focus may be clearer if I add a subtitle such as: "The Effects of Silence on the Moral Development of the Church." My concern is with moral discourse in the Christian community and, more specifically, the Roman Catholic community. My concern is, moreover, with the long-standing tendency of official church leadership to deal with moral controversy of any serious nature by disallowing any voice but its own in the public arena of the church (and any voice but its own as an identifiable Roman Catholic voice in the larger public arena of the world).

It is, of course, not unique to Roman Catholicism to deal with conflicting beliefs by silencing opposition to official teachings. Nor would it be accurate to imply that the Roman Catholic Church has always and everywhere related to diversity and controversy in this way. This has been, however, and remains, a strong tendency in the tradition. From the first lists of forbidden books under Innocent I in 405 to the pressures on church-related publishers to discontinue publication of certain books on sexual ethics in the 1980s, efforts have been made to keep voices suspected of lack of orthodoxy away from the ears of the faithful. And though the wisdom and mood of the Second Vatican Council brought to an end the *Index of Forbidden Books* (first

Originally a lecture given at Catholic University in Washington, DC, a version of it was published in *Vatican Authority and American Catholic Dissent*, ed. William W. May (New York: Crossroad, 1987), 168–86. Used with permission.

named as such in the sixteenth century), theologians are still carefully monitored; leaders of religious communities are pressured to withdraw proposals for policy changes that oppose official episcopal directives; clergy are removed from pastoral ministries if their views are divergent from specific hierarchical church moral teachings, and so on. The importance of the *public* nature of any dissent as a warrant for silencing it is clear when, for example, censure follows popular publication but not publication in a scholarly journal, or when exclusionary measures are more severe following attention by public media.

It is not my intention here simply to critique, let alone to bemoan, this policy or strategy within the church. Nor do I wish to caricature it or to imply that it lacks any serious rationale. It needs to be examined, however, as a way of dealing with controversy about Christian beliefs—in particular, Christian moral beliefs in our own contemporary church and world. I want ultimately to maintain that it constitutes an ineffective strategy (an ineffective moral pedagogy); that it can entail an unjust treatment of persons; and that overall it does not serve the common good of the church or the world. Such arguments can, I think, be supported best by taking seriously at least some of the aims of the strategy and some of the values it has sought to uphold.

The Case for Silencing

Though efforts to silence or to exclude diverse and opposing voices have often entailed the imposition of power as a means of setting questions of truth (the confusion of the authority to govern with the authority to teach, of the *clavis jurisdictionis* with the *clavis scientiae*), it cannot be assumed that these efforts were always motivated by self-protective desires to retain power and privilege. The explicit rationales offered for silencing or excluding opposing viewpoints point, of course, to a view of authority-with-responsibility lodged uniquely in the hierarchical offices of the church. The history of these ideas is perhaps easiest for us to see in the aftermath of Vatican I. The centralization of supreme teaching authority in the hierarchical magisterium carried with it the perceived responsibility of safeguarding revealed truth and providing moral guidance with peaceful certitude for the faithful. The task assigned to theology was primarily to assert and explain the authoritative pronouncements of the official church; in the case of moral theology, it was to elaborate manuals of moral guidance that subordinated all moral doctrine to this authority.[1] Even those principles of the natural law that as such could be known without the special teaching of the church became the province of the hierarchical magisterium. Revelation, it was said, was needed to confirm and complete what the human mind, weakened by sin, could not reach or sustain by itself.

It was maintained that submission to authority not only brought *content* in terms of moral action guides; it produced a kind of necessary *disposition for understanding* the action guides. "A willing acceptance by intellectually able men [*sic*] initiates a personal human reflection upon these truths which often leads to a genuine intellectual *insight* into their inner content and causes."[2] Above all, receiving moral guidance from the authoritative teaching of the church was thought to provide a form of security, freedom from the fear of error, peace of mind, for the faithful struggling to live morally good lives. Acceptance in one's heart of the word of the official church could deliver one from the "feelings of mercy and compassion [that] prevent the mind from maintaining its calm and necessary detachment."[3] Only with this kind of guidance could "most of the problems of our lives, private or public . . . be solved in the light of the natural law." Thus could Catholic moralists, economists, and politicians "go to work with a strong consciousness of [their] mission," precisely because they could rely on an authority believed to be far higher than any human authority.[4]

The maintenance of such benefits for the believer depended, it was thought, on protecting her or him from views counter to official church teachings. This was the theme struck, for example, in *Casti connubii* in the 1930s and in *Humani generis* in the 1950s. In the latter it was explicitly asserted that when a pope goes out of his way to speak on a controverted issue, the subject is no longer matter for theological debate. Only silence befits the authoritative conclusion of the authoritative teaching, and only silence (regarding any other or further views on the matter) will preserve the peaceful certitude of the believer.

While Vatican II went a long way toward rejecting the notion that every question treated by a pope must be considered forever settled,

---

[1]See Franz Bockle, *Fundamental Moral Theology*, trans. N. D. Smith (New York: Pueblo Publishing, 1980), 251–52.
[2]Joseph Fuchs, *Natural Law* (New York: Sheed and Ward, 1965), 159.
[3]Ibid., 160.
[4]Ibid., 160–61.

the theme has reappeared again and again.[5] Its emergence is occasioned today in the context of two issues in particular. The first of these is the issue of the appropriateness of political ministry for clergy and members of religious communities. From Leo XIII to Vatican II, and then again in the strong views of John Paul II, it has been asserted that clergy (and, more recently, nonordained members of religious communities as well) should not participate in secular politics. One major reason offered in support of this position is that the church must provide a unified witness to society regarding fundamental moral principles. Politics, however, involves "contingent matters" regarding which bishops and priests may disagree. If, then, clergy participate in politics, they may be perceived as not in unity with the whole of the official church, and the church's witness will be compromised.[6] By extension, members of religious communities are also identified as special representatives of the church—so that they, too, must be in complete and absolute unity with hierarchical teaching. The ultimate point of a unified witness in regard to all authoritative teaching is that anything less than this will disturb the faithful, confuse them, and weaken the impact of the teaching in their concrete lives.

The second issue that today occasions the explicit emergence of an appeal to the well-being of the faithful as a ground for silencing views not in harmony with official church teaching is the issue of moral norms for human sexual behavior. The *Vatican Declaration on Sexual Ethics* (1975) is a case in point. It argues that when theologians put forth views contrary to official teaching, the result is that "teachings, moral criteria, and modes of living hitherto faithfully unquestioned have been very much unsettled, even among Christians. Many people, confronted with so many opinions contrary to what the church had taught them, nowadays wonder what truths they must cling to."[7] Therefore the official teaching authority of the church has the responsibility

---

[5]The important discussions in this regard occurred in the development of the Vatican II document, *Lumen Gentium*. See Joseph A. Komonchak, "Ordinary Papal Magisteriums and Religious Assent," in *Contraception: Authority and Dissent*, ed. Charles E. Curran (New York: Herder and Herder, 1969), 101–26.

[6]This is one of the arguments traced in papal encyclicals by Leslie Griffin, "The Integration of Spiritual and Temporal: The Development of Roman Catholic Church-State Theory from Leo XXIII to John Paul II" (Ph.D. diss., Yale University, 1984).

[7]Sacred Congregation for the Doctrine of the Faith, "Declaration on Certain Problems of Sexual Ethics," in *Vatican II: More Postconciliar Documents*, ed. Austin Flannery (Grand Rapids: William B. Eerdmans, 1982), 2:487.

to keep intact the doctrine formulated from its interpretation of divine revelation illuminating the natural law. It has the responsibility to do this out of concern for the well-being of the faithful. Protecting the faithful from anxiety and ambiguity in this way serves, moreover, to enhance rather than hinder the capacity of persons to make their own moral choices. The *Declaration on Sexual Ethics*, for example, ends (however paradoxically) with this reminder:

> The sacred Synod affirms that children and young people have the right to be stimulated to make sound judgments based on a well-formed conscience and to put them into practice with a sense of personal commitment, and to know and love God more perfectly. Accordingly, it earnestly entreats all who are in charge of civil administration or in control of education to make it their care to ensure that young people are never deprived of this sacred right.[8]

Thus we are given clearly articulated reasons for limiting controversy and debate, for silencing opinions contrary to the certain teaching of the hierarchy: there is a divinely ordained *authority* on which the church can depend; its own concern is for *truth* as truth, and for the pastoral consequences of compromising the communication of that truth; silencing voices that would falsely challenge that truth is necessary to secure the *well-being* of believers and of the church as a whole, and to respect the *freedom* and potential maturity of believers; all who have the kind of status in the church that makes them in a special way *representatives* of the church have a particular *responsibility to uphold and bear witness to* the authoritative teaching of the hierarchy. It is just these reasons (for silencing or excluding any who oppose this view of authority or who interfere with its pastoral function) that must be met if one is to argue ultimately for the inefficacy and injustice of the strategy of "silencing."

Before I begin to try to do this, however, two other sorts of arguments should perhaps be taken into account. The first is not one generally able to be found in the documents of the official teaching church itself. It is, however, an argument suggested by anyone who maintains that the Roman Catholic tradition should now recognize that its strength no

---

[8]Ibid., 498.

longer lies in struggling to maintain the kind of universalistic ethic that a traditional natural law theory would undergird. Rather, on this view, the strength of the tradition lies in recognizing that it offers a truly sectarian Christian ethic—one that is not for all persons, one that should not be open to counterviews precisely because by its own authority it claims a special revelation not accessible to those who do not receive it. This is an ethic that is wholly dependent upon the story of the community in which it arises—in this case, the Roman Catholic community. Within this community, hierarchical leadership has a specialized role in interpreting the story and articulating the community's moral insight in a way that brooks no opposition. This combines a sectarian view of the Roman Catholic Church with an authoritarian view of moral discernment in the church. It is not a traditional position, but it may be at least implicit in current arguments for "silencing" as a response to controversy.

The second sort of argument that may be added to a rationale for prohibiting public diversity of positions regarding matters of moral teaching is one that is at least pointed to here and there in the documents of the hierarchical magisterium. It is the argument that contemporary forms of communications media are themselves dangerous to the accurate and adequate sharing of Christian insight regarding the moral life. When, for example, the 1976 Synod of Bishops expressed its concern over dissident and false opinions on moral matters, it deplored "the fact that some actually call into doubt some truths of the faith," and that among those who do are especially persons "of more advanced education, because of their special difficulties in reconciling faith with reason," but also persons from among the "working classes," and (in missionary lands) "a few groups of priests and laymen." The causes of this state of affairs include "the fact that publications and other means of communication immediately spread any news of a religious nature to the whole world."[9]

One does not have to be overly cynical to appreciate the dangers to moral understanding from false reporting, sensationalized headlines, and superficial television interviews. The media industry itself acknowledges the need for greater ethical sensitivity and professional ethical rules.[10] Stories multiply in which television networks are sued

---

[9]Synod of Bishops, *On Dangerous Opinions and on Atheism*, in *Vatican II*, 664–65.
[10]See, for example, Robert Schmuhl, ed., *The Responsibilities of Journalism* (Notre

for libel; investigations yield reports of taping interviews twice with the same person to elicit a strong view, editing interviews so that replies to several questions can be combined into one answer, and so on.

There is a ready analogy to the problem of media and moral teaching in the media reports on medicine. Here medical professionals complain of headlines that give half-truths, of premature publicity on research that remains inconclusive (for example, cancer cures), or on diseases that do not threaten public health through casual contact but are reported as if they do (for example, AIDS or herpes simplex). Questions of the appropriateness of the media as means for education regarding medical matters are not unlike questions of appropriateness regarding moral guidance. And just as the medical profession wants control over its own publicity, so officials in the church may well argue for the need for some control over the dissemination of information and opinions regarding church teachings. There is no doubt that some of the difficulties of communication can be minimized if all news is controlled from one source—in this case, relevant members or agencies of the hierarchy. With this kind of control it is in fact less likely that moral communication will be distorted by "one shot" stories, superficial interviews and analyses, or, in general, a news media whose agenda may be very different from that of the church.

With all of these questions and arguments in mind, I turn nonetheless to the thesis that "silencing" is neither effective nor ethical as a way to deal with diversity of views in matters of Christian morality.

The Case Against Silencing

I shall begin with some general reflections on relevant aspects of the Roman Catholic tradition and then move to what seem to me to be crucial considerations in favor of encouraging and sustaining

Dame, IN: University of Notre Dame Press, 1984); William A. Tillinghast, "Slanting the News: Source Perceptions after Changes in Newspaper Management," *Journalism Quarterly* 60 (1983): 310–51; Michael Ryan and David L. Martinson, "Ethical Values: The Flow of Journalistic Information and Public Relations Persons," *Journalism Quarterly* 61 (1984): 27–34; S. M. M. Haque, "Is U.S. Coverage of News in the Third World Imbalanced?" *Journalism Quarterly* 60 (1983): 521–24; "Fresh Attacks on TV News," *U.S. News and World Report*, September 5, 1983, 55–56; Gary Steiner, *People Look at Television* (New York: Knopf, 1963); Robert T. Bower, *Television and the Public* (New York: Holt, Rinehart, and Winston, 1973).

open moral discourse in the public arena, and especially in regard to controversial issues.

The Tradition: Some General Directions

It is impossible to think seriously about the question of church authority and moral beliefs in the Roman Catholic tradition without considering the central place of natural law as a method and a theory. Whatever examples of other approaches to moral theology there are in Roman Catholic history (and there are important ones, such as the voluntarism of Duns Scotus and of Suarez), natural law has dominated the scene at key points since the time of Augustine. Of particular importance has been the tendency since the mid-nineteenth century for natural law to constitute a major source of appeal in papal documents on moral matters. Given this emphasis, it is difficult not to be struck by a historical irony: a tradition that has never really repudiated a central role for human reason (in "making sense" of the moral life) has nonetheless pushed toward an extrinsic authority (the hierarchical teaching office) as the ultimate source of each person's moral understanding. Even if it is argued that because human reason is weakened by sin, it needs divine revelation to restore its power (and an extrinsic authority may be the instrument of divine revelation), the point has seldom been lost that the goal of reason is not juridical submission but understanding. Thus, when revelation provides an "answer" to one of reason's moral puzzles (primarily by revealing reality), reason is thereby enabled to discern the "way" to that answer (just as, analogously, when one learns the answer to a difficult mathematical problem, one can sometimes then, but only then, "figure out" how one gets to that answer). The search of reason for truth cannot be satisfied by an encounter only with institutional power.

Roman Catholic moral thinking has thus not been known for an allegiance to a "divine command theory" but for a continuing affirmation of the ultimate intelligibility of reality and the moral imperatives that emerge from reality. However partial, inadequate, and historically conditioned may be the understandings of reason, it nonetheless never capitulates to a final dichotomy between *is* and *ought*, between reality and the demands of reality for respect. Moreover, there is the potential in every person's reason, every person's mind and heart, to seek to understand reality, and to come to recognize the fundamental moral claims of human life. A tradition that takes these sorts of considerations seriously cannot without grave inconsistency close off (that is, rule out a priori) diverse ways of trying to understand reality; it cannot simply silence voices insofar as they call for a more careful exploration of reality and the moral life.

A second consideration is also important here. Despite a tendency to centralize all teaching authority in the hierarchy, there is room in the tradition for understanding the exercise of this authority in a way that affirms a teaching role for others in the church; that is, the tradition itself provides grounds for multiple voices in a process of ongoing discernment. Central authority can be understood, for example, to be functioning faithfully as an interpreter of revelation only insofar as it takes account of the many sources of wisdom in the church, speaking authentically for the community only when it discerns the faith of the community (as known through general belief, through tradition in the broad range of its expressions, and through the interpretations of multiple theologians in the church). What may at times look like absolute authority is, in fact, relative in many ways. Even an acknowledgment of infallibility in the teaching office of the church carries with it a necessary relativization of papal authority—as, for example, when historians trace a conceptual incompatibility between some forms of infallibility and some forms of papal sovereignty.[11] Moreover, in the teaching of morality there is long-standing and serious doubt as to whether any appeal to infallibility can ever be made regarding specific moral rules. Indeed, as infallibility has been generally understood, there is little likelihood that it can, without self-contradiction, be used to settle highly controversial moral questions.

In a third general consideration, we may note that institutional loyalty on the part of clergy and members of religious communities is a complex matter. Included in it are questions of the general status of nonordained persons and the forms of institutional identity that belong to persons by reason of baptism; the relation of individual conscience to institutional roles; the possibility of pluralism even among

---

[11] See Brian Tierney, *Origins of Papal Infallibility, 1150–1350: A Study on the Concepts of Infallibility, Sovereignty, and Tradition in the Middle Ages* (Leiden: E. J. Brill, 1972). For other helpful treatments, see the spring and fall issues of the *Journal of Ecumenical Studies* 19 (1982); Charles E. Curran and Richard A. McCormick, eds., *Readings in Moral Theology No. 3: The Magisterium and Morality* (New York: Paulist Press, 1982); Gerard J. Hughes, "Infallibility in Morals," *Theological Studies* 34 (1973): 415–28; Francis A. Sullivan, *Magisterium: Teaching Authority in the Catholic Church* (New York: Paulist Press, 1983).

members of the hierarchy; responsible representation of the church as distinct from uncritical repetition of current church policy and already formulated dogmas. The very identification of such questions reveals the inadequacy of simple silencing as a way to deal with diversity in the moral understandings of the hierarchy, the clergy, the laity, and members of religious communities.

But let me move from general directions suggested by the tradition to more specific issues regarding the church's moral discourse. As I have said, my contentions are that silencing diverse or opposing views is an ineffective strategy for moral communication and for the pursuit of truth; that it can entail unjust treatment of persons; and that it does not serve overall the common good of the church or of the world. My support of these contentions will take the positive form of an argument *for* moral discourse in the public arena—moral discourse in which the whole church has a possibility to participate (to think, to communicate, to contribute to and benefit from shared understanding). This argument can be made in at least three ways. (1) Public moral discourse is a necessary condition for a faithful search for truth regarding moral behavior (whether we call this a search for truth or for what is right and good). Without it Christian inquiry into the meaning of the moral life (revealed through nature or scripture or the overall historical life of the Christian community) will not be accurate or adequate. (2) Public moral discourse is necessary in order to avoid unjust injury to persons and groups—injury entailed when the lived experience of persons is not taken into account in the development and communication of moral doctrine. (3) Public moral discourse is necessary in order to prevent unjustified coercion of persons who are called and capacitated by grace for true moral agency as members of the Christian and human community. Let me explore briefly each of these assertions.

The Search for Truth

When I say that public moral discourse is a necessary condition for the faithful search for moral truth, I mean several things. First, what is at stake here is our understanding of the moral life, not just speculative theology. Morality is not an esoteric subject; it concerns everyone. Everyone in some sense has tools for understanding it. Reflection on the morality of human action ought to be, therefore, in an important way an egalitarian enterprise. It is not the prerogative only of bishops or moral theologians. This is not to deny special roles and responsibilities for both bishops and moral theologians in the Christian community's ongoing moral discernment. Nor is it to say that moral questions are simple questions, mere child's play. Yet moral discernment is in some respects everyone's responsibility, and it ought not to be an active, public enterprise for some and a passive, wholly private enterprise for others.

More than this, persons generally are not only able to participate in moral reflection; their participation is *needed* if the community is to attain moral wisdom. Understanding of moral choices cannot come merely from receiving laws or rules. It entails at the very least a discernment of the meaning of laws and rules in concrete situations. It also requires insight into human goals and needs, capabilities and limitations, history and possibility. Such understanding requires reflection upon human experience—personal, social, religious, institutional. In a tradition that affirms a natural-law approach to morality, it is inconceivable that moral norms can be formulated without consulting the experience of those whose lives are at stake. Even where the tradition is more sectarian in its approach to morality, the convictions of the community must be forged and tested in each age by the community as a whole. And even where it is a divine revelation that is being interpreted, someone's experience of God must be understood. We know the dangers of universalizing one group's experience without taking account of others' (as when we impose culturally based norms on persons of other cultures, or when we universalize the experience of one gender as if it were the whole of human nature). We know, also, the dangers of interpreting moral principles without taking account of *anyone's* experience (as has seemed to be the case in the formulation of some principles for human sexual activity). Indeed, then, it could be argued that shared public moral discourse is *most* necessary wherever institutional structures or social barriers would otherwise exclude certain groups of persons, and hence exclude particular aspects of human experience from the moral discernment of the community.

The fear of such discourse, as I have noted, is that strange and new voices will undermine the unity and authority of the official teaching of the church—that diverse voices will produce "a welter of confusion," obscuring the truth, creating anxiety for many persons, and encouraging immorality. And admittedly, the marketplace of contemporary communications media has no "hidden hand" to prevent manipulation of public opinion and distortion of shared beliefs. Hence there are risks for the church in allowing freedom of expression in the public forum. But the risks of not allowing it are much greater.

We need only recall the gaps in credibility that yawn between the members of the church and its official teachings when it becomes clear that the relevant experiences of the faithful have not been taken into account in the formulation of these teachings. We can remember, too, the historical evidence that authoritarian unity does not always assure either adequacy of insight or freedom from error. (To argue that changes in church teaching are never corrections of past errors but only developments of what was previously implicit in the tradition is, as Brian Tierney suggests, "surely to strain human credibility too far." It is impossible, for example, to see mere "development" in the shift in church teaching on religious liberty from the thirteenth to the twentieth centuries. Anyone "who believes that will believe anything."[12]) But when only those with hierarchical teaching offices are responsible to push back the horizons of moral insight, error can persist for a longer time without challenge. Public silence supports it and helps it to endure. There is more accuracy than irreverence in our noting that unless voices can be heard even from unexpected corners of the arena, we may never in a given instance believe our eyes even though we see quite clearly that the emperor has no clothes. The Christian community must preserve the capacity to correct its error, and sustained and open discourse in public arenas is crucial to that capacity.

It is possible to affirm the need for open public discourse regarding moral matters without thereby assuming that sheer tolerance of every opinion leads inevitably to the emergence of truth.[13] Open discussion of issues in the public forum can be a necessary, but not a sufficient condition for a faithful search for understanding. And even "necessary"

---

[12]Tierney, *Origins of Papal Infallibility*, 277. See also Francis Oakley and Bruce Russett, eds., *Governance, Accountability, and the Future of the Catholic Church* (New York: Continuum, 2004).

[13]There are, of course, important analogies between the question of silencing opposition in the church and the long-debated questions of free speech and censorship in liberal society. The issues are not simply translatable from one context to the other, though an examination of either one sheds important light on the other. For a discussion of freedom of speech in liberal society that is conducive to comparisons (and contrasts) with freedom of speech in the church, see Lee C. Bollinger, *The Tolerant Society: Freedom of Speech and Extremist Speech in America* (New York: Oxford University Press, 1985).

conditions have their limitations and their risks. The church, like the nation, must be willing to struggle with difficult questions of what to do, for example, with vocal advocates of anti-Semitism or racism; and the issues of "who speaks for the church" will be with us always.

Unlike the university or the political arena in a liberal society, the church believes it is responsible to the word of God, and that there are substantive truths and moral obligations to which it must be faithful. But precisely because these truths are believed to "make sense" in the moral realm, and because their "sense" must be probed ultimately by each person and by the community as a whole, fidelity to the truth is served, not thwarted, by open public discourse. Despite the risks of disagreement and conflict, then, the church's ongoing moral inquiry, as well as its steady guidance and prophetic moral teaching, requires at the very least toleration of diverse voices. More than this, active collaboration may be required among those who are committed to the same search and to the same goal of living a fundamentally human and Christian life.

The conclusion that I have reached constitutes a modest claim. It does not in itself prejudge fundamental questions of ecclesiology. It rules neither in nor out the possibility of a strong centralized teaching authority; it neither affirms nor denies the need for an official church teaching on fundamental moral matters or an official position on controversial questions. What it does is rule out the strategy of silencing diverse voices. Indeed one might argue that, paradoxically, the greater the centralization of teaching authority in the church, the greater the need for arenas and structures whereby all voices in the church can be heard.

Do No Unjust Injury

Public moral discourse is necessary in order to avoid unjust injury to persons and groups. If silencing is aimed at protecting the well-being of the faithful, it misses its mark. As a strategy it is more likely to harm persons than to help them. At the most obvious level, it can be argued that however good it might be to keep persons innocent and ignorant of controversies (over moral matters), it is simply not possible today. Whatever the drawbacks of modern communications media, major issues will appear in them no matter what. What is published in an obscure theological journal in Germany, for example, is as accessible to a reporter for the *New York Times* as it is to European scholars. Efforts to preserve faith by keeping believers innocent and ignorant of controversies cannot, then, succeed; and it would be better to participate in the moral discourse than to try to censor it.

At another level, it can be argued that protecting individuals from "confusion" (were it possible) retards rather than fosters their moral development. What may be necessary in the training and nurturing of children is not appropriate for ordinary adult members of the Christian community. If moral questions are complex and on the frontiers of human experience, and if moral understandings are ambiguous and not completely certain, no one is helped by being excused from this complexity and ambiguity. Indeed moral maturity is in part constituted by a capacity for ambiguity, by courage in the face of uncertainty, by humility honest enough to eschew self-righteousness.

The injury that may be done to persons through a strategy of silencing, however, includes more than overprotection of individuals or counterproductive uses of media. Another form of injury is a consequence of the perpetuation of falsehoods or partial truths regarding moral action guides (perpetuated because silence is either imposed or chosen in regard to new insights or new moral options). Examples clarify this best. A particularly troubling one can be found in the disparity between public teaching and pastoral practice regarding divorce and remarriage. As moral theologians and pastors are aware, it was for some time possible for divorced persons in stable second marriages to participate in the sacramental life of the church. The pastoral option of resolving legal difficulties through appeal to conscience, to the "internal forum," became more open. Yet official resistance has been strong not only against changing the law of the church regarding second marriages but against publicizing (through public teaching and preaching) the availability of the internal forum solution. Dissent, favoring either a change in law or in the policy regarding public teaching about extralegal options, has been actively discouraged on the grounds that a clear and simple understanding of the law against divorce and remarriage must be maintained. The result of this, however, is that persons who could benefit from knowledge of the internal forum solution are often left ignorant of this possibility. That is, they are left without access to the sacramental life of the church, or what access they have remains pastorally limited because of the continuing split between what the church teaches publicly and what it allows (or at times allows) to be practiced privately. Moreover, the whole church is deprived of hearing openly the serious reasons offered on all sides of an exceedingly complex question.

Consider, too, the tenacious problem of contraception. While for many (perhaps most) in the church this question seems to have long since been put to rest, for others its resolution is far from peacefully assured. The fact that public discussion of this issue persists despite continual efforts to silence key voices has not obviated the need for a different climate for dissent. Although here an internal forum solution is officially available (and publicized as such), the problem of conscience formation remains. Overall the history of silencing opposition to official church teaching on this issue has contributed to a pervasive loss of respect for church law in general. Individuals, still without an opportunity to understand both sides of the issue, are also left without the "certainty of conscience" required for the internal forum solution. It is not difficult to argue in this case that unjust injury is being done both to individual persons and to the common good.

The silencing of religious communities who have attempted to initiate dialogue about the accessibility of tubal ligations in Roman Catholic hospitals provides a third example. The leadership of at least one community was required, under threat of severe sanctions, to forgo any public expression of disagreement with official church teaching in this regard; to cancel plans for discussion of the question within medical institutions; and to express acceptance of the official church position.[14] Here, too, the issue is not only speculative truth, but possible unjust injury to real persons—to women who need justifiable tubal ligations for their medical well-being and the fullness of their married lives. The point is that the prohibition of dialogue on such an issue—the silencing of any serious questions, the presumption that every aspect of the truth is already sufficiently perceived—constitutes a strategy that is not only morally ineffective but arguably unjust.

Contemporary counterexamples exist that point to another kind of strategy for moral inquiry and moral teaching in the church. In these examples, too, what is at stake is not only truth but the well-being of persons—perhaps of all persons. I refer here to the pastoral letters of the U.S. bishops on nuclear disarmament and on economic justice.

---

[14]See Margaret A. Farley, "Power and Powerlessness: A Case in Point," *Proceedings of the Catholic Theological Society of America* 37 (1982): 116–19.

The processes employed in the development of these letters provide crucial evidence of the feasibility of forms of moral communication in which many voices are not only heard but sought. The result is moral discernment that is more than a report of majority opinion, and moral teaching that aims to interpret both divine revelation and human experience. Moral authority is asserted, but disagreement is not silenced. Of course we do not yet know the ultimate effectiveness of these processes. Nor would I want to argue that all moral communication in the church should be limited to these forms. Different issues in different spheres of human life are not only lived but researched in different ways, and varying institutional involvements can require not only the enunciation of church teaching but the stipulation of church policies. Nonetheless, there are elements in these last two examples that offer important clues for the development of strategies for all moral discernment and persuasion. Not the least of these is the willingness to identify and oppose, but not to silence, voices of dissent.

Unjustified Coercion

In relation to public moral discourse, issues of freedom and coercion are closely related to the issues of injury and well-being we have just seen. The case for open public discourse can also be supported for the sake of preventing unjustified coercion of persons called and enabled to be true moral agents. Two kinds of coercion are involved when dissident voices in the church are silenced: coercion of those who are silenced and coercion of those who, no longer able to hear the silenced voices, are thereby prevented from access to possibly viable moral options.

Consider, first, those who are silenced. The matter may be for them one of simple (though agonized) surrender, of trusting in the power of truth to manifest itself in the long run, of acknowledging the limits of their own insights and the need for a church whose overall wisdom can be expected to exceed their own. But it may entail more than this. The matter about which they are required to keep silent, or to "re-say" what they have said, retracting their former words, may be judged by them to involve the continuation of unjust injury to others (as, for example, in the case of hospital policy regarding tubal ligation). Surrender to repressive power in such a situation raises the question of justified opposition to coercion, even coercion within the church.

Consider again those who are kept from hearing both sides in a moral controversy. The effort to prevent their hearing can be construed as a benevolent protection of them, a kind of "soft paternalism" to which they would agree if they could see the whole picture—presumably as those who are responsible for authoritative teaching see it. Like all paternalism, then, the effort fails to respect persons as full moral agents; but in so doing, it aims thereby to safeguard them from their own potential mistakes. Justification of paternalism is difficult in any case, but the difficulties are exacerbated when it occurs in the content of a faith that seeks to enhance, not retard, moral growth. Establishing the premise of paternalism is even more problematic on the hypothesis that some official moral teaching can be in error.

The complexity of the argument regarding these forms of coercion places it beyond what I can treat adequately here. I am reminded, however, of the tensions and even contradictions visible in the work of some of the greatest moral thinkers of the church on issues similar to this one—tensions and contradictions that have haunted the church through the centuries. We have, for example, in our memory the early words of Augustine regarding coercion and faith:

> I do not propose to compel [persons] to embrace the communion of our party, but desire the truth to be made known to persons who, in their search for it, are free from disquieting apprehensions. On our side, there will be no appeal to persons' fear. . . . Let us attend to the real matter in debate, and let our arguments appear to reason and to the authoritative teachings of Divine Scriptures, dispassionately and calmly, so far as we are able.[15]

> My desire is, not that any one should against his will be coerced into the Catholic communion, but that to all who are in error the truth may be openly declared, and being by God's help clearly exhibited through my ministry, may so commend itself as to make them embrace and follow it.[16]

---

[15]Augustine, *Letter* 32.7, in Philip Schaff, ed., *A Select Library of the Nicene and Post-Nicene Fathers of the Church*, vol. 1 (Grand Rapids: William B. Eerdmans, 1983), 244; CSEL 34(1): 71–72. See the discussion of this and other texts in the context of church and state relations in Herbert A. Deane, *The Political and Social Ideas of St. Augustine* (New York: Columbia University Press, 1963), 173–220.

[16]*Letter* 44.1, in Schaff, *Select Library*, 1:262; CSEL 44(2): 23.

But these words do not sit by themselves in our memory, for we have tended to recall in our tradition even more clearly the words of the "later" Augustine:

> I said that I was not in favor of schismatics being forcibly constrained to communion by the force of any secular power. And indeed at that time I did not favor that course, since I had not yet discovered the depths of evil to which their impunity would dare to venture, or how greatly a careful discipline would contribute to their emendation. . . . I have therefore yielded to the evidence. . . . Originally my opinion was that no one should be coerced into the unity of Christ, that we must act only by words, fight only by arguments, and prevail by force of reason.[17]

Augustine moves gradually along a line toward the acceptance of coercion until he one day preaches the famous dictum, " 'Compel them to come in,' saith [the Lord]. Let compulsion move them from outside, and their will will arise from within."[18]

We can recall, too, the arguments of Thomas Aquinas, which affirm the obligation of all persons to follow their own consciences. "We hold, without qualification, that whether the reason be correct or mistaken, the will which is at variance with it is always evil."[19] But we also know that Thomas justified the death penalty for heretics and apostates: "These are to be submitted to physical compulsion that they should hold to what they once received and fulfill what they promised."[20] "[Heretics] deserve not only to be separated from the Church by excommunication, but also to be severed from the world by death."[21] As an alternative to burning at the stake, silencing may seem like a great advance.

Of course, the contexts for these words of Augustine and Aquinas

---

[17]St. Augustine, *Retractionum* 2.5, quoted in Deane, *Political and Social Ideas of St. Augustine*, 186; CSEL 36.137; PL 32.2; and *Letter* 93.5.17, in Schaff, *Select Library*, 1:388; CSEL 34(2): 461.

[18]*Sermon* 62:8 (Benedictine ed., 112, 8), in Schaff, *A Select Library*, 6:449; PL 38.647–48.

[19]Thomas Aquinas, *In Sent.* 2 d. 39, q. 3, a. 3; quoted in E. D'Arcy, *Conscience and Its Right to Freedom* (New York: Sheed and Ward, 1961), 108. See also *Summa Theologiae* I-II.19.5. To put it more plainly, Aquinas was convinced that we must always follow our conscience, even if it should be objectively false.

[20]*ST* II-II.10.8.

[21]*ST* II-II.11.3.

are not equitable with the contexts I have been addressing. Still, the issues are not dissimilar. In the Second Vatican Council these same issues were confronted by the *Declaration on Religious Liberty* (*Dignitatis humanae*). Even there, however, the tensions and contradictions were not finally resolved. The clarity achieved regarding freedom of religious belief within a context of political freedom did not extend to problems of freedom of expression in controversies within the church itself over moral issues. With this document, nonetheless, arguments began to weigh in the direction of Augustine's "early" fundamental insight: force is *not* what causes truth to prevail in the mind or heart. And Thomas Aquinas's doctrine of the binding nature of the individual conscience is given new visibility. From this direction we can hear better the reasons for continued speech rather than silence, for public zones of freedom rather than restricted zones where truth is thought to be so fragile it cannot be trusted in the battles with possible falsehood.

We have had long centuries in which to learn the counterproductiveness of coercive measures when the issue becomes not truth but power, and long centuries to learn the glory of human freedom, as well as its limits and dangers. We have discovered the claim upon us all to listen and to speak, and to love enough to take up the burdens of mutual discernment and shared moral discourse.

Caution should motivate us to monitor systems of communication with guidelines that protect against manipulation and deception. Courage must move us to critique assumptions that experts exist (whether in the Pentagon or among moral theologians or in the church's hierarchy) whose judgments can never be supplemented or questioned. Wisdom may teach us that not every voice can speak for the community, but the truer voices will be better discerned not by excluding dissent but by protecting the most fragile voices in our midst.

CHAPTER 5

Feminism and Universal Morality

Feminists have understandable reasons both to reject and to promote belief in a common or universal morality. The social construction of moral norms is hardly anywhere more evident than in the history of interpretations of women's roles and duties in the family and in society. The suffering caused by what are now judged to be mistaken views of women's "nature" and its laws has moved many feminists to a deep skepticism regarding moral norms in general.[1] Yet insofar as feminism is a movement aimed at the well-being of women, it has an important interest in understanding what truly is for women's good—and in arguing for the basic intelligibility of that good. And insofar as feminism has an ultimate aim of enhancing the well-being of all human persons—women, men, children—its interests extend to understanding human good, individual and social, and to pressing claims that require some agreement on what constitutes and serves that human good. In other words, despite a sharp sense of the historical and social relativity of moral norms, the moral commitments and political agendas of many feminists lead them to articulate (or at least to imply) some version of a common morality. However, simply to

---

A version of this essay was published in *Prospects for a Common Morality*, ed. Gene Outka and John P. Reeder (Princeton, NJ: Princeton University Press, 1993), 170–90. Used with permission.

[1]The feminists to whom I am referring generally in this essay are primarily North American and Western European. Yet more and more feminist theory is being shaped by international and cross-cultural feminist voices. The importance of these voices for the kinds of questions this essay addresses is immense—something that will, I trust, be evident as my discussion unfolds.

attribute to feminists a general assumption about the possibility of a common human morality underestimates the seriousness of feminist critiques of traditional theories of universal morality. It also obscures the quite drastic differences among feminist theories that have emerged in the twentieth century.

On one reading, feminist theorists take as many positions on the possibility of a common morality as might be found in the mainstreams of late-twentieth-century and early-twenty-first-century philosophy, theology, political theory, psychology, and literary criticism. Feminists speak out of and back into classical, analytical, phenomenological, neo-Kantian, Marxist, pragmatist, deconstructionist, hermeneutical, and other waxing and waning traditions and currents of thought. Therefore, they are as cautious, skeptical, ironical, revisionary, deconstructive, or reconstructive as their disciplines have become. Yet there is a difference. Insofar as feminist theory retains a connection with feminism as a movement (a movement against the subordination of women to men and against any basic patterns of relationship that are characterized by the domination of some persons over others), feminist theory is never without a strong challenge not only to relate to particular women's experiences but also to mediate some universally sharable moral insights. This, however, may turn out to be an impossibly conflicted task.

This essay aims to explore the possibilities for a feminist theory that will include a coherent notion of universal or common morality. This is an important project for feminist theory and, I think, generally for both moral philosophy and theological ethics. On the one hand, if a theory of common morality is to be sustained, it needs to satisfy a specifically feminist critique (a critique that incorporates gender analysis). On the other hand, if feminist theory is to accommodate some of feminists' deepest concerns, it must at least ask about the universal relevance and intelligibility of its own moral claims.

I do not propose here to survey all of current feminist theory, looking for signs of a theory of common morality. Nor will I test the many historical and contemporary theories of universal morality against a feminist critique. I will try to locate in feminist theory some key criticisms of possible theories of common morality and some central reasons why a common morality must be sought. I will then attempt to frame some elements for a feminist theory of common morality.

The Feminist Case against a Common Morality

Feminists have resisted theories of common morality primarily because they have been harmful to women (and to some men). In the name of universality, of a totalizing view of human nature and society, such theories have in fact been exclusive, oppressive, and repressive of women and of men who do not belong to a dominant group. Whether consciously or unconsciously, the formulators of such theories have often inaccurately universalized a particular perspective. As a result, the needs and moral claims of some groups and individuals have been left out, their roles and duties distorted, and their full voices silenced. What is thought to be "common" morality, when examined with an eye for gender bias—or for class, race, religious, or other deep-seated biases—turns out not to have universal extension and to incorporate seriously mistaken moral requirements.

At least some theories of common morality, then, are not, in fact, universal; more than this, they distort what should be valid moral claims. They are not only inadequate, but false; not only false, but injurious. Such charges do not by themselves rule out the possibility of a valid universal morality. They only challenge the ones that have been developed thus far. For some feminists, this means that a moral theory can be corrected, expanded, improved upon; indeed, for these theorists the very possibility of a feminist critique implies a more adequate perspective for discerning universal moral norms. For other feminists, the problems with any theory of universal morality are more radical, even to the point where such a theory must simply be ruled out—if not in principle, at least in any foreseeable historical practice.

Feminist theories have diverged through the last four decades on some very fundamental questions. They have agreed that the subordination of women to men is unjustifiable and that it is sustained by false and inadequate interpretations of what and who women are—what they can do, what they desire, what kind of relationships they ought to be able to form. But feminist theorists have disagreed on the causes of gendered hierarchy, on its remedies, and on the nature of its interaction with other forms of dominance and subordination. Some of these disagreements stem from the varying philosophical alignments that have marked feminist analyses all along, and others have emerged in conjunction with changes in feminism as a movement. The bases of disagreements often go as deep, and are as comprehensive, as whole worldviews. In its own considerable pluralism, then, feminism provides formidable obstacles to a common morality; yet it may instance the potential of plural perspectives to allow and even support some common moral norms.

Philosopher Alison Jaggar's categorization of contemporary feminist theories was useful, at least for a time, for understanding the variety of feminist descriptive and normative proposals.[2] Jaggar's focus is on theories of society, but she argues that feminist theories of society have developed along with understandings of human nature, which in turn have involved commitments regarding the nature of human knowledge. She identifies four major categories (or what she sometimes calls paradigms) of feminist theories: liberal, traditional Marxist, radical, and socialist. Each general category encompasses numerous variations but has its own unitary focus. In the twentieth century these categories tended to follow one another in importance within feminist thought; that is, they emerged chronologically in terms of attention and number of adherents, though they all represent points of view still held by some feminists today.

Liberal feminism, in Jaggar's sense, incorporates a view of human nature that emphasizes rationality, autonomy, and individual fulfillment.[3] Its central moral principle is traditional philosophical

---

[2]Alison M. Jaggar, *Feminist Politics and Human Nature* (Totowa, NJ: Rowman and Allanheld, 1983). There are numerous other twentieth-century typologies for feminist theory, but Jaggar's seems particularly relevant to the questions of a common morality. I am using her categories heuristically, however, so that the features of each as I identify them sometimes go beyond (and sometimes fall short of) the descriptions Jaggar offers. See alternative typologies in Josephine Donovan, *Feminist Theory: The Intellectual Traditions of American Feminism* (New York: Frederick Ungar, 1985); Elisabeth Schussler Fiorenza, *In Memory of Her: A Feminist Reconstruction of Christian Origins* (New York: Crossroad, 1983), 7–36; Beverly Wildung Harrison, *Our Right to Choose: Toward a New Ethic of Abortion* (Boston: Beacon Press, 1983), chap. 3; Carol S. Robb, "A Framework for Feminist Ethics," *Journal of Religious Ethics* 9 (1981): 48–68; Rosemary Radford Ruether, *Sexism and God-Talk* (Boston: Beacon Press, 1983), 214–34; Linda Alcoff, "Cultural Feminism versus Post-Structuralism: The Identity Crisis in Feminist Theory," in *Feminist Theory in Practice and Process*, ed. Micheline R. Malson et al. (Chicago: University of Chicago Press, 1989), 295–326. All of these typologies are somewhat dated today, but they remain useful for understanding theoretical developments in twentieth- and even twentieth-first-century feminisms.

[3]Individual feminists cannot easily be assigned to these categories because feminist theories are continually developing and because the categories indicate elements of theories (methods, sources, particular concepts) that turn out to be separable from a theory as a whole—elements that then are able to appear in more than one category of theory. Jaggar herself (whether intentionally or not) sometimes assigns an individual feminist to more than

liberalism's respect for persons, based on the equal dignity of rational agents and on the requirements of rationality itself insofar as reason identifies unconditional moral obligations or provides the warrants for a social contract.[4] Like traditional liberalism, the feminist version has believed in the possibility of objectivity in scientific and moral knowledge; it has seen its own critical function as that of challenging liberalism to consistency and to true impartiality in its recognition of and respect for every human person. Feminists' particular task has been to demand acknowledgment of the full humanity of women and, with this, the extension of principles of liberty and equality to women as well as to men.

Liberal feminism, then, more than any other major form of feminist theory, has tended to support the possibility of a universal morality. Since the 1792 publication of Mary Wollstonecraft's *Vindication of the Rights of Women*, mainstream feminism has struggled to complete what it assumed to be a truly human moral point of view by (a) "adding" insights drawn from women's history and experience, (b)

---

one category, as, for example, when she instances Christine Delphy for traditional Marxism, radical feminism, and socialist feminism. This is why it is difficult to provide a list of feminist thinkers who would now willingly wear the label "liberal." An early and utterly clear representative of Enlightenment liberal feminism is, of course, Mary Wollstonecraft's *A Vindication of the Rights of Women* (rpt., Baltimore: Penguin, 1975). Others who are often remembered as launching historically significant liberal feminist appeals include Elizabeth Cady Stanton, Sarah Grimké, Susan B. Anthony, Sojourner Truth, and Harriet Taylor. Currently it may be more helpful to indicate some of the important feminist explorations of liberal theory (which have varying degrees of sympathy for a liberal feminist point of view, and some of which embody serious criticisms of traditional liberalism). These include Jean Grimshaw, *Philosophy and Feminist Thinking* (Minneapolis: University of Minnesota Press, 1986); Zillah Eisenstein, *The Radical Future of Liberal Feminism* (New York: Longman, 1981); Lenore Coltheart, "Desire, Consent, and Liberal Theory," in *Feminist Challenges: Social and Political Theory*, ed. Carole Pateman and Elizabeth Gross (Boston: Northeastern University Press, 1986), 112–22; Christine Di Stefano, "Liberalism and Its Feminist Critics," *American Philosophical Association Newsletter* 88 (June 1989): 35–38; Genevieve Lloyd, *The Man of Reason: "Male" and "Female" in Western Philosophy* (Minneapolis: University of Minnesota Press, 1984); Susan Moller Okin, *Women in Western Political Thought* (Princeton, NJ: Princeton University Press, 1979); Iris Marion Young, "Impartiality and the Civic Public: Some Implications of Feminist Critiques of Moral and Political Theory," in *Feminism as Critique: On the Politics of Gender*, ed. Seyla Benhabib and Drucilla Cornell (Minneapolis: University of Minnesota Press, 1987); Jean Bethke Elshtain, *Public Man, Private Woman: Women in Social and Political Thought* (Princeton, NJ: Princeton University Press, 1981).

[4]Among the more obvious current representatives of this tradition are John Rawls, *A Theory of Justice* (Cambridge, MA: Harvard University Press, 1971); Alan Donagan, *The Theory of Morality* (Chicago: University of Chicago Press, 1977); Ronald Dworkin, *Taking Rights Seriously* (Cambridge, MA: Harvard University Press, 1977); Alan Gewirth, *Reason and Morality* (Chicago: University of Chicago Press, 1978).

claiming for women a "sameness" with men as human persons and as full citizens, and (c) asserting the autonomy of individual women and the rights of self-determination for women as members of a group. Discouragement with liberalism has grown among feminists (as among others), however. Its perceived failure to emancipate women (after two centuries of theoretical critique and political action) has convinced many feminists that an "additive" approach to political theory is not sufficient. While few feminists want to lose civil liberties or a newfound sense of individual selfhood, they nonetheless have come to demand of liberal norms and ideals more than a simple extension to include women. The content of liberalism itself requires major change, and its claims as an impartial, objective, universal moral theory are in serious doubt.

To many feminists, this form of liberalism fails to take account of the particular historical situations of women. It has sometimes been content to tolerate the divides between public life and private, so that even where liberal ideals appear to alleviate women's oppression, alienation remains in sexual relations, child rearing, and the support services of ordinary housework. Aristotle's *polis* depended on a sexual division of labor, and modern liberal societies seem to need it no less. Appeals to neutral reason are ineffective before the convictions of the powerful, and where they are heard, they leave out whole spheres of human life and dimensions of the human personality. Many feminist critics of liberalism target, then, its remaining tendencies to dichotomize and to rank mind and body, reason and emotion, public and private, autonomy and community. Its theoretical deficiencies mask its support of the subordination of some persons to others on the basis of gender, class, race, and other human particularities that liberalism claims to have transcended.

Not surprisingly, *Marxist feminism* has provided a significant alternative for some of the feminist critics of liberalism.[5] Traditional

---

[5]Among feminists who have explored the possibilities and limits of a Marxist feminism are Michele Barrett, *Women's Oppression Today* (London: Verso, 1980); Jane Flax, "Do Feminists Need Marxism?" in *Building Feminist Theory*, ed. The Quest staff (New York: Longman, 1981); Lydia Sargent, ed., *Women and Revolution: A Discussion of the Unhappy Marriage of Marxism and Feminism* (Boston: South End Press, 1981); Angela Davis, *Women, Race, and Class* (New York: Random House, 1981); Linda Nicholson, "Feminism and Marx: Integrating Kinship with the Economic," in Benhabib and Cornell, *Feminism as Critique*, 16–30.

Marxism offers an explanation for the failures of abstract rationality.[6] It contends that moral norms and ideals are not universal and ahistorical, the achievement of a neutral and solitary observer; they are socially constructed. Even human nature is a historical construction, fashioned out of the interaction of biology, society, and the physical environment—limited by material needs in a concrete and particular situation, subject to the purposes of a ruling class. Relational but not completely relativist, Marxism allows for some objectivity in the physical sciences and a *telos* for moral understandings. For while moralities are conventional, they are part of the human struggle for liberation. The dominant class determines the moral and political norms of a society (and the structures that make norms convincing), but the voices and actions of the oppressed can bring about revolutionary change. The introduction of a feminist point of view will not, then, be irrelevant to the liberation of women and the achieved equality of all persons.

As attractive as Marxist analysis has been for some feminists, and as helpful as it has been in addressing the problems of liberal philosophy and political theory, it has nonetheless not satisfied many feminists as a theoretical basis for understanding the social construction of gender. In its concern for economic analysis, there are strands of Marxism, like liberalism, that leave intact the separation of the public world and the private. In its preoccupation with production, it fails to take seriously the historical nature of reproduction. But above all, traditional Marxism has insufficient theoretical room for either gender or racial analysis. Within its framework, women as women cannot constitute a class, nor is race as such a determinant of class. The tools are missing, therefore, for some of the needs of a feminist theory.

Radical feminism challenges both liberal and Marxist feminism. If Marxism fails to take gender seriously enough, radical feminists make it the central problem. If liberal feminism appreciates the perspectives of women as starting points on the way to understanding women's full humanity, radical feminists begin and (to an important extent) end with the experience and the ways of knowing that are particular to women. These challenges go a long way toward specifying what is

---

[6]In addition to Marx's own writings (especially his early writings), feminists have tended to take most seriously such Marxist interpreters as Georg Lukács, *History and Class Consciousness: Studies in Marxist Dialectics*, trans. Rodney Livingstone (Cambridge, MA: MIT Press, 1971); Karl Kautsky, *Ethics and the Materialist Conception of History*, trans. J. B. Asken (Chicago: University of Chicago Press, 1907).

otherwise an unwieldy category.[7] For whatever else radical feminists are, they are convinced that the most basic form of all oppression is patriarchy, and that patriarchy is neither a mere anomaly in an otherwise liberal justice nor a form of domination that is solely derivative of economic power.

Gender provides the (often invisible) framework for every social relation. Hence, the radical feminist task is to understand how gender is socially constructed and to explore its influence, especially in the private sphere of family life, sexual relationships, and spirituality. For some earlier radical feminists the goal was to eliminate gender differences; for many later radical feminists the goal has been to reclaim the differences between women and men—to retrieve women's culture, to revalue woman-identified emotion in relation to reason, embodiment in relation to transcendent mind, and caring in relation to abstract principles of justice. No longer afraid that acknowledging gender differences will inevitably result in discrimination, many radical feminists are as concerned with the repression of women as with their oppression.

The radical feminist agenda, then, is both to free women's bodies from the power of men and to free women's minds and hearts from the cultural and psychological bonds of patriarchy. This turns out to be one task, for the human person is an organic whole. The task depends importantly, however, on the recognition and release of women's special powers of knowing. For some this takes the form of spiritual insight,

---

[7]Radical feminism is the broadest of Jaggar's four categories. There is, as she acknowledges, no single radical feminist analysis. Jaggar even wonders whether in a short time the category may have to be elided with socialist feminism. But whatever the evolution of theory in this regard, it is still helpful to talk about radical forms of feminism with some historical status. For my present purposes, this category stretches to include elements of the work of such diverse feminists as Shulamith Firestone, Ti-Grace Atkinson, Charlotte Bunch, Kate Millett, Adrienne Rich, Mary Daly, Susan Griffin, Catherine MacKinnon, Carol Gilligan, and Luce Irigaray. My characterization of the category should make it clear which elements I am identifying. As for the individual thinkers (as we shall see), other elements in their works—sometimes because their work has developed and changed—make them representatives of socialist feminism as well. For a fuller perspective on radical feminism with important added assumptions and configurations, see Bell Hooks, *Feminist Theory: From Margin to Center* (Boston: South End Press, 1984), especially chaps. 1–4, 11–12.

It should also be noted here that some religious traditions and organizations (for example, the official voices of Roman Catholic Church leaders) seriously distort whatever meanings have been given to "radical feminism." In doing so, they mislead those who follow them, and ironically, attempt also to co-opt the term "feminism" into a new category they name "Christian feminism."

made possible by participation in communal rituals.[8] For others it is the less mystical process of consciousness-raising, the sharing of women's experience in a way that leads to new self-understanding and insight into human (especially women's) possibility. Variously inspired by the analysis and literary innovations of Mary Daly, the psychological studies of Carol Gilligan, the bold and mysterious *écriture féminine* of French feminists, and the powerful theories and expressions of countless other feminists, radical feminism makes women themselves the focus of exploration and the organizers of their own liberation.[9]

Still, many feminists are not satisfied with what radical feminism has been able to provide thus far by way of theory. While it pays attention to gender and to women's experience and to the integration of body and mind, affectivity and knowledge, and the private sphere with the public, it has finally not been sufficiently historical for some feminists, not sufficiently political for others. Some fear that the new emphasis on differences between women and men is neither warranted nor wise, for it slips too easily into traditional stereotypes and threatens to reinforce once again the subordination of women to men. Moreover, it ignores the diverse histories of individual women and groups of women. And finally, however special women's ways of knowing may be, there remain troubling questions of the social construction of knowledge, the dichotomization of (for example) justice and care, the particular or universal relevance of woman-identified values as the human ideal.

Feminist theory has continued to develop, however, and Jaggar's last category incorporates key elements from both traditional Marxist

---

[8]A good deal of the growing movement in feminist spirituality illustrates this. See, for example, Starhawk, *The Spiral Dance: A Rebirth of the Religion of the Great Goddess* (San Francisco: Harper and Row, 1979); and *Dreaming the Dark* (Boston: Beacon Press, 1982); Margot Adler, *Drawing Down the Moon*, rev. ed. (Boston: Beacon Press, 1986).

[9]See, for example, Mary Daly, *Gyn-Ecology: The Metaethics of Radical Feminism* (Boston: Beacon Press, 1978); Carol Gilligan, *In a Different Voice: Psychological Theory and Women's Development* (Cambridge, MA: Harvard University Press, 1982); Carol Gilligan, Janie Victoria Ward, and Jill McLean Taylor, eds., *Mapping the Moral Domain: A Contribution of Women's Thinking to Psychological Theory and Education* (Cambridge, MA: Center for the Study of Gender, Education, and Human Development, 1988); Luce Irigaray, *Speculum of the Other Woman*, trans. Gillian C. Gill (Ithaca, NY: Cornell University Press, 1985); Hélène Cixous and Catherine Clément, *The Newly Born Woman*, trans. Betsy Wing (Minneapolis: University of Minnesota Press, 1986); Sara Ruddick, *Maternal Thinking: Toward a Politics of Peace* (Boston: Beacon Press, 1989). Not everyone would consider all of these writings to be representatives of radical feminism, but they are all concerned with what they identify as aspects of women's experience, nature, and ways of knowing that are particular to women (different, therefore, from those of men).

and radical feminist theory.[10] What Jaggar calls *socialist feminism* is like Marxism in its assertions that understandings of human nature and society are socially constructed and that prevailing worldviews reflect the interests of the dominant class. It also agrees with traditional Marxism that the perspective of the oppressed is epistemologically privileged because it is more likely to be impartial (though not disinterested) and comprehensive, since its interests are more likely to serve the wider social good. Like radical feminism, socialist feminism believes Marxism to be mistaken in not taking particular account of gender in its analysis of oppression. Radical and socialist feminists have stood together in considering patriarchy to be the major social problem in both private and public arenas. But socialist feminists want to address the interconnections of gender and class and race and age, and they require more systematic and critical studies of women's experience, particularly in the shared social practice of the struggle for liberation. Like radical feminists, socialist feminists want to raise the importance of emotion as a source of knowledge as well as affective power, but at least for Jaggar this involves a critical analysis of historically structured emotional responses.

With these four versions of feminist theory, the possibilities for a theory of universal morality are clearly limited but not eliminated. Insofar as adherents to these versions of feminism still exist, they suggest clues to a feminist common morality. Liberal feminism, sobered by the recognition of its capacity to conceal oppression as well as to reveal it, still looks to a basic set of rights and responsibilities for all human persons. Traditional Marxist feminism, appreciative of the role of power in sustaining historically situated worldviews, still aims at overcoming alienation in the attainment of a universally intelligible

---

[10]At the time of writing her book *Feminist Politics and Human Nature*, Jaggar indicated that socialist feminism was perhaps the "most questionable" of her four paradigms, since it seemed a small modification of either Marxist feminism or radical feminism. She included in it feminist thinkers whose systematic work on gender or class contributed to the kind of analysis described here. Hence this category included Juliet Mitchell (who also qualifies as a traditional Marxist feminist), Nancy Chodorow (who can also be considered a radical feminist), Sandra Harding, Ann Ferguson, and Jaggar herself. Exploration of and from this perspective can be found in Iris Young, "Beyond the Unhappy Marriage: A Critique of the Dual Systems Theory," in *Women and Revolution*, ed. Lydia Sargent (Boston: South End Press, 1981); Zillah Eisenstein, "Some Notes on the Relations of Capitalist Patriarchy," in *Capitalist Patriarchy and the Case for Socialist Feminism*, ed. Zillah Eisenstein (New York: Monthly Review Press, 1979); Christine Delphy, *Close to Home: A Materialist Analysis of Women's Oppression*, trans. Diana Leonard (Amherst: University of Massachusetts Press, 1984); Hooks, *Feminist Theory*.

human social good. Radical feminism trusts the capacities of women to discover or to create who they are and what they need—sometimes even in an essential sense. Socialist feminism, historical and material-ist, pragmatic and provisional, aims nonetheless at a more adequate systematic explanation of oppression for the sake of an ultimate trans-formation of society. Another category may now have superseded all of these—that is, a category that might be called "strategic feminism."

Developments in feminist theory, however, emerging out of each of the four types and out of the interaction among them, have generated sharper obstacles to formulations of universal morality.[11] Two develop-ments in particular call into question the possibility of any overarching feminist theory of morality. The seeds of both are in the call by many feminist theorists for a critical revaluation of human embodiment, af-fectivity, and the ordinary "housekeeping" of life, and in the insistence by all feminist theorists on the inclusion of a woman's perspective.

The first development marks an intensification of the long-standing concern that feminists have had to pay attention to women's bodies. While early forms of feminism attempted to prescind from women's embodiment (opposing, for example, the strictures of "anatomy is destiny"), women soon began to "reclaim" their bodies. With such reclaiming has come the recognition that feminist analysis is irrevo-cably bound up with the historical, the particular, the situated, the contingent—all of which effectively resist universal interpretation. That which had been considered most "natural," abstracted as it was from women's experience and therefore easily universalized by its interpret-ers, now seems almost completely subject to social construction for its meaning. The last bastion for some versions of universal morality seems lost before sustained feminist critique.

The second development is not unrelated to the first. It involves the deconstruction of "women's experience" by women whose ex-perience is marginal to that of the dominant class of women, and by postmodernist feminists who are suspicious of any grand narratives, even those that include the perspectives of women. The critique that

---

[11]Jaggar does not follow these developments very far in *Feminist Politics and Human Nature*, though she does signal them from the beginning (see p. 12). In a later work it is clear that the developments have progressed very far indeed; see Alison M. Jaggar and Susan R. Bordo, eds., *Gender/Body/Knowledge: Feminist Reconstructions of Being and Knowing* (New Brunswick, NJ: Rutgers University Press, 1989).

feminist theorists have lodged against false universalization from men's experience to "human" experience has been turned on feminism itself, with the charge that the experience of some women—white, middle-class, Western, heterosexual—has been falsely universalized to represent all women. Women of color, lesbian women, working-class women, women from across the world have pressed the question of whether there is anything common in women's experience, or whether the delineation of a "women's perspective" must simply replicate the situation in which those with power always privilege their own voices while silencing the voices of others.

The issue is again not simply one of adding many voices in order to make what is partial more representative of a whole. It is the issue of whether women as women do have anything in common, and, again, whether there can be "any account of 'human nature' that, in the guise of a universal account, doesn't end up conflating the situation of one group of humans with the situation of all."[12] It is the issue, moreover, of why gender analysis without class, race, and cultural analyses can only be distortive, why the abstraction of gender from the full situatedness of persons conceals the patterns of their relationships. Feminists increasingly insist, for example, that patriarchy in Western culture cannot be understood without an analysis of why marriage determines a woman's class but not a man's; that a slave woman's situation is not understood simply by adding together what it means to be a woman and what it means to be a slave; that the race of white women as well as black women determines their experience of sexism; and that invisible but "compulsory" heterosexuality must be recognized if all the forms of sexism are to be seen.

Postmodernist trends in contemporary feminist theory coalesce (despite tension) with the challenges of women whose experiences have been heretofore undervalued or ignored.[13] Along with Lyotard,

---

[12]Elizabeth V. Spelman, *Inessential Woman: Problems of Exclusion in Feminist Thought* (Boston: Beacon Press, 1988), 79. For similar formulations of the problem of the interconnectedness of identity factors and the necessity of seeing their interconnections for understanding human oppression, see the groundbreaking study of Okin, *Women in Western Political Thought*; hooks, *Feminist Theory*, chap. 1; Hester Eisenstein and Alice Jardine, eds., *The Future of Difference* (New Brunswick, NJ: Rutgers University Press, 1985); Delphy, *Close to Home*, especially chap. 2; Elizabeth Meese and Alice Parker, eds., *The Difference Within: Feminism and Critical Theory* (Philadelphia: John Benjamins, 1989); Pateman and Gross, *Feminist Challenges*.

[13]Helpful insights into postmodernist philosophy and its uses in feminist theory can be

Derrida, Foucault, and others, some feminists have come to doubt whether any theory can transcend particular power relations and historical situatedness to critique large social and institutional structures. Perhaps no one can attempt to identify common elements in women's (or men's) experience without suppressing voices different from his or her own and without mistaking the contingent for the essential. The dangers of abstraction may finally outweigh any cognitive or political advantage it once seemed to have. To move in this direction, of course, threatens to leave feminism without the tools for a universal critique of structures of domination and subordination. Even categories like "gender," "race," and "class" must be deconstructed, possibly to the point where they are useless for social and ethical theory. At this extreme in feminist theory, all theory as theory is vulnerable.

The Feminist Case for a Common Morality

Nevertheless, feminists continue to theorize, and arguments for a common morality continue to be made. If theories of universal morality have been distortive and harmful, theories of unmitigated relativism are no less so. The problem of representing particulars as universals is bound up with the problems of coercion and violence. But the problem of recognizing no universals at all is also a problem of conflict and power, and it limits or eliminates the possibility of a common cry for justice. Thus Sandra Harding is not alone in believing that "relativism is not a problem originating in, or justifiable in terms of, women's experiences or feminist agendas."[14] Feminists tend to appreciate the observation of Mircea Eliade that historicism is promoted

---

found in Linda J. Nicholson, ed., *Feminism/Postmodernism* (New York: Routledge, 1990); Barbara Johnson, *A World of Difference* (Baltimore: Johns Hopkins University Press, 1987); Benhabib and Cornell, *Feminism as Critique*; Ann Garry and Marilyn Pearsall, eds., *Women, Knowledge, and Reality: Explorations in Feminist Philosophy* (Boston: Unwin Hyman, 1989); Joan W. Scott, "Deconstructing Equality-versus-Difference: Or, the Uses of Poststructuralist Theory for Feminism," *Feminist Studies* 14 (Spring 1988): 33–50; Evelyn Keller, *Reflections on Gender and Science* (New Haven, CT: Yale University Press, 1985); and Jane Flax, *Thinking Fragments: Psychoanalysis, Feminism, and Postmodernism in the Contemporary West* (Berkeley: University of California Press, 1990).

[14]Sandra Harding, "Introduction: Is There a Feminist Method?" in Harding, ed., *Feminism and Methodology: Social Science Issues* (Bloomington: Indiana University Press, 1987), 156.

in nations where history has not been a "continuous terror."[15] So long as oppression, hierarchies of power, and relative visibility of lives are part of human society, it is not possible to conclude that everyone's analysis is equally plausible, that everyone's voice carries equally adequate "truth." Indeed, to adopt historical and cultural relativism as a solution to the inadequacies and falsehoods of universalism may be to abandon the field to the powerful or to struggle for position on a model of human relationship that offers nothing more ultimate than conflict—a model that feminists have consistently rejected.

A feminist case for common morality stands on more than the needs of a political agenda, however. It stands primarily on the convictions that human persons can and ought to experience moral claims in relation to one another, and that some of these claims can and ought to cross (though not ignore) the boundaries of culture and history. These convictions presuppose some commonality in human experience—in the experience of what it means as a human person to rejoice and to be sorrowful, to be protected or violated, nurtured or stifled, understood or misjudged, respected or used. Whatever the differences in human lives, however minimal the actuality of world community, however unique the social arrangements of diverse peoples, it is nonetheless possible for human persons to weep over commonly felt tragedies, laugh over commonly perceived incongruities, yearn for common hopes. And across time and place, it is possible to condemn commonly recognized injustices and act for commonly desired goals. The range of universal moral norms may be narrower than traditional ethical theories supposed, but it does exist. The content of universal morality may be modest and in many ways provisional, but it is not empty. Beyond the critique of universal norms lie caution and care but not arbitrariness or indifference, and not completely isolated moral systems.

The dissonance between such convictions and the new awareness of differences among women is probably more apparent than real. Feminist theorists are wary of identifying commonalities in women's experience, but they do not dismiss them altogether. Thus, Josephine Donovan and others insist that there are some "determinant structures of experience under which women, unlike men, have nearly univer-

---

[15]Mircea Eliade, *Cosmos and History: The Myth of the Eternal Return* (Princeton, NJ: Princeton University Press, 1954), 151–52.

sally existed."[16] These structures include the political subordination of women to men, the assignment of women to major tasks in the domestic sphere, women's participation in economic production for use but not exchange, and significant physical events of the female body such as menstruation, childbirth, and breast-feeding. The meaning of these structures is socially constructed, and hence variable, but women who reflect on them across cultures and classes usually find something in their language and in their consciousness (and therefore in their experience) that is shared.

Those who have done the most to challenge an assumed commonality in contemporary women's experience are women who belong to minority groups in the United States and women from areas of Africa, Central and Latin America, and the many parts of Asia. The goal of their challenge, however, has not been to isolate women from one another, as if differences were eternal barriers. Nor has it been to offer particular stories of particular histories that are simply parallel to every other history—entirely relative in their meaning to the contexts in which they have developed. Rather, they have spoken of themselves as "long-suffering custodians of truth," bringing from their parts of the world protests against cruelty, violence, and injustice.[17] They have presented what they believe to be serious feminist theories of universal significance.[18] They have argued that differences can make community possible, but only if the differences are confronted and respected.[19] These writers are as opposed to unmitigated moral relativism as to false and inadequate universalisms.

If feminist theory is to incorporate some form of common morality, however, it is of course not enough for it to interpret moral norms and ideals only for women. It must incorporate or transcend not only the differences among women but the differences between women and men. If it is a theory of common morality, it must somehow be accessible to men, somehow cross the boundaries of gendered experi-

---

[16]Donovan, *Feminist Theory*, 172–73. See also Emily Martin, *The Woman in the Body: A Cultural Analysis of Reproduction* (Boston: Beacon Press, 1987), 4, 201.

[17]Katie G. Cannon, foreword to *With Passion and Compassion: Third World Women Doing Theology*, ed. Virginia Fabella and Mercy Amba Oduyoye (Maryknoll, NY: Orbis Books, 1988), vii.

[18]See the analysis of women's role in Salvadoran society presented in *A Dream Compels Us: Voices of Salvadoran Women*, ed. New Americas Press (Boston: South End Press, 1989).

[19]See, for example, hooks, *Feminist Theory*, chap. 4.

ence and understanding as well as the boundaries of culture and race and class. Some feminist theories are therefore less suited to address issues of common morality than others. For example, proposals like Carol Gilligan's regarding the moral development of women came close (despite repeated caveats) to sanctioning one set of norms for women and another for men.[20] Still, most feminists who bring women's perspectives to bear on questions of morality rely on the general (and potentially universal) intelligibility and moral force of the arguments they make. They do not assume that these arguments are plausible only to women. In articulating moral claims and ideals, in advocating the transformation of society, they presume some analogy in the experiences of differently situated persons—some basis for perceiving moral challenges and possibilities, some inkling of similarity even in difference.[21]

What feminists think about universal morality is perhaps clearer when the issues are concerned less with method than with moral behavior and social policy. Here the lessons of particularity are not forgotten, but neither are the compelling needs and rationales of universality. The demystification of moral rules in spheres historically important to women is profound. Evidence mounts for historical social construction of the meaning of sexuality, parenthood, marriage and family, technology, war, birth and death. What counts as courage, honesty, loyalty, integrity becomes open to exploration. The loosening of taboo moralities and the relaxation of moralisms are welcome and freeing to women. Some behaviors are no longer interpreted primarily

---

[20]Gilligan, *In a Different Voice*. This is not to question the usefulness and importance of Gilligan's findings in respects other than universal relevance. It must also be noted that Gilligan qualifies her conclusions in this study and succeeding ones, emphasizing that the justice and care perspectives are precisely that—perspectives, and they can be part of women's or men's approach to morality. Nonetheless, her work has been interpreted by many others to show a fundamental (however socially constructed) divergence in women's and men's moral sensibilities. This emphasis is clear in, for example, Nel Noddings, *Caring* (Berkeley: University of California Press, 1984). Sara Ruddick's theory of "maternal thinking" allows more explicit room for men's access to understanding and acting from this moral perspective; see Ruddick, *Maternal Thinking*, 44–45.

[21]For a treatment of analogy as model of relationship and basis of moral epistemology, see Caroline Whitbeck, "A Different Reality: Feminist Ontology," in *Beyond Domination: New Perspectives on Women and Philosophy*, ed. Carol Gould (Totowa, NJ: Rowman and Allanheld, 1984), 64–88. For examples of straightforward ethical analysis from a feminist perspective but obviously offered for general understanding, see Harrison, *Our Right to Choose;* Barrett, *Women's Oppression Today;* Sharon D. Welch, *A Feminist Ethic of Risk* (Minneapolis: Fortress Press, 1990).

as moral matters—as in the evaluation of many sexual arrangements. Other behaviors are newly understood as morally required, even though their meaning is deeply culture-relative—as in the forms that honesty takes in culturally shaped interpersonal relations.[22] Moreover, disagreement among feminists on specific moral questions sometimes relativizes perspectives, and the political arena becomes the appropriate setting for the adjudication of conflict and the struggle with uncertainty, as with the issues of abortion, eugenics, pornography, prostitution, and so forth.[23]

But as relativism rises in importance for feminists, so in a way does a feminist commitment to universal morality. If there is demystification of taboos, for example, so is there demystification of double standards for women and for men. This is as true in decisions about medical treatment as it is in traditional patterns of sexual activity, and it prompts calls for unitary systems of morality.[24] In addition, feminist respect for particularity and diversity is not criterionless, and feminism works hard to sustain some critical distance from every context. Hence

---

[22]See Adrienne Rich, "Women and Honor: Some Notes on Lying," in *On Lies, Secrets, and Silence: Selected Prose, 1966–78* (New York: Norton, 1979), 185–94.

[23]One of the most interesting issues in this regard is prostitution. Feminists have been outraged by the growth of sex industries, especially in, for example, Southeast Asian countries. It seems impossible from a feminist point of view not to condemn the blatant exploitation of women whose economic dependency (and often the economic dependency of their countries) makes them vulnerable, and whose experience is of relentless terror. On the other hand, the voices of women prostitutes in very different circumstances are beginning to be heard, and the last word does not yet seem to be in. See, for example, Gail Pheterson, ed., *A Vindication of the Rights of Whores* (Seattle: Seal Press, 1989). On other issues, see Jean Bethke Elshtain, "The New Eugenics and Feminist Quandaries," *Lutheran Forum* 23 (1989): 20–29; Celeste Michelle Condit, *Decoding Abortion Rhetoric: Communicating Social Change* (Urbana: University of Illinois Press, 1990); Linda Gordon, "Feminism and Social Control: The Case of Child Abuse and Neglect," in *What Is Feminism? A Re-examination*, ed. Juliet Mitchell and Ann Oakley (New York: Pantheon, 1986), 63–84. Other studies of interest to feminist analysis include Charles Bernheimer, *Figures of Ill Repute: Representing Prostitution in Nineteenth-Century France* (Cambridge, MA: Harvard University Press, 1989); Alain Corbin, *Women for Hire: Prostitution and Sexuality in France after 1850*, trans. Alan Sheridan (Cambridge, MA: Harvard University Press, 1990); John Boswell, *The Kindness of Strangers: The Abandonment of Children in Western Europe from Late Antiquity to the Renaissance* (New York: Pantheon, 1988); Daphne Read, "(De)Constructing Pornography: Feminisms in Conflict," in *Passion and Power: Sexuality in History*, ed. Kathy Peiss and Christina Simmons (Philadelphia: Temple University Press, 1989), 277–92.

[24]A survey of court decisions in the United States has turned up a revealing pattern of gender differentiation in acceptance of patient wishes regarding refusal of medical treatment. See Steven H. Miles and Allison August, "Courts, Gender and 'The Right to Die,' " *Law, Medicine and Health Care* 18 (Spring–Summer 1990): 85–95.

it is difficult to imagine a feminist perspective in which sexism could be approved, although to some extent what counts as sexism may be culture-relative. And while feminists have failed (and still can fail) to critique racism or classism, most feminist theorists today would call for self-criticism in that regard. Again, while something is fundamentally contextual about the experience of embodiment, feminists have universalized bodily integrity as a reality and a value that ought not to be violated. While the meaning of sexuality is importantly socially constructed, and gender is understood differently in various historical contexts, feminists have not hesitated to critique—across cultures—actions such as footbinding, female genital circumcision, spouse abuse, sexual harassment, reproductive coercion, slavery, and rape.[25] The critical perspective needed for rejecting such practices is itself dependent upon social influences, but neither feminism as a movement nor feminism as a theory has accepted complete identification with a society or a culture. To acknowledge a point of view is not necessarily to relinquish some claim to universal validity.

The vantage point for a feminist critique of individual actions as well as social practices—women's as well as men's—is a commitment to the well-being of women, and within and beyond that to the well-being of all human persons (and, for many feminists, within and beyond that to the well-being of all the world). These commitments motivate both respect for diversity and a desire for universality. Insofar as refinement of theory serves this commitment today, feminism is searching for a more adequate theory of differences and a more integrative theory of universal norms. The search is not a sectarian one, but one that has much to do with a common morality. As part of that search, I want to consider briefly two possible elements in a feminist theory of common morality. The first is a view of the human person, women-persons or men-persons or differently gendered persons, that tries to take account of feminism's concern for both selfhood and relationship. As such it risks the charge of essentialism, the dangers of abstract universalism, and a form of naïveté in affirming still a "subject." Yet it seems worth considering. The second is an approach to moral action-guides that

---

[25]The tension that some feminists experience, however, in seeming to judge a culture other than their own can be seen in the study of the practice of clitoridectomy among African women. See Hanny Lightfoot-Klein, *Prisoners of Ritual: An Odyssey into Female Genital Circumcision in Africa* (Binghamton, NY: Haworth Press, 1989).

tries to move beyond current feminist theoretical tensions between justice and care. It will encounter the problems of "realism" and again the dangers of universalism. But it will aim to integrate context and principle.

Elements for a Feminist Theory of Common Morality

Autonomy and Relationality

The commitment of feminism to the well-being of women implies, as I have noted earlier, some understanding of what constitutes women's well-being. An early conviction of contemporary feminism was that at the heart of what is good for women is autonomy, in the sense of both self-legislation and self-determination.[26]

Women needed to take hold of their own lives, to refuse the subordinate position that rendered them passive in relation to an active male, to trust their own insights and articulate their own self-understanding. Because autonomy belonged to women as personal beings with the capacity to determine the ultimate meaning of their own lives, they could make claims for respect as persons, valuable in themselves and not merely as instruments in the service of the community—or of the human species, the family, or men. An important part of the claim of respect for autonomy was the right to bodily integrity, the right not to be touched or invaded or used as embodied beings without their own free choice or consent.

An affirmation of autonomy as a central feature of the human personality is not without its theoretical and practical limitations, however. As we have seen, feminists (along with others) have been critical of the connotations of exaggerated individualism, detached spectatorship, and Faustian desires for control that Western notions of autonomy have carried. Therefore, throughout the development of contemporary feminist theory there has been a strong tendency to consider another feature of persons (and another aspect of women's

---

[26]The importance of autonomy (or a capacity for free choice) and relationality is a theme that can be traced throughout several other essays in this volume, as well as in my other writings—such as *Just Love: A Framework for Christian Sexual Ethics* (New York: Continuum, 2006). It does a lot of "work" in relation to diverse questions. Hence, despite some overlap, the meaning of these aspects of human persons is illuminated by seeing their moral status and function in varied situations.

well-being) as important as autonomy—the feature that can be called "relationality."

The tendency of women to emphasize relationships in their approach to morality provides the focus for much of feminist moral theory today. The general response to Gilligan's work testifies to the importance of this approach, as does the interest in earlier studies by Nancy Chodorow, Dorothy Dinnerstein, and others. At stake here, though less clearly articulated than descriptions of psychological patterns of relating, is a view of women, but also of men, in which the capacity for relationship is as significant a characteristic of human persons as the capacity for self-determination. Like autonomy, relationality underlies the value of persons in themselves. Because persons can know and be known, love and be loved, they are both self-transcendent—expansive beyond what they are in any given moment—and self-possessing—capable of knowing and loving themselves, not in spite of knowing and loving others, but through it and in it.

But also like autonomy, relationality has its theoretical and practical limitations. Feminists tend to be aware, for example, of the destructiveness of an emphasis on relationship that fails to respect autonomy. They are more critical of situatedness in communities and traditions than are many recent communitarian philosophers.[27] Women's experiences of submersion in roles, the tyranny of traditions, and the potential oppressiveness of communities warn them of the need for moral limits to community.

Feminist moral theory, then, needs both autonomy and relationality. Against "modernist" rationalism, it can show that autonomy is ultimately for the sake of relationship; against conservative forms of communitarianism, it can argue that relationships without respect for individuality and autonomy are destructive of persons—and, historically, especially destructive of women; against postmodernist diffusion of the self as subject into a network of systems and the womb of language, it can maintain that enduring relationships make an autonomous self ultimately possible.

The meaning of both autonomy and relationality will be importantly influenced by history and by culture. Feminist theory offers neither a "view from nowhere" (unsituated and therefore universally entirely

---

[27]For an overview of feminist theory insofar as it converges and diverges with communitarian thought, see Benhabib and Cornell, *Feminism as Critique*, 12–13.

true) nor a "view from everywhere" (protean and uncommitted, dancing from one conversation to another).[28] Yet feminist notions of autonomy and relationality suggest necessary directions for a common human morality.

Beyond Care-versus-Justice

Closely aligned with considerations of relationality and autonomy is another set of questions generated by the present emphasis on "caring" in feminist moral theory. I have already signaled some difficulties with the current formulations of an ethic of care, but it bears further probing. The issues it raises are in a way critical for a feminist theory of universal morality.

On the basis of empirical studies, Carol Gilligan has argued that there are two very different moral systems, two independent approaches to moral questions, that cannot be combined.[29] They are gender-specific in that men largely prefer a "justice" ethic, while women most often prefer an ethic of "care." In contrast to an ethic of justice—which Gilligan characterizes as concern for individual freedom, social contracts, a ranked order of values, fairness, and an emphasis on duty—an ethic of care in Gilligan's sense focuses on relationships between persons, cooperation, communication, and caring. Justice, in this view, is the value that reinforces individuation and separation of persons, and care is the value that represents connectedness.

On the face of it, Gilligan's ethic of care responds to many feminist concerns. It takes seriously the experience of women, and it gives credibility to considerations of affectivity. It balances individualistic tendencies in Western society with an equal appreciation of relationship. Despite its original popularity among feminists, however, it has provoked some serious feminist disagreement. Critics have raised at least two questions about its descriptive and interpretive adequacy. They ask if, insofar as there are these different approaches to moral questions, they are gender-identified, and if "justice" and "care" ac-

---

[28]For a succinct critique of deconstructionism and the "view from everywhere," see Susan Bordo, "The View from Nowhere and the Dream of Everywhere: Heterogeneity, Adequation, and Feminist Theory," *American Philosophical Association Newsletter on Feminism and Philosophy* 88 (March 1989): 19–25.

[29]Gilligan, *In a Different Voice*; see also Gilligan, "Moral Orientation and Moral Development," in *Women and Moral Theory*, ed. Eva Feder Kittay and Diana T. Meyers (Totowa, NJ: Rowman and Littlefield, 1987), 19–33; and Gilligan et al., *Mapping the Moral Domain*.

curately describe the kind of moral reasoning in which most people engage. Responses to the first concern have been more numerous, and many of them cast serious doubt on the validity of Gilligan's conclusions.[30] I am, however, more interested in the second problem, since it anticipates the first and addresses directly the question of the possibility of a universal morality.

To some extent the participants in Gilligan's and related studies do offer identifiably different sorts of answers to questions about moral situations. They give different reasons for sometimes different solutions to the problems presented. It is not so clear, however, that the reasons differ precisely because some are appeals to justice and others to care. Nor is it at all clear, as Gilligan implies, that some appeal to principles and others to relationships. It is possible, for example, to interpret references to what is "fair" as a way of being faithful to a relation, and to regard references to worries about preserving a relationship as worries about being accepted, judged fairly, and so on. It is certainly the case that *nonviolence*—the most mature consideration in moral choices according to Gilligan's ethic of care—is as much a *principle* as fairness is. There is, in other words, a lack of conceptual clarity in Gilligan's findings.

The major questions to be pursued, however, are how do persons reflect on moral questions and make moral choices—and, beyond that, how ought they to carry out these activities. The more persuasive feminist response to this question would be one that did not insist on the *inevitability* of a dichotomy between reason and emotion, justice and care, principles and persons. My own conviction is that all human choices are choices of both reasons and emotions, and that we evaluate both our reasons and our emotions according to some norms.[31] Whenever we are confronted with alternative actions, we consider the alternatives only if we have some desire to do them, whether out of care or a sense of duty, fear, or some other already-present emotion; the desires—the leaning toward pleasure or duty or fear or care or

---

[30]For a summary of empirical studies challenging Gilligan's conclusions, see Martha T. Mednick, "On the Politics of Psychological Constructs: Stop the Bandwagon, I Want to Get Off," *American Psychologist* 44 (August 1989): 1118–23.

[31]I only suggest here what obviously needs careful elaboration and justification. A more substantive outline of the theory at the basis of these ideas can be found in my *Personal Commitments: Beginning, Keeping, Changing* (San Francisco: Harper and Row, 1986), especially chaps. 3 and 7. Also in *Personal Commitments*, rev. ed. (Maryknoll, NY: Orbis Books, 2013).

whatever—arise from some more fundamental affective response (call it fundamental care, or love, or affective affirmation), some fundamental relationship with ourselves or with someone or something else.

But affectivity, emotions of whatever kind, are not, when they are *chosen*, morally neutral. That is, not even caring is necessarily morally good. There are forms of care that have destroyed individuals and groups. There are forms of relationship, based on whatever reasons and emotions, that are harmful to persons. The problem for our moral lives and our moral theories is how to evaluate our care, our love, our relationships: According to what norms is care helpful and not harmful? The problem, one might say, is whether and how caring may be just.

This question, however, poses another hurdle in the formulation of a common morality. What can count as "justice"? Surely not only fairness, surely not only fidelity to a social contract. In its most general and classical sense, justice means giving to each her or his "due." Broadly speaking, this would seem to require that justice take account of the concrete reality of the one to whom it is due, whether what is relevant in this concrete reality is a contract or a basic human need or the history of a shared commitment or all of the above and more. But theories of common morality have dwindled precisely because we despair of knowing the concrete reality of anything.

There is a sense, however, in which feminist theory almost always incorporates some "realism" in its moral epistemology. The assumption is that real persons and real things not only exist apart from the perceptions of human ideas of them, they also require respect and set a kind of limit to the meaning that can be imposed on them. Feminist skepticism regarding knowledge of concrete reality is not total, nor does acknowledgment of the social construction of reality rule out efforts at discovery of aspects of reality that are in some sense "already there." This is not surprising in a theory generated by a movement whose goal is, at least in part, that women's concrete reality be attended to. Perhaps in spite of some philosophical commitments, feminists persist therefore in trying to understand better the society in which they live, the experience that is theirs, the people with and for whom they struggle. The kind of realisms they oppose are those that reify ideas or that presume total explanations, that require no mutual search and admit no particular relative perspectives. But otherwise feminism asks for attention to reality—for the unmasking of hidden powers, the making visible of what has been ignored, the acting on at least what is less false in human interpretation.[32] For most feminists "reality" is not infinitely malleable, not neutrally open to an infinite number of interpretations at any given point in time. Even deconstruction is used for the sake of better understanding, and it can serve a wiser care. Gender analysis itself is necessary if the concrete reality of persons is not to be falsified or unjustly distorted. Like the human body, the meaning of almost everything is socially constructed, but there are limits beyond which some constructions will end in destruction.

To attend to reality and to care for it justly may seem too general a requirement to satisfy our need for a common morality. Yet if this obligates us to respect autonomy and relationality, particularity and shared needs, embodiment and human hope, we shall have more morality in common than we have perhaps ever had. The very task of specifying our obligations, and the form of its process, will be part of our just care.

---

[32]The phrase is Sandra Harding's in "Feminism, Science, and the Anti-Enlightenment Critiques," in Nicholson, *Feminism/Postmodernism*, 83.

CHAPTER 6

Feminism and Hope

Theological hope as both an attitude and a virtue has been integral to the Christian tradition. Concerns about anchoring this hope and nurturing it have been central to Christian spirituality. Christian women, as well as men, have lived in hope; they have tried to share their hopes; they have "hoped against hope" for themselves and those they love. Yet some Christian and post-Christian feminists have been critical of traditional understandings and functions of Christian hope, just as they have found it necessary to critique traditional formulations of nearly every key doctrinal formulation of faith. My purpose in this essay is to consider carefully the feminist critiques of Christian theological hope and to propose a feminist retrieval and reconstruction of a theology of hope.

Preliminary Clarifications

Let me begin with two clarifications that will help to shape what I want to say about feminism and hope. First, I want to indicate what I mean when I use the term "feminism." This is, of course, a contested term—even among feminists; and among those who oppose feminism, it is almost always seriously misunderstood. Moreover, there are many feminisms; that is, feminism today appears in significantly diverse forms. What I shall mean by it here, therefore, is simply this: Feminism is a position (a conviction and a movement) that is opposed to dis-

A version of this essay was originally published in *Full of Hope: Critical Social Perspectives on Theology*, ed. Magdala Thompson (NY: Paulist Press, 1989). Contributors to the volume: Mary Aquin O'Neill, Margaret A. Farley, M. Shawn Copeland, Rosemary Luling Haughton, Lisa Sowle Cahill, Christine E. Gudorf. Copyright © 2003 by Magdala Thompson. Reprinted by permission of Paulist Press, Inc. www.paulistpress.com.

crimination on the basis of gender.[1] It is therefore opposed to sexism in all of its forms, including institutional structures and practices that are discriminatory (such as gendered role differentiations). Since sexism has been and remains pervasively discriminatory against women, feminism opposes women's unequal access to basic goods and services, and it struggles to eliminate barriers to women's participation in decision-making in church and society. Feminism is also opposed, therefore, to ideologies, beliefs, attitudes, and behaviors that establish or reinforce these discriminating structures, systems, and practices. In addition, it is opposed to other forms of unjust discrimination and patterns of domination; it includes in its analysis the socially constructed connections between gender, race, and class, as well as age, sexual orientation, and other particular characteristics that can be interpreted in ways that form a basis of discrimination and oppression.

Positively, the form of feminism that I am describing seeks to bring about equality and concrete well-being for women and men in all spheres of human life, interpersonal and institutional. It is not anti-men, but it is necessarily pro-women (precisely because, as I have already indicated, gender discrimination worldwide remains largely against women). Feminism therefore incorporates a strategic bias for women. It is, however, ultimately pro-human, for it affirms the fundamental claim of all persons to be respected as persons who are characterized as having basic needs, a capacity for freedom, and deep desires for fulfillment.

Given this meaning of feminism, there are nonetheless many forms that feminism now takes—diverse theories and theologies, even diverse feminist ethics. I do not attempt to sort these out here, but my rendering of feminist critiques of Christian theological hope, as well as my effort to provide a reconstruction, will give some indication of the diversity of feminist perspectives.

The second clarification I want to make relates to the starting point for feminist theology and ethics—and therefore the starting point for a feminist theology of hope. Feminist theologies generally appeal to the standard sources for Christian theology—that is, sacred scripture,

---

[1]For fuller renderings, see Margaret A. Farley, "Feminist Ethics," in *The Westminster Dictionary of Christian Ethics*, ed. James F. Childress and John MacQuarrie (Philadelphia: Westminster Press, 1986), 229–31; and Farley, "Feminist Ethics," in *Feminist Ethics and the Catholic Moral Tradition*," ed. Charles E. Curran, Margaret A. Farley, and Richard A. McCormick (Mahwah, NJ: Paulist Press, 1996), 1–10.

tradition, other (secular) disciplines of human knowledge, and contemporary experience. What is unique about feminist theology, however, is that it begins (like all feminist theory) with women's experience. We can expect, then, that both the critique of traditional ideas about Christian hope, and responses to this critique, will begin with women's experience—diverse, yet in some ways shared.

What are the experiences of women that constitute the "social location" in which the word of God's revelation must be heard if this word is to be a source of life and hope for women? Women know them well, because they include all of the experiences of women's lives—in families, churches, societies. But feminist theology begins most specifically with women's shared experience of struggle—against poverty, exploitation, marginalization, domination, repression, and oppression. The stories of women worldwide are stories of the struggle for liberation from racism, unjust family structures, sexual abuse. They are stories of the frequent failure of educational systems to take women seriously, the refusal by many religious traditions to acknowledge the full humanity of women, the rejection of women whose sexual orientation does not fit the conventional expectations of church and society, and the marginalization of women through unyielding interpretations of secular and sacred traditions.

Women do not, in and through such experiences, see themselves only as victims, without any strength or without possibilities for fullness of life. Nor do women interpret their lives (except in the most dire situations) as without joy and achievement and beauty. Nevertheless, until there is a home in this world for all—women, children, and men; until the world awakens to the plight, for example, of massive numbers of women with AIDS (especially in developing nations); until attention is paid to the rape of women as a strategy of war; until religious traditions recognize that the faith of all is stifled as long as women are excluded from roles of leadership, the work of feminist theology must go on. In particular, Christian feminist theologies must continue to critique interpretations of divine revelation and formulations of Christian faith that serve to perpetuate these kinds of situations. Feminist theologians must continue to reinterpret their traditions—to retrieve lost treasures and forge better insights—until these traditions offer genuinely "good news" for women everywhere.

The Critique

What, then, is the problem with Christian understandings of hope? How is it that sometimes feminists find Christian theologies of hope inadequate, even harmful, to women? No one—least of all feminist theologians—argues that women (or men) ought not to hope. No feminist analysis aims at taking away hope from women. Indeed, feminism as a movement has represented women's efforts to take hold of their lives and move them forward in hope and hopefulness. Years ago, Doris Lessing placed a line on the frontispiece of one of her novels, in the voice of a woman: "I am so tired of it; and also tired of the future before it comes."[2] It was against this experience of weariness and despair that women mobilized, in many generations, first to reflect on their reasons for hope, and then to awaken hope as a sustainer of their actions for justice—for themselves and their children.

Feminist critiques of a Christian construal of hope parallel in many respects the critique of religion promoted by key modern theorists. That is, like Marx, Nietzsche, and Freud, some feminists have argued that Christian hope has all too often been "pie in the sky" hope—a hope in another world that makes people passive and all too patient in the face of injustice and oppression in this world. Suffering and death, they say, have been romanticized by Christian teachers and preachers, as a holy way to reach a world beyond. Feminist (later post-Christian) theologian Mary Daly, therefore, joined Nietzsche in declaring Christianity a religion for victims, a religion that obsessed about pain and death and that made submission rather than resistance a virtue—especially for women.[3] Religious hope, agreed other feminists, gives a false sense that all is really well, and "all shall be well." Belief in an ultimate future, in this view, short-circuits commitment to a proximate future. Desires are thus restrained (repressed), and they become only wishful thinking. The moral demand to alleviate situations of oppression goes therefore unheeded.

---

[2]Lessing attributes this statement to Olive Schreiner. See Doris Lessing, *Martha Quest* (New York: Harper Collins, 1962), 1.

[3]See Mary Daly, *Beyond God the Father: Toward a Philosophy of Women's Liberation* (Boston: Beacon Press, 1973), 70, 146.

Some feminists have noted, further, that this kind of hope works especially against women. It has a gendered face. That is, cultures have frequently conditioned women more than men to passivity; and though this can be a courageous and in some ways noble passivity of endurance, it nonetheless remains drastically ineffective in the face of tragedy. When, contrary to this, women have been active in resisting the causes of the suffering of their children, a resigned hope has nonetheless continued to characterize responses to their own burdens and powerlessness.

Of course, many Christian women, including feminists, do not recognize this as a description of their present experience. These women do not shy away from strong active involvements in movements for justice around the world. But then, many of them also do not think much about hope in a world other than this one. Nor have the young among them, as women, yet encountered the kinds of burdens, limitations, relentless obstacles that may yet await them insofar as they take this world as their primary and even sole concern. Hence, many Christian feminists have developed an eschatology that is resolutely this-worldly, aiming to correct any bias toward another world and refusing to be deflected from the moral imperatives that confront our time.[4]

A feminist critique of traditional notions of hope goes even deeper, however. It reaches, for example, to the charge that Christian hope, based as it is on the death and resurrection of Jesus, is in essence a denial of finitude. Post-Christian biblical and theological scholar Carol Christ has argued that Christian hope therefore constitutes a failure to affirm "this life on this earth, in these bodies."[5] While we need not absolutely rule out the possibility of life after death, Christ says, we ought not to live here in the light of it. Hope in another life should above all not prevent women from recognizing their real home in this world and affirming precisely here their power and potential for action. This is more than a call to resist injustices. It is an assertion that one should in every way "forget" a future that is unlimited and place one's energies and hopes in what can be accomplished here in the world of our experience.

---

[4]This sort of eschatology characterizes, for example, a great number of the essays in *Liberating Eschatology*, ed. Margaret A. Farley and Serene Jones (Louisville, KY: Westminster John Knox Press, 1999).

[5]Carol Christ, *Laughter of Aphrodite: Reflections on a Journey to the Goddess* (San Francisco: Harper and Row, 1987), 214.

More than this, Christian feminists like Rosemary Radford Ruether argue that unless we are willing to focus on this world we will not attend effectively to the vulnerable ecological future of earth.[6] Hope in an unending future for ourselves can obscure our present responsibilities for the survival of this planet and the well-being of the universe. In this view, hope for an end to this world, and ultimate happiness in a world beyond, is a form of self-preoccupation that needs to be transcended or broken. This means that belief in personal immortality must, at least in practice, be relinquished. Only thus will we succeed in the kind of decentering of ourselves that is necessary for the future of the whole of creation. Surrender to the possible loss of our own selves in this sense[7] will empower us to attend to creation as we know it, and to care for all who participate and dwell therein. The call, therefore, is to go beyond what are sometimes called "male models" of individual autonomy, desire for continuity of personal identity, and obsession with one's own absolute future.[8]

These are some of the critiques that feminists offer regarding traditional understandings of Christian hope. The critiques are salutary, whatever our final judgment of their validity. We may, however, need more than this from feminist theology if the hope of Christians, especially Christian women, is to be renewed. To some extent, the problem with Christian hope is whether hope is only of things "unseen,"[9] or whether it also "sees," in some way, the object of its hope; whether hope is only for the future, or whether it also commits us to the present; whether to hope implies—or leads to—powerlessness or power. Let me turn, then, to a feminist response to these critiques—to a feminist retrieval and reconstruction of elements deep in the Christian tradition.

A Response

Before we can consider a response and revision, we need to ask what there is about hope that makes all of this so important. Why should this be a concern for feminists or anyone else? A clue lies in

---

[6] Rosemary Radford Ruether, *Gaia and God: An Ecofeminist Theology of Earth Healing* (San Francisco: Harper Collins, 1992), 250–53.

[7] This form of self-surrender is not to be confused with the denigration of the self that most feminists have resisted; that is, it is not to be confused with a willingness to be used as a mere means by and for an other, a resignation to the role of a "doormat."

[8] Ruether, *Gaia and God*, 253.

[9] See, for example, Rom. 8:24–25.

our manifest *need* of hope—of belief in a future, if you will. For better or for worse, human persons are the kind of beings who cannot live without a *sense* of a future. Our lives are lived not all at once. They are stretched out in time. Being alive for us includes, requires, an experience of past and present moving into a future. When we experience our lives as futureless (closed, stifled, stopped), we find them intolerable. "Hope is for the soul what breathing is for the living organism," wrote Gabriel Marcel.[10]

Simply to be alive is for us to experience the desire and need for more life—just as to love is to experience the desire and need for fuller union, greater affirmation of the beloved, and an extended future for the love. Hence, hope may appear in the form of trust, belief, hope that the deep relationships that are the fabric of our lives and the structure of our hearts will last forever; that they can live into an unlimited future. Creation in us groans—not just in travail of evil and pain but in yearning for fullness of life.[11] If, with Carol Christ and others, we accept a finitude that needs no life after death, then consent to our death is precisely consent to a final limit to our personal future, not only for ourselves but for our relationships.[12] We need hope, then, because of who and what we are. We need hope lest we despair of life and love itself.

Insofar as our present is marked by suffering—whether our own or that of those we love—hope takes the form of believing that things will change, that there is a future, immediate or remote, when something of the suffering will change.[13] The opposite of "pie in the sky" illusion is not despair of any new possibility. To hope is to believe that what looks like a closed and settled fate is not really, not totally, completely, so. We need at least a sense of potential for a "next step." Without some hope we are crushed. We wither and die even while we live. Without hope in a change that can lessen suffering, or alter its

---

[10]Gabriel Marcel, *Homo Viator*, trans. Emma Crauford (New York: Harper and Row, 1965), 10–11.

[11]Rom. 8:22-23.

[12]This is why people—perhaps men more than women—have through the centuries in some cultures (not all), including Western culture, been concerned with genetically related offspring as a way to immortalize themselves. This may not be a hope in unlimited life, but it derives from it.

[13]See my consideration of these same concerns in, "Feminist Theology and Ethics: The Contributions of Elizabeth A. Johnson," in *Things New and Old*, ed. Phyllis Zagano and Terrence W. Tilley (New York: Crossroad, 1999), 1–19.

meaning, or provide us with the strength to resist it or bear it or move us beyond it, we ourselves are forced to make another kind of change. We capitulate to despair, perhaps cursing God (or all reality), perhaps seeing the world as a drama of absurdity that needs no change because it is meaningless in any case. Or perhaps we settle for what others tell us *is supposed to be* our life, but which leads to our premature death.

Nonetheless, once again, we need hope because we are alive, and we experience our lives as needing, desiring, a future. Christian hope is part of human hope in this sense. But it also transforms human hope, not only grounding it and strengthening it but giving it a different future.

But what can be said about Christian hope from a feminist perspective, chastened as we must be by a feminist critique?

My own proposal is that Christian hope need not give up hope in "another world" where lies what as yet "eye hath not seen nor ear heard."[14] Christian hope must, however, include also hope for this present world. The key to all of this is twofold. It includes the connection between these worlds and the requirement of our commitment to one another in the course of our life together. We have important clues to this connection and to the nature of the commitment required.

The most crucial clue is to be found in a feminist interpretation of God's relationship to us and the connection between this and our relationship to one another. Elizabeth Johnson argues that language about the triune God, spoken from a feminist theological perspective, illuminates central elements in classical Trinitarian doctrine. It places in relief the radical equality, mutuality, and community that characterize God's life. This in turn offers us the "ultimate paradigm" for our own personal and social lives.[15] Johnson does not pursue the paradigm in relation to the questions of human hope I am addressing here. Yet it nonetheless offers insight for these questions precisely because it sheds light on the connections between another world and this one. As such, it may provide us with a theological warrant for hope (in this world and the next), and it may guide our action in accordance with this hope.

Think, for example, of our questions of theological hope in the light of the Gospel attributed to John, especially John 15:9–12. Despite John's apparent limitations in understanding inclusive community,

---

[14]1 Cor. 2:9.

[15]Elizabeth A. Johnson, *She Who Is: The Mystery of God in Feminist Theological Discourse* (New York: Crossroad, 1992), 222.

chapter after chapter of this Gospel records Jesus' view not only of a model of being but a model of loving and acting.[16] Climaxing in chapter 15, we are given the words of Jesus: "*As* God has loved me, *so* I have loved you," and "*As* I have loved you, *so* you are to love one another." "As God has loved me," or in other words, *as love flows in the life of God's own self*, so I love you and you must love one another. But how does love flow in the life of God? This is a life and a love of infinitely receptive activity and infinitely active receptivity—a love and a life of utter equality and mutuality, consummate giving and receiving, distinguishable yet one in a life of perfect communion.

It is this, Jesus says, this life and love that provide the *model according to which God also loves us*. "As God loves me, so I have loved you." A self-emptying God raises up the beloved and offers to all a share in the fullness of God's life. But there is more: this model becomes in turn the *model required for our relationships with one another*. "This is my commandment, that you love one another *as* I have loved you." A model, a graced possibility, and a command are signified together.

Nothing, then, is as we might have assumed; business is not "as usual" in the sociological unfolding of our roles and relationships. We are not given a pattern of superiority and subordination; we are not told of a dominating God who exacts submission from a people; we have not here a model in which men are to be superior to women, clergy to laity, pastors to congregations, teachers to students, one nation or race to another. In all human relationships, equality and mutuality are to be at least the goal, if not yet a completely applicable ethical norm. Even relationships that must be unequal for a time (as between parents and children) have as their ultimate fulfillment a friendship between equals.

This is a model for this world, but embedded in it is a revelation of our possible future. No more radical goal is imaginable for us than the goal of universal communion—each of us with God and with one another in God. We have in Jesus' portrayal of his life and ours a news so "good" that it is difficult to believe. We have a proclamation and a promise, a command and a gift; and it stretches from this world to another.

What I am trying to say here, then, is that our understandings of Christian hope (a hope that need not leave us diminished or disem-

---

[16]See my short commentary on this text in, "Feminist Theology and Ethics," 6–7.

powered for action or without insight into the form our own actions should take) should be lodged in our understandings of God's own life and of God's relationship to us—in the connection between God's life and ours. And in this, there is to be found a connection between the present and the future, between "another" world and this one.

Let me try to unfold this in three steps: First, the ground of Christian hope is God's promise and God's action toward us. Second, this promise and this action turn us to this world and not only a world beyond. And third, there is nonetheless continuity between this world and the next.

1. First, then, *the ground of Christian hope is God's promise and God's action toward us.* Theological hope is, after all, hope not ultimately in human individuals or human institutions, governments, churches, or even movements, but in God. It is, of course, not unconnected with hope for persons, things, activities, efforts, and social arrangements in this world. It is hope in God for us—and for those we love. If we are criticized for wishful thinking about an unlimited future, or for simply projecting what we want to be true into an illusory hope, how can we respond? Perhaps our only response is to look to the promises of God in relation to which we take our stand. The biblical record of God's word to us—in both the First and Second Testaments—is filled with promises that our sufferings will be healed and that longings will be fulfilled. Here is recorded again and again the promise that things can change.

In a deep sense, our hope remains in things as yet "unseen." There is no other assurance for us than what we can find in a revealed word. There is no other way to receive this assurance than by trusting this word, throwing our lot in with it, letting go our objections in order to experience its presence. Ours is a hope for a future that is not yet realized. And yet, and yet, what is revealed in the promise is what is "already," along with "not yet"; what is made possible through this revelation is that we can "see" as well as "not see" the object of our hope. Take as a key example what is revealed to us in and through the cross of Jesus Christ. There are indeed those (some feminists among them) who say that the cross, central to Christian faith, signals Christianity's preoccupation with suffering and death. The cross cuts off our energy and our urgency for action regarding what can be hoped for here and now. But those who say this are wrong. The meaning of the cross is precisely *not* death, but, rather, that *a relationship holds.*

No matter what the forces of evil can do to break the bonds of love, a relationship can hold. And this relationship becomes our life—already present, historically accomplished.

The relationship holds even in the face of death, for death no longer has the last word. Christianity has as its center not death but life. We can know our own possibility of death—of the many ways of laying down our lives or having them taken from us—but we can also know our own possibilities of resurrection. Hope, therefore, is *not* always and only of things completely unseen. In our experience there are connections between what we see and cannot see, what we feel and cannot touch, what we hear and what is still silent. We are at times given an inkling that the joy we need and yearn for, the justice and peace, freedom and wholeness, are not afterthoughts on God's part; that though there is discontinuity between our lives of mourning and the life for which we hope, there is also continuity. Sometimes, at least, "our hearts are burning" as we recognize God's presence, as we feel the surge of life within us, and glimpse the horizon of an approaching future. God's promise and action in and toward us are "already," even though more is surely "not yet."

2. Second, *God's promise and action turn us to this world and not only to a world beyond.* The biblical record of God's word to us is filled with promises, but it is also filled with calls, even imperatives, to change some things now. It is, then, simply wrong to think that we are merely to wait patiently, passively, without resistance or hard work or risk of almost everything in order to bring about change. It is also not adequate to think that the ideal of Christian love is to live and work as if we did not hope that our work will make a difference. God does not play games with us. Our labor is not some kind of test for us, in response to some rules of some game.

Feminist (and other) critics are right to charge that Christianity in some of its developments has been too "otherworldly." Overall, however, Christianity cannot be said to be a world-denying religion. Whatever the importance of "other worlds," the Christian tradition has incorporated key beliefs and insights that should continually counter tendencies of apathy toward this world—toward its possibilities and its needs. Christianity, for example, has affirmed (though not always without some difficulty) the importance of human desire—not only for God, but for the world as bearer of revelation, embodiment of beauty, a place where God dwells. The problem with loving the world is loving it well—neither exploiting it nor encouraging domination of some peoples over others; not fleeing it, without giving our lives to mend it, to liberate its peoples, to be true to ourselves. Christian hope is not mere resignation, nor is our task to "swoon in the shadow"[17] of the cross when we should be laboring in its light.

Though death will come, it is not only not the last word; it does not undo the importance of life in this world. Though "in the twinkling of an eye" everything can change (God can come quickly, and sorrows can pass away), it makes a difference what we do in the meantime. If our goal is communion, and we are called to walk along the way to that goal, then it matters more, not less, that we begin and sustain relationships of justice and friendship here and now; that we protect bodies and ease spirits; rear our young wisely and care for those who are old; and that we awaken to the needs and possibilities of our near neighbors and far.

Since our lives together are embodied in this world, we shall not ultimately leave it behind for a disembodied communion. The world around us, and not only ourselves, will be transformed as a whole, as our home forever. Or at least this is theologically plausible—enough so that we need not sacrifice personal identity in order to see our profound obligations to the world as a whole. Our need to decenter ourselves in order to love the whole of creation does not require, nor will it be secured by, abandonment of our hope in personal immortality or the unlimited future of those we love. If the communion to which we are called is with God and with all others in God, then all is at the center,[18] if we let our hearts see it so. Whatever the discontinuity between this world and another, there is a profound continuity between what we begin here, do here, and its fulfillment in an unlimited future.

(3) This brings me to my third and final step (already suggested above) in trying to unfold a Christian and a feminist understanding of hope. It leads me even further in my claim that *there is continuity between this world and the next.* If it is a mistake to hope in another world but not in this one, it is also a mistake to hope only in this world and not in another—especially if the "other" world is finally one with

---

[17]Pierre Teilhard de Chardin, *Essai d'integration de l'homme dans l'univers*, 4th lecture, 1930, cited in Christopher F. Mooney, *Teilhard de Chardin and the Mystery of Christ* (New York: Harper and Row, 1966), 119.

[18]Note the expansion of imagery in this regard in C. S. Lewis, *Perelandra* (New York: Macmillan, 1944), 230–33.

this world-transformed. "As God has loved me, so I have loved you." "As I have loved you, so you are to love one another." This is the starting point. This is the goal. This is to be our one life, for now and forever. How we live it now makes "all the difference in the world" for its ultimate future—not because we earn a future reward, but because what we do now is constitutive of the future. And that there is a future makes "all the difference in the world" for the present.

Feminist theologians and ethicists have argued that we must be willing to stand in solidarity with the marginalized, and willing to take concrete actions for change. They have insisted that we must search for a "usable past" for women (in our experiences and in our traditions), and that we must project a future that learns from the underside of history. Feminists have argued further that we need to understand a "usable *future*" in order to interpret the past and the present, in order to direct our actions in the light of God's promises and God's presence.

Whether we are trying to interpret (and liberate) our traditions or transform our social structures, we can "think from the other end,"[19] which is revealed and experienced in "inklings" of what will be. In so doing, we sharpen our obligation to build community in which none are isolated, to struggle for justice with everyone poor or oppressed, to heal the multiple forms of human suffering, and to assist in the release and nurture of life so abundant that not even death can stop it.

Theological hope, then, is hope in God, for all of us. It relies on the relationship between God's love and our own, on the connection between our own actions and God's promise, and on the continuity between this world and the next. It is a hope accessible and intelligible to feminists and all Christians. I end with Jesus' words to the women who followed him to his death: "Daughters of Jerusalem, weep not for me but for yourselves and your children" (Luke 23:28). Jesus recognized that women know at least two kinds of tears: tears of desolation, which when they have all been shed, leave the well dry; and tears of consolation, which water our hearts and give us strength, and then water us all the way to the sea of action.[20] These latter are the tears of hope.

---

[19]See Letty M. Russell, *The Future of Partnership* (Philadelphia: Westminster Press, 1979), 51-53.

[20]This metaphor was first suggested to me by Beverly Gouaux, in a letter many years ago.

CHAPTER 7

A Feminist Version of Respect for Persons

My central concern in this essay is with what I shall call *obligating-features of persons*. What is it about persons that requires respect? Does a requirement of respect for persons include enough content to tell us not only *that* we must respect one another but *what* it means to give this respect? These questions, I believe, are crucial for current developments in feminist ethical theory, despite some appearances to the contrary.

Concern for a ground of moral obligation may seem anachronistic and even harmful in a time when much of Western ethical theory has discredited or at least moved beyond so-called foundationalist interests. To try to locate a basis for respect for persons is reminiscent of rationalistic projects that seek to tie every moral obligation to one or two indisputable principles. To look for "features" of human persons that bind us to moral actions and attitudes is to run up against problems of essentialism, anthropocentrism, and an abstract universalism that all too easily ignores the particularity and diversity of persons in concrete contexts. Feminist ethical theorists, precisely on the basis of feminist analysis, are skeptical of sheer universalizability as a ground of moral obligation. The modern notion of what it means to be a person all too often either excludes women or makes them disappear into a "generalized other."[1] The better theoretical way may be the postmodernist

A version of this essay was originally published in *Journal of Feminist Studies in Religion* 9, no. 1–2 (Spring/Fall 1993): 183–98. Used with permission.

[1]See the carefully nuanced treatment of this concept provided by Seyla Benhabib, "The Generalized and the Concrete Other," in *Feminism as Critique: On the Politics of Gender*, ed. Seyla Benhabib and Drucilla Cornell (Minneapolis: University of Minnesota Press, 1987), 77–95.

rejection of the personal subject and self, a dissolution of "person" into a plurality of differences. We would look, then, not for features of personhood but for a solidarity among fragmented, partial, separate, even oppositional, socially constructed temporary selves.

To try to identify something that is the same in all persons, male or female, whatever their diversity of history and experience, may be dangerous, but it remains nonetheless important. The risks are that we will once again lose sight of human differences, or once again devalue whatever appears as "other" in relation to our norm. We may even end up with one more theory that justifies self-interest on a grand scale, that isolates individuals in their rights to noninterference and to competition, that allows rejection of the social claims of those identified as other.[2] Or we may repeat the mistake of theorizing about persons in a way that collapses the individual into a "collective singular," an organic ideal in relation to which groups and individuals are subordinated to a developing community without regard for their own needs or demands for respect. Despite these risks, there are strong reasons why feminist ethical theory needs to engage the question of obligating-features of persons.

One such need, it seems to me, is at the heart of recent vigorous developments in feminist ethical theory. Here there has emerged a tension between freedom of choice and social determinism.[3] Contemporary feminism is ambivalent toward freedom in the sense of individual autonomy (or the capacity for free choice), especially if it is considered the central feature of the human personality. On the one hand, claims to autonomy have been important bulwarks in women's struggle against exploitation and oppression. Freedom of choice is valued as the capacity to fashion one's own self, and its exercise is claimed as an inalienable right in relation to bodily integrity, equality of opportunity, and so forth. But on the other hand, feminists are generally critical of individualistic notions of autonomy as the power of self-legislation and the possibility of a solely self-generated personal self. Many feminist theorists are sympathetic to social constructionist views of the self, convinced by the diversity of women's experiences

---

[2] A helpful addition to the growing literature on these problems is the collection of essays in George Levine, ed., *Constructions of the Self* (New Brunswick, NJ: Rutgers University Press, 1992), esp. Agnes Heller, "Death of the Subject?," 269–84.

[3] For an example of the debate on this issue, see Diana T. Meyers, "Personal Autonomy or the Deconstructed Subject: A Reply to Hekman," *Hypatia* 7 (1992): 124–32.

to forgo generalizations even about the value of self-determination. Feminists know that freedom turns up empty when abstracted from social histories and concrete, specific bonds. The theoretical tension between feminist versions of a self-determining and socially constructed self can perhaps be resolved simply by a notion of freedom limited within historically given possibilities. Yet it remains unclear in much of current (especially postmodernist) feminist theory whether the personal self fragments into its roles, is diffused within a web of social forces, and disappears in a protean process of changing personae. Thus it is at least still worth asking about the status of autonomy as a feature of persons.

A second area of feminist ethical theory illustrates the need to consider obligating-features of persons. Central to the concerns of many feminists today are questions of moral development and an emphasis on what is called an ethics of "care." The fruitful studies of Carol Gilligan, Nel Noddings, and now many others have provided rich fare for feminist theory both in method and substance. The descriptive beginnings of these theories, however, as well as the normative debates that have followed, leave largely unexplored the underlying issues of why care should be a moral requirement or a developmental ideal. Often included in an ethics of care is a critique of the grounding of an ethics of justice in principled logic and a preference for the grounding of an ethics of care in the concrete reality of persons and relationships. Yet why persons are valuable, or why caring is a sign of moral maturity, are questions whose answers are more often assumed than examined.[4]

A third reason for feminist theory to explore obligating-features of human persons lies in a troubled set of questions about the possibility or impossibility of a common or universal morality. Feminists have identified serious reasons both to reject and to promote belief in a common or universal morality.[5] The social construction of moral norms is evident in the history of women's roles and duties. Identification of inadequacies and errors in views of women's "nature," as well as the growing feminist appreciation of cultural and historical diversity

---

[4]A beginning effort to probe these assumptions can be found in Robin S. Dillon, "Care and Respect," in *Explorations in Feminist Ethics: Theory and Practice*, ed. Eve Browning Cole and Susan Coultrap-McQuin (Bloomington: Indiana University Press, 1992), 69–81.

[5]See my discussion of this issue in "Feminism and Universal Morality," in *Prospects for a Common Morality*, ed. Gene Outka and John Reeder (Princeton, NJ: Princeton University Press, 1992), 170–90. This essay appears in this collection.

among women, have yielded a deep skepticism among feminists about the universality of any moral claims. Yet the moral commitments and political agendas of many feminists make it unacceptable for them to settle for total relativity in moral norms. Thus the question of a basis for a requirement to respect persons remains an important one—especially insofar as it can help to interpret the meaning of respect across, but without indifference to, boundaries of time and culture.

The larger question of this essay might then, be formulated in terms like these: Is there anything intrinsic to persons that inspires us to care for them, that claims our respect, that awakens our love? Is there anything inherent in persons that forbids us to reduce them to what they can do for us, that prohibits us from invading their bodies or their lives, that requires us to pay attention to their needs and their beauty? There are, of course, additional questions: Do our ethical obligations to one another rise ineluctably from our own dynamism to self-actualization? Are they lodged only in the concrete special relationships we already have? Are there only extrinsic warrants for our obligations to human persons, warrants like the command of God, or our own decision to obligate ourselves through some form of contract, or our vision of a society we are trying to create?

The larger question of love must wait for another day. So must the alternative questions about the grounds of our obligations. Here I will address only what it is about persons that requires our respect. In pursuing this question, I want to consider two "features" of persons that appear to me to require our respect. The first is autonomy, and the second is relationality.

Obligating Features of Persons

If persons are worthy of respect, they are so as integral beings. That is, everything about human persons seems to call for our respect. What could it mean to talk of respecting persons if all we intended by that was respect for one or two features of their being? This would be abstraction, ahistorical and acultural in the extreme. Yet surely not every characteristic of a person requires respect. Some aspects of persons may, in fact, call for our disrespect (as, for example, cruelty in a person's character). We may affirm other aspects but not consider ourselves bound to do so (as in the case of some idiosyncratic habit a person may have). Because personal beings are complex, some aspects of a person may conflict with other aspects, so that our very respect requires that we acknowledge a priority of one aspect over another (for example, the priority of an individual person's freedom of choice, as expressed in informed consent in a medical context, over her physical well-being).

We are obligated to respect persons, not features. Yet if there are intrinsic grounds for this obligation, there must be something *about* persons that claims our respect and tells us what respect must mean. It is according to features, aspects, of persons that we can both establish a general principle of respect for persons and specify its content. The first candidate for such a feature is the one identified by Immanuel Kant, namely, autonomy.

Autonomy

However maligned Kant's principle of respect for persons has become, and whatever the shortcomings of his focus on rationality and autonomy, Kant's theory stands as a powerful and in many ways still persuasive effort to identify an obligating-feature of persons. Its continuing importance for feminist theory is, of course, under suspicion, and yet it deserves reconsideration. As we have already noted, an early conviction of contemporary feminism was that at the heart of what is good for women is autonomy, or the freedom of self-determination. Because autonomy belongs to women as personal beings with the capacity to determine the ultimate meaning of their own lives, they make claims for respect as persons, valuable in themselves and not only as instruments in the service of the family or community or the human species or men.

Kant argued that every human being is absolutely valuable as an end in itself.[6] Persons are ends in a radical sense (not simply the last in a series of means) because they are autonomous. They are autonomous because of their rationality—more specifically, because of their capacity to recognize in and by themselves what counts as a moral obligation

---

[6]Immanuel Kant, *Groundwork of the Metaphysic of Morals*, trans. H. J. Paton (New York: Harper and Row, 1964), 95–96, 102–3 [427–29, 434–36]. "Absolute" here means unconditional, not necessarily "unrelated," for example, to God. For the difficulties in interpreting what Kant is saying in this and similar passages, see George Schrader, "Autonomy, Heteronomy, and Moral Imperatives," *Journal of Philosophy* 60 (1963): 65–77; Thomas E. Hill Jr., "Humanity as an End in Itself," *Ethics* 91 (1980): 84–99; P. C. Lo, *Treating Persons as Ends* (Lanham, MD: University Press of America, 1987), chaps. 3–4.

and to resolve to act in accordance with it or not. Autonomy is, therefore, that feature of persons whereby they are not solely determined in their actions by causes external to their own reason and will, not even by their own internal desires and inclinations. Negatively free (undetermined, uncoerced) in this sense, persons can recognize their own law (reason "legislates" for itself); they are thereby also positively free (self-governing) to determine the meaning of their own lives in an ultimate (moral) sense. This is the basis of human dignity.[7]

The moral response appropriate to and required by this radical personal dignity or worth is respect. To respect persons as ends in themselves is to *relate* to them as valuable in themselves, not just valuable for me; to *treat* them as absolutely valuable, not just conditionally and contingently valuable. To be an end in oneself is, as Kant put it, to have no market price—to be "not for sale," because nothing else can be of equivalent value; nothing can substitute for a human person whose dignity is of "unconditioned and incomparable worth," whose value is permanent and nonreplaceable.[8] Hence, Kant's famous formula: "Act in such a way that you always treat humanity, whether in your own person or in the person of any other, never simply as a means, but always at the same time as an end."[9] That is, persons are not ever to be used as mere means to other persons' ends; no one is to be wholly subordinated to another's agenda. Individuals and groups are not to achieve their purposes at the expense of other persons' basic needs and purposes. Each and every person is to be respected, whatever their achievements, roles, moral integrity, or any other aspect of their being.

Feminist dissatisfaction with Kant's grounding of human dignity in rationality and freedom echoes the criticisms made by Hegel and Marx, Nietzsche and Lacan, Habermas and Foucault, MacIntyre and Sandel. The problems of Kantian autonomy begin with the disembodied self that it represents. Here, seemingly, is a freedom that needs no social context, no affective ties, no history of desire. Here is a rational freedom that opposes duty to inclination and remains deaf to claims from anything but its own logic. The charges are formalism, indifference to human vulnerability, the delusion of a self-generating self. Finally, insist some feminist theorists, the Kantian self is a model of domina-

---

[7]Kant, *Groundwork*, 102, 103, 107 [435–36, 440].

[8]Kant, *The Doctrine of Virtue*, part 2, *The Metaphysics of Morals*, trans. Mary J. Gregor (New York: Harper and Row, 1964), 101 [436].

[9]Kant, *Groundwork*, 96 [429].

tion; its task and its goal are self-repression within and mastery of all that is without.[10]

But it may be possible to retain Kant's intuition regarding a capacity for self-determination and a human claim for respect without at the same time adopting Kant's pessimistic view of affectivity, and without following some Kantians into a morality of principles apart from persons and communities. Like most of Kant's critics, feminists may affirm the significance of individual agency and the dignity of individual persons while insisting on a more integrated and more social view of the human self. The first sign that this is possible lies in a fuller reading of Kant himself. Autonomy need not be completely over against affectivity, given Kant's description of the experience of the law;[11] autonomy is not fulfilled in Hobbesian self-protectiveness, but in a "kingdom of ends";[12] human dignity translates into equality, with respect inclusive of the self as well as others, adversaries as well as friends;[13] there are positive duties to persons as well as negative duties of caring as well as of noninterference;[14] for all of the abstraction from history and from concrete relations, Kant's turn to the self effects (or can) at the same time a turn to others, in sameness but also in embodied diversity.[15]

Kant's notion of autonomy may be useful, even necessary, for a feminist principle of respect for persons, but it is nonetheless inadequate. Its problems remain multiple, impossible to address here. We can, however, pursue one line of thought suggested by Kant's critics, a line that will allow us to hold on to freedom while exploring its context

---

[10]See, for example, Seyla Benhabib, *Critique, Norm, and Utopia: A Study of the Foundations of Critical Theory* (New York: Columbia University Press, 1986), 187; Luce Irigaray, "Any Theory of the 'Subject' Has Always Been Appropriated by the 'Masculine,' " in *Speculum of the Other Woman*, trans. Gillian C. Gill (Ithaca, NY: Cornell University Press, 1985), 133–46; Judith Butler, "Gender Trouble, Feminist Theory, and Psychoanalytic Discourse," in *Feminism/Postmodernism*, ed. Linda J. Nicholson (New York: Routledge, 1990), 324–40; Margaret A. Farley, "Review of Alan Donagan's *The Theory of Morality*," in *Religious Studies Review* 7 (July 1981): 233–37.

[11]See, for example, Kant, *Critique of Practical Reason*, trans. Lewis White Beck (New York: Liberal Arts Press, 1956), 161 [158].

[12]Kant, *Groundwork*, 101–2 [433–35].

[13]See the formulation in ibid., 96 [429].

[14]Kant, *Doctrine of Virtue*, 44–47 [385–88]; *Groundwork*, 96–98 [429–30].

[15]In the *Doctrine of Virtue*, 45 [469] Kant takes up briefly the issue of particularities in individuals (such as age, health, sex, wealth, etc.). While they do not of themselves ground a requirement of respect, there is a need, Kant says, to take them into account in the application of ethical duty. This is hardly sufficient to provide the full ethical approach needed in a feminist ethic, but it may at least not finally oppose it.

and its purpose. To do that, we need to examine a second candidate for an obligating-feature of persons: relationality. For feminist theory, relationality is as primordial as is autonomy, though it may be as problematic as well.

Relationality

The relation of human persons to one another is not a new preoccupation in Western philosophy and theology, nor is it particular to feminist theory. Aristotle argued that the human individual is "by nature a social and political being."[16] For Augustine, "there is nothing so social by nature" as human beings (though they are political only as a remedy for sin).[17] Even Kant thought that the goal of the moral life included community.[18] Hegel, Feuerbach, and Marx attempted to show the dependency of the person on the "other" for her or his own personhood, the capacity (and need) for community as structurally fundamental to the person. In the twentieth century there was a persistent concentration on the person as interpersonal and social. It is generally acknowledged that individuals do not just survive or thrive in relation to others; they cannot exist as human persons without some form of fundamental relatedness to others. George Herbert Mead articulated a theory of the social self that critics describe as submerging the individual so completely in the social that identity is lost. Martin Buber turned dramatic attention to the dialogue at the heart of human reality (and strongly influenced the theologies of, for example, H. Richard Niebuhr and Karl Barth). Contemporary communitarianism (as represented in the work of Alasdair MacIntyre, Michael Sandel, Robert Bellah, Stanley Hauerwas, and others) has different interests than continental social ontology or philosophies of dialogue, but it aims no less to place an otherwise autonomous self in the context of relationships.

Among feminists, relationality and community are central personal

---

[16] Aristotle, *Nicomachean Ethics* 1097b10–11. For an interesting perspective on this in the context of contemporary ethical concerns, see Martha Nussbaum, "Aristotelian Social Democracy," in *Liberalism and the Good*, ed. R. Bruce Douglass et al. (New York: Routledge, 1990), 203–52.

[17] Augustine, *City of God* 12.28.

[18] For example, see Kant, *Religion within the Limits of Reason Alone*, trans. Theodore M. Greene and Hoyt H. Hudson (New York: Harper and Row, 1960), 85, 88.

and political concerns.[19] But, as Marilyn Friedman warns, "Communitarian philosophy as a whole is a perilous ally for feminists."[20] Feminist theorists cite a number of reasons for this caution. First, to give traditional communities and relationships normative weight is to risk perpetuating the tyranny of unchosen roles, patterns of domination and subordination, and overall normative complacency regarding the inhumanity of individuals and groups in relation to one another.[21] Second, communitarian ideals (as they are articulated today) may be essentially exclusionary. As Iris Young argues, in privileging unity over difference, the ideal of community both excludes those who are different and suppresses the differences of those who are considered the same.[22] Third, if an emphasis on autonomy leads to a devaluing of the "other," an uncritical focus on community may do nothing to correct this or redeem it.[23] Everything will depend on the kind of relationships one finds or creates and the way in which one participates in them. Feminist ethics needs an understanding of relationality that will yield a *normative* theory of community.

Once again we have a set of questions too numerous and complex to address here. But our central question remains: What are the obligating-features of persons? And now: How is relationality, along with autonomy, to be understood as an obligating-feature of persons, and can we find in it some clues for an ethic that will guide human relationships?

The philosophy of Jean-Paul Sartre is in many ways a strange place to look for insight into the moral significance of relationality. Few

---

[19]Beverly Wildung Harrison identifies this as one of the methodological "basepoints" for feminist ethics in *Our Right to Choose: Toward a New Ethic of Abortion* (Boston: Beacon Press, 1983), 15ff. Important discussions range across disciplines, as, for example, Carol Gilligan, *In a Different Voice* (Cambridge, MA: Harvard University Press, 1982); Nel Noddings, *Caring: A Feminine Approach to Ethics* (Berkeley: University of California Press, 1984); Isabel Carter Heyward, *The Redemption of God: A Theology of Mutual Relation* (Lanham, MD: University Press of America, 1982); Iris Marion Young, *Justice and the Politics of Difference* (Princeton, NJ: Princeton University Press, 1990).

[20]Marilyn Friedman, "Feminism and Modern Friendship: Dislocating the Community," in Cole and Coultrap-McQuin, *Explorations in Feminist Ethics*, 89.

[21]See ibid., 89. See also Rita Manning, "Just Caring," in Cole and Coultrap-McQuin, *Explorations in Feminist Ethics*, 45–54; Margaret Farley, "Feminism and Universal Morality," and Farley, *Compassionate Respect: A Feminist Approach to Medical Ethics* (New York: Paulist Press, 2002).

[22]Young, *Justice and the Politics of Difference*, 12.

[23]Nancy Hartsock, "Foucault on Power: A Theory for Women?" in Nicholson, *Feminism/Postmodernism*, 157–75. Part of Hartsock's point in this essay is that an alternative view of the world is needed.

thinkers have been so negative in interpreting interpersonal relations. Few, however, have taken them more seriously. Building on Hegel and Heidegger, on Husserl and finally on Marx, Sartre offered a systematic and original description and appraisal of being-for-others, of sociality or relationality. What is particularly to the point in our explorations is that Sartre was as concerned about autonomy as he was about relationality. In a way, the line from Kant to Sartre is clear and direct.[24] Despite Sartre's interest in relationality, he probably represents an extreme development of the potential in Kant's theory for an atomistic, isolated, competitive individual freedom. And despite Sartre's commitment to autonomy, he finally shows us how destructive relationships can be if they are completely without ethical anchoring. Sartre's philosophy, then, may serve heuristically to help us sort out the relationship between autonomy and relationality, not because he offers us an adequate view of this relationship but because he unwittingly shows us what is at stake if we cannot find a more integrative way. To examine Sartre's analysis is also to remember the profound influence he had on Simone de Beauvoir, and perhaps to understand why her own theory was both a remarkable contribution to feminism and yet has been criticized and even rejected by so many feminists.[25] The problems it incorporated from Sartre may not yet, however, be fully resolved.

For Jean-Paul Sartre, as for Kant, the autonomy of the individual is of central importance.[26] Human reflective consciousness functions in

---

[24]The line is interestingly and persuasively drawn in Frederick A. Olafson, *Principles and Persons: An Ethical Interpretation of Existentialism* (Baltimore: Johns Hopkins University Press, 1967).

[25]Simone de Beauvoir insisted throughout most of her professional life that she wore "the mantle of disciple and chief spokesperson for Sartre's philosophy." See Deirdre Bair, *Simone de Beauvoir: A Biography* (New York: Summit Books, 1990), 307; also 269. Most starkly relevant here are de Beauvoir's incorporation of a radical notion of freedom in her overall philosophy and her development of women as "other" in *The Second Sex*, trans. H. M. Parshley (New York: Vintage Books, 1952), esp. chap. 6.

[26]Here I will draw almost exclusively on Sartre's early thought as articulated in *Being and Nothingness*. It is debatable whether he ever significantly departed from the particular ideas I am examining. Simone de Beauvoir thought he did, apparently, and she resisted this. See Bair, *Simone de Beauvoir*, 466, 516, 580. Other scholars disagree. Michael Theunissen, for example, argues, "Nothing has been altered in the *Critique* with respect to the leading thesis of *Being and Nothingness*, in accordance with which the interhuman relation is primarily a subject-object relationship. Correspondingly, Sartre further affirms that the original intersubjective situation is 'conflict' which can turn into acute 'warfare.'" See Theunissen, *The Other: Studies in the Social Ontology of Husserl, Heidegger, Sartre, and Buber*, trans. C. Macann (Cambridge, MA: MIT Press, 1984), 246. There is a difference, however, in that interhuman conflict becomes no longer a matter of ontological structures but, rather, historical conditions of scarcity. An inchoate treatment of nonconflictual human relations

Sartre's theory in many ways like rationality in Kant's. Like rationality, consciousness makes the difference between being a person or a thing. Because of consciousness, a person is negatively undetermined and positively self-determining, radically free. Unlike Kantian reason, however, Sartrean consciousness is not so closed in on itself, generating only its own ideas, recognizing the power only of its own law. Indeed, consciousness is born as freedom only when it encounters another person (another consciousness) in the world. In Sartre's view, things that are not conscious exist in the world as passive objects, to be given meaning, used, transformed, "worked" by the freedom of the person. Conscious beings (other persons) are, however, encountered not as passive objects but as centers of freedom, centers of power. Each person, with her freedom, organizes the world into a system of meaning according to her own chosen ends. The encounter with an other threatens this world, for here is another system of meaning, another set of ends. Two worlds of meaning do not simply exist side by side; they encroach on one another, for it is the very construal of one person's world that can be given a different meaning by another person.

Sartre's telling example is familiar by now even to those who have never read him.[27] Human relations are like this: I am outside a door, listening, perhaps peering through a keyhole. I hear footsteps behind me, and I feel the eyes of another on me. However I have understood my own action (whatever meaning I have given to it until now), the other who approaches will give it a different meaning. Even if I am responding to the request of someone on the other side of the door to test what can be heard or seen through the keyhole (in which case I believe it is quite reasonable for me to be peering through it), I feel profoundly threatened, "unjustified," by the suspicious stare of the other who comes upon me from behind and who now interprets my action and passes judgment on me as a keyhole-peeper. No longer can I simply determine my own meaning for my actions; someone else threatens psychologically to imprison me, to take away my freedom by imposing a judgment on me, by locking my action and thereby my self into a meaning that is not mine.

According to Sartre, only in and through my encounter with another

can be found in Sartre's posthumously published *Notebooks for an Ethics*, trans. David Pellauer (Chicago: University of Chicago Press, 1992), esp. 274–94, 368–76, 496–500.

   [27]Jean-Paul Sartre, *Being and Nothingness*, trans. Hazel E. Barnes (New York: Washington Square Press, 1966), 348–49.

person do I become reflectively conscious and therefore truly free. In concrete relation, autonomy is born. Only through an other do I become a person. But the person-becoming encounter is of a particular kind: My awareness of my capacity and my need to determine myself (through determining my action and meaning) is awakened when my freedom to do so is threatened. It is in experiencing myself being made into an object that I come to know myself as a subject. For Sartre, then, the most fundamental human relations are relations of conflict.

So potentially devastating is the block to my freedom in every suspicious stare from an other that it is necessary for me to respond. The threat of objectification is unbearable. I have two options, says Sartre. I can either overpower the gaze of the other, or I can submit to it so fully, absorb it so completely, that I no longer see it. I do the first by psychologically (or even physically) striking out at the other's eyes, overwhelming the other's judgment, taking away the other's meaning. My freedom prevails. I do the second by choosing to objectify myself in the same way that the other has objectified me. This I can do by, for example, identifying myself with a role, deceiving myself into believing that the whole meaning of my self is exhausted in this part that I play, the part that is expected of one. The power of the other's gaze prevails.

For Sartre, it is of the utmost theoretical importance that persons are encountered as embodied beings; it is as body that the individual receives the other's stare. Hence, the paradigm of human relations is to be found in the sexual sphere.[28] Sexuality represents the most basically structured attempt to overcome the subjectivity and freedom of the other. The two fundamental responses to the suspicious state are sadism or masochism. I can try to manipulate the other's suspicious gaze by seduction (attempting to change it into the appraisal I want); failing this, I can turn upon the gaze, making the other my object, subduing the other even through violence and pain. This is the sadistic response. Alternatively, I can let myself be lost in my desire so fully that I am lost in myself, masochistically absorbed by the other (even though I know that the other does not see me as I am), so completely given over to the other that I no longer have to endure the other's gaze. In a conflict of freedoms, I move to suppress the consciousness of the other or to hide from the consciousness of myself.

We have in Sartre's theory a picture of human absurdity. Autonomy

---

[28]Ibid., 471–556.

and relationality are both fundamental to persons, yet they finally cancel each other out in a futile effort to achieve personal identity. Autonomy needs relationships in order to be actualized; yet in relationships freedom must either crush the autonomy of the other or surrender the autonomy of the self. In either case the relationship is finally destroyed, and autonomy is compromised or at least remains alone, perpetually yearning for itself in an impossible struggle or dream.

The critical question for feminist theory is not whether Sartre has accurately described a large part of human experience, but whether autonomy is inescapably hostile to any but instrumental relationships. We know Kant's answer to such a question: Autonomy requires respect for persons; it requires and makes possible relationships that are more than instrumental. For Sartre, the other is always only the other for me. Freedom's value is only *my* freedom's value. I am not required to treat anyone else as an end; I am compelled to treat everyone else as a means.[29] How, if Sartre is in any way in the tradition of Kant, can he have retained autonomy but lost respect for the other?

In the view of many feminists, the problem lies not only with Sartre but also with Kant. As Nancy Hartsock has put it (though not speaking specifically of Kant), "The philosophical and historical creation of a devalued 'Other' was the necessary precondition for the creation of the transcendental rational subject outside of time and space."[30] Why? Kant's concern for respect for persons was not sufficient to counter the stronger drift of the whole Enlightenment toward the self-defining agent. Moreover, concrete differences in individuals and groups were always "other" to the agent who controlled not only action but meaning. Rationality was never as pure and impartial as it claimed to be, and the myth of incorporating all moral concerns under one perspective has in fact generated exclusion and conflict as much or more than inclusion and harmony of interests. From Kant to Sartre is not as long a way as it seems nor as circuitous.

But can autonomy still require respect for all persons, and can it be correlated with a notion of relationality that requires respect for differences among persons? Can obligating-features of persons call

---

[29]"Insofar as my project is a transcendence of the present towards the future, and of myself toward the world, I always treat myself as a means and cannot treat the Other as an end" (Sartre, *Critique of Dialectical Reason*. trans. Alan Sheridan-Smith [London: NLB, 1976], 112). Both self and other are Hobbesian and, later, Marxian means.

[30]Hartsock, "Foucault on Power," 160.

us to move beyond conflict to care, and within care, to justice that is both personal and political?

Respect Revisited

The Value of Persons

Whatever the variations in feminist theory, feminism as a movement has generally presupposed and even been grounded in the conviction that persons are of unconditional value. Insofar as caring for others has been part of women's lives, it has been perceived by women as a commitment to the incomparable worth of those for whom they care. This commitment is renewed when feminists claim the importance of caring and argue for active participation in it not only by women but by men. Feminist critiques of women's caring call into question not the value of persons or the good of care but the social construction of women as caregivers—their sometime adoption of an identity under the historical pressure of gendered power, expectations, and roles.[31] This critique in turn is part of the central claim of feminists that women themselves are of unconditional value, as persons and as women-persons. The buying and selling of women, by whatever cultural disguise, violates the dignity of women who are each and all ends in themselves.

It is important, then, to keep trying to articulate the unconditional value of persons. If persons are to be valued as ends in themselves, there must be a way to avoid abstracting from their histories and their present needs. If relationships among persons are to incorporate respect, there must be a way to address otherness without devaluing whoever is the other. We must at least try to correct for the kind of theoretical difficulties we have seen in Sartre and Kant.

Persons are ends in themselves because in some way they both transcend themselves and yet belong to themselves. They transcend themselves because their meaning is inexhaustible; they are more than

---

[31]Catherine MacKinnon offers this caution: "Women are said to value care. Perhaps women value care because men have valued women according to the care they give. Women are said to think in relational terms. Perhaps women think in relational terms because women's social existence is defined in relation to men." See MacKinnon, *Toward a Feminist Theory of the State* (Cambridge, MA: Harvard University Press, 1989), 51. For a similar suggestion regarding women's interpretation of their experience in general, see Joan W. Scott, "The Evidence of Experience," *Critical Inquiry* 17 (1991): 773–97.

anyone's judgment of them, more than their past and their present, more than the causes that have shaped them, more than the context that allows them to be what they are. In the midst of all the givens of their lives, persons can introduce something new, whether in meaning or action. They alone can take their stance in relation to what happens to them, what they have done, what they will do or commit themselves to do. They can, in a sense, determine the center of themselves and the direction they will take. Because they are capable of this, persons also belong to themselves; their selves and their actions are in some sense their own.

Yet persons, as we know them, do not exist in the world by themselves. No one today would argue that persons are as autonomous as either Kant or Sartre thought they were. To be self-transcendent and self-possessing is neither to be, nor to be inside, a vacuum. Persons are in the world, and the world is in them. They are in society, and society is in them. They are in biological, psychological, cultural history, and their history is in them like the rings of a tree. We are who we are within social, cultural, linguistic contexts, formed in our understandings and our desires. We do not produce our own meaning out of nothing, nor are our actions wholly our own. We take our stance, but who knows what causal forces, or what moral luck, make any stance possible? Thus, if we are free, if we are autonomous, it is not in spite of our world but because we are capable of interaction with our world. In hearing and receiving, knowing and loving, speaking and doing, surrendering and resisting, we become ourselves—able (always more or less) to understand our desires, express our intentions, organize our plans, and reveal our loves.

By freedom, but not only by freedom, persons are both self-transcendent and self-possessing; they are so also by knowledge and love. These are not separable capacities, but mutually qualifying ways of existing—of being and relating. Persons are ends in themselves not only because they can freely determine themselves but because they can know and be known, love and be loved, as both embodied and free. By knowledge, love, and freedom, persons transcend themselves even as they possess themselves. Paradoxically, persons who are terminal centers of life are capable of being centered beyond themselves, finding their home in what they love. The capacity of persons to love one another and the world, and (as theologians and philosophers of religion must surely add) their capacity to love and to love freely what is sacredly transcendent and immanent, makes them worthy of respect.[32]

How can we know that any of this is true, that it is more than rhetorical assertion? And even if it makes sense as a characterization of persons, why should any of it create in us an experience of moral obligation? How can persons, ends in themselves, claim respect? Kant had reasons for insisting on autonomy as a central feature of persons, but he did not think it admitted of an a priori demonstration. Relationality may equally defy demonstration as an obligating-feature of persons. Reasons can be given (as I am trying to give), and descriptions can be offered. But the claim itself may have to be experienced. Kant noted that "two things fill the mind with ever new and increasing admiration and awe, the oftener and more steadily we reflect on them: the starry heavens above me and the moral law within me. I do not merely conjecture them and seek them as though obscured in darkness or in the transcendent region beyond my horizon: I see them before me, and I associate them directly with the consciousness of my own existence."[33] If Kant had to contemplate the moral law, feminists may have to do no less; only now it is not only a law but concrete persons that must be seen.

Freedom in Relation

We need a way of interpreting autonomy not as sheer self-dependence but as a response to what we already are and to what has become possible for us in terms of where we are.[34] In other words, we need an understanding of autonomy as situated. Here, perhaps, is a way to begin: Freedom is not opposed to desire (as Kant thought it

---

[32]Basil Mitchell maintains, for example, that it is human persons' "capacity to love one another and to love God, rather than their powers of self-legislation" that makes them "proper objects of respect." See Mitchell, *Morality: Religious and Secular* (Oxford: Clarendon Press, 1980), 134. This may be an important place to add a clarification about the limits of this essay. While my focus is on an ethical obligation to respect persons, I do not thereby in any way want to imply that we have no obligation to love God/dess or that we have no obligation to respect and to love beings that are not perceived as persons. Both of these dimensions of a feminist ethic need to be dealt with, though not here.

[33]Kant, *Critique of Practical Reason*, 161–62 [158–59].

[34]Charles Taylor concludes his remarkable analysis of the trends in modern philosophy with the observation that Hegel's criticism of the autonomous self was a harbinger of the contemporary attempt "to situate subjectivity, by relating it to our life as embodied and social beings, without reducing it to a function of objectified nature." Hegel did not and cannot do it for us, but the task seems clear. See Charles Taylor, *Hegel and Modern Society* (Cambridge: Cambridge University Press, 1979), 167–69.

was), but desire is not in the first instance free. Shaped as we are in the fabric of our lives, our desires rise not from our free choice but out of what we already are—including our needs and loves, fears and hopes, deprivations and fulfillments. These desires, rising unbidden, nonetheless present themselves to our freedom. Our desires mediate for us the options of freedom. For whenever we are confronted with alternative possible actions, these actions become viable choices only if we desire them in some way.

But desires have not only a history; they arise not only out of the past that has generated our present selves. Here and now desires rise out of some deeper affective response; they rise out of our loves. Loves, too, have a history, and they rise unbidden by our choice. But, like the desires that express them, loves present themselves to our freedom. Every action that we choose is for the sake of some love, whether for ourselves or for another, whether for persons or for things. When we choose our actions, we ratify, identify with, some of our loves (deferring, or refusing to ratify, other loves that are thereby not expressed in action). And the same is true for the desires that come from our loves; we affirm some and refuse to affirm others, letting the ones we affirm issue in action or commitment to action.

Freedom, then, is possible not in spite of our loves and desires, but because of them—because they express who we are and present what can be chosen, because they do not always compel us to remain as we are. Becoming truly one with our loves, and in that process shaping them—sustaining or changing, strengthening or weakening, integrating or fragmenting—that is the possibility and the task of our freedom. Freedom, then, rises out of relationality and serves it. Freedom is for the sake of relationship—with ourselves and with all that can be known and loved.

But what are the possibilities for our love, the possible forms of our relationships? In particular, what are the possibilities of our relating with other persons? Can freedom find and shape relationships whose core is not conflict, whose pattern is not dominance and subordination, whose goal is not exclusion of some for the sake of being included with others?[35]

---

[35]For a fuller (though still only in sketch form) description of freedom of this sort, see my *Personal Commitments: Beginning, Keeping, Changing* (San Francisco: Harper and Row, 1986), chap. 3.

It is true, as Sartre suggests, that some of our experiences of others are experiences of being threatened; that we sometimes seek self-justification whether by mastery or by submission; that we are likely to project on those who are different from us what we ourselves lack (not-I) or what we fear (passion) or do not understand (the "mysterious") or need (the complement or the narcissistic mirror).

But these are not the only possibilities for relating to others. However serious the threat of absurdity and tragedy among us, there are multiple testimonies to the experience of shared struggle and the achievement of mutual understanding; and there are continuing proposals for theories that will sustain liberating praxis.[36] An obligation to respect persons requires that we honor their freedom and respond to their needs, that we value difference as well as sameness, that we attend to the concrete realities of our own and others' lives. We *can* risk considering seriously the meaning the other gives to the world; building communities of support that have openness to the other at the center of their strength; surrendering our tendencies to (and pretenses of) omniscience without surrendering to despair; learning the particular content of just and fitting care. In a feminist ethic, respect for persons is both an obligating and a liberating call.

---

[36]Examples of such theories from a feminist perspective can be found in the work of bell hooks, Seyla Benhabib, Iris Marion Young, and many others. What is particularly helpful is the effort to find a theory that will address both interpersonal and political relations. The problem of otherness in the area of religious pluralism is creatively treated by David Tracy in *Dialogue with the Other: The Inter-Religious Dialogue* (Grand Rapids: William B. Eerdmans, 1990). This work has important implications for a general theory about human differences.

CHAPTER 8

How Shall We Love
in a Postmodern World?

In the process of preparing this address I came to appreciate why Socrates and his friends told stories to one another after their banqueting. A leisurely dinner is not always conducive to abstract considerations or rigorous philosophical argument. I decided, therefore, to follow the example of some of the participants in Plato's *Symposium* and to begin with stories—or, more accurately, small pieces of stories. I do not propose to generate a theory from these tales, nor will I say a great deal about them as I move eventually to more theoretical issues. They are simply stories, bits of narratives, that were burned into my mind when I first encountered them at various times in the past, and that now intrude themselves periodically when I think about abstract questions such as my topic for tonight: How shall we love in a postmodern world?

An image from the first of these stories was inscribed in my memory some years ago when I saw the Brazilian film *Pixote*. This is a story of countless numbers of children and young adults who fend for themselves in the streets of great cities and little towns in Brazil. Not tied to families, these children struggle for life, alone and with each other. The film follows one small boy, Pixote, as he moves through his experiences in a reformatory, back into the streets, playing with others a deadly game (a child's game, nonetheless) of survival through stealing, prostitution, the sale of drugs, and murder. Pixote's is not a

This essay was originally the Presidential Address given by Margaret A. Farley at the 1993 Annual Meeting of the Society of Christian Ethics. It was later published in the *Annual of the Society of Christian Ethics* (Washington, DC: Georgetown University Press, 1994), 3–19. Used with permission.

highly dramatic tale; indeed, his own emotions and those of all the other characters are thinned, flattened, almost nonexistent. That is, in part, the point. The children appear incapable of feeling much at all—not horror, not guilt, not fear, not compassion, not even desire. They show little reaction to the violence, the contempt, the squalor of their outcast existence. Ordinary life is engaged only by the need for cunning, and even this is perfunctory most of the time. Yet in a final scene, Pixote accidentally shoots and kills one of his companions. At first, his response is the same as it always is to deaths he causes and death that threatens. Observing the results of his shooting, he simply sits on a bed with his usual impassive expression. A few moments pass. Then he vomits, into the camera. This is followed by what is for the film a most extraordinary but fleeting interaction, a small gesture of comfort. The film ends with Pixote walking down one more railroad track, heading once again for nowhere in particular.

The second story, or suggestion of a story, is more positive. It appears in a poem called "Aria," by Delmore Schwartz. I first saw this text placed on a page opposite a photograph of a magnificent glass sculpture of two nude figures: a woman and a man, as beautiful as a Greek goddess and god, glorious and shining in naked strength and splendor, standing in mutual embrace. The lines of the poem were not gender assigned, and it does not really matter which figure speaks which lines (or, for that matter, whether the figures were male and female):

> "—Kiss me there where pride is glittering
> Kiss me where I am ripened and round fruit
>   Kiss me wherever, however I am supple, bare
> and flare
> (Let the bell be rung as long as I am young;
>   let ring and fly like a great bronze wing!)
> Until I am shaken from blossom to root."
>
> "—I'll kiss you wherever you think you are poor,
> Wherever you shudder, feeling striped or barred,
>   Because you think you are bloodless, skinny
> or marred;
>   until, until
> your gaze has been stilled—
> Until you are shamed again no more!

I'll kiss you until your body and soul
the mind in the body being fulfilled—
Suspend their dread and civil war!"[1]

The third and final story is a factual account presented at a women's conference designed as an alternate to the Conference of Bishops of Latin America in Puebla, Mexico, in 1979. Speaking of the experience of peasant women in Venezuela, Leonor Aida Concha reported the following dialogue between a Venezuelan Indian woman and a priest:

Father Gumille, scolding a woman who killed her daughter deliberately during birth, received the following answer: "God grant, Father, that when I was born, my mother had loved me well and would have had pity on me for all the trials we endure, poor Indian women among Indian men. They go with us to plant the fields, carrying their bow and arrow, no more; we go with a basket full of dishes on our backs, one child nursing and another in a basket. They go to kill a fish or a bird, and we dig and drop [give birth] in the fields. In the afternoon they return to the house carrying nothing, and some of us, besides the load of our children, bring roots to eat and corn for cold drink. When they arrive home, they go to talk with their friends, and we go to look for firewood. Then we spend the whole night grinding corn for *chichi* [cold corn drink], and what is the end of all this trouble? They drink, get drunk, and when they are beyond reason they beat us. They take us by the hair and stamp on us. If only, Father, my mother had buried me when I was born. You know well that we complain legitimately, because you can see what I am telling you every day; but our greatest affliction you cannot know. You know, Father, for the Indian woman death is serving her husband as a slave, sweating in the fields and at home without any sleep. After twenty years he gets another girl without sense; he loves her, and even if she beats our children, we can say nothing, because the husbands do not pay any atten-

---

[1]Delmore Schwartz, "Aria," in *Poetry in Crystal* (New York: Steuben Glass, A Division of Corning Glass Works: 1963), 52. This poem appeared in three different versions in various periodicals. It was designated as part of a sequence of poems entitled "Kilroy's Carnival: A Masque." See *Last and Lost Poems of Delmore Schwartz*, ed. Robert Phillips (New York: New Directions Books, 1989), 7.

tion to us. The young girl can command us and treat us as her maids, and if we speak, they silence us with a stick. How can we suffer like this, Father? The Indian woman cannot do her child a greater favor than to liberate her from these trials, to take her out of this slavery that is worse than death."[2]

I intend these stories, these images, to constitute a background as well as a central presence in relation to which my considerations of love in a postmodern world can be interpreted and assessed. At the very least, let them stand as a reminder that questions of love ought not be abstracted from real persons who love and are loved, who are not loved and do not love, whose love is shaped by the groups to which they belong, who cry out sometimes across the centuries against the expectations of duty and love.

My title, "How Shall We Love in a Postmodern World?," signals my intention to concentrate on a set of questions that have escalated in interest with the challenges to moral philosophy and theology by so-called postmodern thought. What is so interesting about these questions, and so urgent, is that they take us once again to the heart of our understandings of human freedom, moral agency, interpersonal and social connectedness, and love.

A Postmodern World

The trouble with beginning with postmodernism, as if it were an ordinary school of thought or social and political program, is that it is amorphous, a massive mixture of heterogeneous theories—about art and architecture, literary criticism and linguistics, philosophy and religion.[3] It combines substantive proposals with skeptical method,

---

[2]Margarita Gamio de Alba, "The Indigenous Woman of Central America," transcribed in Leonor Aida Concha, "The Indigenous Woman in Latin America," in *Women in Dialogue*, trans. Ruth Fitzpatrick (Notre Dame, IN: Catholic Committee on Urban Ministry, 1979), 11.

[3]For helpful history, mapping, and interpretation of multiple postmodern representatives and themes, see Harry R. Garvin, ed., *Romanticism, Modernism, Postmodernism* (Lewisburg, PA: Bucknell University Press, 1980); Kenneth Baynes, James Bohman, and Thomas McCarthy, eds., *After Philosophy: End or Transformation?* (Cambridge, MA: MIT Press, 1987), esp. "General Introduction" and part 1, 1–158; Reed Way Dasenbrock, ed., *Redrawing the Lines; Analytical Philosophy, Deconstruction, and Literary Theory* (Minneapolis: University of Minnesota Press, 1989); Andreas Huyssen, "Mapping the Postmodern," in *Feminism/Postmodernism*, ed. Linda J. Nicholson (New York: Routledge, 1990), 234–77. One key text (but by no means a fully representative one) to which commentators frequently

and the sensibilities it evokes are varied though they bear a family resemblance of sorts. Postmoderns have been both iconoclastic and apocalyptic, both elitist and aligned with mass culture. They have been accused of being neoconservative, yet they are heatedly repudiated by most standard neoconservatives. Postmodernism largely despairs of the emancipatory potential of Enlightenment modernism, but sometimes it appears with at least a limited emancipatory agenda of its own. It challenges much of ethical theory, though from its perspective morality frequently modulates into aesthetics.

Postmoderns and their critics are, I think it is fair to say, generally agreed that what postmodernist philosophy is *against* includes the universalizing tendency of the Enlightenment, the philosophical project of establishing general moral norms, the search for a stable reality behind historical contingencies, the assumption of individual inwardness and self-possession, an ahistorical subject beyond the constituting influences of language, the notion of a transcendent entity underneath fluid appearances. Of course, postmodernism is not the first philosophical movement to be suspicious of universal theorizing, to challenge the unity of the human self, to object to the idea of transcendent reason or transcendent reality. Indeed, there is plausibility in the observation that Derrida, Lyotard, Foucault, Kristeva, and others continue the skeptical traditions of thinkers like Hume, Marx, Nietzsche, Freud, and Dewey. Yet the project of demythologization in the hands of postmodernists seems more focused, more total—more revolutionary, if you will. There is the claim on the part of at least some postmodern thinkers that all past theory is swept away; a radically new way of thinking is now at hand; the very possibility of theory is now gone.

It is not difficult to appreciate the salutary aspects of postmodern thought—to acknowledge the ongoing need for deconstruction of theoretical idols and illusions of isolated individuality. It has been a major contribution of postmodernism to lift up the importance of particularity and difference, historical situatedness, the dynamics of power, false security in settled views of society and the world. The virtue of epistemic humility ought to develop more readily in a postmodern world.

It is less easy to follow with appreciation the movement of post-

---

return is Jean-Francois Lyotard, *The Postmodern Condition* (Minneapolis: University of Minnesota Press, 1984).

modern thought to the extremes of deconstruction and the borders of a new construction. Iris Murdoch may be justified in her judgment that what some self-proclaimed antimetaphysical postmoderns are finally about is offering a new metaphysics.[4] It is not just that we are to question the existence of an ahistorical self or an unimpeachable self-identity, for example; it is that language is the ultimate structure of reality. Like traditional metaphysics, postmodern thinkers search for a hidden a priori that determines the form of everything. Reality is in the medium, not beyond it. As for human persons, it is not just that we are shaped, influenced, by social forces beyond ourselves, as every behaviorist would hold; it is not just that the individual is subordinate to the community, as Marxists or theorists of the social self might maintain; it is not just that the ideology of the subject as male, white, and middle-class must be challenged, as feminists would agree; it is that we seem to disappear altogether as centered selves. Individual experience is illusory; even our bodies, so important for our situatedness, appear boundaryless and hence disembodied. The whole of human activity emerges from a matrix of linguistic codes, but it is not our own activity. So pervasive is the reality of language in which we are submerged, and the hidden networks of power by which we are controlled, that individual consciousness may not really exist. Perhaps we do have here a new metaphysics, what Murdoch is willing to call linguistic idealism, linguistic monism, linguistic determinism.[5]

It is in a world so understood that we may ask: How shall we love? What can it mean to love as a human individual? What sort of love is called for by individuals who are "only" social constructions, whose identity is "only" a protean self subject to impersonal dynamics of power, nonpersonal linguistic codes? What kind of love can come from persons whose agency is diffused? Is it finally meaningless to ask how we should love as if there were guidelines and choices to be made regarding our loves?

To answer these questions we have several alternatives. We can address the questions in terms of the postmodern world as I have so far described it, in which case most of the answers will lean toward the negative and will almost certainly (and intentionally) come up

---

[4]See Iris Murdoch, *Metaphysics as a Guide to Morals* (New York: Allen Lane, Penguin Press, 1992), 6.

[5]Ibid., 185.

empty of an ethic of love. Or we can sidestep postmodern thought, either because it mistakenly opposes the advances of modern theories or because modern theories, too (upon which postmodernism is parasitic), have little to say about how we should love. Hence, perspectives that are either antimodern or simply after-modern can hardly be expected to offer much wisdom regarding our loves. We can, in this case, return to premodern insights or try to forge something entirely new but more adequate than postmodern efforts to date. Or, finally, we can take postmodern thought more seriously. We can, like some postmoderns,[6] be eclectic (expecting helpful insight from the old and the new, the premodern, the modern, and the postmodern); and in so doing, we can pay more attention to the relevant postmodern concerns, bringing them into focus not just as critiques of modern theory but as potentially illuminative of our experiences of ourselves and of one another. I want to pursue this last alternative—that is, relying not on postmodern perspectives alone, nonetheless taking seriously some postmodern concerns.

To this end, then, let me acknowledge that what I have described thus far as a postmodern world of thought may be something of a caricature, despite my caveats regarding the amorphousness of postmodernism as a development in many fields. Even if the assertions of some postmodern thinkers accord with this view of a postmodern world, they can be intended as exaggerations, motivated by disenchantment with the moralistic excesses of some forms of modernist thought; they may be strategies to achieve tolerance of differing views. In any case, it is impossible without gross oversimplification and distortion to ascribe univocal positions to all of the thinkers who have been designated as postmodern. It is no wonder, for example, that Richard Rorty expresses surprise at Sabina Lovibond's inclusion of his writings and Alasdair MacIntyre's along with those of Jean-François Lyotard under the term "postmodern." Though Rorty acknowledges some similarities between his thought and that of the other two, he lets stand his demurral: "I am not fond of the term 'postmodernism.'"[7]

Not only are there significantly different agendas among thinkers who may be gathered under the large umbrella of postmodernism,

---

[6]See, in particular, Edith Wyschogrod, *Saints and Postmodernism: Revisioning Moral Philosophy* (Chicago: University of Chicago Press, 1990), xvii–xx.

[7]Richard Rorty, "Feminism and Pragmatism," in *The Tanner Lectures on Human Values*, vol. 13, ed. Gretchen B. Peterson (Salt Lake City: University of Utah Press, 1992), 13n18.

but it is also sometimes difficult to reconcile even within one thinker the various aspects of his or her thought. Rorty, among others, notes internal inconsistencies in much of what is considered "postmodernism," nowhere more apparent than in the mixing of rejections of representational views of knowledge with the rhetoric of "unmasking."[8] I have here neither the occasion nor the desire to adjudicate different interpretations of postmodernist thought. It is clear to me that there are certain tensions and even fissures within it, but I will follow the lines of thought that seem to me useful for discerning whether and how to love in a postmodern world.

First, however, let me identify a basic premise of my own: There are what I will call "locations" in our experience where we can recognize something real and enduring in other beings and something real and enduring in ourselves. There are experiences in which we connect with the "real" beyond us and the "real" within us.[9] That we are able to love in a postmodern world, and how we shall love in this world, can at least be glimpsed in these locations. I will consider only two of them (though there are more): the experience of love and the experience of the suffering of others.

Like postmodern thinkers, I concede the elusiveness of the very notion of "experience." Experience is not a "pure, positivist, nonlinguistic reality that determines the shape of language apart from ideology and culturally systemic shaping."[10] Like premodern and postmodern theorists, I acknowledge that whatever is received is received according to the mode of the recipient. Like postmoderns, I recognize that experience is not self-interpreting; it is constituted for us and interpreted by us within the limits and possibilities of the languages we already have, the worldview we already hold. Our experiences are, therefore, diverse, socially shaped, difficult to understand without some tools of

---

[8]Ibid., 12–13n17.

[9]I use quotation marks for "real" to signal the same challenge to a positivistic sense of the "real" that prompted David Tracy to repeat Vladimir Nabokov: "'Reality' is the one word that should always appear within quotation marks." See David Tracy, *Plurality and Ambiguity: Hermeneutics, Religion, and Hope* (San Francisco: Harper and Row, 1987), 47. To repudiate positivism's reality is not (as I hope will be clear in my context) to jettison the "real" except in the sense of brute facts, the knowledge of which requires no interpretation by us.

[10]George Levine, "Introduction: Constructivism and the Reemergent Self," in *Constructions of the Self*, ed. G. Levine (New Brunswick, NJ: Rutgers University Press, 1992), 6.

deconstruction. Unlike some postmoderns, however, I allow that there are limits to the meaning of our experiences that are not reducible to the limits of our cultural formation. Something can be given in experience that resists our projection of meaning, challenges our purposes, modifies our language, and changes our understanding. We can make mistakes about what experiences mean. Our very judgments of error, as well as our reflective confirmations of at least partial accuracy, tell us that the reality at the heart of an experience may not always be only the product of our language; left to itself, this reality need not evaporate into nothingness.

Experience and Reality

Love, as a central concern of human individuals and societies, comes upon hard times when there is less and less access to what is lovable. Certain ways of thinking about love tend to distance us from what is loved, to disallow our contemplating, receiving, and responding to what is lovable precisely as lovable. When, for example, we believe that love should be motivated only by duty, or that, having nothing to do with duty, love counts as love only when it is in the form of unfettered, spontaneous desire, we in significant ways disengage love from the beloved. A duty to love, whether generated by authoritative command or by ineluctable logic, may sustain a preoccupation with loving but not a real nurturance of love (though, of course, duty can also play an important role in both bringing us to love and holding us faithful to a love once it is begun). Desire may disguise itself as love, but in the process miss loving the beloved who is desired (though desire can be both an occasion for love and an important consequence of love). Theories of human affectivity that focus only on duty or desire, rather than on love as a response to what is lovable, can thus undermine the theoretical and practical priority of love. This is what much of both modern and postmodern thought has tended to do, the former by an emphasis on duty and the latter by an emphasis on desire. In both cases, there has been little room to consider the experience of love that I want to identify as a location for an experience of the reality of the self and the other.

A more likely location for both a modern and postmodern sighting of the connection between the self and the other, grounded in something enduring and real, is the experience of suffering, particularly the suffering of others. Almost every philosopher has identified the importance of sympathy and compassion in human relations, and a few have even made these responses central to their moral theory. Schopenhauer, for example, located the ground of moral obligation in what he considered to be natural compassion.[11] Contemporary feminists (whether liberal, socialist, or radical) have tended to begin moral theory with the experience of someone's oppression, the violation of someone's freedom, deprivation of basically needed goods, injury or loss calling for human care, and premature and unnecessary death. Postmodern thinkers have not ignored the stark claims that suffering places on us. Rorty, for example, presents the "liberal ironist" as *noticing* (though not reasoning about) the pain and humiliation of others, experiencing by "imaginative identification" a responsive desire to prevent it and to care for the sufferers.[12]

These two kinds of experience are often closely connected. When we love someone, our attention to their suffering is formed by our love. When individuals or groups suffer, our "noticing" of their wounds can lead us to see them for the first time and perhaps (though by no means necessarily) to love them. But my point is that in these experiences we encounter reality—in others and in ourselves. The point may be clearer if I can describe further the ways in which we are affected by love (of the kind to which I refer) and affected by the suffering of others.

The kind of love I have in mind is the kind that depends on being awakened, touched, tapped, by the lovableness of what is loved. Such love is by no means limited to romantic love; it may, indeed, in some ways characterize all love (though I will not argue that here). Call it Thomas Aquinas's *passio* or Jules Toner's "response" or Irving Singer's "appraisal," it is love that arises or is at least specified by an experience of affective receptivity and response.[13] What is loved reveals itself as

---

[11]Arthur Schopenhauer, *On the Basis of Morality*, trans. E. F. J. Payne (New York: Library of Liberal Arts, 1965).

[12]Richard Rorty, *Contingency, Irony, and Solidarity* (Cambridge, MA: Cambridge University Press, 1989), 93.

[13]See Thomas Aquinas, *Summa Theologiae* I-II.26.2; Jules J. Toner, *The Experience of Love* (Washington, DC: Corpus Books, 1968), chap. 5; Irving Singer, *The Nature of Love*, vol. 1., rev. ed. (Chicago: University of Chicago Press, 1984), chap. 1. These are, of course, not the only writers to describe love in this way, but they offer clear examples of the kind of love in question.

lovable (as beautiful, valuable in some way), so that love is activated in the one loving. It is at once passion (the other is "received") and action (love is awakened, a responding affective affirmation of the beloved). This is not the only experience that theorists and nontheorists have called "love." There are other important forms or aspects of love, ways in which love expresses itself in our experience; there is love that is commanded, love that is a bestowal of value, love that is the practical exercise of loving deeds in response to the call of duty, love that is an emotional upsurge in search of an object. In all of these forms of love there may be an experience of the self and of what is loved; but where love is a response to the lovableness of the beloved, there the reality of the beloved and the self is experienced as most clear. Since it depends on a perception of the beloved (as well as on all kinds of dispositions that may enhance or obscure this perception), it may be a "mistaken" love. The "reality" at the heart of the experience may be an illusion. Or, as Martha Nussbaum puts it, we may deceive ourselves about what is given in love, "about who; and how; and when; and whether."[14] But the possibilities of error, of illusion and delusion, do not eliminate the possibilities of accuracy, of receiving and responding to what is real. "We also discover and correct our self-deceptions";[15] at least sometimes we do.

A second location in our experience where we may encounter the reality of others and ourselves, I have said, is our experience of the suffering of others. This is no doubt most apparent in what might be identified as paradigm experiences of suffering—what some have called "tales of terror" and "whirlpools of torment,"[16] where bodies are destroyed, minds ravaged, and spirits broken. These are the sufferings that go on in human history generation after generation—a "voice heard in Ramah weeping" (Jer. 31:15), peoples subjugated by peoples, families rent asunder, stories of rape and starvation, abandonment, confusion, violence, and relentless dying. This is the sort of human pain that Simone Weil named "affliction," differentiating it

---

[14]Martha C. Nussbaum, *Love's Knowledge: Essays on Philosophy and Literature* (New York: Oxford University Press, 1990), 261.

[15]Ibid.

[16]The phrases belong to Phyllis Trible and James Crenshaw. See Trible, *Texts of Terror: Literary-Feminist Readings of Biblical Narratives* (Philadelphia: Fortress Press, 1984); Crenshaw, *A Whirlpool of Torment: Israelite Traditions of God as an Oppressive Presence* (Philadelphia: Fortress Press, 1984).

from "suffering" in the ordinary sense.[17] It is, she said, always both physical and spiritual; it is never only physical (like a toothache that is soon over and gone) but it is also never only spiritual. With this kind of suffering, there is no competition between miseries of the body and miseries of the soul. For affliction when it is spiritual also afflicts, leaves wounds in the body; and when it is bodily, if it goes on long enough, it always also afflicts the spirit.

This is the kind of suffering that has the power to uproot life; that can be in itself the equivalent of death; that almost always includes some form of humiliation, some social degradation; that has the potential to attack the self—chaining down thoughts to become a "state of mind" that persons can live in sometimes twenty, thirty, fifty years, a lifetime; and in which one's very soul threatens to become its accomplice, pulling to inertia and despair.[18] This kind of suffering, when we see it in others, has the power to grasp us so that we cannot avoid the reality of the sufferers or the reality of ourselves.

To behold acute suffering can, of course, just as well distance us from one another, lead us to build an illusory world in which we mask reality, tempt us to retreat from the claims of others and the intolerable aspects of ourselves. Moreover, if love can be mistaken, so can our perception of suffering be false. I cannot argue that every experience of the suffering of others puts us in contact with what is real in and for the others. Yet we do have some experiences of the suffering of others where their suffering is revelatory, where it holds our gaze inescapably upon what is real.

How we think about and anticipate experiences both of love and of the suffering of others influences the experiences themselves. This is why philosophies have some potential either to facilitate our experiences of the real, or to get in the way—by denying the possibility of such experiences or by blunting their starkness with theories that explain them too well. Probably every philosophy holds elements that both facilitate and threaten the kind of experiences I have been describing. I want still to pursue the lines in postmodern thought that shed light on these experiences, that perhaps facilitate them even as they render them problematic.

---

[17]Simone Weil, *Waiting for God*, trans. Emma Crauford (New York: Harper and Row, 1973), 117–25.

[18]Ibid., 118–19.

Love's Requirements

Despite the fact that methods of deconstruction tend to undermine notions of a unitary self and dismiss theories of knowledge as presence, there is much in postmodern debates that is useful for exploring our experiences of love and of the suffering of others. This is particularly true of debates about the status of the self and the other, and about the connections between self and other through knowledge and love.

Postmodern critical philosophy is said to have accomplished the death of the self, the end of subjectivity. But the self that is dead is a certain version of the self; it is the self that modern philosophy characterized as disengaged, disembodied, wholly autonomous, and self-transparent. And the subject that has disappeared is the isolated bearer of signs, the conscious knower of clear and certain ideas, the self-governing and self-responsible agent whose task was to instrumentalize body and world.[19] The stability of this subject and self had long ago been shaken by Freud, whose identification of unconscious dimensions of the self divided it and rendered it opaque. The self isolated from the world was challenged by Marx as well, who substituted an active, effective, humanity for the self-sufficient observer. Nietzsche ridiculed the notion of a subject perceiving an objective reality, or an agential self with any core other than its own will to power. Already in the nineteenth century linguistic paradigms began to displace paradigms of consciousness as the subject of knowledge.

Strong lines of postmodern thought have, so to speak, finished the job of erasing an "essential" self, a "true" self. Jacques Lacan, for example, pursued the part of Freud's thought that emphasized radical decentering.[20] Jacques Derrida, Michel Foucault, Julia Kristeva,

---

[19]For succinct overviews of the "history of the self" in Western thought, see Charles Taylor, "Overcoming Epistemology," in Baynes, *After Philosophy*, 464–88; Agnes Heller, "Death of the Subject?" in Levine, *Constructions of the Self*, 269–84; Seyla Benhabib, "Feminism and the Question of Postmodernism," in *Situating the Self: Gender, Community, and Postmodernism in Contemporary Ethics* (New York: Routledge, 1992), 202–41.

[20]See Jacques Lacan, *Ecrits: A Selection*, trans. A. Sheridan (New York: W. W. Norton, 1977); Lacan, *The Four Fundamental Concepts of Psychoanalysis*, trans. A. Sheridan (New York: W. W. Norton, 1964); John P. Muller and William J. Richardson, *Lacan and Language: A Reader's Guide to Ecrits* (New York: International Universities Press, 1982). For an alternate reading of Freud, see Ernest Wallwork, *Psychoanalysis and Ethics* (New Haven, CT: Yale University Press, 1991).

and Luce Irigaray[21] have all in various ways presented a diffused self, submerged in forces not so much within it as outside of it in society and culture, desiring breakthroughs into new matrices of language, power, and thought. Rorty argues for the rejection of a "core self" in favor of a "web of relations to be rewoven," replacing the notion of a "formed, unified, present, self-contained substance" with a "tissue of contingent relations," stretching into the past and into the future.[22] Oddly enough, postmodernism (as in at least some stages of the thought of, for example, Derrida, Lyotard, and Foucault) offers views both of a decentered, nonoriginary, socially constructed and controlled self, and of a newly released Nietzschean self that is aggressively self-inventive, self-creating, attempting to break all boundaries of theory, obligation, or tradition.

If the "self" is really dead; if there is only process and relation without agency; if there is indiscriminate desire and no real choice of affective response issuing in action; if there are only protean masks and not even a Proteus behind the masks; then there is not much point in asking how we shall love in a postmodern world. Either we will not love in any recognizable sense at all, or we will not be responsible for our socially constructed loves. We will all be like Pixote, moving as in a dream, indifferent to love or compassion, fear or contempt.

But the debates about the self, fueled by postmodern critique, may indeed have given it new life. Three proposals seem to me to be particularly significant in this regard, and particularly helpful in pursuing my question of how we shall love. The three proposals I have in mind are from disparate sources, but they all relate to the issues of the self that have preoccupied modern and postmodern thinkers. I can do no more here than cite them briefly.

The first proposal comes from Charles Taylor's important work not only on the sources of "modern identity" but on the need for a "strong sense" of the self.[23] Taylor argues that the modern understanding of the self as disengaged, representing to itself an objective world which it can instrumentalize, is too "thin" a conception of the self. In opposition

---

[21]I am uncertain whether Julia Kristeva has modified her view of the self in her essay, "Psychoanalysis and the Imaginary," in Levine, *Constructions of the Self*, 285–97. There is some hint here of the possibility of a resurrected subject.

[22]Rorty, *Contingency, Irony, and Solidarity*, 41–43.

[23]See Charles Taylor, *Sources of the Self: The Making of the Modern Identity* (Cambridge, MA: Harvard University Press, 1989); Taylor, *Human Agency and Language: Philosophical Papers*, vol. 1 (New York: Cambridge University Press, 1985).

to this notion of the self, Taylor proposes a "strong sense" of the self, a sense in which the self is not merely a "bearer of preferences" but a subject of "significance." That is, human persons are beings for whom things matter, have meaning, in a way that accounts for responses of shame, self-esteem, appreciation, love, and so forth. As such, personal agency is more than mere planning, directing, controlling. Here is a self that is not isolated from the rest of the world, not over against what it knows. Here is a self, we can surmise, that can be affected by what is not itself, that can respond with both spontaneity and freedom—a self that is engaged yet not thereby wholly lost as a self.[24]

A second proposal is the one contained in Seyla Benhabib's considerations of what feminism can find useful in postmodern thought. Benhabib distinguishes "strong" and "weak" versions of the postmodern thesis of the death of Man (the death of the subject or self).[25] In the strong version, the subject dissolves into a "web of fictive meaning," becoming "merely another position in language."[26] There is left no trace of autonomy, purposiveness, self-possession, responsibility. The weak version, on the other hand, recognizes that subjectivity is contextually situated, socially structured (by language, narrative, culture); yet the subject is not reducible to heteronomous determination. Selfhood, in this version, is not merely a series of performances, not merely a process without any self-determination. We are, in other words, not only characters in our own stories but to some degree authors as well. Benhabib's point is that feminist theory can align with the weak version of this aspect of postmodern thought, but not the strong; for only the weak version allows room for ongoing critical theory. Whether or not one's concern is for a viable feminism, the weak version of the death of the self seems to accomplish more than the strong. It radically modifies the Enlightenment notion of autonomy (by incorporating the limits of cultural embeddedness), and it opens to new understandings of relationality; yet it does not (against reason and experience) relinquish freedom, intentionality, and accountability.[27]

---

[24]Taylor, *Human Agency and Language*, 1:97–114.

[25]Benhabib, *Situating the Self*, 213–18.

[26]Ibid., 214–15. The phrases belong to Jane Flax, who along with Judith Butler, Benhabib is opposing. See Jane Flax, *Psychoanalysis, Feminism, and Postmodernism in the Contemporary West* (Berkeley: University of California Press, 1990), 32ff.

[27]Postmodern philosophical writings are not without support for Benhabib's "weak" version. Rorty, for example, argues that individuals, while containing within themselves multiple roles, personalities, sets of belief and desire, can nonetheless "harmonize" these

The third proposal regarding the status of the self is lodged in Edith Wyschogrod's study of the relevance of stories of saints for a postmodern ethic.[28] Wyschogrod's problem is less the social construction of the self than the self inventive, self-creating notion of "self" that finally is no-self. Postmodernity's "language of desire," "libidinal economy," yields to no boundaries (not laws, not the past, not a charactered self). The decentering of the subject by unlimited desire makes individuation (and hence also unity) of the self impossible; the saint and the sufferer disappear. Wyschogrod's solution to this problem is not to jettison the language of desire but to give it a boundary when it meets the Other. The saint, responding to the Other, achieves selfhood only in relation to the Other. The source of decentering becomes the possibility of new centering; the death of the self yields the life of the self. For Wyschogrod, the saint is the model for postmodern love.

Wyschogrod is not alone in focusing on the Other. While unselfish love is not of much interest to most postmodern writers, there are ways in which the modern concern for otherness is advanced by postmodern considerations.[29] Indeed, postmoderns steadfastly privilege otherness, difference, concrete particularity rather than sameness and universality. In a variety of contexts, they do not allow us to turn away from what is different from ourselves, even different within ourselves; that is, they challenge the complacency of our ordinary and familiar interpretations of everything. Barbara Johnson, for example, says of a deconstructionist reading of a text: "A reading is strong . . . to the extent that it encounters and propagates the surprise of otherness."[30] What deconstruction aims to do is to demystify our familiar understandings, but its goal is not necessarily an infinite regress into nothingness. The surprise that an encounter with otherness can hold is a discovery of error and of an ignorance we did not know we had. Ignorance, in turn,

---

various roles. Moreover, such harmonizing, integrating into a "unifying story about oneself," is desirable. Freedom is thereby achieved (though not unfolded as if it always already existed within the self). "Personhood" is a "matter of degree." See Rorty, "Feminism and Pragmatism," 15n22, 25–35.

[28]See Wyschogrod, *Saints and Postmodernism*, 233–57. For my own development of some of these ideas, see Margaret A. Farley, "A Feminist Version of Respect for Persons," *Journal of Feminist Studies in Religion* 9 (Spring 1993): 183–98; also in this volume.

[29]For a careful history of the development of concern for the Other in twentieth-century philosophy, see Michael Theunissen, *The Other: Studies in the Social Ontology of Husserl, Heidegger, Sartre, and Buber*, trans. C. Macann (Cambridge, MA: MIT Press, 1984).

[30]Barbara Johnson, *A World of Difference* (Baltimore: Johns Hopkins University Press, 1987), 15.

can be not merely a gap in knowledge but an imperative.[31]

If there are, after all, selves in a postmodern world, and if we become selves in relation to others, can we finally answer our questions about love? Probably not yet, at least not without a few more exploratory steps. For one thing, we need to consider more carefully how the self can be *affected* by the Other. The Other is a limit that aids self-definition and self-individuation, but can the postmodern Other awaken love? Can the pain of the Other awaken compassion?

Despite the fact that Nietzsche's influence on postmodernity cuts deeply against receptivity (in favor of active self-making), there are ways in which some strands of postmodern thought are at least amenable to the kinds of experiences of love and of the suffering of others to which I have pointed above. The modern subject cut off from the world is now immersed in the world; no longer preoccupied with self-certainty in settled truth, the subject is freed for relationship. The self has a capacity for being affected by an Other. Against Nietzsche, and against the kind of influences on the self that have to do only with impersonal power, there are some postmodern voices (or at least participants in postmodern discussions) that speak of the importance of sympathy, solicitude, and compassion. As Rorty puts it, pain is nonlinguistic, and not only can we "notice" it but we can respond to it with compassion.[32] Wyschogrod's saints are what they are (and exemplars for the rest of us) because they render themselves vulnerable to the suffering of others. "What is other than the self can affect the self through pain or wounding."[33] For Paul Ricoeur (not, of course, a postmodern in any narrow sense of the term, but in conversation with postmodern writers), solicitude for the suffering of another is a location for relationship that is both receptive and active, receiving and giving.[34]

That we can love in a postmodern world seems to me beyond ques-

---

[31]Ibid., 16.

[32]See Rorty, *Contingency, Irony, and Solidarity*, 94. Although I agree with Timothy Jackson that a Christian concept of *agape* is both fuller and different from anything proposed by Rorty, I think Rorty the "postmodern" may offer more than Jackson finds in Rorty the "liberal." See Timothy P. Jackson, "Liberalism and *Agape*: The Priority of Charity to Democracy and Philosophy," *Annual of the Society of Christian Ethics* (1993), 47–72.

[33]See Wyschogrod, *Saints and Postmodernism*, 98 and passim.

[34]Paul Ricoeur, *Oneself as Another*, trans. K. Blarney (Chicago: University of Chicago Press, 1992), 190–91. Ricoeur takes pains to differentiate his analysis from that of Emmanuel Levinas, even as he writes appreciatively of Levinas's work in this regard.

tion, even though there are winds of philosophical thought that blow other ways. As to how we ought to love in this world, however, we have in the end only clues. One of them is to value stories, and through stories to pay attention to the concrete lives of individuals and groups. A second, emerging from the first, is not to suppress difference; to meet the other as really other, not simply as another of myself. A third may be to take seriously the embeddedness of human life—embodiment in all its layers of flesh, of dwelling, of relationships, of culture; to take seriously both beauty and pain, of the body and the spirit, of the individual and the culture. Yet another clue might be to care for potentiality, not only actuality—for what someone has not yet been allowed to be or even think to become, for what has been oppressed or repressed by whatever forces of ignorance or power. And a final clue: across the premodern, modern, and postmodern worlds, never to underestimate the form of decentering that comes from reverence in the beholding of beauty and compassion in the face of pain.

I began with some stories. They remain as my measure and my challenge. Pixote tells us not only that we have certain possibilities but profound needs; and when these are not met, there comes a contradiction in our being, a wound that cannot remain hidden. Schwartz's "Aria" sings of love's power to awaken to beauty and to bring it to newness; it is the song of the self in a "strong sense," full of yearning for wholeness and union. The woman in the Venezuelan fields will not let us turn from the limits of human endurance, will not let us forget that pain needs no language and responsibility crosses borders that we do not expect.

Do I thus do violence to a postmodern taboo, moving from the arguments of experience to the arguments of principle? Perhaps, though my intention has been to appreciate the contributions and the problems of a postmodern age. In so doing, it seems fair to conclude that we should love in a postmodern world in the same way we should love in any world—where Pixote must not be ignored; where lovers are to heal one another of shame; where the cry of sufferers is not to be silenced. I end where I began, for this is still only a banquet, and our own concrete lives, in whatever our world, remain to be lived.

CHAPTER 9

Ethics, Ecclesiology, and the Grace of Self-Doubt

What is the influence of ecclesiology on ethics, or ethics on ecclesiology? The tempting answer to both of these questions, framed almost anywhere we want to look in the long history of the Roman Catholic Church, is simple: There is no influence, one way or the other. Theological construals of what the church is or should be have little to do with the content of moral theology, and moral theology (or ethics) is seldom brought to bear on our understandings of church. If we limit the questions to the recent history of Catholic theology, say from the middle of the twentieth century to the beginning of the twenty-first, the answer seems even clearer. Ecclesiology and ethics share a common context, the church, but they seldom if ever interact.[1]

However tempting such a response may be, the historical and contemporary situations are much more complex. In the past or the present, if theologies of church as such do not shape moral theology and vice versa, the actual mode of life in the church does influence its moral discernment and teaching. And—at least to some extent—our understandings of church have an influence on its life. We can say more than this, however. In an important sense, the

A version of this essay was originally published in *A Call to Fidelity: On the Moral Theology of Charles E. Curran*, ed. James J. Walter, Timothy E. O'Connell, and Thomas A. Shannon (Washington, DC: Georgetown University Press, 2002), 55-75. Copyright by Georgetown University Press. Reprinted with permission. www.press.georgetown.edu.

[1]Unless otherwise indicated, Farley uses the terms "ethics" and "moral theology" interchangeably. Without burdening the text with descriptives, both will refer to the theological discipline of reflecting on questions of morality within the Roman Catholic tradition. This is, of course, a kind of shorthand, and when necessary, is augmented with clarifying distinctions or designations.

twentieth century was the century for ecclesiology, and the last third of the century has frequently been described as the "age of ethics." It was therefore inevitable that theological paths would cross—that ethical assessments would be made of the church itself, as well as of theologies of church, and that interpretations of the nature and function of the church would play a role in ethical debates.

It is instructive to trace twentieth-century interactions between ecclesiologists and church leaders and between church leaders and moral theologians. The most dramatic interactions are adversarial, and the debates turn less often on issues of morality than on issues of church authority. Though some of the participants play more than one role, the adversaries are frequently church leaders and moral theologians, with ecclesiology providing the main lines of the no-longer-surprising plot. A more sobering interpretation of the drama, however, recognizes this as only a subplot. The major story is about what happens to the vast numbers of faithful members of the Catholic Church—largely observers of the subplot, though relentlessly drawn into it, with their lives at stake. A key question raised by this story is: Why is the church's teaching on many ethical issues so divisive or so ineffective? Or, to narrow the question more fairly: Why does the official teaching of the church on certain ethical issues appear to be unconvincing to so many of its members?

The answer to this question may be embedded in the story itself, or it may be obscured by the more visible onstage actions that are part of the subplot. This essay explores the lines of the subplot, but in search of an understanding of the main one. It begins with the work of Charles E. Curran, the moral theologian whose life and writings, more than any of his peers, have been at the center of the subplot, and whose own work suggests interpretations of the story as a whole. The essay then moves to the broader stage of developments in the Roman Catholic tradition since Vatican II—developments in ecclesiology, moral theology, the writings and actions of church leaders, and the general life of the church. The final section of the essay addresses directly the question of "reception" on the part of the faithful—the internalization, or not, of official church teachings. Here I examine the concept of "self-doubt" on the part of everyone involved in relation to the experience of moral obligation—a set of considerations whose relevance will, I hope, become clearer as we proceed. These are all large tasks, so I make no pretense in this essay of pursuing them further than to suggest possible renderings of the story and interpretations of its meaning.

Charles E. Curran: The Meeting of Ecclesiology and Ethics

Of the more than three dozen books authored by Charles Curran as well as the dozen and a half edited or coedited by him, on my count only a very few do not address some aspect of the relationship between ecclesiology and ethics. Throughout most of his more than forty years of thinking about this relationship, Curran provides brief, sometimes repeated, considerations that nonetheless add up to a whole that he himself has not yet drawn together completely.[2] These considerations cover methodological issues in moral theology, a basic theology of the teaching function and office of the church, the relation between theologians and the hierarchical magisterium, justification of dissent from noninfallible but official church teachings, and general considerations of power in the church (including considerations of church/state relations). Curran provides historical overviews of these issues, critical analyses, and constructive recommendations for the ways in which church leaders and theologians should relate. Overall, it seems fair to say that for Curran the ultimate issue in all of this is moral discernment in the church—the capacitation of the church as a moral community that lives in the world.

Curran's path to this central issue is direct but not simple. At the very beginning of his academic career, he wrote doctoral dissertations on the limits of moral knowledge available through natural law[3] and on the medical treatment of women after rape.[4] His attention is later drawn to the troubling questions of the relation between ecclesiology and ethics and between church leaders and ethicists because of the difficulties encountered by theologians and others regarding the teaching of the church on artificial contraception. His own experience of

---

[2] I say this despite the more lengthy treatment Curran gives to these matters in at least three of his later works: *The Living Tradition of Catholic Moral Theology* (Notre Dame, IN: University of Notre Dame, 1992), chaps. 5–6; *Church and Morality* (Minneapolis: Fortress, 1993); and *The Catholic Moral Tradition Today: A Synthesis* (Washington, DC: Georgetown University, 1999), chaps. 1, 2, and 8.

[3] Charles E. Curran, *Invincible Ignorance of the Natural According to St. Alphonsus* (Rome: Academia Alfonsiana, 1961).

[4] Curran, *The Prevention of Conception after Rape: An Historical Theological Study* (Rome: Pontificia Universitas Gregoriana, 1961).

struggle with church authorities over this and other normative ethical questions stands as a kind of defining moment for the post–Vatican II church, and surely for his own professional life. The documentation of this shared struggle is itself a significant contribution to any efforts to address these troubling issues.[5]

Limitations on the roles both of church leaders and moral theologians are at the heart of Curran's theological perspective on the teaching function of the church. Although he has never hesitated to affirm the need for some kind of hierarchical structure in the church, Curran has long been opposed to "hierarchology"—or the theological commitment to a "pyramid" structure of the church whereby absolute authority exists at the top. Consistent with and part and parcel of this rejection of total hierarchy, Curran again and again reiterates a view of the teaching function of the church as broader than the church's teaching office.[6] Function and office are not to be conflated; they are not identical. Rather, the teaching function includes all of the church's members in a way that is analogous to the priesthood of all believers. Just as there are "different kinds of sharing in the priesthood of Jesus," so "all share in some way in the teaching function of Jesus."[7] Correlatively all are learners, one from the other. "There can be no absolute division between the hierarchy as the teaching church and the rest of the faithful as the learning church."[8] If there is some role for everyone in the teaching function of the church, then all roles have their limits; all are part of a whole.

The task of theologians is carried out within the whole of the teaching and learning church. It is a limited task—limited by its very nature (as a discipline of learning), by the diverse ministries of theology and church leadership, and by its dependence on and service of the faithful. Theologians must look to the sources of insight into Christian faith—scripture, tradition, reason, and experience (not just their own experience, but the experience of others in the church).[9] They must

---

[5]Charles E. Curran and Robert E. Hunt et al., *Dissent in and for the Church: Theologians and Humanae Vitae* (New York: Sheed and Ward, 1969); Curran, *Faithful Dissent* (Kansas City, MO: Sheed and Ward, 1986).

[6]See for example, Curran, *Themes in Fundamental Moral Theology* (Notre Dame, IN: University of Notre Dame, 1977), 114; *Moral Theology: A Continuing Journey* (Notre Dame, IN: University of Notre Dame, 1982), 4; *Catholic Moral Tradition Today*, 197–98.

[7]Curran, *Moral Theology*, 4.

[8]Ibid.

[9]Curran, *Catholic Moral Tradition Today*, 47–55.

also listen to and respect the judgments articulated by hierarchical church authorities as they, too, interpret scripture and tradition and relate to the whole church.

Similarly, the task and authority of those who hold teaching offices in the church are limited—by the same sources to which theologians must turn, by the need to listen and learn from all members of the church, and by important dependence on the work of theologians in the past and in the present. The limited nature of the church's teaching office correlates with Curran's general understanding of the nature of the church. His is a post–Vatican II ecclesiology that emphasizes the sacramental and communal aspects of the church and that seeks to move from a juridical model to a model imaged as the People of God.[10] It remains important for the Roman Catholic tradition to affirm the visible nature of the church, and hence the significance of structure. Yet this is a pilgrim church, "between the times" and in continual need of reform, including a reform of its institutional structure. In the aftermath of Vatican II, Curran was arguing for the decentralization of power in the church, fuller participation by all members, and collegiality with co-responsibility—within the hierarchy and between the hierarchy and theologians.[11]

The issue of dissent, including public dissent on the part of theologians, was the issue that sharpened Curran's articulation of the limits of the teaching office of the church. He interpreted his own positions regarding artificial contraception, divorce and remarriage, homosexuality, and related issues (particularly in sexual ethics) as faithful, justifiable dissent from official church teachings of the time. Vatican authorities judged that his dissent was not legitimate, and their discipline was to deny him his faculty position as a Catholic theologian at Catholic University of America. Curran's defense of his and others' dissent was not an appeal to freedom of conscience but to a theology of the church's teaching function and office.[12] He and

---

[10]Curran and Hunt, *Dissent in and for the Church*, 96–97; Curran, *Critical Concerns in Moral Theology* (Notre Dame, IN: University of Notre Dame, 1984), chap. 1; *Toward an American Catholic Moral Theology* (Notre Dame, IN: University of Notre Dame, 1987), 150–57; *Living Tradition of Catholic Moral Theology; Catholic Moral Tradition Today*, chap. 1.

[11]Curran and Hunt, *Dissent in and for the Church*; Curran, *Catholic Moral Theology in Dialogue* (Notre Dame, IN: Fides, 1972; repr. University of Notre Dame, 1976), chap. 5.

[12]Charles E. Curran, ed., *Contraception, Authority, and Dissent* (New York: Herder and Herder, 1969), 11.

other theologians, canonists, and church historians argued that there is a long and honorable tradition of Roman Catholic theology and practice that allows and can even welcome dissent that is both respectful of the hierarchical teaching office and offers carefully reasoned alternative positions.[13]

What lies behind a theological justification of dissent, as well as behind the limitations of the teaching office, is ultimately the nature of moral knowledge. Curran notes repeatedly throughout his writings the many ways in which knowledge of specific moral norms is contingent, limited, subject to error, not conducive to certitude. In a tradition that has generally eschewed voluntaristic divine or ecclesiastical command theories, there is a long-standing and deep conviction that moral obligation depends on moral insight.[14] That is, the sheer will of a lawgiver is not a sufficient ground for moral obligation. Even God's commands—from God's wisdom as well as God's will—have a content whose meaning is ordinarily and at least to some degree accessible to those who receive them. Creation is revelatory of moral claims; scripture and tradition provide lenses for interpreting God's will; grace heals in part the injuries to mind and heart that are the result of sin; graced human reason, therefore, is capable of moral discernment. Yet moral discernment is difficult, imperfect, likely to be diverse, and never completed. Except for extremely important general moral convictions, the church and each person in it must continue the process of discerning and deliberating about what we should do and how we should live together.

Like Thomas Aquinas, Curran believes that moral knowledge is more subject to contingencies the closer it gets to particulars. Hence, whatever infallible powers the teaching church may have, they do not reach to the problems of particular ethical norms. Processes of discernment and deliberation inevitably include disagreement, mistakes,

---

[13]Ibid., 9–15; Curran and Hunt, *Dissent in and for the Church*, 133ff.; Curran, *Themes in Fundamental Theology*, 111.

[14]Curran frequently notes two strands in the Catholic tradition—strands identified with Aquinas on the one hand and Scotus and Suarez on the other. The former strand views law primarily as an ordinance of reason, and the latter sees it primarily in terms of the will of the legislator. It is the former that has prevailed in the Catholic tradition overall, certainly in the contemporary period. See, e.g., Curran, *A New Look at Christian Morality* (Notre Dame, IN: Fides, 1968), 128–30; *Contemporary Problems in Moral Theology* (Notre Dame, IN: Fides, 1970), 138–42; *Directions in Fundamental Moral Theology* (Notre Dame, IN: University of Notre Dame, 1985), 200–202; *Toward an American Catholic Moral Theology*, 157–58; *Catholic Moral Tradition Today*, 1.

reversals, new insights, conversions of both heart and mind.[15] Moral certainty, therefore, comes in degrees, and dissent against noninfallible official church teachings can be not only justifiable but beneficial for the process as a whole. This does not mean that moral insight is finally unattainable, or that the church must be timid in articulating basic moral obligations and aspirations. It means that "the church can and does speak with a greater degree of certitude on the level of more general values, goals, attitudes, dispositions and norms" than when it speaks on specific issues; for the latter, it "must realize that its statements cannot claim to have absolute certitude."[16]

If the teaching and learning functions of the whole church are to serve effectively the church's mission to the world, it will not be because human limitations in moral knowing are completely transcended. The assistance of the Holy Spirit is real, but it does not work by magically overwhelming human capacities. The truth that the church as a community holds and shares with generations of believers is not the totality of all truth, not a truth once and for all fully possessed.[17] The moral insight that believers achieve is always partial, always the object of further search in ever new human situations. There is a legitimate presumption in favor of the church's official teachings, but it is not sufficient to begin and end with this presumption. For if this teaching is about particular moral norms, then it is noninfallible teaching, which is to say that it may be wrong. Moreover, the presumption will be weakened if those in a teaching office do not properly carry out their role in relation to the roles of others in the church.[18]

Given these understandings of the church, its participative teaching function, and the nature of moral knowledge, Curran recommends strategies requisite for communal moral discernment. First is epistemic humility. The church, in particular its leaders, must remove the "albatross of certitude" that prevents it from relating the gospel message more effectively to the modern (and postmodern) world.[19] Accepting the limits of moral insight, the church can more graciously acknowledge the legitimacy of disagreement and dissent. It can live as

---

[15]Curran, *Directions in Catholic Social Ethics* (Notre Dame, IN: University of Notre Dame, 1985), 119-23; *Living Tradition of Catholic Moral Theology*, 114-20.

[16]Curran, *New Perspectives in Moral Theology* (Notre Dame, IN: Fides, 1974), 154–55.

[17]Curran, *Living Tradition of Catholic Moral Theology*, 112.

[18]Ibid., 120.

[19]Curran, *New Perspectives in Moral Theology*, 155.

a community of moral conviction (regarding basic moral obligations such as love of enemies, compassion for the poor, prohibitions against genocide, and so forth); but this church can also risk recognizing itself as a "community of moral doubt," in need of the insights of others on troubling particular moral issues.[20] In accordance with this, the church can shape and use its structures in ways that best serve the requirements of learning as well as teaching—activating all levels of its life, local and universal, and enabling the voices of its members. Its laws can be assessed and valued insofar as they genuinely build the life of the community and bear witness to its faith and its love.[21]

Not surprisingly, Curran's more specific recommendations address the all too frequent tensions between hierarchical authorities and Catholic theologians. He wrote in 1982 that the primary responsibility for checking errors in theology rests with the theological community, whose obligation as a community of scholars is to assess rigorously the work of its members. The hierarchical teaching office does have a "judicial function" in relation to the work of theologians, but judicial interventions should (1) be reserved to a category of "last resort"; made only after consultation with theologians of more than one school of theology; (2) begin at the local level, so that diversity in cultural experience and praxis can be taken into account; and (3) follow due process in every case.[22]

Curran insisted, then, that theologians must be self-critical and open to dialogue with all other theologians in the church. But in 1992 he followed Richard McCormick in also identifying corrective attitudes and actions required of the hierarchy.[23] Holders of the hierarchical teaching office must acknowledge different levels (of gravity) of church teaching, admit past mistakes, refuse to collapse the teaching role of bishops into the teaching role of the papacy, consult widely on moral matters, recognize that discernment is a process, revise procedures for overseeing theological work, and overall introduce a more communal form of discernment in the church.[24]

I suggested earlier that Charles Curran's ultimate concern in all of

---

[20]Curran, *Church and Morality*, 10–11.

[21]Curran, *Directions in Fundamental Moral Theology*, 199.

[22]Curran, *Moral Theology*, 9–10.

[23]Richard A. McCormick, *The Critical Calling: Reflections on Moral Dilemmas since Vatican II* (Washington, DC: Georgetown University, 1989), 142–45.

[24]Curran, *Living Tradition of Catholic Moral Theology*, 126–29.

his considerations of the relationship between ecclesiology and ethics has been the capacitation of the church as a moral community with internal responsibilities and a mission in and to the world. We may now be at a point where the force of that judgment becomes clear. Church structures serve a "discerning church"[25] when they facilitate effective and creative moral discourse and when they nurture the moral lives of individuals and the church as a whole. Because of the limited nature of moral knowledge as well as the intrinsic significance of communal participation, teaching and learning thrive when church leaders, theologians, and all the faithful collaborate in the discernment and fulfillment of moral obligations. No longer theorized as a "perfect society" sufficient unto itself with an unchanging and absolute hierarchical order, the church is nonetheless a "unique community,"[26] one in which moral deliberation and action can be nurtured. Inerrancy in moral matters is not guaranteed by the grace of office; but a decentralized church in which inclusive "catholicity," functioning through different levels of authority and diverse ministries, offers an "antidote" to many of the risks of error that beset even graced humanity.

For these reasons, Curran laments the inattention given to the moral formation of the church community, or even to theological reflection on the "ecclesial context" of the moral life of believers.[27] He insists on the utter importance of the role of the faithful in discernment and action[28] and provides brief analyses of relevant aspects of moral experience, decision-making, judgment, and the formation of conscience in the context of the church.[29] It is to these concerns that I will return in the final section of this essay. For now, however, it is useful to turn to the broader stage on which ecclesiology and moral theology have been developing since Vatican II. This will help to place Curran's work in theological and ecclesial context, but it will also provide a fuller background for pursuing questions of the requirements for moral discourse in a discerning church.

---

[25]Curran, *Church and Morality*, 46.

[26]Curran, *Directions in Fundamental Moral Theology*, 199; *Toward an American Catholic Moral Theology*, 167. For the rejection of "perfect society" notions of the church, see Curran, *New Perspectives in Moral Theology*, 146; *Critical Concerns in Moral Theology*, 26.

[27] Curran, *Catholic Moral Tradition Today: A Synthesis*, 2–3.

[28]Curran, *Living Tradition of Catholic Moral Theology*, 120–22.

[29]Curran, *Catholic Moral Theology in Dialogue*, 174; *Living Tradition of Catholic Moral Theology*, 120–22; *Catholic Moral Tradition Today*, chap. 7.

Ecclesiology and Ethics: The Post–Vatican II Struggle

The twentieth century marked an extraordinary move by ecclesiology to the center of the theological stage. Surveys of the important writings abound, some focusing on the relationship of ecclesiology to ethics.[30] There is no need to repeat these surveys here, but it is important not to underestimate the ecclesiological sea changes that have taken place as well as the intensity of the theological conflicts that surged before and in the aftermath of Vatican II. This council produced two constitutions focused entirely on the church, one dogmatic (*Lumen gentium*) and the other pastoral (*Gaudium et spes*), and most of its other documents address ecclesiological issues as well. The council did not happen in a vacuum, nor did the sea-changes it brought about begin or end with the council itself. One needs only to think of names like Emile Mersch, Henri de Lubac, Yves Congar, Karl Rahner, and later Hans Küng, Edward Schillebeeckx, Avery Dulles, Rosemary Radford Ruether, Leonardo Boff, Hans Urs von Balthasar, and many others, to remember the kind of theological work, precisely in ecclesiology, that preceded and followed the council. Though the fortunes of theologies of the mystical body, historical studies of church reform, and critiques of church structures have risen and fallen more than once, this work informed the council and became part of the debates in its wake.

The council said very little explicitly about ethics, but what it said about the church—its life and its practices—had great influence on developments in the method and substance of ethical thought. Issues like the meaning of church as the People of God, the role of the laity in the church, the church as a world church, religious liberty, the func-

---

[30] I am particularly dependent on essays by Avery Dulles, "A Half Century of Ecclesiology," *Theological Studies* 50 (September 1989): 419–42; Mary E. Hines, "Community for Liberation," in *Freeing Theology: The Essentials of Theology in Feminist Perspective*, ed. Catherine Mowry LaCugna (New York: HarperCollins, 1993), 161–84; and Richard A. McCormick, "Moral Theology, 1940–1989: An Overview," *Theological Studies* 50 (March 1989): 3–24. Charles Curran also provides many useful historical overviews throughout his writings, as in *Transition and Tradition in Moral Theology* (Notre Dame, IN: University of Notre Dame, 1979), 3–28; *Toward an American Catholic Moral Theology*, 157–61; *The Origins of Moral Theology in the United States: Three Different Approaches* (Washington, DC: Georgetown, 1992); *Moral Theology at the End of the Century* (Milwaukee: Marquette University, 1999). An excellent overall resource is Charles E. Curran and Richard A. McCormick, eds., *Readings in Moral Theology No. 3: The Magisterium and Morality* (New York: Paulist, 1982).

tion of the local church in relation to the church universal, openness of the church to the world, ecumenism, development of doctrine, the church as pilgrim church—each yielded new questions about a theology of communion, cultural diversity, freedom of conscience, the core and peripheral status of truths, the "sense of the faithful" as source and confirmation of church teaching, the church's mission, corporate responsibility, and on and on. All of these questions are questions not only for ecclesiology but for ethics. They have been extended with an urgency pressed in political theologies, liberation theologies, and the many forms of feminist theology, where the line between systematic and moral theology has been usefully blurred for some time.

In pursuit of the overall questions of this essay, I will focus on only two of the major ecclesiological issues that have preoccupied the church and its theologians since Vatican II and that are today still fraught with difficulties and conflicts. These issues are of clear importance for moral theology, and they have implications for just about every other issue, large or small, that I have identified above. The first has to do with ecclesiological concepts of "communion." The second is embedded in the many debates about teaching authority in the church. These two issues are not unrelated because church structures and functions are inseparable from whatever it means for the Roman Catholic Church to be a community.

Communion and Its Discontents

By far the dominant paradigm for the church coming from Vatican II was that of the People of God.[31] Countering the narrowly institutional representations of the church that held sway through most of the second millennium, this image represented new understandings of the church's relation to God and, even more importantly, the possibility of newly structured relationships among its members. It was not in opposition to an earlier-twentieth-century Mystical Body of Christ theology, though it added historicity, visibility, and mission to what might otherwise be too mystical, organic, and spiritual a view of the church. Moreover, while both Body of Christ and People of God im-

---

[31]Others have noted this, but the landmark work of Avery Dulles helped to situate this in the context of the council as well as in a broader historical and theological context. See Dulles, *Models of the Church* (New York: Doubleday, 1974), esp. chaps. 1 and 3.

ages could accommodate democratic tendencies, organic metaphors (frequently part of the meaning of "Body of Christ") generally proved less conducive than covenantal ones (frequently intrinsic to understandings of "People of God") in this regard.

The concept of "communion" has in some ways worked well with the People of God paradigm. It provided "interiority" comparable to the Body of Christ metaphor; it could combine respect for the dignity of the individual with a concern for the common good; and it incorporated notions of diversity in community. Significant contributions to a theology of communion (or *koinonia*, community) were made by Catholic theologians such as Charles Journet, Henri de Lubac, Yves Congar,[32] and later Heribert Mühlen[33] and J. M. R. Tillard.[34] For all of these thinkers, an ecclesiology of communion included a vertical meaning (the church and its members in communion with God) and a horizontal meaning (the members called to communion with one another in the church). It therefore was lodged in and incorporated doctrines of the Trinity and incarnation on the one hand and the risen Christ and Eucharist on the other.[35]

The richness of the concept of *communio* has had wide appeal, but its very breadth and depth can mask serious differences in theological perspectives. When focused on "community," for example, it has served a new theological communitarianism, particularly in ecumenical circles. It has also shown the limits of too narrow an appeal to communitarianism. Since 1992 the World Council of Churches has attempted to address the divide between its projects on Faith and Order and on Life and Work. Concern to achieve a unified voice on issues of peace and justice prompted a study of the relationship between ecclesiology and ethics.[36] Strongly influenced by ethicists such as Stanley Hauerwas,

---

[32]For succinct but thoughtful overviews of the relevant works of Journet, de Lubac, and Congar, see Dennis M. Doyle, "Journet, Congar, and the Roots of Communion Ecclesiology," *Theological Studies* 58 (September 1997): 461–79; and Doyle, "Henri de Lubac and the Roots of Communion Ecclesiology," *Theological Studies* 60 (June 1999): 209–27.

[33]Heribert Mühlen, *Une Persona mystica*, 3rd ed. (Paderborn, Germany: Schöningh, 1968).

[34]J. M. R. Tillard, *Church of Churches: An Ecclesiology of Communion*, trans. R. C. Peaux (Collegeville, MN: Liturgical, 1992); see also his "The Church of God Is a Communion: The Ecclesiological Perspective of Vatican II," *One in Christ* 17 (1981): 117–31.

[35]See, e.g., Tillard, "Church of God Is a Communion," 118–25.

[36]For useful insights into the WCC process, see Lewis S. Mudge, "Ecclesiology and Ethics in Current Ecumenical Debate," *Ecumenical Review* 48 (January 1996): 11–27;

John Howard Yoder, and John Milbank, this work focused on the question of the formation of community, of *koinonia*. The insights from this study have been valuable for Protestants, Orthodox, and Roman Catholics alike.[37] Yet the tendency of the study to cede discussion of church-dividing ethical issues to discussion of the church itself *as a* social ethic did not fulfill the hopes of all WCC participants. And for many Roman Catholic readers of the study, the integration of mission in the world, solidarity with the poor, and universal concerns for justice was not yet adequate. Missing, too, were many of the creative insights of feminist scholars, both Catholic and Protestant, on the nature of the church community and its tasks in relation to the world.[38]

Theologies of *communio* have had other important implications for ecumenism—some of these equally relevant to ethics and equally controversial. There is, for example, the question of the relationship of all the Christian churches to one another. Congar argued that a view of the church that gives priority to communion can accommodate both unity and diversity among the Christian traditions.[39] From an eschatological point of view, there are degrees of unity. But there is a unity already present among Christians, a unity sufficient to be named "communion" and, as I have maintained elsewhere, sufficient to allow Christians to welcome one another to their table.[40] This view, of course, is disputed and is not represented in current official Roman Catholic Church teachings. It remains a troubling issue for communion ecclesiology and for ethics.

Mudge, "Towards a Hermeneutic of the Household: 'Ecclesiology and Ethics' after Harare," *Ecumenical Review* 51 (July 1999): 243–55; Werner Schwartz, "Church and Ethical Orientation: Moral Formation in the People of God," *Ecumenical Review* 51 (July 1999): 256–65; Arne Rasmusson, "Ecclesiology and Ethics: The Difficulties of Ecclesial Moral Reflection," *Ecumenical Review* 52 (April 2000): 1880–94.

[37]Reports of the consultations of the study are available in Thomas F. Best and Martin Robra, eds., *Ecclesiology and Ethics: Ethical Engagement, Moral Formation, and the Nature of the Church* (Geneva: WCC Publications, 1997).

[38]See, for example, Rosemary Radford Ruether, *Women-Church: Theology and Practice of Feminist Liturgical Communities* (New York: Harper and Row, 1985), esp. chap. 5; Letty M. Russell, *Church in the Round: Feminist Interpretation of the Church* (Louisville, KY: Westminster/John Knox Press, 1993); Serene Jones, *Feminist Theory and Christian Theology: Cartographies of Grace* (Minneapolis: Fortress, 2000), chaps. 6–7.

[39]Yves Congar, *Diversity and Communion* (Mystic, CT: Twenty-Third Publications, 1982).

[40]Margaret A. Farley, "No One Goes Away Hungry from the Table of the Lord: Eucharistic Sharing in Ecumenical Contexts," in *Practice What You Preach*, ed. James Keenan and Joseph Kotva (Kansas City, MO: Sheed and Ward, 1999), 186–201, included as chapter 10 in this volume.

Finally, a theology of communion has exacerbated some already disputed questions about relationships intrinsic to the Roman Catholic Church. These range from the relationships of local churches with one another and with the papacy, to relationships between the hierarchy and Catholic theologians. They are simultaneously issues of structural viability, diversity, and doctrinal development in a church that is deeply, if mysteriously, communal. They take us to the second major issue for ecclesiology and ethics that I have said I would address.

Authority and Its Afflictions

Ironies abound in the history of the Roman Catholic Church, but the ironies of the post–Vatican II era are surely among the greatest. Two theologies of church battled with each other prior to the Second Vatican Council. One appeared generally more persuasive in the council. To some extent, these same two theologies continue to battle after the council. "Descending" ecclesiology affirms the centralization of authority and power in the church, favors expanding the reach of claims of infallibility, views some church structures as absolutely unchangeable, is wary of pluralism, and continues to see the church as a bulwark against the dangers of much of contemporary society. "Ascending" ecclesiology (the approach generally taken in Vatican II) presses for important decentralization, resists what it calls "creeping infallibility," sees structure in the church as a modifiable instrument, views pluralism as inevitable in a "world church," and wants openness to the world both in its radical need and some of its achievements. Such descriptions are overly simple, no doubt, and no theologian would feel comfortable being placed completely in one school or the other. Yet at least the issues of development of doctrine, reform of the papacy, the relative authority of *Humanae vitae* and *Evangelium vitae*, historical aspects of church structure, uniformity and diversity, the hierarchy of truths, and so on, are often debated precisely along these lines.[41] Current struggles over the implementation of John Paul

---

[41]See, e.g., Avery Dulles, "Catholic Doctrine: Between Revelation and Theology," *Catholic Theological Society of America Proceedings* 54 (1999): 83–91; Richard A. Mc-Cormick, "Moral Doctrine: Stability and Development," *Catholic Theological Society of America Proceedings* 54 (1999): 92–100; John R. Quinn, *The Reform of the Papacy: The Costly Call to Christian Unity* (New York: Crossroad, 1999); Francis A. Sullivan, "The Doctrinal Weight of Evangelium Vitae," *Theological Studies* 56 (September 1995): 560–65; Congar, *Diversity and Communion*, parts 1 and 3; Tillard, "Church of God Is

II's 1990 *Ex corde ecclesiae* exhibit the divide as clearly as anything else—a divide in which, on the one hand, *communio* is interpreted in interior spiritual terms amenable to decentralization of authority in the church, and on the other, communion theology is aligned with juridical structures and a centralized, hierarchical view of the teaching function of the church.[42]

While sharp debates engage theologians on both sides of issues, attention has been focused in recent years on what I earlier described as a subplot in the story of the relationship between ecclesiology and ethics—that is, the theological and political struggle between many church leaders and many moral theologians. The ecclesiological spotlight here is on authority, both teaching and governing. As the action unfolds, we see a mounting effort on the part of church leaders to maintain one official voice on controversial moral (and other theological) issues. Document after document has attempted to settle once and for all the moral questions that continue to divide the teaching office of the church from the work of many theologians.[43] Along with multiple investigations of individual theologians, there have been still more documents aimed precisely at tightening the reins on theologians in the exercise of their craft.[44]

---

a Communion," 124–25; Hines, "Community for Liberation," 164–67; Germain Grisez and Francis A. Sullivan, "Quaestio Disputata: The Ordinary Magisterium's Infallibility," *Theological Studies* 55 (December 1994): 720–38. It is sometimes observed that the 1985 Synod of Bishops attempted to accommodate various ecclesiologies, though it did not by any means resolve the major divide. See Synod of Bishops, "The Final Report," *Origins*, December 19, 1985, 444–50.

[42]The first view is anticipated in the 1990 *Report of the Catholic Theological Society of America on the Profession of Faith and Oath of Fidelity*. The second is articulated in J. Augustine Di Noia, "Ecclesiology of Communion and Catholic Higher Education," *Origins*, October 7, 1999, 268–72.

[43]Consider, for example, not only *Humanae vitae* but the 1992 *Catechism of the Catholic Church*, *Ordinatio sacerdotalis* in 1994, *Evangelium vitae* in 1995, and countless papal letters and documents from the Congregation for the Doctrine of the Faith regarding issues in sexual ethics.

[44]Dramatic examples include the revised "Profession of Faith and Oath of Fidelity" mandated by the CDF in 1989; *Veritatis splendor* in 1993, which identified not only non-negotiable moral teachings but attacked whole schools of thought that were judged to foster departures from official teachings; *Ad tuendam fidem* in 1998, which established new canonical categories to restrict dissent; and the Vatican insistence on specific ordinances for the implementation of *Ex corde ecclesiae*, approved by the American bishops in 2001. An exception to this list of examples is the set of guidelines worked out between U.S. bishops and theologians, "Doctrinal Responsibilities: Approaches to Promoting Cooperation and Resolving Misunderstandings between Bishops and Theologians," *Origins*, June 29, 1989, 97–110.

However one interprets or evaluates these documents, they relegate to the shadows the deeper questions that press the church, its leaders and its theologians, regarding moral discernment and teaching. For example, should moral disputes, questions of moral truth, be settled by the command of those currently holding hierarchical power, or does this kind of ecclesiastical discipline contradict the very nature of moral discernment and moral insight? Is the ultimate authority of the church located in a central *sedes* that extends with absolute power to all corners of the church and to each individual's conscience? Or is the church first a community and second a structured community whose roles and offices derive their authority only as they serve the community well? Is the Catholic Church built on a tradition wherein moral insight must be informed, critiqued, nurtured, chastened, but finally freed for communal and individual moral action? Moreover, can moral questions have different answers in diverse cultures (all part of a world church) without yielding a full-scale moral relativism? And can disagreements be accommodated, sometimes within the same (even dominant) culture of the church without a loss of unity so serious that the church's prophetic witness is compromised?

As we have seen, much of the hard work on such questions has been done by systematic theologians and church historians like Tillard, Congar, Rahner, and Dulles.[45] But the questions are of utmost importance for moral theologians who along with colleagues in other theological disciplines continue the work of Häring, Curran, McCormick, and many others. A small essay like this is no place to adjudicate large questions, but I turn now to an issue that is relevant to them all—the issue of the reception of moral teachings by the faithful members of the church. My interest, however, is not finally in reception as such but in what it provides as a vantage point for an ecclesiology of a morally discerning and acting church.

---

[45]Only the space limits of this essay keep me from incorporating the monumental work of persons like Francis A. Sullivan in his *Magisterium: Teaching Authority in the Catholic Church* (New York: Paulist, 1983); and *Creative Fidelity: Weighing and Interpreting Documents of the Magisterium* (New York: Paulist, 1996); as well as John W. O'Malley, *Tradition and Transition: Historical Perspectives on Vatican II* (Wilmington, DE: Michael Glazier, 1989); and Ladislas M. Örsy, *The Church: Learning and Teaching* (Wilmington, DE: Michael Glazier, 1987). It is also hard to overestimate the contribution of biblical scholars such as Elisabeth Schüssler Fiorenza, *Discipleship of Equals: A Critical Feminist Ekklesia-logy of Liberation* (New York: Crossroad, 1993).

The Grace of Self-Doubt

While "reception" as a theological concept has various historical and contemporary connotations,[46] I will assume it to mean the acceptance and internalization of church teachings by the faithful members of the church. In this sense it is essentially connected with an active notion of the *sensus fidelium*—that is, the whole church searching for and sharing insights into what it believes and how it should act on what it believes. My concern is the reception of the moral teachings of the church and the participation of the faithful in the discernment and deliberation that lead to these teachings. The first step in my brief analysis is to consider once again the nature of moral knowledge.

We have already noted in relation to Charles Curran's work the generally accepted Catholic conviction that human reason is capable of some genuine moral insight, especially when it is graced by the power of the Holy Spirit. We have also noted that moral insight, rather than a blind surrender to a command, is at the heart of Catholic traditional understandings of moral obligation. But it is important to say more than this—for example, that a descriptive analysis of the experience of moral obligation reveals the following elements: (a) an experience of a *claim* that is (b) addressed to one's *freedom*, (c) experienced as *unconditional*, (d) perceived to be *justifiable*, and (e) experienced as both a *liberating appeal and an obligating demand*.[47] Insofar as moral obligation emerges in this kind of experience, moral obligations "make sense" to those who have these experiences; in other words, they are in some way and to some degree intelligible. For those who stand in the Catholic tradition, this "making sense" has almost everything to do

---

[46]For a succinct discussion of its meanings, see Lucien Richard, "Reflections on Dissent and Reception," in *The Church in the Nineties: Its Legacy, Its Future*, ed. Pierre M. Hegy (Collegeville, MN: Liturgical, 1993), 6–14. We need here, of course, a full-scale discussion of Canon 750, which on some readings gives very little importance to "reception," but on others points to the essential role of "Christ's faithful" in the very possibility of an ordinary universal magisterium.

[47]Of course, this means that any particular experience of moral obligation could be a mistake. That is, the claim might be misinterpreted; one might not be actually free to respond to the claim; it might not be unconditional; and it might prove to be unjustified. I am not here trying to describe the grounds for unconditionality, freedom, justifiability, but only to describe what does occur in our experience. A full description of this experience must wait for my forthcoming work on the experience of free choice. However, the elements I note here should not be surprising in that they intend to integrate what many others have partially identified.

with interpreting concrete reality in the light of reason and revelation.[48]

Because there is something that must be understood or recognized (something intelligible) at the heart of the experience of moral obligation, it is not possible to separate the question of moral "authority" from the question of moral "truth" (or "content" or "meaning").[49] Unless an individual recognizes the moral claim as a genuine one (based in the concrete realities that are confronted), there will be no experience of obligation; or if there is one, it will be the pragmatic (not moral) obligation to avoid punishment or to reap a reward depending on one's response to what is perceived as a (nonmoral) claim. Similarly, it is not possible for persons to experience moral obligation in response to the teaching or command of another unless they recognize the "truth" in what is being communicated—unless it makes some "sense." This does not mean that we need to discern for and by ourselves the answer to every moral question before we can recognize it when it comes from another, or that we cannot learn from others—those we recognize as "authorities" because we have learned to trust their wisdom or their experience or even their designation as authorities within our communities. Ultimately we learn from others because they help to make transparent the truth for which we seek.

If moral insight comes in a recognition of some moral truth, then it is not possible for persons (especially persons in a tradition that affirms this approach to moral matters) to experience moral obligation simply because they are told that they ought to.[50] They may do something only because they have been commanded to do so, but their response is a moral response only if they recognize a moral claim. The

---

[48]I am not unique in taking this position. It is what can be generally understood as one form of a Catholic natural law approach.

[49]I put "truth" within quotation marks to indicate its generally contested meaning and possibility. The questions surrounding this term are beyond the scope of this essay, but I do not think they vitiate the use I make of it here. I have treated this at somewhat greater length regarding the use of scripture as a source for theology and ethics. See "Feminist Consciousness and the Interpretation of Scripture," in *Feminist Interpretation of the Bible*, ed. Letty M. Russell and Shannon Clarkson (Philadelphia: Westminster, 1985), 41–51.

[50]I do not dispute the fact that those who believe that the root of moral obligation is solely or primarily in the authority of the commander will not necessarily need the command to make sense. This is certainly true of those whose religious and moral framework is based on a full-blown divine command theory. In this case, however, the basis of a moral command "making sense" is precisely that it comes from a recognized legitimate commander. This is not what characterizes much of the Roman Catholic tradition of moral theology. Hence, it is even notable that traditional Catholic interpretations of the Abraham and Isaac story tend to differ from traditional Protestant ones.

truth or genuineness of a moral claim—no matter how difficult its content—makes a nonviolent appeal to the human subject.[51] As such, it does not coerce the human person but obligates her, and in this, it also frees her to do what is most true to herself.[52]

If we add to this interpretation of moral obligation an acknowledgment of the limitations in all moral insight (Curran's position but also affirmed by most, perhaps all, contemporary Catholic moral theologians), we come close to explaining the pluralism among Catholics regarding particular moral questions. With some key issues such as artificial contraception, same-sex relationships, and second marriage after divorce, the diversity among Roman Catholics is not merely a matter of differing intellectual opinions but of profoundly divergent experiences of moral obligation. How, then, shall a discerning church accommodate such differences? Shall it tolerate them? Engage them in an ongoing process of moral discernment? Or repudiate those that differ from the present teachings of central church leaders? Theological and moral pluralism on such matters seems inevitable, even though consensus is a worthy goal for the church to pursue. Insofar as unanimity is desirable, however, how may it be sought in ways that respect the nature of moral knowledge and that capacitate a faith community for moral discernment?

Participants in the Catholic tradition believe that they are assisted by the Holy Spirit in their efforts to discern actions faithful to God's plan for creation. But one of the least recognized gifts of the Spirit may be what I call the "grace of self-doubt." If all co-believers are to participate in moral discernment in the church; and if the limited contribution of each requires the participation of the other; then all—laity, clergy, theologians, church leaders—have need of the grace of self-doubt. There are obvious objections to be made to such an assertion: for example, self-doubt is hardly grace-ful; it is a debility that can distract us, undermine our capacity for discernment, and cut the nerve of our action. Those with real power never yield to self-doubt, and those who do yield are doomed to ineffectiveness and despair. How, then, can the church raise a unified prophetic voice if it is infected with self-doubt?

---

[51]I draw here on a characterization of "truth" provided by Paul Ricoeur. See his *Essays on Biblical Interpretation*, ed. Lewis S. Mudge (Philadelphia: Fortress, 1980), 95.

[52]I realize I prescind here from many urgent philosophical questions about the nature of the human subject and the very possibility of becoming a self. In this brief essay, I can do no other.

These objections may be accurate. But there are different forms of self-doubt. There is the kind that must be overcome and the kind that must be achieved with grace. Often they are correlated with positions of powerlessness and power. It is *not a grace* for anyone to doubt fundamentally his or her own self-worth or the value of her experience and the possibility of his insight. Some forms of insecurity require transformation into strength. But there *is also a graced self-doubt*, needed perhaps especially by those who are in positions of power. If the greatest temptation of religious persons is self-righteousness, then the second-greatest is the grasping for certitude—fighting self-doubt in ways that shut the mind and sometimes close the heart. The grace of self-doubt is what allows for epistemic humility, the basic condition for communal as well as individual moral discernment (affirmed not only by Curran but by all who have understood the lessons of our age and the limits of moral epistemology). It is a grace accessible to those who struggle for understanding, those who have come to see things differently from what was once seen, those who have experienced the complexity of translating convictions into action.

This is not a grace for calling into question every fundamental conviction we have achieved. It will not foster doubt, for example, about the dignity of human persons or the trustworthiness of God's promises. It is a grace for recognizing the contingencies of moral knowledge when we stretch toward the particular and the concrete. It allows listening to the experience of others, taking seriously reasons that are alternative to our own, rethinking our own last word. It assumes a shared search for moral insight, and it promotes (though it does not guarantee) a shared conviction in the end. Absent such grace, it is not surprising that a church's teaching will remain divisive and ineffective, unconvincing to many within the church and without. We have come, then, perhaps to a clue for interpreting the main plot of the story of ethics and ecclesiology in the twenty-first century of the Catholic Church.

It is unlikely that official moral teachings can be received and affirmed by members of the church whose experiences of moral obligation are dismissed or denied. Theologians oppose one another and/or church leaders, reaching impasse after impasse, slowing the process of genuine discernment. Church leaders judge those who disagree with them as "dissenters," legitimate or not, rather than as needed participants in the search for moral truth. And ironically, the voice of the church is muted because it does not represent the wisdom of a genuinely discerning church. But is this last claim really so? No amount of the grace of self-doubt will solve all of the problems of moral disagreement, so is it not better to raise a voice that is unified, even if it can be so only by the silencing of opposition?

The response to this objection can only be that one voice cannot in fact speak for a divided church. The responsibility of church leaders is to hear all voices, mediate them, and finally speak with humility, even—on some questions—provisionally if necessary. This can constitute in itself an important witness in a church and a world that know all too well how complex are the specific moral issues to be faced. Such an approach need not compromise a prophetic response to massive problems of war, racism, dying refugees, a threatened environment. It need not soften the Catholic tradition's commitments to respect human life, promote human well-being, and honor the sacred in all created realities. It can forge cross-cultural discourse and sustain a mission of justice in the world. The unanimity that emerges from diversity is powerful and will not be broken by the best of efforts at moral discernment.

The church needs the structural flexibility to serve such an aim and a process. Curran and major ecclesiologists have pointed in the right direction. The central and minor plots of the large drama of ecclesiology and ethics need not be either institutionally or personally tragic. Infused with the grace of self-doubt as well as the courage of conviction, this ought to be a story of faithful discernment, corporate responsibility, and persuasive guidance for a future whose moral questions can only be more and more demanding.

CHAPTER 10

No One Goes Away Hungry
from the Table of the Lord

Eucharistic Sharing in Ecumenical Contexts

Case: *Christian ecumenical gatherings—whether for dialogue, study, social action, or prayer—frequently occasion a desire for and questions about sharing Eucharist. This is particularly true in ecumenical theological schools where students from various Christian traditions study, live, and work together for two or more years. In one ecumenical divinity school, there is a weekly community Eucharist, led on a rotating basis by members of different denominations. The questions that arise for each generation of students, particularly (but by no means only) Roman Catholic students, include: Ought we to participate in a Eucharist of another denomination? Should a Roman Catholic Eucharist occasionally be celebrated as the school's weekly community Eucharist? And if so, how will those from other Christian traditions be invited to participate? These questions are experienced not only as theological and canonical questions, but as sometimes deeply anguished ethical and pastoral questions, questions of a shared faith and community life. What can be said in response?*

This essay expresses Farley's response to this and similar troubling questions raised primarily by her students, now for more than thirty-six years. Some of her views were first published as "No One Goes Away Hungry from the Table of the Lord," in *Practice What You Preach: Virtues, Ethics, and Power in the Lives of Pastoral Ministers and Their Congregations*, ed. James F. Keenan and Joseph Kotva (Franklin, WI: Sheed and Ward, 1999), 186–201.Used with permission.

My response to this case, after more than thirty-five years of teaching in an ecumenical theological school, is expressed in the title of this essay: "No One Goes Away Hungry from the Table of the Lord." Although my response is focused on a particular context, it represents the position I want finally to defend concerning the general practices of intercommunion among the Christian churches. Three preliminary clarifications regarding my own perspective and assumptions may be useful. First, even though my concerns are for each Christian tradition's approach to these questions, this essay focuses primarily on the Roman Catholic tradition. Any light shed on the problems raised by this tradition will, I think, add some light to analogous problems in other traditions. Moreover, insight into these questions may prove relevant to internal church questions of eucharistic sharing in contexts of intermarriage and of stable second marriages after divorce—both crucial issues especially for the Catholic tradition.

Second, I approach these questions with a very "high doctrine" of Eucharist. I myself believe, for example, in the "real presence" of Jesus Christ in the transformed bread and wine; in the unspeakable encounter with God and with one another by the "taking and receiving" of this bread and this wine; in the eucharistic sharing of Christ's sacrificial offering and the gift of God's life. I even take seriously the genuinely sacramentally inspired forms of reverence for consecrated "reserved" elements. Hence, when I argue that no one should come away hungry from the table of Jesus Christ, it is not because I reduce the meaning of this table to a lowest-possible common denominator.

And third, although the case described above requires an appraisal of principles and rules, it also opens to questions of disposition (character or virtue), both personal and communal. The defense of my own position does not entail a judgment of the wisdom or good will of those who agree or disagree. It aims, however, to show the need for prudence, faithfulness, courage, and liberty of spirit on the way to Christian unity. Both those who yearn for sharing at the table of Jesus Christ, determining all the while that they must wait, and those who yearn for it and discern that they may come forward, can be transformed by eucharistic grace. Neither churches nor individuals, however, can afford to act out of unexamined experiences of power or fear.

In order to explore the question of intercommunion, therefore, and to respond to this case, I will do three things. First, the question needs to be put in some kind of historical context so that both its difficulty and its importance can be seen. I do not attempt to trace its overall history but only to situate its current possibilities and perhaps urgency. Second, I explore ways of thinking about intercommunion that may make my thesis ("No one goes away hungry from the table of the Lord") theologically plausible. And third, I reflect on why and how all of this is a matter for ethical concern.

Historical Ecumenical Developments

Major efforts to reunite separated Christian churches go back at least to the Middle Ages, when conciliar attempts were made to heal the breach between Eastern and Western churches. The sixteenth-century break in Western Christianity was followed almost immediately by at least some efforts to overcome the divisions between Protestants and Catholics. None of these efforts ever reached, however, the proportions of the ecumenical movement that developed in the twentieth century. The establishment in 1948 of the World Council of Churches (WCC) stands out as a major achievement as well as a dynamic new force within this movement—not only because it concentrated efforts at unity among the Protestant churches, but because it included both Protestant and Orthodox participants. And, of course, the importance of the Second Vatican Council in the mid-1960s for the opening of the Roman Catholic Church to ecumenical dialogue and activities can hardly be overestimated. Even in the years following the sixties, when the movement came to have a low profile and seemed almost to lie dormant, remarkable progress was made in the careful work of bilateral and multilateral theological commissions, in the sharing of ministries of social justice by many of the churches, and in the ongoing transformation of attitudes among the faithful. The Roman Catholic Church came to participate importantly with other churches through the World Council. Though not an official member, Catholic representatives shared in the work of the WCC Faith and Order Commission, in various bilateral commissions facilitated by the WCC, and the Catholic Church held full membership in several national Councils of Churches.[1]

---

[1]For a succinct but detailed history of some of these developments, see George Tavard, "Ecumenical Relations," in *Modern Catholicism: Vatican II and After*, ed. Adrian Hastings (New York: Oxford University Press, 1991), 397–421. Key documents are available

Through all of this, however, there remained a "bleeding wound in the ecumenical movement—the divided eucharist."[2] At first a difficult issue for all of the churches, its resolution was easier among many (though not all) of the Protestant and Anglican churches in Western Christianity than it was for either the Roman Catholic or the Orthodox churches. Despite major achievements in theological agreement regarding the Eucharist (most notably in the 1982 WCC Faith and Order Commission's "Lima Report," *Baptism, Eucharist, and Ministry*[3]), the fissures have not been mended. The starkness of this ongoing question has become more and more apparent as concord grows on other issues, as intermarriage of individuals in the diverse churches increases, and as full communion becomes a possibility for many of the Christian churches in the United States.

Recent developments include efforts at "full communion" among five mainline Protestant churches in the United States. Proposals in this regard follow historically upon mergers within the Lutheran Church and the Presbyterian Church, signaling a growing movement toward unity in the Protestant churches. A proposed Concordat between the Evangelical Lutheran Church in America (ELCA) and the Episcopal Church continues to be explored, and the Concordat between the ELCA and three Reformed churches—the Presbyterian Church (U.S.A.), the Reformed Church in America, and the United Church of Christ—is now in place. "Full communion" means that each church confesses a common faith; members of the churches may take communion in each other's church and transfer membership; clergy can be exchanged; and joint efforts in evangelism, witness, and service are possible (including starting congregations, produc-

---

in Harding Meyer and Lukas Vischer, eds., *Growth in Agreement: Reports and Agreed Statements of Ecumenical Conversations on a World Level* (New York: Paulist Press, 1984); and, more recently, Michael Kinnamon and Brian E. Cope, eds., *The Ecumenical Movement: An Anthology of Key Texts and Voices* (Grand Rapids: William B. Eerdmans, 1997).

[2]Kondothra M. George, "Editorial," *Ecumenical Review* 44 (January 1992): 1.

[3]See World Council of Churches Commission on Faith and Order, *Baptism, Eucharist, Ministry*, in Meyer and Vischer, *Growth in Agreement*, 465–503. For an overview of agreements, see Kinnamon and Cope, *Ecumenical Movement*, 129–210. For historical and contemporary liturgical forms across Christian traditions, see Max Thurian and Geoffrey Wainwright, eds., *Baptism and Eucharist: Ecumenical Convergence in Celebration* (Grand Rapids: William B. Eerdmans, 1983), 99–255. Of course, along with agreements, there are still strong disagreements as well. Not specific to issues of Eucharist, but nonetheless relevant, are current conflicts within the WCC between Orthodox churches and Protestant churches.

ing materials, and so forth).[4] The Concordats propose theological resolutions of heretofore divisive issues, including issues of the meaning of the Eucharist and apostolic succession of clergy. Beyond their significance for the churches directly involved, they stand as a salutary challenge and painful reminder to the Roman Catholic and Orthodox Churches to address again the serious issues that divide them from other churches.

In the context of an ecumenical divinity school, these movements in the synods and assemblies of the Protestant churches have had enormous effect on the experience of shared Eucharist. New theological formulations have set the minds of many to rest, but new openings to intercommunion have increased the spiritual distress of those who believe they still ought not to approach the table of a church that is not their own, nor invite to their own table those whose membership is in another church. For Roman Catholics, it becomes necessary to review the present possibilities of both adhering to the letter of the law and sharing the Eucharist with Christians of other traditions.

I have sometimes argued that there is more flexibility in the Roman Catholic position than is commonly assumed. This is not a wholly successful argument, especially if one is looking for a general magisterial or canonical approval of intercommunion. The 1983 Code of Canon Law certainly moved beyond prior absolute prohibitions of shared Eucharists. Though the general principle articulated in Canon 844 is that Catholic ministers give sacraments only to Catholics, and Catholics may receive sacraments only from Catholic ministers, some exceptions are allowed.[5] The key criteria for exceptions are spiritual necessity or spiritual benefit, the avoidance of error or indifferentism, the validity of the sacraments, a shared common faith, and a proper disposition. What circumscribes the exceptions so narrowly, however,

---

[4]For identification and discussion of issues involved in the Concordats, see *The Lutheran* 9 (November 1996) and 10 (May 1997). See also *A Formula of Agreement: Between the Evangelical Lutheran Church in America, the Presbyterian Church (U.S.A.), the Reformed Church in America, and the United Church of Christ on Entering into Full Communion on the Basis of "A Common Calling,"* https://www.rca.org/sslpage.aspx?pid=434. See also William A. Norgren and William G. Rusch, eds., *"Toward Full Communion" and "Concordat of Agreement"* (Minneapolis: Augsburg Fortress, 1991); Daniel F. Martensen, ed., *Concordat of Agreement: Supporting Essays* (Minneapolis: Augsburg Fortress, 1995).

[5]See *The Code of Canon Law*, trans. the Canon Law Society of Great Britain and Ireland in association with the Canon Law Society of Australia and New Zealand and the Canadian Canon Law Society (London: Collins Liturgical Publications, 1983), Canon 844, 156–57.

are first, the required "emergency" nature of spiritual need (a situation in which one cannot physically or morally approach a minister of one's own church; one is in danger of death or some other "grave and pressing need"[6]), and second, the requirement of a Roman Catholic assessment of the validity of the sacrament. What all of this means in practice is that, for example, according to the letter of the law, Catholics may approach the table of Eastern churches (even, in some circumstances, Eastern churches still separated from Rome) but not the table of Protestant churches in the West; individuals in so-called mixed marriages may not, after their wedding ceremony, partake of the same Eucharist through a lifetime of the shared sacrament of marriage; and so forth. In relation to the particular case with which we began, it is generally not possible (apart from further exceptions sometimes made under the rulings of local bishops) for Roman Catholic divinity school students, who take seriously the letter of the law, either to approach the "open table" of a weekly Eucharist offered by Protestant, even Anglican, ministers; or for a Roman Catholic priest to preside at one of these weekly Eucharists and, with the Catholic assembly, invite Protestants to the table.

It is difficult to invoke even the "spirit" of the canons for broader interpretation or relief from what may seem to be a contradiction in one's participation in an ecumenical community of worshiping Christians. What can be done, however, is to appeal to the larger spirit of nonlegal yet significant Roman Catholic texts that articulate an openness to new dimensions of sharing, and on this basis develop a theological and ethical rationale for a more open table. In what follows, I propose a way of thinking about eucharistic sharing that begins to argue for my thesis: No one, at least not because of ecumenical barriers, should go away hungry from the table of the Lord. This proposal, as I have already indicated, is applicable in particular to situations of ecumenical divinity schools, but it has broader implications at least for mixed marriages, and beyond this to other serious ecumenical activities.

---

[6]The descriptions of need are not exactly the same for Roman Catholics, for members of churches in communion, and churches not in communion with the Catholic Church. Still, the emergency nature of the need tends to predominate as a theme in all the descriptions. See Canon 844.1–4; see also *Directory for the Application of Principles and Norms on Ecumenism* (Vatican City: Pontificium Consilium ad Christianorum Unitatem Fovendam, 1993), sections 129–36.

New Theological Possibilities

My theological proposal moves in three steps: (1) the formulation of a theological principle, (2) the development of this principle in terms of the problems it must address, and (3) a brief view of the underlying theological considerations that are at stake in the principle and the proposal. Principles here are not merely abstract formulations. Rather, they inform and give shape to relationships; insofar as they govern and inspire practice, they are part of the development (either upbuilding or diminishing) of the faith and the life of participant individuals and communities.

First, then, the formulation of a theological principle. Vatican II's *Decree on Ecumenism* identified two principles that have been the basis for ecumenically shared Eucharist: Eucharistic sharing presupposes and therefore should signify the *unity* of the church; and sharing in the Eucharist should provide a *means* of grace, including grace that *leads to unity.* For many Protestants, the Eucharist as a means to unity is emphasized, and it is sufficient to justify intercommunion. For the Orthodox churches, unity itself is the absolute condition for participation in the Eucharist (that is, Eucharist must be coextensive with membership). For Roman Catholics, as the Decree goes on to say (and as has been reiterated many times since the Council), "The fact that it [eucharistic worship] should signify unity generally rules out common worship. Yet the gaining of a needed grace sometimes recommends it."[7]

The principle I want to propose turns this approach, in a way, upside down. That is, without denying the importance of a condition of achieved full unity or Eucharist as a means to this unity,[8] I want to shift the focus from an ultimate unity to the unity, however partial, that already *is* among Christians. From an eschatological point of view, there are degrees of unity. No unity presently achieved (even through shared church membership) is complete; it is not yet full Christian unity. But among the Christian churches, and among Christians, there

---

[7]*Decree on Ecumenism,* in *The Documents of Vatican II,* ed. Walter M. Abbott (New York: Guild Press, 1966), 8.

[8]That is, I do not want to deny the importance of Eucharist shared specifically by co-members of a given church. I am addressing the question not of who participates in every Eucharist, but of the possibility of ecumenical participation in some Eucharists.

is nonetheless already a unity. On the basis of *this* unity, Eucharist may be shared. Or better, the Eucharist can be the point of unity, the one deepest form of unity available to Christians. I do not mean by this (as I have already indicated) that our understanding of Eucharist or our enactment of it should represent a "lowest common denominator" among Christians or their churches—quite the opposite, which I hope will become clear as I move to develop my principle in terms of the potential difficulties it must resolve.

The kind of unity usually required by the Catholic Church for sharing of Eucharist includes a common faith, common understanding of the Eucharist, apostolic succession in the churches offering Eucharist, and valid orders on the part of the eucharistic minister. When exceptions of any sort are made, a shared Eucharist must not, negatively, imply a denial of one's own faith (by seeming to agree with whatever the other believes, even if it is considered by the Roman Catholic Church to be heretical or schismatic) or cause scandal (by giving a deceptive impression that full unity has already been achieved) or occasion indifferentism regarding the need to keep working for a unity that will not be a mere homogenization of differences.

The principle of my proposal would not require unanimity of belief regarding all formulations of Christian faith, nor even regarding the nature of Eucharist. It would not require uniformity of polity, or ecclesiastical structures, among all the Christian churches. It would, rather, accept diversity anchored in the deep unity of a shared commitment to the God of Jesus Christ, to discipleship in relation to Jesus, to a life whose source and end are a participation in the salvific action of Jesus Christ for all the world.

It is generally acknowledged that we face today a very different situation and a different set of questions regarding church unity than at any other time in the past. Our concerns for "recognizing the body" of Jesus Christ are not Paul's; they are also not the fourth-century church's concerns for heresy and schism; they are not the post-Reformation concerns for the scandals of Christian conflict (although contemporary scandals of sex abuse may rival the scandals of the past); they are not even the pre–Vatican II concerns for maintaining absolutely unique and separate ecclesial identities. With the experience of more than a half century of ecumenical interaction, we have learned, as Yves Congar said, that "no church or communion has succeeded in convincing the rest," that it and it alone is the true church with which all should join in a unity that is the reduction of others to itself.[9] Perfect unity remains in the "not yet" of the eschaton. But imperfect unity—the unity whereby heretofore unthinkable agreements have been reached on doctrinal questions, and heretofore unimaginable commonality has come to be in the rituals of worship—this unity is already ours. It is a "pluralist unity," a "reconciled diversity," a universal church, if you will (not a homogenous whole of which dioceses are quantitative parts), in which diverse traditions can be valued as historically shaped strands without which the richness of the whole of Christianity could not now be.[10]

Such a pluralism, of course, a diversity in unity, would require a recognition of some form of equality among the ecclesial communities of a whole Christianity. We have moved, reluctantly and perhaps confusedly and fearfully, toward this possibility. The Vatican II *Decree on Ecumenism* says poignantly, for example,

> Undoubtedly the differences that exist in varying degrees between . . . [members of separated churches] and the Catholic Church—whether in doctrine or sometimes in discipline, concerning the structure of the Church—do indeed create many and sometimes serious obstacles to full ecclesial communion. . . . Nevertheless, all those justified by faith through baptism are incorporated into Christ. They therefore have a right to be honored by the title of Christian, and are properly regarded as brothers [and sisters] in the Lord by the sons [and daughters] of the Catholic Church.[11]

And Pope John Paul II, in his 1995 encyclical *Ut unum sint*, wrote,

> In the spirit of the Sermon on the Mount, Christians of one confession no longer consider other Christians as enemies or strangers but see them as brothers and sisters. . . . Today we speak of "other Christians," "others who have received baptism," and "Christians of other communities."[12]

---

[9]Yves Congar, *Diversity and Communion*, trans. John Bowden (Mystic, CT: Twenty-Third Publications, 1985), 162.

[10]Ibid., esp. 149–52.

[11]*Decree on Ecumenism*, 2.

[12]John Paul II, *Ut Unum Sint*, 42, in *Origins* 25 (June 8, 1995): 59.

To respect the many Christian churches as equal partners in the life and mission of the whole church does not entail a simplistic belief that "one is as good or true as another." Adherents to each of the diverse traditions will necessarily believe that their own tradition is for them (and in some objective sense as well) a fuller way to follow Jesus Christ, the most life-giving way. Pluralism in an energetic sense does not mean indifferentism. Indeed, when diversity is respected within a deeper unity, diversity is enhanced.[13] Only so does the maintenance of diversity necessitate neither competitive pluralism nor loss of distinctiveness in relatively superficial forms of unity.

Diverse beliefs regarding the nature of Eucharist itself remain, however, a troubling problem for many. Whatever unity there is among Christians, how can they partake of the same table if they understand so differently the reality of what they enact? Even here, however, both the degree of diversity and its significance may be exaggerated. To a remarkable extent, theological agreements have been reached among the many Christian churches. No longer do debates rage about Eucharist as sacrifice or Eucharist as a meal. Almost all Christian traditions today acknowledge the participation of eucharistic ritual in the salvific action of Jesus Christ, the graced presence of God in the sharing of the eucharistic meal, the profound meeting with God and with one another in the "taking and eating" that is essential to the rite of Eucharist.[14] Where differences remain, they are more than semantic but less than failures to recognize the grace of God in Jesus Christ and in the church's action done in memory of his redemptive offering.[15]

---

[13]My own observation of faculty and students in an ecumenical divinity school is a strong case in point. As individuals come to know and genuinely understand traditions other than their own, they come to know and value their own tradition more deeply. As they come to see the richness of the whole of Christianity, they become more deeply committed to their own historical tradition within Christianity, even as they profoundly appreciate the whole.

[14]It must be acknowledged that these agreements have been forged primarily between mainline Protestant (Lutheran and various Reformed churches), Roman Catholic, and to some extent Orthodox theologians. The issues are of less intense interest to "free church" traditions and have therefore not occasioned the same efforts at adjudication.

[15]For historical perspectives as well as contemporary assessments of ecumenical similarities and differences regarding Eucharist, see Congar, *Diversity and Communion*; Horton Davies, *Bread of Life and Cup of Joy: Newer Ecumenical Perspectives on the Eucharist* (Grand Rapids: William B. Eerdmans, 1993); John Kent and Robert Murray, eds., *Intercommunion and Church Membership* (London: Darton, Longman and Todd, 1973). For historical overviews of theologies of Eucharist, see Gary Macy, *The Banquet's Wisdom:*

If the degree of diversity is less than it is sometimes assumed to be, its significance as a barrier to breaking eucharistic bread together may also be less than is sometimes assumed or feared. One might appeal, for a useful perspective, to the apparent lack of common understanding on the part of the apostles at the Last Supper, and no doubt thereafter if the orthodoxy test put to them were to include specific formulations of what they believed. But other appeals might be made as well today, relativizing the importance of specifically articulated shared understandings. For example, in the Roman Catholic tradition the Eucharist has many meanings—sacrifice, presence, encounter, nourishment, reconciliation, remembrance, enactment, opening to salvation history. In this tradition, it is essential that these meanings be held together. But many of these meanings—if not always all—are essential in other Christian traditions as well. Is it, therefore, not possible to come together within the deep unity of relationship to Jesus Christ, as long as *some* of the multiple meanings of Eucharist are shared?

If the meaning of Eucharist is indeed inexhaustible (though not thereby without any recognizable content), cannot Roman Catholics come to the table of a Protestant church when they are invited, entering into the Eucharist in terms of the understanding of that particular tradition? Must the whole of the meaning important to Catholics be expressed at every tradition's table? And cannot Roman Catholics invite Protestants (as well as members of the Eastern churches) to the Catholic table, assuming at least partially shared understanding of the ritual and the event? Insofar as Catholics believe in the overwhelming, transforming grace of this sacrament, why should they withhold it or, indeed, worry about it, when they are joined by those whom they have recognized as Christian?

A Short History of the Theologies of the Lord's Supper (New York: Paulist Press, 1992); Paul H. Jones, *Christ's Eucharistic Presence: A History of Doctrine* (New York: Peter Lang, 1994). For historical interpretation of particular relevance to Roman Catholic beliefs, see David N. Power, *The Sacrifice We Offer: The Tridentine Dogma and Its Reinterpretation* (New York: Crossroad, 1987); David N. Power, *The Eucharistic Mystery: Revitalizing the Tradition* (New York: Crossroad, 1992); Edward J. Kilmartin, "The Catholic Tradition of Eucharistic Theology: Towards the Third Millennium," *Theological Studies* 55 (September 1994): 405–57; David N. Power, "Roman Catholic Theologies of Eucharistic Communion," *Theological Studies* 57 (December 1996): 587–610.

Intercommunion as an Ethical Issue

Whether Christians can share in the Eucharist across their many traditions or not is a question for ethics as well as for theology. Four brief considerations will serve to outline an ethical perspective that takes account of the theological proposal I have offered above. First, not even the Roman Catholic Church has ever maintained that intercommunion, while generally ruled out with separated churches in the West, is intrinsically reprehensible or intrinsically immoral.[16] This suggests that there are ways of understanding it, of at least clarifying exceptions, that can and should be worked out—particularly if an ethical obligation to participate in ecumenical Eucharists can be discerned.

Second, what divides the churches most intensely today, as much within themselves as between or among them, are ethical questions. Unlike prior centuries of controversy in Christianity, we are more likely to be faced with serious conflicts over moral rules and behavior than we are over doctrines of incarnation and redemption, virgin birth, the communion of saints, or even church polity and Eucharist. Issues such as population policy, divorce and remarriage, and same-sex relations are tearing many churches apart today.[17] Hence, insofar as church unity is a pressing concern within Christianity, there is a grave need to reach to a deeper bedrock of unity, a stronger basis for covenant, from which differences can be negotiated yet respected. A sharing of the eucharistic table offers that bedrock, that covenantal possibility.

Third, deep in the Roman Catholic tradition (and others) are insights about moral growth and development. There is a dynamism in being that inclines to fuller being, in love that yearns for fuller love, and in unity that desires greater unity. The actions, practices, of individuals and communities actualize (or diminish) potentials for fullness of being, love, and unity. Insofar as unity *already exists* among the Christian churches, it has motivated practices such as the search for theological

---

[16]See Richard A. McCormick, *Notes on Moral Theology, 1968–84* (Washington, DC: University Press of America, 1984), 21. McCormick is here referring to the claim made in this regard by Wilhelm de Vries in his essay, "Communicatio in sacris," *Concilium* 4: *The Church and Ecumenism* (New York: Paulist Press, 1965), 18–40.

[17]This is true within individual churches and among them. A case in point is the intensely growing rift in the WCC between Orthodox and Protestant churches over issues of the ordination of women and of gays and lesbians.

agreement (through the work of bilateral and multilateral commissions); these practices have in turn effected greater unity. Similarly, intercommunion based on an already existing unity (deeper even than particular church membership) offers a graced transformative practice leading to unity (perhaps in diversity) that can still come to be. Intercommunion is not merely a means to a missing unity but an unfolding and actualizing of a present unity that has a future.

For this practice to be possible, all the virtues and graces integral to religious and moral discernment will need to flourish. Until rules are explicitly changed, practice will be determined by the theological understandings and moral convictions of individuals and churches. These cannot be clarified without at least prudence, patience, wisdom, courage, freedom of spirit, and faithfulness to the process wherever it leads. Whatever virtues are required of individuals in concrete situations, these same virtues are required of local faith communities and of churches as a whole. On the way, even imperfect unity and imperfect love can help us to cast out fear.[18]

Finally, what is at stake in these questions goes beyond the shared self-offering and covenanting of individual Christians and churches. Christian traditions acknowledge that Eucharist is not merely an intramural affair; its grace is not only for the Christian community or even the diverse Christian communities. Through the Eucharist, Christians are integrated into a salvific whole. Christians come to the table not for our own sakes alone, but for the salvation and liberation of all the world. To be welcomed to the table is also to be sent forth. The Eucharist is a sacrament by which we are incorporated into the life of God and into the redeeming activity of Jesus Christ. In the Eucharist we are strengthened and gradually transformed into oneness with the whole Body of Christ—*Christus amictus mundi*; we are transformed therefore also into bread for the world, the risen Body of Christ. Insofar as Christians are divided, separated, in this communion, we are limited in the sharing (social, political, economic, spiritual) that is demanded of us as a way of living in the world.

I end, therefore, where I began: No one should go away hungry

---

[18]Were there space here, it would be important to consider the relevance of what are called "pastoral" solutions in the Roman Catholic tradition. Strong analogies are to be drawn between what is required of individuals for these solutions and what is required of communities and institutions in their considerations not only of exceptions to general rules regarding intercommunion but ultimately of changes to be made in the rules themselves.

from the table of the Lord. Yet there is here a paradox: Insofar as we do come to the table and are fed, we will nonetheless in one sense go away hungry from the table of the Lord—because we live in the already/not yet of unity, of transformation, of fullness of Life. This latter hunger, however—*not the hunger of being turned away from the table*—is a holy hunger: It is both nourished and intensified precisely by participation in the Eucharist. As it grows, we need the Eucharist more. If we recognize the hunger of others because it reflects this hunger of our own, we shall know the moral "ought" of not closing our own table and not forbidding ourselves the food that is offered to us at the tables of the diverse Christian traditions.

CHAPTER 11

Sermons on the Themes of Holy Week

Dignity and Humiliation:
Palm Sunday

Texts
Zechariah 9:9–12
Hebrews 12:1–6
Mark 11:1–11

"Those who went in front and those who followed were all shouting, 'Hosanna! Blessed is the one who comes in the name of the Lord!'" (Mark 11:9). And thus it was that Jesus entered Jerusalem the week before the celebration of Passover.

This is a dramatic, but in some ways puzzling, event in the story of the life of Jesus. It is very old as part of the tradition. It appears in all four Gospels, in John as well as in the synoptics. Whether it actually happened or not, whether Jesus actually rode into Jerusalem on a colt or not, it is clearly important to the earliest formulations of the narrative about Jesus. It may have served, as an element in the tradition, primarily (perhaps only) to make a point about the messiahship of Jesus. But it is not unreasonable for us to take it in its own terms in Mark's Gospel and to ask: What is its meaning? Why does Jesus, in the story, decide to ride into Jerusalem in a way that invites acclaim? Why at this point in his ministry does he make an almost triumphant entry into Jerusalem? What is it that we remember today, on this Palm

---

This sermon was delivered in Battell Chapel, Yale University, March 31, 1985.

Sunday, as a result of this story that has held firm so long within the Christian biblical tradition?

The Irony of the Messianic Destiny

One way to look at the event is to see the irony of its telling.[1] Jesus and the readers (or hearers) of the story know something that the other persons involved in the narrative do not seem to know. We know its ending. Jesus and we are the only ones who know that when he enters Jerusalem on this day, he enters it for the last time; this is the road to his death. Indeed, the irony is stark. On three previous occasions Jesus tried to tell his disciples that his destiny was to suffer grievously—to be rejected, delivered into the hands of his enemies, condemned to death, and then to rise again (Mark 8:31–32; 9:30–32; 10:32-34). But this is the one thing his disciples have not seemed able to hear. They have not understood that he himself is going to die, and they have not grasped that his call to them is to follow him to the cross. Just prior to today's story, for example, James and John showed that they had not learned that the identity of Jesus as the Christ would be irrevocably bound up with his identity as the crucified Messiah. They who agreed to drink the cup of which Jesus would drink did not yet understand that it would be the cup of suffering and death.

Up until now Jesus has cautioned the disciples and others not to say anything publicly about the great works he did in their presence. Insofar as anyone understood who he was, they were warned to say nothing of what they knew or had seen. At least seven times in Mark's Gospel up to this point Jesus repeated his request, his "strict order," to tell no one about him or who he was. But now, in this week before Passover, he decides to enter Jerusalem with full publicity; to receive the acclaim of the crowds; to appear before the world fulfilling one of the messianic prophecies. Gone is the pattern of avoiding popular enthusiasm; gone the seeming discretion that protected him from the people's desires for a leader they could follow. With careful premeditation, he arranges for this entry into Jerusalem. Luke tells us that when he is cautioned by some to restrain his disciples, he answers only, "If these were silent, the stones would shout out" (Luke 19:40).

---

[1] See Mary Rose D'Angelo, "Images of Jesus and the Christian Call in the Gospels of Mark and Matthew," *Spirituality Today* 36 (Fall 1985): 220–36.

So Jesus now openly is signifying his messiahship (or at least so the writers of the Gospels want us to understand). "Hosanna! Blessed is the one who comes in the name of the Lord! Blessed is the coming kingdom of our ancestor David! Hosanna in the highest heaven!" (Mark 11:9–10). Jesus and we know that he is a messiah of the sort the crowds do not expect and will not want. We who know the end of the story know the irony of an acclaim that will turn within a week into mockery and humiliation. This is a triumphal procession that will lead to gross indignities and finally killing. Of all the things we need to ponder on the hearing of this story, I focus for a moment on just this: on the nature of the event insofar as it holds together the experiences of honor and dishonor, dignity and condemnation. The problem it offers for us may be different from what it offered the early disciples of Jesus, but the meaning it offers may be very close to the one Jesus tried so hard to help them understand.

The Source of Glory

It is true that within a week, honor will have turned into humiliation. Palm Sunday leads ineluctably to Good Friday. But we who know this know also that it is not Palm Sunday as such that transforms Good Friday; it is not this day's festivity and acclaim that will reach over to soften the harsh and terrible death that is to come. It is, rather, Good Friday that transforms Palm Sunday; it is in the mystery of Friday's death, Friday's cross, that today's honor will ultimately be understood. In the end, therefore, Palm Sunday will also help to interpret Good Friday. In the center of what looks like utter humiliation will be revealed a dignity so sure that it finally overwhelms what would contradict it. In the center of seeming foolishness will shine wisdom; out of what appears as utter tragedy will emerge final hope; in death will be shown the ultimate power of life.

This means that today we do not simply anticipate Good Friday. Or for that matter, we do not only anticipate Easter Sunday (the light of which we need to understand it all). But on a day like today when the question of honor and loss of honor presses itself upon us, we may see (in the light of the whole story of salvation) how the glory of God shines in the humiliation of Jesus Christ and, moreover, how it transforms or has the power to eliminate what might otherwise appear only humiliating in our own lives and the lives of one another. In other words, the experiences of both humiliation and dignity must be held together if we are to understand either Palm Sunday or Good Friday.

But what *is* humiliation? What constitutes it? And is it to over-dramatize the situation in the Gospel to say that the honor accorded Jesus in his entry into Jerusalem turned to humiliations by the end of the week? After all, were we to make a film of the story, would we not portray Jesus as emanating dignity through it all—so that what looks humiliating will be really only the behavior of his opponents? But the story is itself shocking enough. In an important sense Jesus *is* humiliated. Have we ever seen an otherwise dignified person fall down? Especially stumble, or lurch? And suppose such a one has been brought to that point by the actions of others—or by the very burdens of their own lives? And what if, as in Jesus' case, this person's clothes are taken from them? What if a foolish crown is put on her head? Or he is tortured not only with great physical pain and debility, but with endless indignities?

But again, what *is* really humiliating? Just as we do not adequately understand the suffering of Jesus Christ unless we see it as it reaches down through the centuries to the suffering of individuals and groups of today, so we do not adequately understand the sufferings of Jesus, and the truth of dignity within indignity, unless we see them in the lives of those who are otherwise judged among the humiliated today.

What is it that appears humiliating to us today? Is it not a kind of powerlessness, a perception of "difference" in another, an incongruity with our own sources of self-esteem? And do we not impose humili-ation precisely by determining from the "outside" the meaning of the life or self of others, by looking upon them with our indifference or our derision, or our trivialization or their plight? Do we not demean them precisely because they threaten the categories of our world, make vulnerable our own fragile sense of acceptance in the acclaim of the crowd, in the honor of society, in our own self-image? Think of who it is we count among the "humiliated" today: those on the margins of human society because they are mentally ill, or their economic welfare needs the support of the state, or a form of disablement blinds us to their human powers, or their educational background is not the same as ours, or their familial arrangements are different from ours. Under the sign of the cross, their dignity may claim our song of praise, but all too often our songs are of another sort. What Jesus tried again and again to teach his disciples openly remains still largely unrecognized by us. Yet in the identification of Jesus with the "humiliated" of the world lies the possibility of their and our understanding of a dignity that transforms what should otherwise contradict it.

I am reminded, for example, of the account Rosemary Radford Ruether has given of the experience of a student of hers who was raped in a woods. During the rape, she says, the woman became convinced that she would be killed and resigned herself to her impending death. When the rapist finally fled, and the woman found herself still alive, she experienced a vision of Christ as a crucified woman. "This vision filled her with relief and healing: 'I would not have to explain to a male God that I had been raped. God knew what it was like to be a woman who had been raped.'"[2]

It may be that not just in our understanding of others, but in our understanding of ourselves, we may come to interpret more truthfully our experiences of humiliation and shame. It is not a small matter to discern whether humiliation is deserved or not; not a small matter to discover whether our desires and fears for honor or dishonor are based on truth or falsehood; not a matter of indifference to distinguish courage from foolishness, dignity from vanity, heroism from grandstanding.

Two questions can be raised, however, in regard to all of this. Both are situated in the heart of the connections between Palm Sunday and Good Friday.

The Problem of Nonresistance

To identify undeserved humiliation with the passion and death of Jesus: Is this not too easy a consolation? Does it not come perilously close to fitting Friedrich Nietzsche's characterization of Christianity as a religion for victims? Is humiliation, after all, to be piously accepted when it is not deserved? Is this not a dangerous prescription likely to be destructive for persons who should at some point resist the false shame imposed on them and who should claim a rightful respect for their dignity as persons?

Another way to formulate this problem is to question something in the model that Jesus offers on his entry into Jerusalem. The Gospel writers tell us he specifically chose to ride into the city on a colt, or an

---

[2]Rosemary Radford Ruether, "Feminist Theology in the Academy," *Christianity and Crisis*, March 4, 1985, 61.

ass—the animal that princes rode on when they wished to signify peaceful intentions as they entered a city (if their intention was warfare, they rode on a horse). Jesus, then, is depicted as coming in peace—coming not to conquer but to teach the ways of peace; coming seemingly not even to resist the forces of his own coming destruction.

When is dignity lost by a refusal to resist the judgments and the humiliating actions of another? When does surrender to the power of another constitute a less than human submission? If we take Jesus' story seriously in this regard, we learn that dignity is sustained with and by integrity; that humiliations cannot destroy us if we remember who we are; that the forces of false judgment and suspicion, of servile fear and violence, are to be named for what they are and opposed, resisted, even if it means our death. But they are to be resisted in terms of what they are, not capitulated to by adopting the patterns of evil they represent, and not surrendered to by believing the deception they impose. They are to be resisted by not believing that to be humiliated means that we are without dignity. Through the death of Jesus, all death is overwhelmed; through the humiliations of Jesus, all humiliation can be transformed. This is not because of the death or the humiliation, but because of the love that held true, the bond between Jesus and God that proved stronger than death, the dignity that proved infinitely greater than the humiliation it suffered. When Jesus entered Jerusalem lamenting that it had failed to understand the things that were for its peace, he did not thereby give up the struggle against the works of war. His passion—his suffering and humiliation—were understood by him to be the continuation of his labor, no less a task than all of his other ministry before the week of his death.

To Stand and Be Counted

This brings us to a second problem, or a second question regarding all of this. Granted all that may be believed about the humiliations of Jesus, and the challenge that these offer for our own experience of humiliation or our own humiliation of others, we can still ask why did Jesus enter Jerusalem with the crowds singing his praises, with an acclaim that he knew would be short-lived and hollow? Apart from simply interpreting this text as the Gospel writers' way of making the point of his messiahship, we can ask: why did he bother? Perhaps so that we would know the irony that only he knew then, and sing of it today, remembering and learning. But perhaps also because it is important for us, no matter what our humiliations or potential humiliations, to know the time to stand before all in a word of truth. Jesus' entry into Jerusalem was less a claim on his part for messiahship than a sign of the fulfillment of God's promise, a witness to the truth of God's word. Here stands a life, a reality, a love, so great that neither death nor anything else can ultimately gainsay it. Here stands a dignity the honor of which is so real that no attempted humiliation can obscure it. Here stands a hope and an accomplishment that no amount of foolishness or malice can take away.

This is what we celebrate on Palm Sunday. We remember that in the face of derision, danger, and death, on this day—and not only after his resurrection—Jesus stood in truth and a revelation of his glory. We remember what it means neither to hide from opposition nor always to withdraw from conflict, but also not to come to it on a charger with drawn swords. We remember and we stand to celebrate the dignity not only of Jesus but of all whom he joined among the lot of the "humiliated," among all those we know who take up this cross. Here is the intersection between Palm Sunday and Good Friday: a "crucified" dignity that remains eternally dignity, and a dignified "humiliation" that is finally not humiliating.

Some of us will sing in the face of life's indignities, and some of us will be silent; some of us will weep, and some will be dry-eyed. But none of us is excused from the task of discerning the meaning of these indignities and the possibility of their transformation. Insofar as we do this, we will have strength to walk into this week of the passion of Jesus Christ, whom we try today to honor with the trust that gives voice to our praise.

Weep for Yourselves and for Your Children

Texts
Luke 23:24–32
Jeremiah 9:16

There are important reasons for pondering texts regarding the passion and death of Jesus Christ outside of the intensity of Passiontide. Some aspects of its mystery emerge more clearly when we are, for example, approaching winter rather than in the heart of spring—especially in a year when autumn has been marked by the violent death of a nation's leader and by new levels of despair in our own people whose lives are further diminished by national policies for the distribution of public funds.

I myself, whether in Passiontide or outside of it, am reluctant to speak about the passion. It seems better simply to hear the story told, and stand before it in silence. It is a tale of sorrow whose own power is great enough to form our hearts. If we must (as we must), however, add our own words to the texts, probing again and again their meaning, perhaps what should be said is this: Behind the words of the Gospel lies a living bond between the passion of Jesus Christ and today. We understand the passion only when we see it stretch to the lives, the suffering, the passion, of persons through the centuries to today. The text that points most explicitly to this bond is the text we have heard, "Daughters of Jerusalem, do not weep for me, but for yourselves and for your children."

This sermon was delivered in the University of Chicago's Rockefeller Chapel on October 18, 1982, which accounts for its references to particular past world and national events. The substance of it, however, remains overall important and relevant in diverse situations. This version of the homily was published in *Criterion* 21, no. 1 (University of Chicago Divinity School, Winter 1982): 19–21. Used with permission.

The women who came to the execution of Jesus, the daughters of Jerusalem, were not the same as the women from Galilee with whom we are more familiar. They may have been simply part of the crowd that always attended executions in Jerusalem, as elsewhere, out of curiosity, delight in the spectacle of a killing, or compassion. They may have been professional mourners, such as Jeremiah appeals to in an earlier day (Jer. 9:16), members of the wealthier classes who were sometimes hired to aid by their special skills in the lamentations of the real mourners. They may have been women who had listened to Jesus in better times. In any case, they wept. They raised a wail of death for Jesus. And Jesus turned to them and raised a death wail for Jerusalem, for the women and their children. The days will come, said Jesus, when they will envy the barren, envy those who do not have the added anguish of beholding the tragic suffering of their own children.

Some scholars say that Jesus is, by these words, predicting the fall of Jerusalem. But he points far beyond any one event. He points to the suffering of us all, to the power and oppression that will cause desolation again and again, to the shattering of human lives, the deep piercing of individuals' hearts by swords of sorrow, the violence pressed against groups and whole societies, the long anguish of emptiness in individual spirits, the disease and diminishment that attacks persons and cultures.

But why should Jesus point at such a moment to the suffering of the future? I do not think he was moved, as some have suggested, by anger and rejection of the women's tears for him. Nor were his words a reproach, as others have thought, for the complicity of the women in the sins of the people. Rather, Jesus spoke of the suffering of the future because he truly grieved for these women and their children. In the midst of his suffering, attention was paid to them. But more than this, and within it and under it, lies a deeper mystery. The suffering of Jesus Christ is one with the suffering of the generations to follow.

Perhaps we understand better than the daughters of Jerusalem that the meaning of the suffering and death of Jesus Christ reaches down through the centuries, touching not only the suffering of these women's children, but our own—giving to it all a new meaning and a different potential. If the doctrine of the Mystical Body means anything at all, it means that Jesus is mysteriously identified with human persons across time and space, and that we have a new reality by reason of his holding us in relation to God while remaining one with us in our continued suffering. To the extent that we understand our own solidarity with all human persons, and the implications of the incarnation of Jesus Christ for that solidarity, to that extent we hear Jesus' words today not finally as, "Do not weep for me," but, "*Weep for me*—in the person of your sisters and brothers."

But something must be said about weeping. Persons wise about the life of the spirit have often told us of different kinds of tears. In relation to the passion, there must be at least two sorts of tears. There are tears of desolation, which, when they have all been shed, leave the well dry. Such tears may rise from a mere sensitivity to the cross, or a preoccupation with its meaning only for ourselves, a sorrow that empties the heart of its strength and prevents real love. But there are also tears that water our hearts and give us strength and peace in real union with Jesus Christ. These are tears that turn us not in upon ourselves, but which open us to union—with Jesus and with our brothers and sisters. Such tears may even move us to action.

We begin to see, then, that the meaning of this text moves in a number of directions. It may touch and help to change our futures in a number of different ways. The first of these we can see by turning to Jesus' final word to the daughters of Jerusalem: "If this is what they do to the green wood, what will they do to the dry?"

Biblical scholars tell us this text records a proverb that means, in one form or another, "If this is what they do to the innocent, what will happen to the guilty?" Insofar as it means this, it can nonetheless offer hope. It is reminiscent of Zechariah's prophecy whereby those who are guilty will nonetheless receive from Yahweh a spirit of kindness that allows them to mourn and so to return to life. In the call to tears is the promise of life. "They will look on the one whom they have pierced; they will mourn for him as for an only son, and weep for him as people weep for a first-born child. . . . When that day comes, a fountain will be opened . . ." (Zech. 12:10, 13). The call to mourn is a sign of ultimate grace for the guilty.

But the meaning of these words goes even further for us. Green wood is still full of life, not easily broken, not easily burned. Dry wood has death within it, is easily snapped in two, consumed by flame, or simply rots back into the soil. In this text, the difference between the green wood and the dry is the life of faith within them: If this is what the forces of evil can do in a time when faith is fresh and new, what can they do when it has faded and almost died?

If Jesus speaks thus to the women, is it not for us a voice of despair? We, after all, can be said to live in the time of the dry wood. How shall we escape, or endure, the tragedies that will lead us to cry out to the mountains, "Fall on us!" and to the hills, "Cover us!"?

The mystery of faith and the mystery of tears come together. We shall escape, or endure, only if we do as Jesus calls the women to do: Water our faith with our tears, so that it cannot be broken like dry wood or burned like kindling. Water our faith with our tears, so that even though we, too, must go into the valley of death, we shall not fear ultimate destruction. Water our faith with our tears, so that the pledge of hope that is sealed in the passion and death of Jesus Christ becomes for us the source of unending life.

Through tears, then, our own hearts can be transformed. Yet it is not enough. The voice heard in Ramah, lamenting and weeping bitterly, was the voice of Rachel weeping for her children because they were no more. The forces of evil not only within them but around them crushed them and took their lives or forced them into exile (Jer. 31:15). We must look in a further direction for meaning in the "Daughters of Jerusalem" text.

Why has this text been a source of consolation to so many women, even in circumstances like Rachel's when forces of evil outside of us endanger or destroy all that we value in life? Consolation has come not just because attention has been paid from the midst of Jesus' own suffering to our pain and tragedy, nor even because forever the connection is made between the passion of Jesus Christ and our own. The text is a source of consolation because it holds within it a call to action. To live the connection between the passion and today is to mourn not with tears that leave us empty and alone, but with tears that move us to struggle against suffering and death, even to the point of laying down our own lives. It is to mourn with tears that water us down to the sea of action, even if the price is living the passion unto death.

We live in a time of growing awareness of the tragic consequences of oppression and injustice, of the distortions and limits that evil structures and systems entail. But we have come to understand that the death of Jesus Christ constitutes an ultimate challenge to an order of things in which persons are exploited or enslaved, or where their basic needs are ignored. However we understand the laying down of Jesus' life as a surrender, we know that it is not a surrender to the forces of evil. It opposes them unto death.

A story is told in the book of Wisdom that sheds light on the "Daughters of Jerusalem" text in this regard. A young man goes to his death, condemned by a society of persons who have decided that life is short and there "is no remedy for dying." They determine that they will "seize the time" by oppressing the needy, the just ones. "As for the virtuous man who is poor, let us oppress him; let us not spare the widow, nor respect old age, white-haired with many years" (Wisd. 2:10). They therefore beset the just man because he is obnoxious to them. His very existence is a reproach to them, a challenge to their thoughts and to their way of life. Their strength, they say, will be their norm of justice. The young man's response to them is like the later words of Jesus. This man, too, says to the women in the crowd that it is better to be childless than to perpetuate such a society. Challenging a fundamental value, he cries out in the face of their inability to see that he who is about to die is better off than they are, they who grasp and perpetuate a life that claims fruitfulness but in actuality yields sterility and death. His words to them challenge not only their attack upon him but the very order and content of the values that constitute their worldview.

Jesus' call to the weeping women may be no less a challenge to a prevailing set of human values, a call to a form of mourning that yields not only self-transformation but transformation of social norms. There are tears that move us to challenge the values, the patterns of behavior, the structures that send women and men to their deaths prematurely, or that so constrict people's lives that their possibilities are choked off unjustly. There are tears that open us, rather than close us, to union with the dispossessed—a union that itself challenges the *status quo*. There are tears that move us and empower us—however limited our capacities—to action.

But the "Daughters of Jerusalem" text moves in one more direction. For we may ask: Why should we not weep, and weep finally in despair? Tears may transform our hearts from evil. They may even move us to try to transform the oppression and evil around us. But finally the people in the story of the book of Wisdom are right. For all their efforts to grasp life, "They invited death, considered it a friend and pined for it, because they said: brief and troublous is our lifetime, and there is no remedy for dying, nor is anyone known to have come back from the nether world" (Wisd. 1:16–2:1). Are there not finally only tears of utter impotence and helplessness left? Does not the well in us finally run dry, so that our resources (and those of all creation, for that matter) exhaust themselves? We for whom an experience of a future is essential, for whom hope is for the soul what breathing is for the body—must we not finally weep in despair before the diminishment of life and the inevitability of death?

Once more another text opens for us the "Daughters of Jerusalem" text. This time it is a text that is not past to the event of Jesus' death, but future to it. It is the text, the texts, which tell of the New Testament experience of the rest of the story of Jesus' death. In these texts women and men have heard of a death that held in itself a future, a death that led to a mysterious undoing of death.

"Daughters of Jerusalem, weep." The darkness of death cannot be avoided. An ultimate powerlessness before the pull of dying cannot be taken away. There are tears of which we shall die. Yet in such weeping our hearts may finally be broken, so that our existence is new; and a joy that is eternally sorrow-consoled may allow us to embrace not only ourselves and our children but a new future for all reality.

We may have an inkling that the possibility of such joy is not an afterthought on the part of God; that though it represents radical discontinuity with our lives of mourning and limited joy, it nonetheless is continuous somehow with the surge of life that our tears also hold. We may have such an inkling through the transformation of life that we and others may even now find in what we know as the "resurrection experience" of Jesus Christ.

If we can live on such an inkling, then we can hear the words of hope whispered and sung to those who wail through the centuries, to Rachel, weeping for her children, but hearing finally the word, "There is hope for your descendents." We can understand the action of Jesus Christ choosing freely to be with us and to lay down his life for us. We can believe, thus, that no one need suffer alone. We can even choose still to bear children, hoping against hope in the face of apocalyptic futures. We can do all of this because we are allowed to see the light of mercy in the shadow of death and nothingness, the light in a mercy that is otherwise darkness to us and that lets bodies be destroyed, minds ravaged, spirits crushed, and does not hinder the cry, "Why hast thou forsaken me?"

By such seeing we catch a glimpse of light, a glimpse of the fullness of light, in the bitter pain of Jesus Christ, whose passion (like our own sometimes) seemed so filled with futility, with senselessness, with the unnecessary cutting off of something in the beginnings of its promise. Only by such seeing may we understand even now, when the pain is softened by the centuries, the light and sweetness in that pain that has filled the world with the possibility of light and sweetness ever since.

So Jesus calls us to weep—for him, but in him, for all of us; to blend our lives by our tears, to live our tears in our action. If in this or any time our hearts are too dry for tears, then we may ask for what Catherine of Siena called the tears of fire, whereby the Spirit of God weeps in us, and the fire of love and the waters of life are one.

The Cup of Suffering and of Love:
Reflections for Holy Week

Texts
Mark 10:35-40

Each year the Christian Lenten season yields a final week that is named "Holy" because in it we remember the passion of Jesus Christ. More than in any other week of the year, we probe our shared memory of this key event that is part of the center of the Christian story. We don't just "bring it to mind"; we try all over again, anew, to understand it, to make sense of the many interpretations given to it, and to discern what it asks of us. We embark on its journey, as into an event that belongs to our present as well as to our faith community's past.

Many of us are reluctant to speak much about what we have come to call the passion of Jesus Christ. It seems better simply to hear the story told, and to stand before it in silence. Yet we *must* speak together, perhaps, for the story has not been in every respect self-interpreting, not even in the light of the resurrection experience that follows it. And troubling questions about its meaning are always with us.

Interpretations of the passion of Jesus are important not only because we have questions, or because our understanding of the event is essential to our spiritual lives, but because some interpretations of the passion and death of Jesus have yielded troubling consequences in the world—from anti-Semitism to quietism, from triumphalism to strange models of life thought by some to be ordered by a God who would send a son to death in order to satisfy a requirement that seems to be arbitrary and cruel. Moreover, we know that we cannot turn to the story of this dying without a critical reminder of the dangers

---

This sermon is adapted from a version delivered at Marquand Chapel, Yale Divinity School, during Holy Week, 1998.

of sentimentalizing the sufferings of Jesus, of being overwhelmed by them in a way that weakens us and prevents our seeing the implications for our own day.

I want, therefore, to explore something of the meaning of the passion and death of Jesus Christ through symbols and concepts that may challenge some ways of thinking about these events, but also to expand some ways of entering into them more deeply.

Can You Drink the Cup?

We have a whole week during which we can ponder the meaning of the suffering and death of Jesus. At the beginning of the week, then, it may be useful to focus not on the cross but on an image similar to the cross, an image that Jesus uses when trying to expand his disciples' insight into what lies ahead. It is recorded in a passage in the Gospel of Mark (10:35–40).[3] Christians know the passage well. James and John come forward out of the group of disciples, and they inquire of Jesus whether he will do for them whatever they ask. Jesus responds, "What is it you want me to do for you?" They say that they want a special place in the reign of Jesus when it comes; they want to sit one at his right hand and one at his left. Jesus tells them they have no idea what they are asking. So instead of answering their plea, he offers another question: "Are you able to drink the cup that I drink?" And they answer, "We are able." Of course, as in so many scenes in the Gospels, we know the irony of their response, for they had still not "gotten the point" of Jesus' question—a point they failed to understand until the last days of Jesus' life began to unfold in all their horror, and a point they may not finally have understood until they saw and could touch the wounds of the risen Christ. We know the irony of their response, but we may have difficulties of our own in understanding the full meaning of drinking the cup that Jesus drinks. Indeed, what can it mean for us to drink this cup? The "cup" we know to be a symbol of the cross, which in turn symbolizes for us the suffering that Jesus is to undergo. But what does it mean for any of us to drink this cup? This is the question we must ponder.

Clearly, the image says something about a call to suffering and even

---

[3]The story also appears in Matt. 20:20–28, although the supplicant here is the mother of James and John.

to death on a cross. But insofar as this is so, we have good reasons in our skeptical age to resist the question, or at least to resist placing it at the center of our Christian self-understanding. Serious critics of Christianity, for example, have charged that it is precisely preoccupation with suffering that has prevented Christians from working for justice, and has encouraged in women and sometimes minority groups a harmful motivation for the acceptance of burdens that should not be theirs, or not theirs alone. We can think that we are to be passive in the face of our own suffering, that we are simply to accept it, bear it, endure it, expecting relief only in another world. Opponents of Christianity have charged that Christians are too preoccupied with suffering and death, that Christianity is a religion for victims, and it can nourish only a spirituality for weaklings. Whatever truth there is in these charges, it is clear that not just any understanding of suffering will enable us to enter the mystery of this week without being weakened, and without—however inadvertently—serving to reinforce injustices.

Chastened as we may be by such criticisms and potential problems, the question nonetheless remains: What does it mean for us to "drink the cup"? To answer this question we need some understanding of human suffering. There is a sense in which it is true, what was said by an old and diminishing man in an Italian film of many years ago: "All suffering is the same." But also, it is true that all suffering is unique. There are, of course, paradigmatic experiences and descriptions of human suffering. Jesus' own suffering is as dramatic as it is salvific. But we also come face to face with human suffering in particular others, whose whole lives seem shattered, whole identities broken, with loss after loss, in one physical or spiritual trauma and tragedy after another. I have elsewhere referred to Simone Weil's dark identification of human pain that seems to break all boundaries of what a human being can bear.[4] She differentiates this kind of suffering by naming it "affliction." In its ultimate forms, this kind of suffering perhaps always also includes an element of the experience of the absence of God–the sense of God-forsakenness that overwhelmed Job and that made Jesus cry out, "My God, my God, why have you forsaken me?"

What does "Can you drink the cup" mean? Perhaps ultimately, "Can you enter into life even unto affliction, even to the point of death?" But

---

[4]See my rendering of Weil's insights in this volume's previous essay, "How Shall We Love in a Postmodern World."

more must be said about it than this. For what Jesus tried to reveal to his first disciples, and through them to us, was not only that they must be willing to suffer, to endure their *own* suffering that might be *like* his own; but rather, "Can you drink the *cup that I will drink?*" The cup to be shared was and is the cup of Jesus Christ. It is intrinsically important to share the pain, the suffering, of Jesus—of one we love. But in this case, it also moves within and beyond this: for the cup of Jesus is the *cup of the suffering of all persons.* If we are to drink this cup, we are to partake of the sufferings of everyone else. And if we are to do this, if we are to do more than look upon Jesus, and others, with pity, we must, paradoxically, know something of affliction in ourselves. We must have at least inklings of the possibility of sufferings that reach all the way to humiliation and degradation, where the lines between body and spirit are no longer sharp and where competition among miseries may be silenced.

We know more about this cup, however. We know that it signifies all kinds of human suffering—suffering in the forms of sickness and tragic accident, aging and diminishment, natural disasters of drought and floods and earthquakes, human misunderstandings and disparities in love, failures and catastrophes great and small. Yet something in particular characterizes those sufferings that are central to the image. Given the context and the nature of the final sufferings of Jesus, there can be little doubt that the centrally imaged form of suffering is, specifically, suffering that is the *consequence of injustice.* Here is the suffering that *does not have to be*, the suffering that results from violence and abuse, exploitation and oppression, human indifference, greed, desire for power, hatred, and abandonment. Here is the suffering that cries out for an end not in death but in *change!*

We know still more about the cup: We know, for example, that those who call Christianity a religion obsessed with pain and death are wrong to think that the ultimate point of the cup or the cross is suffering and death. Rather, the ultimate point is that a *relationship holds.* The divine/human relationship is renewed, and it holds. The cup that Jesus drinks is first of all a cup of love, a cup of covenant that seals the promise of a God who drinks, too, of human suffering, in order finally to transform it. The cup signifies the relationship between God and Jesus Christ; and—in Jesus—the relationship between God and all human persons; and finally the relationships among human persons, held in the life of God. In other words, the meaning of the cup and the cross is that the relationship between God and humans is healed forever in and through Jesus Christ. A relationship holds, and now all relationships have the possibility of holding.

The image, then, comes full circle. The cup is not only a cup of suffering but a cup of love and a cup of life. We come to it not drawn by a delight in suffering but by the love of God for us revealed in the suffering of Jesus Christ, and by the oneness of all persons now forever held in the purposes of this cup. Moved by love to alleviate pain, we can come to yearn for justice; and insofar as it is possible to us, we are moved to do the deeds of justice, which are for us the deeds of love. This is not a call to passivity in the face of suffering. Like Jesus, we must resist suffering and pain as long as we can, remedy it in others as far as we are able, oppose the forces of injustice until we can do no more. We are not to surrender prematurely, before it is time. And when we reach the point of our own surrender (when we die), it need not be a surrender to disease or to violence, not even a surrender to death itself, but to the embrace of God.

Crucified Love

Another image is closely related to the image of drinking the cup. It may seem counterintuitive to most of us, but it holds a further insight into suffering and love. It is the image of a "crucified love." It can be described, demonstrated, revealed. It is a love both commanded and modeled by Jesus Christ, and characterized in its highest degree as, "No one has greater love than this, to lay down one's life for one's friends" (John 15:13). It can be found in every great human love—for God, for one another. It is present wherever relationships are genuinely and profoundly sustained.

But what is it, this form of great love? Or perhaps, first, what is it not? It is not the kind of love that is self-destructive or passive in the face of external forces of destruction. It is not "doormat" love. It is not love that violates human dignity, one's own or another's. It is not love that kills or is killed, that has death at its core. It is not love that clings because of fear. It is not love that weakens the self or the other. It is not a small love, a timid love, a fickle love, but a great love.

What, then, does it mean? What does it mean to say that perhaps every great love is a crucified love? A crucified love is a love that is tried by fire, that is achieved through a baptism of fire; even as it is crucified, it survives and lives. This is a love that is unconditional, that ultimately holds steady and strong no matter what must be borne; no matter what must be overcome, accepted, or forgiven; no matter what limitations are experienced in day-to-day living and working together; no matter what forces of evil threaten to pluck such a love from our hearts. Here is a love that manages to withstand distance, complexity, limitation. It is able to hold suffering even as it struggles to alleviate it. It is the kind of love symbolized by Mary's heart, pierced by a sword of sorrow. It is finally a love that is stronger than death, a love that can move us to lay down our lives for others.

By ourselves, no doubt, we are not capable of such loves, though we desire and aim at them. Nonetheless, we partake in such love because of the love of God in Jesus Christ—the love that was never lost or ended, that sustained a bond that was never broken, the love crucified but not destroyed. Here is indeed a love stronger than death, and strong enough to be shared with all of us. This is the love at the center of the meaning of the cross of Jesus Christ, making it possible for relationships to hold. This is the love that bears all burdens, holds all human suffering in order to transform it. Here is a love crucified that still lives, that does not turn away from swords of sorrow or the groanings of creation, that yearns to transform suffering into a fountain of life. We now have a basis to trust that great loves are possible to us, too, insofar as we partake in the love of God in Christ Jesus, revealed in the crucifixion of Jesus—this love that has lived and poured out life and love to us ever since.

Easter Rejoicing and the Discipline of Nonfulfillment

Texts
Philippians 4:4–9
John 16:19–24

This is the first day after Easter, and perhaps it is enough simply to say to one another again and again, "He is risen as he said. Alleluia. He lives and is with us still. Let us rejoice and be glad." Insofar as we now know, or believe we know, the end of the story of Jesus' life in this world, there is always the possibility that—throughout all of Eastertide and the rest of our lives, for that matter—joy will wash over us, warm and melt our hearts, renew our spirits, and bring us together in love. Even when, in the days to come, it may seem impossible to lift our minds and hearts in joy; even when the burdens of our lives make our hearts again too heavy; even when the tears of others afflict our spirits and turn us to sober and ongoing sorrow: We may still say to one another, "Jesus is risen as he said; let us rejoice and be glad." We can still remind one another that we are meant to receive, in the depths of our spirit, a gift of joy. It is, after all, a part of the Good News in which we believe, that we are meant—at some level of our existence—to be genuinely and profoundly happy.

This could, of course, be a dangerous way to talk. It can strike our cynicism as "cheap grace," or it can sound unfortunately like a gospel of "prosperity." It may even increase our present or future sadness, making our lack of joy worse—as when someone says to us, "Cheer up!"—as if giving us one more obligation we cannot meet. We will be unable, eventually, to avoid the recognition that, despite some profound experiences of Easter joy, there will remain in us agonies

---

This sermon is adapted from a version delivered in Marquand Chapel, at Yale Divinity School, on Easter Monday of 2014.

of ongoing pain; powerlessness before the pull of death will not be over; the injustices among us will not all be righted, not now or then or in our lifetime.

And yet, and yet, there are important reasons for us to rejoice—not only now in the "first fruits" of Eastertide, but in its full and unfolding experience and meaning beyond today. And although *reasons* for joy are not always by themselves sufficient to awaken joy, we may nonetheless help one another by considering them (these reasons)—especially now on a day when gladness is more immediate, and our Easter experiences more clear. Moreover, it is possible that in pondering reasons for rejoicing, joy may be more likely to dawn in us again and again, almost unawares; we may even, in long days from now, find our hearts still burning within us as we remember encounters, in whatever form, with the risen Jesus. What are our reasons for rejoicing? There may be a multitude of them or only one, but we can explore the potential power of at least some.

Reasons for Joy

A first reason to rejoice is because we have learned something about our suffering. The deep truth of Easter is that suffering is not the last word, and even death is not the last word. God *is* present with us still, and makes a home with us; we have not been forsaken. Our hearts and our bodies may again be broken, yet we believe that our existence is new, that we and all others can even now be alive with a hope that is new; and in our sorrows we may experience at least an inkling of the impulses to joy—small, hidden experiences of resurrection.

Creation, redemption, consummation: In a Christian perspective, these are not discontinuous. Nor are they the story of some other world, some other hearts, some other home, than our own. God, we believe, is present everywhere, charging the world with grandeur, hovering over it and dwelling within it, groaning within it for life and glory. And Jesus, the one who emptied himself in order to gather us to himself—who made our world his home and did not abandon it—now transforms (or aims to transform) our hearts and our earth, holding us into what is promised—what is not yet full, but is somehow already here. Perhaps joy wears out only if it forgets the source of its hope; perhaps joy is joy for us only if we remember the groaning; perhaps joy is "cheap grace" ("cheap joy") only if it does not shape our actions.

A second reason for rejoicing is that Jesus himself rejoices. Yes, he still drinks with us the cup of the suffering of each and all of us; yes, it is his Spirit that still groans in all creation. Yet in his resurrected life, in his utterly successful saving love, he is glad to overflowing. We who are also called to drink the cup of Jesus—which includes our own suffering, the suffering of all humankind, and even the cosmic suffering of all creation—are also called into friendship with God in Jesus Christ. *It is a part of friendship to share not only the suffering but the joy of one's friend.* In fact, it may be a greater sign of *love* that we at least want to share the joy of one we love—since it is ironically often much easier to share the sorrow of another than it is to share their joy. It takes a more profound openness, a more deeply anchored humbleness, a more radical conversion of heart, to enter into and to embrace the joy of another. Jesus, whom we at least desire to love with the love of friendship, is full of joy—a joy we desire *for his sake* to share.

There is a correlative (but different) third reason for us to rejoice: That is, *not only is Jesus Christ joyful, but he wants us to share in his joy.* It "matters" to him that we are able to do this. As a kind of echo of words recorded of Jesus, Paul writes to the Philippians: "Rejoice in the Lord always; again I will say, Rejoice" (Phil. 4:4).[5] Why? Because the joy of Jesus is *for us*—no less than his suffering, no less than his labor, no less than his death. *Everything*, if we can only receive it, is for us and all of creation: his love, his incarnation, his divinity, his truth, his pain, his glory, his Spirit, his life in time and eternity, his joy. It is Jesus' own risen life, his own unutterable, bursting joy of being, knowing, loving—it is this life that we are to live, in the hope of what has already begun. Jesus not only wants us to share in his joy, but yearns for it—*for our sakes*, because of the love God has for us. "Abide in my love. If you keep my commandments, you will abide in my love, just as I have kept my Father's commandments and abide in his love. I have said these things to you so that *my joy* may be in you, and *your joy* may be complete" (John 15:10–11, emphasis added). And again: "Very truly, I tell you, you will weep and mourn, but the world will rejoice; you will have pain, but your pain will turn to joy. . . . So you have pain now; but I will

---

[5]*The Jerusalem Bible* translation is, "I want you to be happy, always happy in the Lord; I repeat, what I want is your happiness."

see you again, and your hearts will rejoice, and no one will take your joy from you" (John 16:20–22).

Awakening to Joy

Reasons by themselves may not, however, be enough to bring joy to our hearts. We need also, perhaps, to learn *ways* of receiving joy—"strategies of heart," if you will—for opening to the possibilities of joy. One step in this regard may be pondering the characteristics of experiences of joy, trying to understand what joy is "like."[6] Many years ago I had a friend who seemed to know a lot about joy. It radiated from her, and was shared by many. I asked her, therefore, what the experience of "joy" was like for. She thought for a moment and then said to me: "Joy is not like euphoria; not like elation. It is less like a great burst of laughter than it is like a long, low chuckle." I took this to mean, in part, that joy cannot be had by straining for it. Nor can it be sustained by simply thinking happy thoughts. It is impossible for us to grit our teeth and be joyful. Moreover, we can grow emotionally weary of too much joy, just as we can grow weary of too much sorrow. Joy requires what might be called a "relaxation of the heart," a "letting go," a melting of the heart that in turn makes it possible to receive both the mercy and the joy of God as well as of one another. The kind of joy that extends from "Easter joy" runs deep enough to blend with experiences of peace.

A second "strategy of the heart" for receiving joy is what I call a "discipline of nonfulfillment."[7] To be open to joy, and to sustain peaceful joy, it seems concretely essential to learn such a "discipline." This discipline is not a practice merely of resignation in the face of what we cannot fully possess or achieve; it is not a simple acceptance of disappointment and disillusionment; it is, rather, something like the experience of Mary Magdalene on Easter morning, when in utter

---

[6]Although many philosophical and theological distinctions are to be made between "joy" and "happiness," I do not enter into this particular discussion here. I also do not try to draw a line between grace and learning (as in "strategies of the heart"). The latter can be ways in which grace works.

[7]I have never seen this term in writing except in my own work. The idea for it, however, was, in part, first suggested to me following a conversation with Ursula Niebuhr and Christopher F. Mooney.

joy she beholds the risen Christ, yet hears the loving words, "Do not cling to me."[8] Imagine the transformation of her grief into joy when she heard her name and beheld the one she sought. Yet in that very experience of joy was the paradoxical requirement of the "discipline of nonfulfillment." "Do not hold on to me," Jesus said. In this is the essence of what we know as the "already" but "not yet" of our existence. "Do not hold on to me," even though I know that I am the source and the center of your happiness and your life. "Do not hold on to me, because I have not yet ascended to the Father" (John 20:16–17). This is a beginning joy, not an ending, and the cross remains within it.

Without a discipline of nonfulfillment, our pining for what we do not have undermines our joy in what we have. This is a discipline that sustains our lives and our loves in a situation that is essentially *already/ not yet*, presence but not full presence, presence but also absence, fulfillment but not complete fulfillment, being at home but still on a journey. To open to joy is still to surrender; to love with the power of joy is to follow its call; to allow the flowering of joy is to relax in its presence and to trust in its promise. This is our present experience of resurrected life. If we speak only of the cross, we cannot go on; but if we speak only of resurrection, we cancel out most people's concrete experience. For Christians, there is a deep sense that in every sorrow, there is some joy; in every joy, there is some sorrow.

The discipline of nonfulfillment is what keeps alive our longings and our labors for justice and peace, even though we must cry, "Peace, peace, and there is no peace." As part of what I have elsewhere called a "crucified love," a discipline of nonfulfillment releases, frees, and anchors our committed love. It makes possible the richest forms of sustainable passion, single-minded purpose, and faithful promise-keeping. It also makes possible what, in our experience, might be named crucified hope and even crucified joy. Just as a crucified love is a love that is not destroyed, but lives, so also is a crucified joy one that enacts and nourishes our share in the risen Life of Jesus, the life of the Spirit.

There is one more strategy that might be proposed as a way of receiving joy. It is simply to ask for it—that is, to pray for it. Some

---

[8]My interpretation of this event is somewhat different from many of those offered by other theologians and biblical scholars. For a recent and helpful perspective, see Harold W. Attridge, "'Don't Be Touching Me': Recent Feminist Scholarship on Mary Magdalene," *Essays on John and Hebrews* (Grand Rapids: Baker Academic, 2012), 137–59.

Christians raise objections to this: It seems selfish to them, or presumptuous. It is, they say, better (and easier) to ask only for faith, or for courage, or for hope. But there are good reasons to ask God for joy. One is that we need it; we need it desperately, just as we need wisdom and courage. It is a mistake to think that joy is a luxury. We need its strength and its peace. Another is that Jesus told us to ask for it. In John 16, the imperative is given: "Until now, you have not asked for anything in my name. Ask and you will receive, *so that your joy may be complete*" (John 16:24, emphasis added). If we can let go of our objections, and perhaps also of our fears of disappointment, the very asking for joy may allow us to receive it—to receive it actively as we would receive a guest, as we would receive a gift. The Spirit of God, the spirit of joy, intends to dwell within us, breathing within us the truth that our hearts may indeed rejoice.

CHAPTER 12

Celibacy under the Sign of the Cross

While writing and speaking frequently on issues of sexual ethics, marriage and family, divorce and remarriage, same-sex relationships, and related topics, I have yet to address the question of celibacy. It seems both appropriate and timely to do so now, even though I believe the recent work of Sandra Schneiders, Peter Brown, Jo Ann McNamara,[1] and others, has covered much of the ground I might have explored. Historians (such as Brown and McNamara[2]) have contributed immensely to our perspective on questions of religiously motivated celibacy, both for men and for women; and systematic analyses (set forth by Schneiders, Karl Rahner,[3] and others) have focused issues and argued for positions with which I am largely in sympathy. Nonethe-

---

A version of this essay was originally published in *Sexuality and the U.S. Catholic Church*, ed. Lisa Sowle Cahill, John Garvey, and T. Frank Kennedy (New York: Crossroad, 2006), 126–43. It appears with permission from The Crossroad Publishing Company, Inc., www.crossroadpublishing.com.

[1]Sandra M. Schneiders, *Religious Life in a New Millennium*, 2 vols. (New York: Paulist Press, 2000–2001); and Schneiders, *New Wineskins: Re-imagining Religious Life Today* (New York: Paulist Press, 1986); Peter Brown, *The Body and Society: Men, Women, and Sexual Renunciation in Early Christianity* (New York: Columbia University Press, 1988); Jo Ann McNamara, *Sisters in Arms: Catholic Nuns through Two Millennia* (Cambridge, MA: Harvard University Press, 1998); and McNamara, *A New Song: Celibate Women in the First Three Christian Centuries* (New York: Haworth Press, 1983).

[2]Other useful studies are included in Peter Brooks, ed., *Christian Spirituality* (London: SCM Press, 1975); Elizabeth Abbott, *A History of Celibacy* (Toronto: HarperCollins, 1999); Elizabeth Castelli, "Virginity and Its Meaning for Women's Sexuality in Early Christianity," *Journal of Feminist Studies in Religion* 2 (Spring 1986): 61–88; Ross S. Kraemer, ed., *Maenads, Martyrs, Matrons, Monastics: A Sourcebook on Women's Religions in the Greco-Roman World* (Philadelphia: Fortress Press, 1988).

[3]See Karl Rahner, "On the Evangelical Counsels," *Theological Studies* 8, trans. D. Bourke (New York: Herder and Herder, 1971); Edward Vacek, "Religious Life and the Eclipse of Love for God," *Review for Religious* 57(2) (March-April 1998): 18–37.

less, my agenda and my perspective may be sufficiently different from those taken by other scholars that I will risk adding this essay to the conversation already in place.

I will attempt to do three things, each briefly. Drawing on the massive historical studies of others, I will look to history not for a complete narrative of the Christian practice of celibacy, but to give some context to the concept of celibacy as it has perdured through centuries. Then I will turn to contemporary problems that burden both the concept and practice of celibacy. Finally, but in response to these problems, I will propose an understanding of celibacy that may be fitting and useful for contemporary Christians. I will not explicitly address the question of whether celibacy should be required for the Roman Catholic priesthood (though I think it should not), nor the question of the secular as well as religious importance of celibacy for persons in general, particularly contemporary women (though I think this is of great personal and political importance, especially for feminists). I will focus on celibacy in Western Christianity, because issues of sexuality vary from culture to culture and tradition to tradition, and I cannot here take on questions of so broad a scope. This in no way implies that I think traditional Christian understandings of celibacy cannot cross cultural divides.

It is an understatement to say that celibacy presents key questions for the future of traditionally celibate Christian communities. My goal is not to make recommendations in this regard but to contribute to work that needs to be done prior to such recommendations. My own ultimate interest is in celibacy as understood and practiced by women in Western Christian religious communities with so-called active ministries, though I hope what I say will have useful implications for the practice of celibacy in other contexts as well.

The View from the Past

What I am looking for here is the history of an idea, a creative concept, an imaginative understanding of the meaning of religiously motivated (in particular, Christianly motivated) celibacy. I do not, of course, think that concepts can be divorced from the concrete contexts and specific practices that shape them, but sometimes a concept crosses the divides of time and space, of gender and culture. It becomes part of a living tradition. "Celibacy" is such a concept.[4] It cannot be understood adequately apart from the specific historical contexts in which it was practiced, yet the meanings of one context tend to interact with meanings of another. Peter Brown's study of the practice of "permanent sexual renunciation" among men and women (mostly men) in Christian circles from 40 CE to 430 CE provides a good example of this. Brown pays attention both to context and to the development of a tradition as he weaves a narrative with multiple plots and characters, drawn from letters and sermons, philosophical and theological dialogues, lives of saints and fictional romance literature, polemical treatises and guides to prayer, works of art and inscriptions on tombstones.

Brown offers no incautious and sweeping generalizations, no superficial samplings of profoundly diverse experiences. Rather, what we are asked to examine in meticulous detail is an intriguing variety of places and times, persons and cultures. A repeated phrase of Brown's is "a different world"; this or that was a "different world" from the ones through which he led his readers in previous chapters. The diaspora of Paul was a different world from the Palestine of Jesus. The meanings given to the human body and to human sexuality were therefore different, too. Cappadocia and Pontus were worlds away from the Egypt of the Desert Fathers, and Gregory of Nyssa's understanding of asceticism was a world away from Anthony's. The Latin traditions of sexual renunciation grew out of a world vastly different from either the drastic challenges of the East or the slow and humble patience of the monks at Sinai. Different times, different places, different particular histories, different temperaments: the forms and meanings of sexual renunciation have been myriad—complementary, paradoxical, contradictory, parallel, incompatible. They form a dazzling panorama, an intricately woven tapestry whose threads we can trace without blurring what they portray.

Think, for example, of the vast differences in the experiences of a commitment to celibacy by wandering young radicals, middle-aged postmaritally celibate bishops, desert solitaries, virgin women who remained within the households of their families of origin, wealthy

---

[4]I am not distinguishing "celibacy" here from its sometime term, "virginity." The two terms can have different connotations, with sometimes differently gendered meanings. I am also not going to distinguish celibacy from "chastity," or from "continence" though there are more important reasons for doing this (not the least of which is that "chastity" applies to both celibacy and marriage).

women patrons of monasteries, celibate philosophers engaged in serene study circles, men and women participating in daring experiments of cohabitation, desert communities of women or men. Think of the differences in self-understanding in the experience of permanent continence undertaken in the belief that the soul can transform the body; or the belief that conversion of heart is helped by a celibate integration of affections in relation to God; or the conviction that sexual nonavailability of women to men can overturn gendered expectations; or beliefs that friendship can be greater if it transcends sexual intimacy; that human personal self-bondage can be undone only by rigorous asceticism that includes the repudiation of sex; that the death and resurrection of Jesus Christ can be entered into in a way that makes sex irrelevant. Brown finds all of these forms and rationales (and more) for permanent celibacy—emerging, developing, competing among themselves and competing with a view of married chastity. None of them were lived in a social vacuum; most of them were intensely debated; and thus did the option of sexual renunciation grow more real and more widespread in an unfolding Christian world.

Despite all of this variety—descriptive and normative—in understandings of celibacy, Brown insists that permanent sexual renunciation is a recognizably distinctive element of Christian morality in the four centuries he studies and later; and that it has had far-reaching cultural consequences, including the breaking of the "city's" control over the meaning and activities of the human body. But can these diverse practices of sexual renunciation inform a whole tradition, and if so, how shall it be characterized?

What began with Paul's opinion about celibate freedom in service of the gospel took quantum leaps when through the years it came to be seen variously as a substitute for martyrdom, a majestic ideal of virtue, a radical turn away from ordinary lives of marrying and raising children, a form of heroic asceticism that promised mystical experiences of God.[5] Specific contexts gave rise to idiosyncratic practices, but developing theologies both fueled these practices and held them, however loosely, together. Chief among these was a theology of sexuality that made sexual renunciation a logical choice for those who

---

[5] I do not claim that Brown draws these conclusions, but only that his (and others') studies lead to them.

could make it.[6] Christianity, after all, emerged in the late Hellenistic Age when even Judaism was influenced by pessimistic attitudes toward sex. While early Christian writers and preachers affirmed sex as good, a part of creation, they also believed it to be paradigmatically injured by the destructive forces of a catastrophic Fall, caused by an "original sin" (which was a sin of disobedience, not of sexual sin. The fathers of the church shared with Stoic philosophers, therefore, a suspicion of bodily passion and a respect for reason as a guide to the moral life. What prevailed in Christian moral teaching was a doctrine that viewed sex as good but seriously flawed—in that its passion could not as such be controlled by reason. Like the Stoics, Christian leaders taught that sex can be brought back under the rule of reason by discovering and respecting its rational purpose—that is, the purpose of procreation. Its justification could only be found in its service to the species, as a necessary means to human reproduction (hence, there could be no morally good sex without a procreative intent, and in large part because of this, no sex outside of marriage).

Even within marriage, sex was considered a kind of duty, acceptable for its instrumental value; it could even as such still be tainted (a view held by St. Augustine, though not by many others[7]). At the very least, the experience of sexual passion was thought to prevent (for the time it lasted) an undistracted contemplation of God. Hence, marriage was extolled as a graced institution and as a remedy for lust, but it was better to forgo marriage (and sex) in order to free the spirit for union with the divine, as well as to free an individual's time and energies for service of the gospel.

A theology of sexuality was combined, then, with a theology of marriage that heightened the value of celibacy. While mainstream Christianity was never a world-denying or body-denying religion, the early church fashioned theological perspectives that relativized the importance of marriage and family for centuries to come. As Rowan Greer has shown, the church in late antiquity manifested at least three attitudes toward marriage and family, the combination of

---

[6]For general background on the history of sexual ethics, see Margaret A. Farley, *Just Love: A Framework for Christian Sexual Ethics* (New York: Continuum, 2008), chap. 2.

[7]Key primary texts for Augustine's view of sexuality include *On the Goodness of Marriage* (401 CE); *On Holy Virginity* (401 CE); *A Literal Commentary on Genesis* (401–14 CE); *On Marriage and Concupiscence* (419–21 CE).

which yielded a deep ambivalence.[8] (1) There was a seeming rejection of family ties, sometimes even open hostility toward the family. The Christian message was a sword of division, setting family members against one another (Matt. 10:34–39; Luke 12:51–53). All Christians were asked in some sense to leave all things, including father, mother, spouse, children (Matt. 12:25; 22:30; Luke 20:35). Believers lived in anticipation of a new age, which would exclude marrying and giving in marriage. (2) Closely related to this, the early Christians saw the church itself as their family. For those who had to leave their former families, the church was their new home (Matt. 10:29–30). (3) On the other hand, Christians also believed that marriage and family in the ordinary sense could be affirmed, not abolished, within the new life of faith. Against reported teachings of gnostics of various kinds, Christian preachers (Augustine the foremost among them) affirmed the goodness of marriage and its importance in God's plan. But the message remained ambiguous, with attitudes of rejection, substitution, and affirmation continually in tension. In such a context, a rationale for celibacy was not difficult to understand.

Threads in theologies of sexuality and of marriage were pulled forward into a theology of the human person that raised the choice of celibacy into a magnetic ideal. A celibate lifestyle offered a way to heroic virtue, to perfection in the love of God and neighbor. Holiness was connected with bodily discipline and with the heights of contemplation. Relieved of ordinary responsibilities (and in the case of women, freed from coerced marriages, limited lives of drudgery, and the often painful burdens of endless childbearing), individuals could control their own bodies and map out whole new horizons of human freedom. By the second century, Christianity had become a religion for the young; for many, celibacy had become the lifestyle of choice.[9] By the Middle Ages, there was a whole world of celibate priests, monks, and nuns, a whole culture sustained on the assumption that celibates can embrace a holy way in the church and in the reign of God.

Along with theologies of sexuality, marriage and family, and human perfectionism, there grew through the centuries a theological and practical connection between celibacy, community, and the "care of

---

[8]Rowan A. Greer, *Broken Lights and Mended Lives: Theology and Common Life in the Early Church* (University Park: Pennsylvania State University Press, 1986), 77–100.

[9]Brown, *Body and Society*, 191.

souls." Added to this, and gradually transforming it, was the expansion of care of souls to the care of whole persons, especially persons in desperate need. From Basil the Great's "hospitals" in the fourth century to the monastic centers in the early Middle Ages, and from the mendicant friars of the high Middle Ages to the eighteenth- and nineteenth-century orders of nuns dedicated to the care of the poor, celibacy was a way both to union with God and to love and service of one's neighbor. The relentless logic of a way of life that was not only an end in itself but a contributor in helping this world yielded a descriptive concept of celibacy and its normative rationale.

At the heart of the concept, in summary, was the belief that celibacy offered a unique and privileged access to union with God, primarily because it was conducive to prayer—to contemplation, meditation, even mystical experience of the presence of God. But access to God was also a matter of wholeness in the individual self, achieved through sexual renunciation as a primary form of asceticism, both negative (the control of disruptive and conflicting desires) and positive (the liberty of spirit that was thereby achieved). Celibacy was, therefore, a way to holiness, to perfection of the highest human capabilities, shaping a readiness for the reception of God's grace in this world, and all the while witnessing to hope for a new world to come. As a way of life, it aimed to refine capacities for love of both God and neighbor. Most of the time it was understood as a higher and better way (than marriage) of imitating the life of Jesus Christ (though it was never considered automatically or absolutely so[10]). Hence, despite its multiple and varied manifestations through the centuries, celibacy in a Christian context came to incorporate the general conceptual elements of a lifelong commitment to sexual abstinence, nonmarriage, *imitatio Christi*, freedom from ordinary familial responsibilities—all for the sake of union with God, perfection of the self, and service to one's neighbor in the context of the reign of God. These conceptual and purposive lines were set and remained with astonishing consistency through centuries of subsequent history in the church.

Both the concept and its rationale have been subject to critique,

---

[10]Augustine, for example, insisted many times that the disobedient or unfaithful virgin was not to be considered as holy as the faithful wife. One's "state of life" did not guarantee one's achievement of its goals.

however, from individual Christian (as well as secular) thinkers, political leaders, and in the twentieth century, proponents of psychological theories that judge celibate lifestyles to be unhealthy. In the history of Christianity, there is no doubt that the paradigmatic critique of celibacy was rendered in the sixteenth century by leaders of the Protestant Reformation. Not only the concept and the rationale of celibacy made it vulnerable, but the concrete historical failures in its practice readied it for the broadsides delivered by the major Reformers.

Theologies of sexuality, marriage and family, perfectionism, and even forms of neighbor-love came under particular attack by Martin Luther.[11] In fact, questions of sexual behavior played an important role in the whole of the Reformation. Celibacy was challenged not just in its scandalous nonobservance but as a Christian ideal. Marriage and family replaced it among the Reformers as the center of sexual gravity in the Christian life. Luther (as well as John Calvin, for that matter) was deeply influenced by the Augustinian tradition regarding original sin and its consequences for human sexuality. Yet Luther developed a position on marriage and sex that was not dependent upon the traditional procreative ethic. Like most of the Christian tradition, he affirmed marriage and sexuality as part of the divine plan for creation. But he shared Augustine's pessimistic view of fallen human nature and its disordered sex drive. Like Augustine, Luther thought of sex as an indomitable drive, difficult to control and tainted by sin. Luther was convinced, however, that the best remedy for disordered desire is not celibacy but marriage, wherein sex can be domesticated, tamed, by the multiple responsibilities of wedded life and children. Luther was not the first to advocate marriage as the cure for unruly sexual desire, but he took on the whole of the tradition in a way that no one else had.

In Luther's view, sexual pleasure itself in one sense needs no justification. The desire for it is simply a fact of life. It remains good so long as it is channeled through marriage into the meaningful whole of life. What there is in sex that detracts (or distracts) from the knowledge of God is indeed sinful, but even a procreative aim cannot provide it with a special "justification." If it cannot be justified, it has simply and

---

[11]Relevant writings of Martin Luther include *Two Kinds of Righteousness* (1519), *Sermon on the Estate of Marriage* (1519), *Treatise on Good Works* (1520), Estate of Marriage (1522), *How God Rescued an Honorable Nun* (1524), *On Marriage Matters* (1530).

finally to be forgiven, as do the sinful elements that are inevitable (according to Luther) in all human activity. The "place" of its forgiveness is only within marriage and a family.

The Protestant Reformation, then, did little to change fundamental Christian assessments of sex. Yet it drastically altered the assessment of celibacy. The paradigm for Christian daily life was now marriage and family. A lifelong commitment to celibacy became thoroughly suspect as a realistic possibility for individuals (the indomitability of sexual desire precludes sexual abstinence for all but a very few). And since (by the higher Middle Ages) it was frequently associated with a life of supposed poverty, but one that depended on alms from the genuinely poor, celibacy was judged to be not only unrealistic but marked by laziness and moral turpitude.

Even more importantly, Luther rejected perfectionism on theological grounds.[12] All persons are justified by the grace of God in Jesus Christ, yet all remain sufficiently sinful that progress in internal transformation is not to be expected: *simul justus, simul peccator*. Seeking perfection is, rather, sinful in itself, since it is essentially self-centered. It contaminates faith in God (for it seeks salvation in "works-righteousness") and prevents a full-blown love of neighbor.

The primary *ethical* demand made on Christians is indeed, according to Luther, love of neighbor. But it is in the secular, nonsacramental institutions of marriage and family that individuals learn obedience to God, patience, and the required forms of neighbor-love. After 1523, therefore, Luther shifted his emphasis on marriage as a "hospital for the incurables" to marriage as a "school for character." This did not mean that Luther simply turned desires for holiness in a new direction. Rather, he continued to reject perfection altogether as an authentic Christian concern.

The Catholic Reformation (or so-called Counter-Reformation) absorbed scarcely any of the critiques of the ideal of celibacy or its goals. It did take seriously the quite accurate charges of widespread nonobservance among celibates. Catholic Church leaders moved, therefore, to strengthen the discipline (primarily through "enclosure" to avoid temptation) that might better protect and promote celibacy as a

---

[12]Calvin, unlike Luther, maintained the importance of growth in the Christian life, or what he called "sanctification." See John Calvin, *Institutes of the Christian Religion* 3.3–10.

valid choice among Christians.[13] By and large, however, the Protestant critique remains still to be addressed in the Roman Catholic tradition at practical and theoretical levels alike. Combined with other problems that haunt the concept, rationale, and practice of committed lifelong celibacy, this critique must finally be taken into account in the development of theologies of celibacy. Only so will constructive proposals make sense in the "different world" of contemporary cultures and the church. I turn, then, to problems of the present that are in important ways still problems from the past.

Problems in the Present

Problems with historical theologies of sexuality, of marriage and family, and of the human person are not the only problems to be faced in validating Christian choices of committed lifelong celibacy. Developments in contemporary theology that correct historical inadequacies sometimes serve only to sharpen the questions for a celibacy rationale. A "view from the present" is therefore needed to complement a "view from the past" if we are to clarify the full set of challenges that constructive proposals regarding celibacy must take into account.

First, past theologies of human sexuality no longer serve well the authentication and promotion of lifelong committed celibacy. Pessimistic views of sex have yielded to theologies of embodiment and sexuality that at least aim to integrate reason and emotion, body and spirit, desire and love. Far from being seen as a drain on individuals' strength and power, sex is believed to enhance the capabilities of the person as a whole. Today, sex is not even thought to be a distraction from prayer. On the contrary, it has become a truism that it is not sex that gets in the way of contemplation, but work (or whatever form of pressured and all-encompassing activity characterizes responsible lives in contemporary society).

No one any longer argues that sex is the paradigmatic location of the damage from original sin. Sexual desire can still have negative

---

[13]There is an important story here that is relevant to gendered perceptions of sexuality—the story of the multiplication of rules for enclosure of women celibates (as distinguished from the much fewer rules for the enclosure of men). The presupposition was not that women were more likely to break their vows of celibacy because of their stronger sexual drive, but that men needed to be protected from contact with women so that men could be helped in controlling their sexual desires.

consequences (as in exploitation, repression, oppression, betrayal), but celibacy is not the remedy for all such evils.[14] Moreover, freedom for service may still be secured at the price of celibacy, but there are those whose experience shows that too much "availability" can be as counterproductive as too little. The challenge to celibacy, then, is that there are very fine ways, holy ways—other than lifelong celibacy—to live out the sexual dimension of human life. There are ways, to put it sharply, that appear to be just as conducive to union with God, service of the neighbor, and fulfillment of the human person. Given the personal cost of celibacy, why then should anyone choose it?

Similarly, historical problems with theologies of marriage and family are superseded by contemporary insights and valuations. But in this development, also, traditional rationales for celibacy may be weakened if not destroyed. The twentieth century saw in some sense a giant step taken in the church's positive affirmation of the family. Again and again in papal encyclicals, statements of episcopal synods, documents of Vatican II, and so forth, the family has been hailed as not only the foundation of society but even "the first cell of the church," the "domestic sanctuary" of the Christian community.[15] In the twentieth century, arguments are made (primarily in defense of rights of the family) for marriage, family life, and parenthood as intimate to the identity of the individual, rooted in the core of what it means to be a person.[16]

The very concerns that led Christians of the past to relegate the family to secondary importance in the Christian life have been revisited in the light of new understandings of human relationships, connections between public and private spheres, the secular and the sacred, and

---

[14]It should be noted, in addition, that psychoanalytic theories—however controversial and changing—do not challenge a view of sex as an indomitable drive, but they have yielded the widely accepted belief that this is simply part of human nature. More than this, some theorists no longer see sex as the fundamental basis for all motivation (since it has become more obvious that there can be multiple motivations for sex). The point is that no overly simplified theory of sexuality can serve to bless celibacy (or, for that matter, to condemn it).

[15]For an overall view of this development, see Margaret A. Farley, "Family," in *The New Dictionary of Catholic Social Thought*, ed. J. Dwyer (Collegeville, MN: Liturgical Press, 1994), 371–81; "The Church and the Family: An Ethical Task," *Horizons* 10 (Spring 1983): 50–71. For specific documentation of these and other texts, see, e.g., *Gaudium et spes* 52; Apostolicam actuositatem 11; *Familiaris consortio* 16.

[16]For an overview of some of these arguments, see David Hollenbach, *The Right to Procreate and Its Social Limitations: A Systematic Study of Value Conflict in Roman Catholic Ethics* (Ph.D. diss., Yale University, 1975).

salvation history.[17] Previous assumptions that marriage and family are "things of this world" that must be transcended for the sake of the reign of God, or that they are less conducive (than celibacy) to growth in a whole and absolute love for God and a universal love for all humankind, are now modified and even discarded. Today Christian theology is less likely to think of marriage as involving a "divided heart" and more likely to ponder the ways in which God can be found in creation, whether in nature or in created persons. Theologians are less likely to conceptualize marriage as an "indirect" way to union with God and more likely to see special relationships as participations in and helps toward Christian *agape*. Once again, then, what rationale can be given for lifelong celibacy that fosters it as a choice among Christians?

When it comes to contemporary theologies of the human person, there has been no abandonment of the view that moral development and growth in holiness are possible and even required. Luther's view has not found resonance in the Roman Catholic psyche. The attack on "works-righteousness" has indeed chastened Catholic theology, but the net result has been stronger, more persuasive theologies of grace and theologies of human freedom.[18] Moreover, in both Protestant and Catholic theologies, character development and theories of virtue are once again central to a comprehensive Christian theological ethics. Similarly, postmodern dismissals of the continuity of the "self" are not finally persuasive for human persons whose experience of life includes the promise of an unlimited future in relationship with God.

What does provide yet another challenge to rationales for celibacy, however, is the gradual move in Catholic theology to develop the notion of a universal call to holiness. Always implicit in Catholic belief, it nonetheless was obscured by the emphasis on celibacy as a response to this call. Thomas Aquinas argued in the thirteenth century that it is a matter of "precept," of moral obligation, that all are called to love God with a whole heart,[19] with the implication that this is possible in all walks of life. But it took Vatican II in the twentieth century to identify once and for all the radicality of the vocation of all Christians,

---

[17]One should note, however, that Roman Catholic Church leaders are still quite capable of ranking celibacy over marriage in terms of the "superiority of this charism to that of marriage, by reason of the wholly singular link which it has with the kingdom of God." See *Familiaris consortio* 16. The issue is whether this claim remains supportable.

[18]See, above all, Rahner's many essays in this regard and his *Foundations of Christian Faith*, trans. W. V. Dych (New York: Seabury Press, 1978), part 3.

[19]Thomas Aquinas, *Summa Theologiae* II-II.184.3.

and in one fell swoop the tensions between "precepts" and "counsels" were almost swept away.[20] But if all morally good ways of life can be the "means through which and the basis upon which" an individual grows toward the fullness of her perfection, then it is less clear why anyone would choose lifelong celibacy, given the genuine renunciation that it involves.[21] If "grace is everywhere,"[22] and the way that grace works is through ordinary lives, private or public, in church or family or chosen community, then is there a particular rationale left to be articulated for lifelong celibacy?

Celibacy and Its Future

No doubt the most important Christian response to contemporary questions of whether religiously motivated lifelong celibacy makes sense is that Jesus himself has shown the way. Yet no one thinks she or he can exactly replicate Jesus' life. There are requirements for discipleship, but celibacy is not one of them. Having no general command to imitate Jesus particularly as celibates, Christians must probe the legitimacy of this option in their own time and place and in their own personal circumstances. Hence, it is not superfluous to respond to the problems of celibacy in the face of changing understandings of human sexuality, marriage and family, and the call to holiness.

Celibacy must be an authentic way not only of living but, in particular, of living one's sexuality. What was a difficult life choice for past generations becomes more difficult still in a pan-sexualized culture like our own. Whatever the rationale for such a choice, it must be able to stand when past groundings seem no longer reasonable, or when understandings and practical possibilities of sexual choices are legitimately transformed. Deep in the Christian tradition is a sexual theology and ethic that values marriage and procreation on the one hand and singleness and celibacy on the other. Why is this so? We have come well beyond the view that sex as such is as likely to be evil as to be good, and we can also move beyond the view that a life without genital sexual activity is against nature. Even if all theory should be

---

[20]*Lumen gentium* chap. 5, nos. 39–42; chap. 6, nos. 43–47.

[21]See Karl Rahner, "On the Evangelical Counsels," *Theological Investigations* 8, trans. David Bourke (New York: Herder and Herder, 1971), 142.

[22]Georges Bernanos, *Diary of a Country Priest* (New York: Macmillan, 1937), 298.

for this latter view, the experience of those who lead celibate lives is too often against it. Whether celibacy is chosen or graciously accepted, many of those who live it manifest in their lives not only happiness and well-being but the heightened peace that comes with human self-realization and fulfillment.

Committed lifelong celibacy has always been only an alternative way—an alternative to marriage and to life in a family, and also an alternative to singleness without a focused permanent commitment to celibacy. As such, it has offered a way of relating to God and to neighbor that is of value in itself, but also revelatory of the meaning of sexuality for the Christian community and the wider society beyond. Whatever the aberrations in some past or present historical settings, celibacy has always held the potential of challenging existing power relations, liberating individuals for the unexpected, breaking the bonds of gender stereotypes, and resisting the rigid social constructions of sexual meanings in any era. There is no reason to prevent the option of religiously motivated lifelong celibacy from fulfilling these functions today.

The twenty-first century brings its own sexual problematic, and it is one for which celibacy is not irrelevant. The work of the French philosopher Michel Foucault was preoccupied with a question that his massive history of human sexuality was not finally able to answer: How did contemporary Western culture come to believe that sexuality is the key to individual identity? How did sex become more important than love, and almost more important than life?[23] Celibates have no more of an answer to these questions than anyone else. But the option of celibacy keeps such a question in perspective and perhaps even alive. Celibacy represents the possibility that genital sex need not be at the heart of every profound human relationship, and that sexual intensity, lived celibately, can empower the human person as a whole.

Perhaps particularly for women in the twenty-first century, committed lifelong celibacy holds the possibility of resisting and transcending gender stereotypes that continually threaten to limit the spheres within which women (and men, for that matter) may live and work. In an era when the importance of gender is more and more questioned—whether

---

[23]See Michel Foucault, *The History of Sexuality*, 3 vols. (French ed., Editions Gallimard, 1976–94).

in marriage, partnerships of all kinds, or roles in the family, church, and society—celibate individuals and groups provide perspectives and insights of critical importance to all. Genital sexual renunciation need not (ought not, and probably cannot) render individuals sexless or gender-free, but it can expand the horizons against which gender and sex gain meaning. Moreover, in a time when population growth is less of a need than ever before (when, in terms used by Peter Brown, there is no need to "replace the dead"[24]), celibates can help to make visible the multiple forms of fruitfulness that characterize human relationships and endeavors.

Moreover, despite my previous positive theological review, traditional concepts and rationales regarding marriage and family are themselves under challenge. For whatever reasons (including the greater acceptability of same-sex unions, the volatility of contemporary societies, the development of reproductive technologies), it is difficult to know what counts as "traditional" family. And whatever form a family takes, issues of structural justice have become central to its viability and its worth. Every form of human power—religious, legal, political, economic—is being brought to bear on the family. "Family values" are frequently not pious or innocuous slogans but coercive agendas for controlling the family, as often to its detriment as to its gain. Celibates along with everyone else have a stake in the outcome of this social confusion.

This means that, for example, it will not do for celibate women and men on the one hand, and spouses and parents (or single persons, partners, single parents, etc.) on the other, to compete with one another for some kind of pride of place in the church or society. Contemporary discourse about sexuality, about the nature and roles of men and women, serves all persons ill if it closes off their genuinely legitimate options, determines the limits of their activities, yields yet again gendered hierarchies in every sphere. Hence, if the alternatives open to individuals are pit against each other, both women and men must refuse the temptation to vie for what any others judge to be a "better" way. Oddly enough, if celibates have a stake in a stable outcome of social confusion regarding marriage and family, so also sexually partnered

---

[24]With widespread practices of genocide, and with new threats of plague-proportion disease, there may emerge different needs regarding population growth. But even with this possibility, celibacy may have a lot to contribute as an alternative way of rearing, if not bearing, children.

persons and their offspring have a stake in whatever new understandings emerge for celibacy. After all, most human relationships—all but a limited number in any person's life—are celibate.

Every authentic way of life incorporates relationships that are intrinsically good and hence constitutive of the fullness of life toward which they are also a means. Insofar as love of God requires love of neighbor—not just as a test or a sign, but as a way in which God is to be loved—marriage and family offer particular ways of loving. It is, as Rahner insists, false to say that "two loves, the love for God and Christ on the one hand, and the human love which finds its fulfillment in marriage on the other, are opposed to one another as rivals."[25] God is not one particular among many, not in competition with human objects of love. To love anyone truly is to encounter, in Martin Buber's terms, the "Eternal Thou."[26] Past distinctions, then, between celibate love for God as "direct" and a love for God in and through marriage as "indirect" are no longer adequate. The possibilities we have of union with God are not determined by the ways in which we live our sexuality (except insofar as everything in our lives has something to do with our way of loving God).

Committed lifelong celibacy, as I have already said, has always been only an alternate way of living, but it has been an *alternate* way. Despite newer insights into the shared goals and rationales of every authentic way of Christian living, the different ways are not conflatable. If we are more adequately to *distinguish* yet *value* diverse ways of life—in particular, celibate and married walks of life—a focus on some particular aspects of both ways of life may be useful. These aspects include different forms of intimacy, different witnesses to hope, and different patterns of living.

Briefly, then, we can observe that differences in possibilities for human interpersonal intimacy are more telling than anything else. There are forms of intimacy that belong to sexual partnerships but not to celibate relationships. At the heart of the renunciation that is intrinsic to lifelong celibacy is a letting go of some of the richest, most passionate yet tender, most all-encompassing forms of intimacy given to human persons. This is an intimacy that is not limited to genital intimacy, but overflows into, permeates, the daily sharing of all of life with another

---

[25]Rahner, "On the Evangelical Counsels," 148.
[26]Martin Buber, *I and Thou* (Edinburgh: T and T Clark, 1959).

person insofar as that is possible. Of course, such intimacy frequently encounters the many forms of struggles that are also part of blending lives together. Even and perhaps only through these struggles are the depths of this intimacy discovered and forged.

Not all human interpersonal intimacy is foregone by a commitment to celibacy, since the intensity of friendships—precisely without genital content—can sometimes surpass the intimacy of those who are sexually partnered. Yet at the heart of the renunciation that is intrinsic to lifelong celibacy is a letting go of sexual and marital intimacy. Something is lost for celibates when it comes not only to the intensities of sexual relationship but to a particular kind of sharing of the fabric of everyday life. When a commitment to celibacy is religiously motivated, when it is undertaken in response to a perceived call, then the reasons for renunciation and loss are lodged in a relationship to God and to the People of God, both of which offer new possibilities for intimacy in shared lives and labors. And such a call can include casting one's lot with others, in community, ministry, and friendship. Hence, the processes toward and the realities of intimacy are not the same in different walks of life. Intimacy may not be measured, but it takes diverse forms.

Lifelong celibacy, chosen for the sake of the reign of God, has from early Christian centuries been valued in part as a witness to an unlimited future—an embodiment of eschatological hope in a world to come. In the twentieth and twenty-first centuries, eschatology has turned more to this world than a world beyond, so that marriage and family have become a sign of hope in a new way. That is, the very decision to bear children requires hope in the future of this world, whatever its tragedies and terrors. Both perspectives are important, one must say. The danger that hope will be wishful thinking, a "pie in the sky" kind of hope that never attends to the needs of this world, is countered by eschatological demands that we (whether celibate or married) work for justice and the mending of the world. But on the other hand, and as I have said elsewhere, if hope in another world without care for this one is a mistake, so too is hope in this world without belief in the continuity between this world and its transformation by God into another. Those in either walk of life, married or celibate, are called to hope in both ways. Neither detracts from the other if their primary embodied witnesses coalesce into the kind of theological hope without which we cannot live.

When one focuses particularly on one or the other vocation, there are things to be said that cannot be said only by comparison. In each vocation there is need for a home—if not a material dwelling place, at least a home in the heart of God and the hearts of some others. In each vocation a life is laid down, in love for others, again and again. In each vocation there is fulfillment and nonfulfillment, rejoicing and waiting, in the mystery of what is "already but not yet." In each vocation there is waxing and waning of courage and energy and devotion and love. Each vocation is in itself a life and a ministry.

In the story of each person's life is the story of God-relatedness and neighbor-love. Neither of these loves is reducible to the other, and both are required as the foundation, the integrated way, and the goal of authentic vocation. There is more than one kind of neighbor-love and more than one kind of love of God. Just as there is more than one kind of love in diverse experiences of marriage and family, so there is more than one kind of love in diverse experiences of lifelong celibacy. The fullness of love that God gives to God's people encompasses them all.

But were I to speak primarily (and in general) of lifelong committed celibacy, I would have to emphasize somewhere that such a life is a little like living on a park bench—without a home or a place to lay one's head. Though a Christian celibate life is certainly not "world-denying," nonetheless to embrace it is fundamentally a decision to "leave all things" for the sake of the reign of God. Unlike marriage and family, a celibate vocation is not really first a part of the "order of creation." It may be that there are goods that are attractive to some who choose lifelong celibacy, goods that they respect and love and need not leave behind. Yet the experience of many who make the choice of lifelong celibacy in a Christian context is frequently charged with radicality in a way that most other commitments are not.

This form of choice of Christian celibacy makes sense only for the sake of love—or better, for the sake of at least a desire to love God with one's whole heart and soul and mind and strength, and to love one's neighbor as one's self. That is, it makes sense only if it is a way to refine human capacities for love, to find in faith the union that is love, and to express love in action. The goal of this life is given first in the yearning that prompts it and then in the ongoing desire that sustains it. The central rationale for this life may be found, finally, in the desire to pick up one's very being and place it down again in utter affirmation of God; and in so doing, in profound love of and solidarity with the neighbor near and far. This is true of all vocations in one way or another, for all great loves are in some profound sense crucified loves. In each vocation a life is laid down somewhere along the way, and perhaps again and again. I say again: in each there is fulfillment and nonfulfillment, rejoicing and waiting, in the mystery of the already–not yet. In each and every vocation is both life and ministry, and perhaps also mystery. But a celibate vocation makes sense only under the sign of the cross—which is a sign, after all, not of death but of life; not of betrayal but of relationships that hold.

CHAPTER 13

Prophetic Discourse in a Time of AIDS

When I was originally asked to write about prophetic aspects of global advocacy for prevention of HIV and AIDS, I was conflicted as to whether the term "prophetic" is helpful in describing, or in providing guidance for, the task of preventing the spread of HIV and AIDS in our world today. Prophetic discourse has many meanings, even when it is located paradigmatically in the traditions of the biblical prophets. As Cathleen Kaveny notes in her intriguing work on the values and dangers of prophetic language in contemporary ethical and political contexts, biblical prophets were individuals who were called and commissioned by God, usually to deliver a message to God's people.[1] The divine message frequently took the form of social critique and reform. "The prophet," as Abraham Heschel maintained, "was an individual who said 'No' to his society, condemning its habits and assumptions, its complacency [and] waywardness. . . . His fundamental objective was to reconcile [human persons with] God."[2]

Since biblical times, however, individuals and groups have engaged in "prophetic" discourse without claiming to be prophets in the He-

---

A version of this essay was originally published in *HIV Prevention: A Global Theological Conversation*, ed. Gillian Paterson (Geneva: Ecumenical Advocacy Alliance, 2009), 57–68. The substance of the essay was formulated in the context of an international and ecumenical dialogue with thirty-five theologians and practitioners, held in Johannesburg, South Africa, in January 2008.

[1] See M. Cathleen Kaveny, "Prophecy and Casuistry: Abortion, Torture, and Moral Discourse," *Villanova Law Review* 51 (2005): 499–579. One can add to Kaveny's analysis of contemporary prophets not only skepticism regarding false prophets (there were many of these in the Hebrew Bible) but the tendency for all sorts of persons, with all sorts of motivations, to claim without much justification their own prophetic powers. Effective prophetic discourse will be known by its fruits.

[2] Abraham J. Heschel, *The Prophets*, vol. 1 (New York: Perennial Classics, 2001), xxix.

brew Bible/Old Testament sense—without, that is, claiming to have a message or a commission actually and directly from God. Like the biblical prophets, though, their language and rhetoric typically express religious or moral indictments; they address basic moral concerns; their appeal is to the "heart," not only the "head"; and they offer a vision of a future that is better than the present.[3] Prophetic discourse, therefore, does not ordinarily issue in what today we would call "dialogue"; it aims for changes of heart simply by the power of its message.

Insofar as these characterizations of prophetic discourse are accurate, I have some reservations about its usefulness as a primary form of advocacy regarding HIV and AIDS prevention. Integrating multiple approaches to prevention, and mediating disagreements about both means and ends of preventive actions, require more than indictments, more than "conversation-stoppers," more (though not less) than appeals to the heart. Nonetheless, because HIV and AIDS prevention must ultimately address some of the most profound issues in human life and experience, there is perhaps inevitably the need and the potential for it to become prophetic. No one in biblical times simply "decided" to be prophetic; nor can that be done today. What we can do, however, is to shape the aims and actions of prevention in ways that awaken and change people in response to the HIV/AIDS pandemic. Insofar as those who work at prevention can do this, they may indeed "find" themselves to have been and to be prophetic. What I will offer here, then, are three considerations for the use of prophetic discourse in relation to HIV and AIDS prevention if it is indeed to be "prophetic." These considerations relate to (1) context, (2) manner, and (3) content for such discourse.

Context

Prophetic discourse tends to arise in contexts where needs are massive and injustice reigns. Surely the AIDS pandemic, especially as it is experienced in sub-Saharan Africa,[4] is the result of, as well as the

---

[3]See James M. Gustafson, *Varieties of Moral Discourse: Prophetic, Narrative, Ethical, and Policy* (Grand Rapids, MI: The Stob Lectures of Calvin College and Seminary, 1988), 7–17.

[4]My considerations throughout this essay are informed primarily by my thirteen years of working with women religious in sub-Saharan African countries. Analogies may be drawn, however, with other countries across the globe.

generator of, such contexts. We have sisters and brothers everywhere who are threatened with grave illness, or who are already sick unto death. Lives are disrupted, families are devastated, and ordinary hopes are challenged in every way. I need not detail the multilayered and interlinked problems of which we are already starkly aware. Justice issues abound—from those embedded in aspects of globalization, to those rigidified in culturally gendered and sexual patterns of relationships; from local and international poverty and the sufferings it spawns, to the terrible racial, geographical, and class imbalances in access to lifesaving medicines.

HIV Prevalence: Challenge and Task

For those struggling on all fronts against HIV and AIDS, the *AIDS Epidemic Update* published in December 2007 by UNAIDS and WHO (World Health Organization) offered some new and good news.[5] The number of people living with HIV worldwide appeared to have leveled off; the number of annual new HIV infections was then estimated to have peaked in the late 1990s and to have gone down by 2007. At first glance, this made it look like prevention was working, at least to some degree, and the raging fires of the pandemic may have been contained. At second glance, the news was confusing and not good enough.[6] It was confusing because it reflected better methods of epidemiological and demographic research, but not necessarily any dramatic decline in prevalence itself. It was not good enough because, however the facts were presented, it remained the case that in 2007 at least 33.2 million people around the globe were still estimated to be living with HIV; 2.1 million people died of AIDS; and 2.5 million more people were newly infected. For those who for so many years had experienced the pandemic in the Global South, particularly sub-Saharan Africa, this new information was important, but it did not change the concrete experience of a situation that remained dire. When a Kenyan woman with whom I worked heard of the estimated decline in HIV prevalence

---

[5] *AIDS Epidemic Update* (Geneva: Joint United Nations Programme on HIV/AIDS and World Health Organization, December 2007).

[6] The accompanying 2007 UNAIDS Fact Sheet maintained that the downward revisions were "due mainly to improved methodology, better surveillance, and changes in key epidemiological assumptions." This presumably meant that earlier estimates were somewhat inflated because of less adequate epidemiological and demographic research.

suggested by the new report, she shook her head in puzzlement and said simply, "It may be because we all have died."

In the latest *UNAIDS Global Report* published in 2013, statistics showed that the trends identified in 2007 are continuing in the direction of positive progress in HIV prevention. The numbers of new infections generally are down—both for adults and children; the rates of AIDS-related deaths are down, not only because of more effective strategies for prevention but also because of greater access to antiretroviral treatment. Yet the *2013 Global Report* sounds notes of caution.[7] There are signs of stagnation in progress, and new obstacles to stopping the pandemic once and for all. Among these are the recent emergence of complacency regarding sexual risk behaviors among the young, and the flatlining of financial resources to sustain the needed ongoing work of education, scientific research, and expansion of the means of prevention and treatment. Stigma and discrimination continue to foster the false shame and despair that have marked the pandemic all along. In many countries women continue to bear a disproportionate burden in relation to their own vulnerability to infection and in regard to the responsibilities that fall to them in caring for those who are sick and dying. Draconian laws in some countries (for example, Uganda and Nigeria) raise barriers against the opportunities of especially vulnerable populations to seek HIV and AIDS testing and treatment.[8] And even though great positive strides have been made in many countries, in some countries the situation remains dire.

The news is both good and not good, then. More specifically, since the beginning of the epidemic, which became a worldwide pandemic, approximately 75 million (statistically between 63 million and 89 million) people have become infected with HIV. But from 2001 on, the rate of new infections dropped by 33 percent. Hence worldwide there were 35.3 million people living with HIV in 2012. Still, according to the *UNAIDS 2013 Global Fact Sheet*, 2.3 million people became newly infected in 2012 alone (down from the numbers of newly infected in 2001 by 3.4 million). Simultaneously, the number of AIDS-related deaths has also declined (1.6 million deaths in 2012, down from 2.3 million in 2005, which was considered the peak year

---

[7] See Michel Sidib (UNAIDS Executive Director), "Foreword," *UNAIDS Global Report* 2013, 2–3.

[8] I refer here to factors of poverty, gender violence, laws against same-sex relationships, political volatility, and so forth.

for deaths because of AIDS). To an important extent, this is because of expanding access to antiretroviral treatments. In 2012, an estimated 9.7 million people living with HIV in low- to middle-income countries had access to these therapies.

Regionally, statistics vary greatly, however. For example, in 2012 approximately 3.9 million people were living with HIV in South and Southeast Asia, 1.5 million in Latin America, and 25.0 million living with HIV in sub-Saharan Africa. New infections in these countries in 2012 were estimated to be about 270,000 in South and Southeast Asia, 86,000 in Latin America, and 1.2 million in the sub-Sahara. AIDS-related deaths in that same year were calculated at 220,000 in South and Southeast Asia, 52,000 in Latin America, but 1.6 million in sub-Saharan countries in Africa. Hence, although prevalence figures are surely declining in remarkable ways, even the lowest numbers are still terrible, and the highest numbers remain truly tragic. Moreover, the percentage of those living with HIV who are eligible for antiretroviral treatment does not match (especially in the sub-Sahara) the still large numbers who need it.

World Church: A New Call

The context for prophetic discourse regarding HIV and AIDS prevention encompasses not only societies but churches. Biblical prophets, after all, spoke more to the people to whom they belonged than to other peoples who might be oppressing them. There is no doubt that churches (as well as temples and mosques) have been in the forefront of responses to HIV and AIDS—in some countries providing more than 40 percent of the care of the sick and dying, and also making important strides in education, counseling, and multiple forms of support. More, of course, is needed. As a context for prophetic discourse, however, perhaps the most important element undergirding any widespread responses from religious traditions and institutions is the developing self-understanding of their own reality. For the Christian churches, in particular, this involves new insight into the meaning of Christianity as "world church." Unfortunately, many Christians still understand "world church" to mean that the Christian gospel has been taken to the far corners of the world. But ours is a time when the concept of "world church" has a different content and provides a different call. Now more and more Christians recognize that the Christian gospel was never meant to be only or even primarily a Western European or North American gospel exported like the rest of Western culture to other parts of the world. At last it becomes clear that God's self-revelation can not only be *received* in every language and culture, but *given* out of every language and culture; it can be not only *heard* but *spoken* from across the globe. Its intended possibilities are stifled when any one culture claims nearly total control over its forms.

Two consequences follow from a growing understanding of what it means to be "world church." The first of these is tied to the fact that the church has not always thought about itself in this way. That is, in the past, Western Christianity exported teachings regarding, for example, sexuality and the status of women that are part of the problem now with HIV/AIDS in formerly missionary countries.[9] Imposition of attitudes and practices shaped by Western culture at the very least destabilized traditional cultures in, for example, Africa. These attitudes and practices now intermingle confusedly with traditional practices and with modern secular (and largely Western) practices, all together contributing to the spread of HIV and reinforcing stigma and shame. Recognizing this gives a wake-up call to all Christians to reexamine certain teachings and attitudes, in the light of what is needed to stop the relentless sickness and dying. Insofar as some teachings of the church are part of the problem, we are all responsible for part of the remedy.

The second consequence of developing understandings of what it means to be "world church" is or can be a growing clarity among all Christians—whether in Africa or Europe or China or the United States—that they are *all equal* sharers in the one life of the church, partakers in the one Life of the Spirit of God. All are therefore called to bear the burdens of one another when the church in one part of the world is in dire need. If the church has AIDS, as it is so often said, if the Body of Christ has AIDS, then no Christian is spared this devastation. To the extent that AIDS is a problem for the church of Africa (or of Australia, East Asia, Europe, or the United States), it is a problem for us all. The gospel comes to us and is received by us—all together across this world; and it calls us not just to assist one another but to stand in solidarity with all, especially with those who are most vulner-

---

[9]See Margaret A. Farley, *Compassionate Respect: A Feminist A Feminist Approach to Medical Ethics and Other Questions* (New York: Paulist Press, 2002), Part I; and *Just Love: A Framework for Christian Sexual Ethics* (New York: Continuum, 2006), 77–89.

able or who suffer the most. This truth characterizes the context for prophetic discourse, the context in which co-believers need a prophetic word of challenge as well as comfort.

Manner and Mode of Prophetic Discourse

I turn now to my second consideration, what I have called the "manner," or way or mode, of engaging in prophetic discourse. Respecting the limits of this essay, I will offer what will be rather bare statements, assertions if you will. I do not assume these are all self-evident, but I place them on the table for consideration.

First, although prophets are known for their clarion calls to repentance, social criticism, and even condemnations, their success depends on whether they also *energize and offer hope*.[10] The biblical prophets spoke out of and back into their own communities. Their words were born in humility yet conviction; they aimed finally not at condemnation but at reminding the people of a future dependent upon common memories, shared hopes, and present actions. The community for prophets in the context of HIV/AIDS is the human community as well as the community of the church.

Second, prophetic discourse in a time of AIDS cannot arrogate to itself sole platforms, silencing other voices, as if it alone were sufficient. Indeed, the effectiveness of prophetic discourse today, especially in the context of HIV/AIDS prevention, may well depend on its respect for and inclusion of other modes of discourse, such as social analysis, empirical research, and practical reasoning. In a context where no one has yet succeeded in finding the perfect policy, the certain remedy, prophets do well to *call for dialogue* and not simply obedience.

Third, it is not so very difficult to awaken many people to the demands of the dire situation of HIV and AIDS in the world. What follows this awakening, however, is difficult indeed. For when compassion stirs, it can be overwhelmed by the problem of what might be called the "too much or too little." As it did for the prophet Elijah (1 Kgs. 19:4–9), the mountain can appear too high; or as the army commander Naaman saw it, the Jordan River can appear too lowly and ineffective (2 Kgs. 5:1–19). In the face of the mountain of HIV

---

[10] I draw here on Walter Brueggemann's *The Prophetic Imagination* (Philadelphia: Fortress Press, 1978), 14.

and AIDS, prevention can appear too overwhelming and intractable a problem, so that we are tempted to do as Elijah did, give up and throw ourselves under a broom tree in despair. Alternative smaller efforts at prevention, those strategies that are clearly "at hand," can seem to us too little to make a difference, so that like Naaman we reject them as "not worth doing." Numbness threatens at every turn. Prophetic discourse, therefore, must safeguard its speakers and hearers from the despair that calls them to the broom tree and the skepticism that scorns a little river in a strange land. It must, therefore, include the specification of concrete ways, particular actions, that are present enough and possible for persons and groups to undertake.

Fourth and last, prophets are shaped by their own experience. Whose experience, then, is needed to engage in prophetic discourse in a time of AIDS? Gustavo Gutiérrez once asked: Can theology be done by the poor?[11] Do oppressed and believing people have a right to think and to speak? Is it not the poor themselves who can reimagine and reappropriate the gospel? There is of course no telling from where prophets may arise, yet the question must be pondered: Whoever should bring a prophetic word to the context of the AIDS pandemic, should not those who are most grievously infected and affected be among them? Are their insights into the nonnecessity of the present situation needed if prophetic discourse is to make a difference? If so, how shall they find their voice, and with whom can they stand as they prophesy before the powers of the church and the world?

Content of Prophetic Discourse in a Time of AIDS

I come, finally, to a consideration of the content of prophetic discourse, especially as it relates to advocacy for HIV prevention. Let me begin by affirming that we do have religiously prophetic individuals and organizations among us, and I have no intention of trying either to replicate or substitute for the hard work as well as eloquent prophecy they have given us. I refer to the contributions of Michael Kelly, Robert Vitello, Alison Munro, Kevin Dowling, Musa Dube, and many others from multiple religious traditions who have pondered the re-

---

[11]Gustavo Gutiérrez, "The Voice of the Poor in the Church," in Catholic Theological Society of America, *Proceedings* 33 (33rd Convention, 1978), 30–34.

quirements for HIV/AIDS prevention in the light of faith, of concrete needs, and understandings of the complex and large global picture. I refer also to the faith-based programmatic designs for prevention through reduction of risks and remediation of vulnerabilities that have been developed by, for example, the World Council of Churches, the Ecumenical Advocacy Alliance, the Catholic Agency for Overseas Development, Caritas Internationale, and Catholic Relief Services, as well the massive work of secular international organizations such as UNAIDS and the World Health Organization.[12] Many of these efforts and documents have been made available to all who search for understanding and practical ways forward. All together they reinforce the need for specificity in strategies and action, yet integration and coordination; and they complement one another by providing essential pieces to what would otherwise be an incomplete view.

Here I do not itemize all of these efforts, and need not, even if there were space in this essay to do so. What I will do is much simpler, more suggestive than programmatic, yet signaling something about the content for prophetic discourse in a time of AIDS. I propose, therefore, three somewhat disparate observations.

The first has to do with the approach to prophetic discourse modeled by the prophets in the Hebrew Bible/Old Testament. They began by articulating their own and their people's *grief*—the primary announcement that "things are not right."[13] The substance of what these prophets said was not first a reprimand, but an articulation of sorrow and grieving over death. Theirs was a grief lodged in stories of human suffering—the kind of suffering that goes on for generations—"a voice heard in Rama weeping" (Jer. 31:15), peoples oppressed and injured by other peoples, women violated in their very persons, and in far too many places relentless dying.[14] In the Christian scriptures/New Testament, Jesus, too, spoke of this kind of suffering: "Can you drink the cup that I will drink?" (Mark 10:35–40; Matt. 20:20–28). The cup images the suffering of all persons, hence all kinds of sufferings. But

---

[12]See especially *HIV Prevention from the Perspective of A Faith-Based Development Agency* (London: Catholic Agendy for Overseas Develpment [CAFOD], 2003); *Framework for Action: The HIV and AIDS Campaign*, 2005–2008 (Geneva: Ecumenical Advocacy Alliance [EAA], 2005), esp. Goal II; *Practical Guidelines for Intensifying HIV Prevention: Towards Universal Access* (Geneva: UNAIDS, 2005).

[13]See Brueggemann, *The Prophetic Imagination*, 20–21 and passim.

[14]See Farley, *Compassionate Respect*, 69–71.

at the heart of the image are the sufferings that are the consequence of injustice—the sufferings that do not have to be, the sufferings that cry out for an end not in death but in change.

Prophetic discourse concerned with the AIDS pandemic can begin also in nothing other than grief. It begins with the real stories of real persons and families and villages and cities and churches and nations. From these narratives social criticism must follow, if much of the suffering does not have to be. "No more," the prophets must cry; "no more" to false judgments, stereotyping, blaming, and shaming; "no more" to exploitation, indifference, domination; "no more" to conditions of unfreedom and the denial of dignity and rights; "no more" to infection, sickness, and dying that does not have to be. And hearers will not despair as long as the prophets can imagine with them the "next steps," the "new possibilities" that will bring change.

My second observation is that while prophets must speak to their own communities, the work of preventing the spread of HIV crosses borders; it has become essentially *multicultural and interfaith.* Cross-cultural work has always been difficult, and so very many mistakes have been made in attempting it in the past. Prophetic discourse may include in its task the bridging of what have been insurmountable divides—cultural, racial, gendered, geographic, religious, economic. New forms of learning and acting are required. Prophetic discourses of healing and hope challenge partnerships based on domination and submission; they foster partnerships based on mutual respect, a search for mutual understanding, and trust in interdependence. Prophetic discourse can embody the learnings that (a) it is not possible simply to transplant the beliefs and practices of one culture into another; (b) no one culture should stand in general judgment of other cultures; (c) yet not anyone can unreflectively and unconditionally respect every cultural practice—whether their own or another's; (d) hence, people from diverse cultures can stand in solidarity with those who critique, in their own culture or another, practices from which people die; and (e) all peoples have responsibilities, each for the other and for all. Prophets of prevention must tell the stories that bespeak and effect the hopes of peoples, the possibilities of their coming together to weep over similarly recognized tragedies, to laugh over similarly recognized incongruities, to stand in awe of one another, and to labor for common goals.

My third observation is about aspects of advocacy for HIV prevention that are most commonly accepted as controversial. As many others have noted, the controversies are not only about the use of condoms or needle exchange; they go much deeper. Given limitation of space, I forgo commenting on needle exchange, but focus on issues of *sexuality*. As growing voices of African women theologians are saying, the traditions of world religions in which many of them stand must find better ways to address problems of sexualized stigma, discrimination, and gender bias.[15] The favored response of religious leaders has all too often been simply and vehemently to reiterate strong moral rules which, if they are adhered to, may guard people against risks from sexual activities. Ironically, the sheer repetition of traditional moral rules has frequently served only to heighten the shame and the stigma associated with AIDS, and to promote misplaced judgments on individuals and groups (especially women). The perpetuation of a predominantly taboo morality (which by definition is nonreflective) reinforces the sort of divine punishment motif that the book of Job was against, and it ignores the genuine requirements of justice and truth in sexual relationships.

The AIDS crisis, as I have indicated above, presents a clear situation in which faith traditions must address their own traditional teachings about sexuality, and they must rethink the gender bias that remains deep within their teachings and practices. It would be naive to think that cultural patterns that make women vulnerable to AIDS are not influenced by world religions (and vice versa) whose presence is long-standing in their countries. Fundamentalism takes varied forms, but many of them are dangerous to the health of women. Questions must be pressed about the role of patriarchal religions in making women invisible—even though women's responsibilities are massive, and their own agency can be crucial and strong.

I long ago came to the conviction that the sexual sphere of human life must be governed not by taboos but by considerations of justice. I have also become convinced that what justice means in the sexual sphere is not very different from what justice means in other spheres of human life, whether social, political, or economic. Questions of same-sex relationships, or of the use of condoms to prevent illness and death, or of equality within marital relationships, are questions of justice, and they must be measured by the criteria of justice that govern human

---

[15]See Farley, *Compassionate Respect*, 6–17.

relationships more generally. These are not isolated and individualistic questions; they go to the very roots of morality—including Christian morality.[16] The question to be asked is not whether this or that sexual act in the abstract is morally good, but rather, when is sexual expression appropriate, morally good and just, in a relationship of any kind? With what kinds of motives, under what sorts of circumstances, in what forms of relationships, do we render our sexual selves to one another in ways that are good, true, right, and just?

Prophetic discourse regarding HIV/AIDS prevention must incorporate new understandings of human sexuality and the requirements of justice. Norms for sexual relationships and activities must take into account the concrete reality of human persons, particularly their capacities for freedom and relationality. It is only within a new framework (with roots in traditions of faith, although not always clearly recognized or articulated accurately and adequately in these traditions) that human sexuality as a whole can be understood, and specific questions such as the justifiability of the use of condoms can be resolved.[17]

A sexual ethic that remains too much in the form of a morality of taboos has led to an interpretation and rejection of some means of HIV and AIDS prevention—in particular, the use of condoms—because they are considered forms of contraception. This, however, misses (somewhat tragically) the point that their use in this context has nothing to do with a contraceptive goal; it has only to do with preventing people from grave infection and ultimate dying. I applaud the work of scholars like James Keenan on issues of condom use.[18] His appeals to well-entrenched principles in the Christian tradition (such as material cooperation, toleration, *epikeia*, and double effect) are extremely important and, in my view, sound. Yet we must go further. Issues of condom use cannot be reduced to questions of "lesser evil," or even of "double effect." They arise only because some frameworks for Christian sexual ethics have not been challenged—as they must be. My own proposal in this regard is that justice norms for sexual relationships must include requirements to treat individuals as ends in themselves,

---

[16]See Farley, *Just Love*, chap. 6.

[17]Condoms are a necessary strategy, and should not raise a moral problem as such (except of motivation). They are a necessary but not sufficient strategy. This is an issue that is both exaggerated and underplayed, to the detriment of many efforts at HIV and AIDS prevention.

[18]See James F. Keenan, ed., *Catholic Ethicists and HIV/AIDS Prevention* (New York: Continuum, 2002).

and to do no unjust harm; they also require, more specifically, free consent on the part of both partners, as well as mutuality, equality, some level of commitment, and fruitfulness in some form (though not necessarily biological children). Finally there is a requirement of social justice regarding the rights of persons in their sexual choices and in relation to religious groups and human society in general.

Let me conclude by saying that if religious traditions have anything at all to say to situations like the AIDS pandemic, they must speak of God and of human responsibilities to one another in relation to God. Words of hope and deeds of love will be "true" and effective only insofar as they are shaped by accuracy of understandings of the situation and plausibility in identification of claims of justice. The great human and religious goals of mutual respect, solidarity, fairness, compassion, come slowly. But in some contexts, where responses to human suffering become urgent, where abandonment and death make slow progress "too late," the role of prophetic discourse expands.

CHAPTER 14

Religious Meanings
for Nature and Humanity

The question I have been asked to address in this essay is, "Can religious and spiritual identity contribute to an understanding of nature and humanity?" I will assume that having a religious or spiritual "identity" means holding some religious beliefs and in some way attempting to incorporate these into one's life and actions. So the question becomes, can we have religious beliefs that are relevant to our understanding of nature and humanity, and are there spiritual practices that produce, follow from, or expand such beliefs?

Since "religion" is a very complex phenomenon, and "spiritualities" are numerous and diverse, I hope it will be useful if I narrow this question—focusing primarily on Christianity as a religious tradition, but in a way that may provoke analogous considerations in other religious traditions. Christianity is a likely "test case" for the question—not because it offers the best answers, but because within it there have been many efforts to develop systematic theologies that specifically address the meaning of nature and of the human person, and because it has had—for better or for worse—a marked influence on Western intellectual history as a whole. There are, of course, many traditions of theology and spirituality within Christianity, so that what I say will remain quite general and will not necessarily apply to every individual or group that claims a Christian identity. To some extent,

A version of this essay was originally published in *The Good in Nature and Humanity: Connecting Science, Religion, and Spirituality with the Natural World*, ed. Stephen R. Kellert and Timothy J. Farnham (Washington, DC: Island Press, 2002), 103-12. Reproduced by permission of Island Press.

my rendering of the Christian tradition may be more recognizable by Roman Catholics than by Protestants, but it is not limited to the Catholic tradition.

All major religious traditions become "major" in part because they have something to say about the "large" questions that human persons encounter—the questions of suffering, of the grounds for human hope, of the meaning of personal maturity, of transcendence (historical, personal, communal). Religion, in fact, has a lot to do with "meaning." It is not generally experienced as an irrational activity, but rather as part of the effort of reason to make sense of what it confronts. Though its sources transcend what reason can access by itself, its insights and convictions are believed to complement, not do violence to, what reason can understand. Religions include more than "worldviews" that appear to make sense, but they do include these. Hence, crises may occur within religious traditions when what used to make sense is called into question, when dissonance is experienced between what the tradition has taught and what its adherents find emerging in their experience. This is what happened for many twentieth-century women, for example, when traditional—especially, but not only—religious understandings of themselves came into conflict with their own experience. This gave rise to widespread efforts on the part of women in almost every religious tradition to critique and to reconstrue traditional beliefs—an enterprise on which their continuing to stand within their traditions depended.

To some extent, a similar crisis has occurred for many religious believers, in particular Christians, when confronted not only by the threat (and the reality) of ecological devastation, and not only by the responsibility of humans in this regard; but by the apparent contributions of their own religious traditions to the problem. Many forces, of course, have converged to create this problem—from economic exploitation and political competition to technological imperatives that all too often have exacerbated what we now refer to as the "rape of the earth." But among these forces has been the force of ideas, of convictions, beliefs, ideologies, that motivated or did not check the massive processes that have led to the devastation of life-systems and even ecological collapse. The charge against Christianity in this regard is by now well known, and it has been taken seriously by thoughtful Christians, including many theologians. If Christian theology has not been the primary purveyor of ideas that account for our environmental problems, it has at least for a long time neglected questions of the meaning of nature and of humanity that might have countered them.[1]

The real question before us, therefore, is not just whether religion and spirituality can contribute to understandings of nature and the human person, but whether they can contribute in ways that will help now to protect, not destroy, the earth and all that dwell therein. To pursue this question, we must undertake three tasks—critique, retrieval, and reconstruction. The charges against Christian theology must be taken seriously, which means that construals of nature and humanity must be critically appraised. And if persons are to continue to stand within the Christian tradition, an effort must be made to retrieve neglected or forgotten elements in the tradition, elements that may now transform the dominant Christian understandings of nature and humanity. And finally, some reconstruction of these understandings must be undertaken in order for Christian theology to be part of the remedy, not the problem, in approaches to humanity and nature.

In this short essay, I can only suggest some outlines for these three tasks. Christian theology is complex, and it appears in multiple strands of the Christian tradition. There are many theologies of nature and many theologies of the human person, not one univocal theology. Moreover, it will not be sufficient simply to look at theologies of nature and humanity, since these are intertwined with, for example, theologies of God, creation, freedom, and sin.

Even the sources for Christian theology are multiple—standardly including scripture (the Hebrew Bible and the New Testament), tradition (the history and development of theologies, church teachings and practices), other disciplines of knowledge (for example, philosophy, the natural and social sciences, history), and contemporary experience. Each of these sources requires interpretation; and when it comes to how the insights from these sources will work together and provide guidance for action, each requires decisions regarding how they will be used in the faith community. Hence, critique, retrieval, and recon-

---

[1] For recent and useful discussions of the many issues involved here, see Drew Christiansen, "Ecology, Justice, and Development," *Theological Studies* 51 (1990): 64–81; James M. Gustafson, *A Sense of the Divine: The Natural Environment from a Theocentric Perspective* (Cleveland: Pilgrim Press, 1994); Gustafson, *Intersections: Science, Theology, and Ethics* (Cleveland: Pilgrim Press, 1996); Larry L. Rasmussen, *An Earth-Honoring Faith: Religious Ethics in a New Key* (New York: Oxford University Press, 2012); Gretel Van Weiren, *Restored to Earth: Christianity, Environmental Ethics, and Ecological Restoration* (Washington, DC: Georgetown University Press, 2013).

struction will need to apply to all sources and to their uses in Christian theology and ethics. It becomes clear, then, why all I can do here is to suggest what must be examined.

Critique of the Tradition

Every religious understanding of the natural world and humanity is importantly connected with an understanding of God or of what is considered in some way to be ultimate. The first critique that is relevant to our concerns, therefore, is a critique of some historical versions of a Christian theology of God. More centrally in some Christian traditions than in others, God has sometimes been seen primarily as wholly transcendent, largely absent or hidden to human searching, the goal of human desiring but one that leads beyond this world and sometimes even in opposition to it. A transcendent God, sometimes further understood as requiring a submissive people, is a notion that has played itself out sociologically in human relations of dominance and subordination—God in relation to God's people, men in relation to women, parents in relation to children, teachers in relation to students, and so on. It is not difficult to believe that such a distant God might delegate governing authority to humans over the world of nonhumans, and that such a God would have purposes so hidden that humans remain largely on their own in ruling the world. This view of God is in many respects a caricature of Christian beliefs about God, yet it has captured the imagination of theologians at times, and it has appeared often enough in popular belief. Its consequences have become unacceptable to many Christians, who search for better understandings of the God whom they experience and love.

Whether God is distant or near, uncaring or compassionate, the world that God created was for centuries in Christian theology looked upon as hierarchically ordered, static, a habitat of living beings but not itself living and dynamic. The second critique important for us today, then, is the one that has been made of doctrines of creation insofar as they are contradicted by the findings of modern science, and insofar as they incorporate misleading dualisms between mind and matter, soul and body, rationality and emotion. Much of past Christian theology of nature was based on the going physics, astronomy, and biology of its time. When these sciences changed drastically, theology, too, had to undergo Copernican-like revolutions, incorporating new insights about order amid disorder and chance; massive new information amid growing uncertainties; evolution and its challenge to a human community derived from a common ancestry; challenges to human freedom from the neurosciences and psychology. For some, the dependence of old theologies of nature on old science appeared to be so great that everything heretofore believed about the natural world and the place of persons in it had to be rejected. Moreover, early church repression of theological adaptation to new science prevented much of the creativity that might have emerged in a theology of nature and an ethical understanding of the responsibilities of humans in the world.

The third area of critique important to our concerns focuses more centrally on theologies of the human person, on the relationship between humanity and nature, and on social and political theologies. In many ways, theology has not neglected the human person in the manner it has neglected the cosmos. Centuries-long debates about human freedom are still instructive for contemporary efforts to understand human responsibility in the face of new forms of determinism. Theologies of human embodiment have moved far beyond, though they still learn from, medieval notions of formed matter. Liberation and other political theologies have already introduced correctives that go beyond critiques of earlier social theories. New insights into power relations connect with long-standing concerns about limitless self-interest in fallen human beings. But with all of this, further critiques are under way, offering special challenges to the anthropocentrism of much of Christian theology. Lynn White's scathing critique of Christianity's role in the environmental crises has been taken seriously (if sometimes only to argue against it).[2] No theologian today is satisfied with Francis Bacon's (or Lynn White's, for that matter) interpretation of the Genesis texts whereby humans are given mastery over nature and ordered by God to subdue it. But if this so-called despotic interpretation of Genesis is no longer credible, newer "stewardship" interpretations are found wanting as well. There is more than one creation story in Genesis (and in other books of the Bible), and critical studies now extend to a search for more adequate understandings not only of the shared "citizenship" of humans and nonhumans but of the coherence of scientific discoveries regarding evolution and biblical-theological interpretations

---

[2]Lynn White, "The Historical Roots of Our Ecological Crisis," *Science*, March 10, 1967, 1203–7.

of creation. This leads us to the question and the task of retrieval of lost insights, insights that can relativize, correct, or supplant elements in the tradition that are no longer credible to many of its adherents.

Retrieval of Theologies in the Tradition

It can be argued quite persuasively, I think, that deep within Christian traditions there lie quite other articulations of theologies of God and of the world that are both more central to the tradition throughout the centuries and that are more illuminative of the questions Christians and others raise today regarding nature and humanity. These need to be retrieved in a way that influences not only development of doctrine but of the life of faith in the popular Christian mind. What we are looking for are theological insights that do not justify (or better, that forbid) human assault upon planet Earth, whether in terms of God's supposed command or our interpretation of hierarchies of importance among the inhabitants of this planet.

Just as the creation stories in the book of Genesis provide us with more than directions of mastery over nature (indeed, quite other than these), so the writings of key theologians in the history of Christianity offer us both bad and good news. The bad news—regarding an absent God, an instrumentalized nature, and God-ordered inequality in relations between human beings—needs critique. Much of the good news is still good and deserves to be retrieved.

For example, St. Augustine, writing in the fifth century C.E., is frequently blamed for the beginnings of Christian hierarchical thinking. It is true that Augustine, following Greek and Roman philosophers, did think of creation as hierarchically ordered. Yet his view of nature's order may challenge, not justify, our domination of the earth. In his massive work, *The City of God*, Augustine is noting (as he does elsewhere) the rankings among all creatures. "Those that live are ranked higher than those that do not. . . . Sentient [beings] are superior to nonsentient . . . intelligent [beings] higher than nonintelligent."[3] These lines were oft quoted by Christian thinkers who followed Augustine. Not so often quoted were the lines that followed, in which Augustine, perhaps with tongue in cheek, is nonetheless seriously critiquing the human tendency to value creatures not for what they are but solely for

---

[3] Augustine, *City of God*, trans. G. Walsh, et al. (New York: Image Books, 1958), 11.16.

their utility to humans. "Sometimes we so prefer certain nonsentient things to others that are sentient that, had we the power, we would annihilate these latter, reckless of the place they hold in the pattern of nature or willfully sacrificing them to our own convenience. For who does not prefer to have food in his house rather than mice, money than fleas? This is less astonishing when we recall that, in spite of the great dignity of human nature, the price for a horse is often more than that for a slave and the price for a jewel more than that for a maid."[4]

It is Augustine, too, whose heart was restless for God, but who nonetheless did not consider created beings as mere stepping-stones to God. What all beings *are* is related to God, but they *are* therefore of value in themselves. More than one lyrical passage such as this one in Augustine's *Confessions* sing of the worth of every creature.

> What is this God whom I love? I asked the earth and it answered, "I am not God." And all things that are on the earth confessed the same. I asked the sea and the deeps and the creeping things with living souls, and they replied, "We are not your God. . . ." I asked the blowing breezes, and the universal air with all its inhabitants answered: "Anaximenes was wrong. I am not God." I asked the heaven, the sun, the moon, the stars, and "No," they said, "we are not the God for whom you are looking." And I said to all these those things. . . . "Tell me about my God, you who are not God. Tell me something about God." And they cried out in a loud voice: "God made us." My question was in my contemplation of them, and their answer was in their beauty.[5]

Important, too, among the elements of the Christian tradition are the twelfth- and thirteenth-century attempts at a theology that would integrate God, humanity, and the cosmos. Inspired by ancient Greek scientific works and the works of Jewish and Muslim scholars, Christian theologians sought to articulate a faith grounded in and nourished by two revelatory texts—the Bible and creation. God revealed God's own self, and revealed the nature of humanity and of the world, in both of these "books." But this was a God who created *ex nihilo*, out of noth-

---

[4] Ibid.
[5] Augustine, *Confessions*, trans. R. Warner (New York: New American Library, 1963), 10.6.

ing, not in a long ago beginning time, but throughout the history of the world. This was a God who holds everything in creation, human and nonhuman, so that every being remains utterly contingent, utterly dependent for its very existence and for its activity on the continuing—here and now—creative activity of God. This view takes nothing away from the work of created beings (nor would it later have to be at odds with theories of "big bangs" or theories of evolution), for God intended to share God's being and activity with all creatures—to share God's life and love and beauty. But a God who holds all in being is thereby intimately present to all—more intimate to every being than it is to itself. This is not a distant God, not an absent God—though profoundly hidden, yet gloriously revealed.

Thomas Aquinas offered a theology and metaphysics of ontological "participation," one that drew from Greek understandings but that fit very well with understandings of a personal God who knows and loves all into being; a God who is all being, yet can create many beings; a God in whose being all other beings participate, indeed they "live and move and have their being."[6] Careful to avoid pantheism on the one hand, and any shade of deism on the other (for the God he tried to understand was both immanent and transcendent), Aquinas offered a view of creation in which every being has its own worth. Every being is in some way instrumental in regard to others and to the whole (even humans are so), but every being is of value—of goodness and beauty—in itself as well. Such a theology yields what is sometimes called a "sacramental" view of the world and all that belongs to it. In the words of the twentieth-century scientist and theologian, Pierre Teilhard de Chardin: "Nothing is profane for those who know how to see."[7] God's presence is everywhere, and nothing falls outside God's embrace.

Understandings such as these were, of course, undermined when scientific advances discredited what there was in them that depended on an outmoded physics. Yet long after their losses to better science, they remain potential sources of insight, ready to be made compatible with contemporary findings. What begins in critique and is filled out through retrieval is now ripe for reconstruction.

---

[6]See, e.g., Thomas Aquinas, *Summa Theologiae* I.44.1; *Summa Contra Gentiles* III.25; *De Veritate* 2.11 ad 4.

[7]Pierre Teilhard de Chardin, *The Divine Milieu* (New York: Harper and Row, 1960), 38.

Reconstruction of the Tradition

Deep in the Christian tradition is a view of human persons as created beings whose structure is complex: We are embodied spirits, enspirited bodies (embodied consciousnesses), with structures within structures—chemically, biologically, physiologically—and with capabilities for thinking and feeling, for planning and choosing. We are relational—not only social but interpersonal, deeply dependent upon others for developing our own selves, open in relation to a transcendence that reaches all the way to the possibility of union with God. We are in the world—the world of nature and the world of historical, cultural, political, economic systems and institutions. We have potentiality as well as actuality—possibilities for flourishing, but vulnerabilities for diminishment. Each person is unique, yet we are all common sharers in the human community and in creation.

Ironically, what we may need to do with theological views such as this, perhaps, is for a time to turn away from ourselves and to look around us. Only when we understand better what God is doing in the world of nature may we turn back upon ourselves with greater wisdom about who we are. After all, we might have to admit that though we are part of an ecosystem, we are in a sense "misfits." We are the ones who worry about ecological disasters, and we are the ones who are responsible for them. We are profoundly interdependent with all other beings in nature, yet we are more dependent on the other beings than they are on us (or we would be, had we not already so modified nature that the future of all now depends on us). We think of the rest of nature as vastly inferior to us in achievement, but it possesses a harmony and rhythm that mock the restlessness and anxiety that are ours.[8]

What we need is a new decentering—that is, to find a center beyond ourselves in order to find a center within ourselves. We have many sources in Christian theology for both understanding decentering and helping to effect it. For example, we have strong resources for building a contemporary theology and an ethics of the "common good," expanding our notions of solidarity with humanity and with all cre-

---

[8]See Christopher F. Mooney, *Theology and Scientific Knowledge: Changing Models of God's Presence in the World* (Notre Dame, IN: University of Notre Dame Press, 1996), 150–51.

ation, learning what it means to stretch our hearts in a love of God that requires a love of neighbor and a love of the created universe. In fact, the Christian tradition has thought long and hard about certain forms of decentering. It has cautioned against egocentricity, warned against solely self-centered love, offered judgments against setting up idols, especially the idols of one's own self. Christian theology since the nineteenth century has moved through major changes variously described as "conversions" (in focus) from the "object" to the "subject," from the subject to the "other," from the other to the community, from the community to those at its margins. Each of these has been a form of decentering, taking ourselves in an important way off of center stage.

To turn now to the wider world will, like other conversions, require whole new labors in order to see from a perspective heretofore not taken. Preliminarily, it requires new awakenings that take us out of ourselves and our "business as usual." There is more than one way to begin: with fear—of ecological disaster; with repentance; or with new experiences of awe and joy in response to beauty. We no doubt need all of these ways. Fear is easy to understand, if we take seriously what we know about the threats to our planet, and even terror can be salutary. Repentance may be easy to understand, too. This volume is about "good," or "goodness," about the *bonum*. But implicit in our considerations is concern for the "bad," or "evil," about the *malum*. In the context of theological and ecological concerns, there may be evils we lament—conflicts and disruptions in the world of nature, animal suffering and human disease, deaths that may be part of nature but for which we mourn. In our context today, however, there are also evils for which we repent—evils *that do not have to be*. These are the evils of our own assaults on nature, intentional or unintentional, and the evils of our assaults on one another, because there is a link between our exploitation of the earth and our injustice to human beings. The poor suffer disproportionately from environmental destruction, and racism and sexism have ecologically distorted faces.[9] Conversion and repentance may come only when the face of suffering and loss becomes visible to us—in nature and in humanity; and it is in part the task of theology to make visible that face.

There is another way for conversion to begin: that is, with the be-

---

[9]See, e.g., Leonardo Boff and Virgilio Elizondo, eds., *Ecology and Poverty* (Maryknoll, NY: Orbis Books, 1995).

holding of beauty and its concomitant response of awe and unexpected joy. Perception of the good—if it is clear and full enough—awakens love. It reaches inside of us and taps our capacity to love. Even more so, the perception of what is beautiful awakens us, grasps us and frees us, lifts us out of ourselves and makes possible the "Turning" (the conversion) of which Martin Buber spoke.[10] Beauty taps our capacities both to know and to love, and it enables us to turn our gaze from preoccupation with ourselves to the beholding of what is beyond us—more than we are, even if we share in its being.

Neither terror nor repentance nor joy in beauty should be romanticized. Here is the possibility of life or death. For with the conversion that may come (or the decentering) there comes also the hard work of new ethical discernment and new moral choices. Just as "working the land" is not only a romantic idea but an ongoing struggle (both for and against "nature"), so there is work to be done if we are to move the world of humans in the face of the moral imperatives that are ours.

My answer, then, to the question with which I began, is that a Christian theology of nature and humanity can contribute to our understanding, to our decisions, and to our hope. With all religious traditions we may begin to see and experience (in the words of C. S. Lewis) that for all creation there is no center because all is at the center.[11]

---

[10]Martin Buber, *I and Thou*, trans. R. G. Smith (New York: Charles Scribner's Sons, 1958), 100.

[11]C. S. Lewis, *Perelandra* (New York: Macmillan, 1944), 230–33.

CHAPTER 15

Death Be Not Proud

Freedom and Death in Relation to Life

Death is a problem for human persons in a way that it is not for other living beings. We are the ones who anticipate it, worry about it, try to understand it. In this sense, we transcend it. We stand outside of it and ponder it, fear it, attempt to come to peace with it. We are the ones who rebel against it or accept it—though no matter what, we die. And perhaps even more important to us, those we love also inevitably die. In this essay, and in the one that follows, I attempt to probe some of what might be called the "large" questions surrounding human freedom in relation to death and to life. These are primarily questions of meaning and questions of moral discernment in the face of choices that may be made about our dying.

I have entitled this essay "Death Be Not Proud," and the one that follows it, "Death Be Not Humble." Both titles are, of course, inspired by a poem written by John Donne, published in 1633, two years after his own death. It appears within his nineteen *Holy Sonnets*:

This essay is based in part on a previously unpublished set of lectures, first delivered at the third annual Ernest Becker Summer Institute, sponsored by the Ernest Becker Foundation, Seattle University School of Theology and Ministry, and the Washington State Hospice and Palliative Care Organization, July 24, 2008. This essay also draws on an earlier lecture, published under the title, "Issues in Contemporary Christian Ethics: The Choice of Death in a Medical Context," in *Santa Clara Lectures* 1, no. 3 (Santa Clara, CA: Santa Clara University, 1995).

> Death be not proud, though some have called thee
> Mighty and dreadful, for, thou art not so;
> For, those, whom thou think's thou does overthrow
> Die not, poor Death, nor canst thou kill me.[1]

Donne intended something quite specific in these lines, and I will return to them in due time. I reverse them, in a way, in the title of the paired essay to follow. Although both of these titles may seem vague and puzzling, I appeal to Donne and others primarily because I think we can use the wisdom, clarity, and light that poets sometimes bring to the philosophical and theological analyses of our most complex and difficult questions.

Meanings for Death

Throughout human history, death has been given many meanings. Every religious and cultural tradition has something to say about death; religious thinkers, scientists, philosophers, psychologists, poets, and artists have offered their own insights and convictions; and we all have some relationship to death. It is on the horizon for us all, and it comes closer as our circumstances change—as we grow older, or our health begins to fail, or we feel the threats of outside forces bearing down on us, or we experience the dying of those who are dear to us. We may repress awareness of the reality of death—in ways suggested, for example, by Ernest Becker in his major publication, *The Denial of Death*;[2] or we may come to accept it as a part of life, even though we do not generally "like it" (as Forrest Gump said sadly, in the 1994 film by that name). Whatever meaning we discover for, or give to, death, it is intelligible to us and others only within the larger frame of our ultimate beliefs, or our worldview.

Among many thinkers today, there has been a growing tendency to try to understand human death simply as a part of a life span. Like every other living thing—including the red blood cells within us—we begin, we live, we die. Death is natural, they say, even though we find ourselves pleading, along with Dylan Thomas, "Do not go gentle into

---

[1]John Donne, "Holy Sonnets," X, in *John Donne's Poems*, vol. 1, ed. E. K. Chambers (London: Lawrence and Bullen, 1895), 162–63.
[2]Ernest Becker, *The Denial of Death* (New York: Free Press, 1973).

that good night . . . [but] rage, rage against the dying of the light."[3] Even Christians who for centuries thought of death as a catastrophe, the result of a primal sin, now take seriously the discoveries of modern science and move beyond the idea of physical death as punishment or as some kind of terrible disaster unintended in the original creation of humanity. It is commonplace today to conclude that the natural resources of the life of the individual simply exhaust themselves; and when the author of Genesis tells us that death is the result of sin, we can interpret this to mean that death is *experienced* differently because of some form of "fall," but it would always have been a part of our lives. Moreover, although many Christians believe that insofar as death has been overcome in an order of redemption, this means not that death ceases to be an inevitable and still usually dreaded event, but that it does not hold the last word for human life (which is actually the point of John Donne's sonnet, "Death Be Not Proud").

Nonetheless, however much we try to "naturalize" death, it remains a problem for us—in a way that it is not for other biological beings. Hence, as recently as the mid-1970s, there arose a great quarrel among some ethicists. The renowned Protestant ethicist Paul Ramsey started it, in a way. He was disturbed that his own and others' embrace of the concept of "death with dignity" had fostered too glib an ideology for the promotion of "right to die" campaigns. Ramsey therefore published a broadside against such slogans and ideologies, in an article he titled, "The Indignity of Death with Dignity."[4] Death remains our enemy, he said, and as he said elsewhere, "God means to kill us all in the end." Ramsey worried that efforts to naturalize, and thereby dignify or even romanticize, death would add greater burdens to those who are already dying; and the tragic aspects of death would be covered over.

The Jewish physician and medical ethicist Leon Kass, in response to Ramsey (though he shared many of Ramsey's concerns about death with dignity campaigns), argued that there is at least the *possibility* of a dignified death. "Death *may* be a great evil, but it should not be considered *in itself* an 'indignity.' "[5] He pointed to a Midrash that offers

[3]Dylan Thomas, "Do Not Go Gentle into That Good Night," in *Collected Poems of Dylan Thomas 1934–52* (New York: New Directions, 1981), 128.

[4]Paul Ramsey, "The Indignity of Death with Dignity," in *On Moral Medicine: Theological Perspectives on Medical Ethics*, ed. S. E. Lammers and A. Verhey (Grand Rapids: William B. Eerdmans, 1987), 185.

[5]Leon R. Kass, "Averting One's Eyes or Facing the Music? On Dignity and Death," in Lammers and Verhey, *On Moral Medicine*, 205.

an interpretation of the book of Ecclesiastes 7:1, which differs from conclusions drawn by Ramsey:

> When a person is born all rejoice; when he dies all weep. It should not be so; but when a person is born there should be no rejoicing over him, because it is not known where he will stand by reason of his actions, whether righteous or wicked, good or bad. When he dies, however, there is cause for rejoicing if he departs with a good name and leaves the world in peace. It is as if there were two ocean-going ships, one leaving the harbor and the other entering it. As the one sailed out of the harbor, all rejoiced, but none displays any joy over the one which was entering the harbor. A shrewd man was there and he said to the people: "I take the opposite view to you. There is no cause to rejoice over the ship which is leaving the harbor because nobody knows what will be its plight, what seas and storms it may encounter; but when it enters the harbor, all have occasion to rejoice since it has come in safely." Similarly, when a person dies all should rejoice and offer thanks that he departed from the world with a good name and in peace. That is what Solomon said, "*And the day of death [is better] than the day of one's birth.*"[6]

This interpretation signals a perspective on death not only as the natural end of the life span of humans, something that therefore (according to Kass) can be approached with dignity; but a perspective that sees death as more than a simple ending of life in this world. Rather, our choices regarding what we do in life have a lot to do with whether our death and our life are "worthy of respect." We need to pursue this suggestion, but to do so requires that we move beyond simply a life-span model to consider more specifically the place of freedom and death in our lives.

Death, as I have already emphasized, is a problem for human persons in a way that it is not for other living beings. Although past societies of humans and every major religious tradition have all tried to explain death in some way, for contemporary Western society, it has become and remains an enigma. We try to reduce it to a mere biological fact

---

[6]Ibid., 211n13. Kass is drawing on *Midrash Rabbah Ecclesiastes*, trans. A. Cohen (London: Soncino Press, 1961).

(the life-span model). But death threatens also from terrorists and wars and accidents that have nothing to do with aging or with communicable or genetic diseases or organic anomalies. We try our best to control death—in all circumstances; and if we cannot control it, we are in tears, we are angry, we are in despair. Why? Because we are used to controlling things, perhaps. But more deeply, because we are the ones who desire an unlimited future. We are the ones who love one another in a way that we cannot believe that such loves will end.

Yet death is not only outside of us; it is at the center of our lives. Not many believe anymore that only our bodies die; that we "shuffle off this mortal coil" and do it easily. We know better. Death strikes at, happens to, each of us as a whole person. It is an event for us as spiritual persons, not only as biological persons (by saying this I do not thereby rule out the possibility of immortality for persons). We as embodied spirits, enspirited bodies, die. And whatever death is, it is a finalizing moment. As Emily Dickinson wrote,

> All but Death, can be Adjusted—
> Dynasties repaired—
> Systems settled in their Sockets—
> Citadels—dissolved—
>
> Wastes of Lives—resown with Colors
> By Succeeding Springs—
> Death—unto itself—Exception
> Is exempt from Change.[7]

Whether anything changes yet continues after death, it stands as the limiting condition for our possibilities in this life, the ultimate "given" in relation to which our freedom will take its stand—or not. As such, it is never merely, in a simple sense, a natural biological process. In fact, it can seem ironically "unnatural" to us that our very selves diminish and die, that our relationships are torn asunder, that the wrenching that occurs at the heart of our beings is possible despite all of our efforts against it.

What does this mean? It means that there may be another sense

---

[7]Emily Dickinson, "All but Death, Can Be Adjusted," in *The Complete Poems of Emily Dickinson*, ed. Thomas H. Johnson (Boston: Little, Brown and Company, 1960), no. 749.

(than purely biological) in which death is natural (truly "human") for us. That is, it is not only as biological beings that we must die, but also (and at the same time) death belongs to us as beings who are in some way transcendent of biology, and who are free. Insofar as we are free, capable of self-determination, able to make of ourselves (within limits, of course) who we become, without death we could only live with the possibility that we may constantly undo what we have already chosen, reverse what we have already become. We might never finally "be." We would never know what it means to live out our commitments to the end, for there would be no end beyond which we could not change our mind—to betray or be faithful.

But if our freedom (as the Roman Catholic theologian Karl Rahner and others have insisted) is not merely the power to do this or that, to constantly change our course of action, but rather "the power to decide that which is final and definitive in our lives, that which cannot be superseded and replaced . . . the summons to a decision that is irrevocable,"[8] it needs death for its finality. (This is perhaps why the ultimate witness to a love is to "lay down our lives" in the many ways that this may be called for—lay down our lives for what and who we love.) Rahner does not suggest here that freedom only needs death in the end, but that death is, in a profound sense a part of our life all along. It is our horizon, and we make our choices with this horizon in mind. In this sense, death lies not only in the future, but in the here and now, as a factor of what our present means. Since our life in time is limited, we must ultimately (if only by default, choosing not to choose) in whatever time we have, through childhood, youth, and old age, choose what we will love above all else and how we shall integrate all of our loves in relation to what we love above all else. No matter what kind of life we are living, we must affirm some opportunities and reject others (we cannot do or be everything), sacrifice some things that are valuable to us and seek others. Insofar as life is or becomes irrevocable, our choices, too, will finally become irrevocable. Freedom is not the power always to change our loves but to determine them, to decide what we really want, what it is for which we will live or die.

The meaning of death, in this view, cannot be understood apart from the meaning of life, and the meaning of life is importantly shaped by

---

[8]Karl Rahner, "On Christian Dying," *Theological Investigations*, vol. 7, trans. D. Bourke (London: Darton, Longman and Todd, 1971), 287.

the meaning of death. If every choice that we make during our lives changes us, shapes us, then our final choices ought to be, or we can at least hope may be, our greatest. Perhaps I can clarify this by three observations.

First, it is helpful to reflect on the meaning of human time. Time for us is not like a calendar or a clock; it is not like space, with one part outside the other. Our time is within us—like the time of a tree (its rings of time becoming part of itself); or like a melody (which cannot be known or understood if only one note is heard). Our lives in time become wholes (even if the "whole" is made up of fragments), and only when they are complete (for good or ill) can their meaning be complete, the patterns of our choices finally making us be who we have become.

Second, the experience of old age may shed light on this as well. As Rahner mused (when he himself was in his eighties): not everyone gets to live into old age; but for those who do, it must be a part of their vocation. He wrote, "Old age is a grace (both a mission and a risk) not given to everyone. . . . [It is erroneous to think that it] is a merely external situation . . . like a costume in which a person plays a role in the theatre of life . . . which he simply drops at death. . . ."[9] On the contrary, if we are to take each person's history seriously, we must understand that the period of life that is old age is, if we achieve it, like every other period in life, potentially definitive of the meaning of that life. In other words, if we do indeed live into old age, and we are still with capacities to know and be known, love and be loved, then the final meaning of our life may be determined or ratified by our freedom only when we are old (although it *may* be chosen irrevocably before this).

Third, of course we know that this would not apply to persons whose old age is lived without cognitive awareness, without the possibility any longer of relating to other persons or to God (as, for example, the case may be with persons in end-stage Alzheimer's disease). Moreover, many of us—whether young or old—may die suddenly, seemingly without the possibility of making final choices that ratify our greatest loves. Hence, we need to "practice" (so to speak) making what we want to be our final choices all along as our lives unfold. Thus

---

[9]Rahner, "Growing Old," in *Prayers and Meditations: An Anthology of Spiritual Writings*, ed. J. Griffiths (New York: Crossroad, 1981), 91.

do we give direction to our loves, our lives, our characters. Gradually we may learn that our options for choice include acceptance or rebellion, faithfulness or abandonment, and surrender (or not) to that in which we ultimately hope.[10]

For those in a Christian context (I use this as an example, but I believe there may be analogies in other religious traditions and worldviews), whose understanding of death and life is shaped by the promises of God, who believe that God is their ultimate destiny—their beginning and their end, their holder in life and savior in death: profound acceptance of death can be an acknowledgment of an ending that is finally God's call. Christians can know themselves called, in the face of death, to resist the forces of diminishment and death as far as possible, and to surrender in the end not to evil (or even sickness, or violence) but to God. Dying, as Pierre Teilhard de Chardin puts it,[11] holds the mystery and the hope that death will be truly an "act of communion" with God; that our final choice (if we are able to make it so) will not be mere resignation, but rather, a surrender into the heart of God.

Physical Life in This World: A Relative Value for Humans

Insofar as our considerations of the meaning of death for freedom and the whole of our lives are plausible, they can lead us to another "large" and correlative question—that is, the sheer value of human physical life in this world. Just as all religious and cultural traditions have had something to say about the meaning of death, so they have incorporated moral assessments of choices regarding human life and its preservation. These choices appear in contexts of individual self-defense, war, criminal sanctions, debility and old age, and a variety of other situations where life and death appear to conflict, and the balance between them threatens to tilt in the direction of death. Though

---

[10]Ernest Becker's theory of the "terror" of death is not the same as Rahner's (or many others'), although there are ways in which they are reaching for something similar. Whether Becker is accurate in claiming that the experience of overwhelming anxiety before death is universal, implicit in his view of development of character is something like the everyday choices against the horizon of death that Rahner describes. And Becker's proposal that "nondestructive heroism" can transcend death's terror, that eros drives for unity and meaningfulness in ways that may be epitomized in Søren Kierkegaard's "leap of faith," a surrender to a being, cause, or beloved goal: all of this is not completely unlike Rahner's interpretation of the role of death in freedom, life, and love.

[11]Pierre Teilhard de Chardin, *The Divine Milieu* (New York: Harper and Row, 1960), 90.

clear norms have governed many of these contexts, ambivalence and ambiguity have not always been overcome. Jewish and Christian traditions, so profoundly influential in Western culture, have not escaped ambiguity and internal controversy regarding some questions of human life and death.

Ambivalence in the Christian tradition, for example, has in some respects increased over the centuries. In the first three hundred years of the life of the church, there was a strong prohibition against taking any human life, even in self-defense (though one could lay down one's life in martyrdom, for there was not everywhere a corresponding absolute obligation to preserve life in each and every circumstance). The attitude toward war was generally one of pacifism. Leading thinkers in the early church such as Justin Martyr could write confidently that the Christian must not resist attack. Origen maintained that the Christian lawmaker must not allow killing at all. Ambrose taught that the Christian could not take the life of another even to save his own life. From the mid-fourth into the mid-fifth century, however, when St. Augustine was writing and preaching, the prohibition against killing was less absolute. The commandment "Do not kill" still yielded a prohibition against private individual killing either of oneself or another; but now there could be justification for a Christian's engagement in warfare. With the beginning of a Christian version of a "just war" theory, Christians could be not only soldiers but magistrates leading armies to war; and they could be hangmen performing as agents of the state carrying out what appeared to be justifiable capital punishment. In the Middle Ages, the prohibition against murder (taking the life of an innocent person) was clear, as was a prohibition against suicide; but the right of the state to wage war and to impose capital punishment, and the right of individuals to self-defense, were now formulated and accepted. Indeed, gradually there developed a full-scale casuistry regarding the meaning and application of these rights.

Today, questions about death and dying have become more than ever complex and troubling, perhaps especially in Western culture. Apart from issues of war, revolution, capital punishment, abortion, and even issues of the threat to the lives of whole species, including the human species, its cultures and civilizations, within the threatened demise of planet Earth—apart from these issues, there are multiple and growing questions regarding choices for death in a medical context. These latter issues are, of course, raised in large part by developments in medical technology, the possibilities of which have fueled a cultural need and pressure to expand the horizons of death and the control of our dying through scientific learning and power. But all of these issues and questions turn us to the question of the value of human physical life in this world, and from this to the question of whether there are limits not only to killing one another, but to our obligation to preserve human life.

Such questions are philosophical (and medical and legal), but also religious (and hence theological) issues. They are questions, issues, deep within both Judaism and Christianity (and again, I think, with analogues in other traditions as well). A way to begin probing these questions is to reflect on two convictions that appear to be lodged in our attitudes toward human dying. On one hand, life is a fundamental good. It is a gift from God, to be held as a gift is held, with reverence and respect. It is to be stewarded, cared for as something that is our own yet not only our own to be done with simply as we please. A sign that life is this kind of value for us, this kind of gift, is God's command to us: "Thou shalt not kill" (Exod. 20:13). The command appears in legal and prophetic traditions in the Hebrew Bible and in the teachings of Jesus in the Christian scriptures, articulated along with imperatives neither to kill nor to be angry, and not to despair in the face of suffering. We interpret this command not only as a negative prohibition against killing but as a positive prescription—so that, for example, as the Protestant theologian Karl Barth expresses it, we are obligated to will to live, and even will to be healthy.[12] "The freedom for life to which the human is summoned by the command of God is the freedom to treat as a loan both the life of all persons with one's own and one's own with that of all human persons."[13] Or, as the U.S. Catholic bishops put it in their 1992 document on the provision of artificial nutrition and hydration,

> The Judeo-Christian tradition celebrates life as the gift of a loving God and respects the life of each human being because each is made in the image and likeness of God. . . . Our church views

---

[12]Karl Barth, *Church Dogmatics*, III/4, trans. A. T. MacKay et al. (Edinburgh: T and T Clark, 1961), 356.

[13]Ibid., 335 (inclusive language added to translation).

life as a sacred trust, a gift over which we are given stewardship and not absolute dominion.[14]

The value of human life is, then, revealed in God's command and in the story of God's relationship to humanity. It is also recognized, as many would argue (in religious as well as secular traditions), in our understandings of human nature itself, which manifests a basic drive toward life, a desire to live that is indicative of a moral "law," an obligation to preserve human life. Others have found this valuable good of human life in their loves for one another, experiencing in relation to a beloved a revelation of the value of life such that an intention to kill seems never to be part of what love requires. Still others argue for the value of human life based in a perception of the fundamental worth or dignity of each human person, lodged in the human capacities for free choice and for relationships with others. At the very least, human life (physical life in this world) is considered to be valuable because it is the necessary condition for human persons to have and to enjoy other values. And still others maintain that respect for the life of each individual is necessary for the common good of the human community. On all of these counts, human life is to be preserved—as a good that is precious to God, to community, and to each person within her or his context of creation.

But if this is one conviction, religiously and philosophically affirmed (that human life is a fundamental good), there is a second general conviction: Physical, biological, human life in this world is not an absolute good, not the supreme value for humans. Thus, Barth can qualify the command, "Thou shalt will to live," with the paradoxical formulation, "[but] not will to live unconditionally . . . rather will to stake and surrender [one's life], and perhaps be prepared to die."[15] And the Catholic bishops can write, "As conscientious stewards we have a duty to preserve life, while recognizing certain limits to that duty."[16]

There are thus these two intuitions: Life must not be destroyed, but it need not always be preserved. Every person is utterly valuable, and each one's life is utterly valuable, yet things other than life are

---

[14]U.S. Bishops' Pro-Life Committee, "Nutrition and Hydration: Moral and Pastoral Reflection" (1992).

[15]Barth, *Church Dogmatics*, III/4, 334.

[16]U.S. Bishops Pro-Life Committee, "Nutrition and Hydration."

sometimes more valuable. Human life deserves respect; it even has sanctity; but death may sometimes be welcomed.[17]

When these two intuitions or convictions are held together, they press us with serious questions about life and death. For example, what are the limits of our obligation to preserve life? And are the prohibitions against taking life, against intending death, absolute? If physical life in this world is not an absolute good, to what other goods is it relative? What other values might, under what circumstances, take priority over life? These are the questions I will pursue in the essay that follows, "Death Be Not Humble."

---

[17]Richard Stith, "Toward Freedom from Value," in Lammers and Verhey, *On Moral Medicine*, 127.

CHAPTER 16

Death Be Not Humble

Freedom and Life in Relation to Death

The first essay in this paired set focused primarily on general theological and philosophical concepts relevant to human death. My concern in that essay was with problems regarding death as a limiting condition of life, but also the importance of death as a horizon for the choices we make during our lives. Considering, therefore, the significance of free choice in determining the meaning of our lives, I foreshadowed more specific concerns regarding choices about our very way of dying. I tried also to articulate an understanding of human biological life in this world as a value—a value that is basic but not absolute, intrinsic yet relative to other values. I began to move toward issues not only of taking human life by human hands, but of possibilities for moral limitations on our obligation to preserve human biological life. I turn in this second essay to some of these more specific questions, especially regarding decisions in a medical context about how and when we die.

Decisions about Dying

One of the most urgent issues facing our society, and therefore also our religious traditions, is the issue of ending lives marked by great suffering and caught in a prolonged process of dying—an issue that

---

This essay, like the previous one, draws in part on the unpublished Ernest Becker Lectures that Farley delivered in 2008, and on her 1995 Santa Clara University lecture, previously cited in Chapter 15.

has emerged in our time and culture primarily because of massive advances in medical technology. This issue is today perhaps most acutely focused in terms of movements to legalize euthanasia and assisted suicide. Growing public support for the decriminalization of these options reflects a general cultural (and religious) shift in evaluations of suicide; it also represents deep fears in anticipation of circumstances that surround sickness and death. Although some have a realistic fear of not being treated adequately or at all, the fears that are most relevant to issues of euthanasia and assisted suicide are fears of being given too much medical treatment, being kept alive too long, dying not at peace but in a wild frenzy of efforts to secure for us a little more time to live. To many persons, it appears that the only way to retain some control over our death—so that we are able to die a death marked by conscious self-awareness, with knowledge of our ending, surrounded by those we love—is to take death into our own hands. It begins to make sense to many that while science has made death an enemy to be fought on the battlefield of medicine, so science must come to befriend death, to assist us scientifically in dying as we choose.

Issues at the heart of choices regarding our own dying are, of course, complex; and they cannot all be addressed in this short essay. Insofar as these issues are moral or ethical issues,[1] they have to do with not just *whether* we are free to choose our own way of dying, but *when and how* our choices regarding death are good choices, choices able to be justified in relation to the value of human persons and the value of human life in this world. As is generally known in Western culture today, the range of options possible in response to the use of medical technology near the end of life includes everything from preserving life as long as possible no matter what, to ending life by our own hand (or with a physician's, family member's, or friend's assistance) before it becomes what we fear will be intolerable; from various formulations of "Do Not Resuscitate" orders in hospital settings to "Limitation of Treatment" orders that cover everything from the use of antibiotics to ventilators to medical provision of nutrition and hydration; and from developing "Living Wills" to granting "Medical Durable Power

---

[1] The terms "moral" and "ethical" are often used interchangeably. Technically, insofar as there is a difference in their usage, the term "moral" (or "morality") tends to apply to more concrete experiences, questions, etc., while "ethical" or "ethics" refers to more theoretical ways of thinking about morality or moral questions. I do not distinguish them in this essay with any strict consistency.

of Attorney" to someone we ourselves designate, so that we will not be left without some "say" in our treatment at the end of life. Moral discernment about the appropriateness of some of these options has to do not only with our convictions regarding relevant moral principles and rules, but with the circumstances in which these options arise.

Some choices regarding death can be morally justified; some cannot. And among the choices that are potentially justifiable, some are more easily justified than others. So general a statement is hardly controversial, but a great deal of controversy surrounds every effort to specify it. Some conceptual and moral distinctions have been traditionally useful in specifying justifiable and nonjustifiable options. But these very distinctions are part of what is controversial today. We are therefore faced with multiple serious questions, such as: Are there indeed limits to our obligation to preserve life? And is the prohibition against taking life, against intending death, truly absolute?

When we begin to reflect on these questions, we tend to do at least two things, or engage in at least two preliminary analytical strategies. First, we identify *limits*, boundaries, to our obligations regarding human life. In order to do so, we ask what are the conditions under which life must always be preserved? If human physical life in this world is not an absolute good, to what other goods is it relative? What other values might, under what circumstances, take priority over life? And second (though relatedly), we do consider *distinctions*. We differentiate between kinds of choices in order to see whether some of them may be morally justified though others may not. We distinguish, for example, between choices to kill and choices to let die. In beginning our moral discernment, it is useful (even if controversial) to consider each of these strategies or analytical tasks.

Limits to the Obligation to Preserve Life

Although I have said that my primary focus here is on choice in a medical context, it is nonetheless helpful to consider more generally the limitations that have been proposed or acknowledged regarding the obligation to preserve human life. None of these is without complication or controversy, but they indicate the willingness of most persons to relativize in some way the value of human life. It is, actually, difficult to find anyone who finally wants to make of human biological life in this world an absolute value. For example, when it comes to war, those who think that some wars can be justified are willing to relativize the value of the lives of their enemies; those who are absolute pacifists are willing to relativize the value of their own lives.

Some of the traditional candidates for limits to the obligation to preserve life (which is not to be equated with limits to the obligation not to kill) include the following:

1. *Personal integrity and moral or religious witness.* When fidelity to personal convictions and beliefs cannot be sustained without risk of one's life, it is permitted to bear witness to truth or loyalty or specific commitments even if the actual cost becomes one's own death. The history of Christian martyrs is a clear case in point. Of course, all sorts of values must be taken into account before concluding easily that one is called to lay down one's life in this way.

2. *Conflict between human lives.* There are situations in which the value of one or more individuals' lives comes into conflict with the value of another's. Criteria have been developed to justify the limiting of efforts to preserve some lives when all cannot be preserved. Examples of situations where these criteria apply can include self-defense, defense of others, scarcity of resources (when some form of triage is inevitable); conflict between individual lives and a common good.

3. *Personal autonomy.* Sometimes values such as freedom are considered so important that loss of life can be risked to maintain them. While examples of this can be subsumed under the previous two limits, there is a particular sense in which human autonomy is unique. That is, the capacity in human beings for self-determination, for free choice, can be valued in a way that sets some limits to our obligation to preserve another person's life. This is the case when an individual's refusal of medical treatment takes priority over the beneficent wishes and actions of medical caregivers. Such a limitation is ensconced in U.S. legal protection of a right to refuse treatment; or put positively, a legal requirement of freedom of consent to medical treatment implies also an individual's right to refuse it.

4. *Quality of life.* Though historically this has sometimes been a more controversial limitation than others, nonetheless there has emerged a general recognition that the obligation to prolong life can be limited when the burdens of treatment become significantly greater than the benefits of continuing to live. A conflict of values can occur

within an individual person for whom there is a "totality" of value. Physical life is a condition for every other value enjoyed by the individual in this world, but as a condition it is for the sake of the person as a whole. Thus, for example, the loss of present and future conscious awareness, of the very capacity to relate consciously with others or even oneself, or of the possibility of a life free from intractable and personality-changing pain, may relativize the value of ongoing sheer biological existence and hence limit the obligation to preserve one's own or another's life.

5. *Medical futility.* The ineffectiveness of some forms of activity (for example, medical treatment) to extend the life of a patient (or to extend it with a reasonable quality of life for the person as a whole) sets a limit to the obligation to preserve that life. "Medical futility" is, of course, a frequently contested term and concept. There is a sense in which it correlates closely to the "quality of life" limit already described, yet it bears particular identification. Its meaning is clearest when it is restricted to cases in which no benefit from any treatment whatsoever seems possible for a patient, neither in the present or the future. In other words, available treatments cannot serve any of the goals of care for this particular patient in this particular situation. In such situations, there is no longer an obligation to continue what are essentially futile treatments; indeed, there may be an obligation to cease such treatment. This does not mean that the patient is no longer to be valued and respected; nor does it mean that a patient may be abandoned, without companionship and care for her or his comfort.

To identify limits to the obligation to preserve life helps us see how human life is a value but a relative value; it is a way of gaining clarity on what the value of life is relative to; it provides a perspective from which we may ask whether or not we are truly obliged to preserve a particular life, our own or another's, in a particular situation. Yet categories of "limits" in this sense do not by themselves resolve the questions about preserving life and staving off death in concrete circumstances. They are necessary but not sufficient for our moral discernment in this regard. Additional conceptual tools such as descriptions of moral actions in terms of their intentions and circumstances are needed. Descriptions allow distinctions, and distinctions serve discernment. I turn, then, to a another analytical task and strategy—the making of moral distinctions.

Distinctions among Choices Regarding Death

There is an ironic twofold problem with making distinctions regarding the moral status of different choices regarding death. On the
one hand, relying too strongly on such distinctions to solve our moral
questions regarding death can obscure the real problems we face. This
happens when distinctions become rigid, predominantly legalistic,
formulas seemingly providing easy application to every situation.
But on the other hand, blurring the distinctions among these moral
options can compound the problems we face. This is most dangerous,
for example, when attempts are made to lump together all sorts of
end-of-life choices, in a medical context, under one category and call
it "euthanasia." This is sometimes a temptation for advocates on the
left and on the right regarding some of the most troubling issues. Even
those who otherwise take distinctions seriously may contribute to
confusion when they define euthanasia as, for example, "an action or
omission which of itself or by intention causes death, in order that all
suffering may in this way be eliminated."[2] Important distinctions are
contained in this definition (based on concepts such as "intention" and
"cause"), but they are all too often invisible under the large umbrella
of the oversimplified category, "euthanasia."

On the contrary, the kinds of careful distinctions I have in mind
appear in long-standing theological as well as philosophical traditions, and they have been incorporated into many formulations of
contemporary secular medical ethics—though not without some
serious opposition. The most important of these moral and ethical
distinctions, as I identify them, are on three levels: (1) a distinction
between taking life (killing) and allowing someone to die; (2) a distinction between so-called ordinary and extraordinary means of medical
treatment; and (3) a distinction that divides what is sometimes called
"direct" killing from "indirect" killing. All of these distinctions are
sometimes included under the general concept of "euthanasia," but if
taken seriously, they change drastically the landscape of its meanings.
Terminologically euthanasia has two radically different forms—one
"active" (killing) and the other "passive" (allowing to die). This is why

---

[2] See Vatican Congregation for the Doctrine of the Faith, *Declaration on Euthanasia*
(1980).

the term "euthanasia" should always be qualified as either "active euthanasia" or "passive euthanasia," or perhaps in general usage come to be understood always and only to mean "active euthanasia." My interest here, however, is not finally in terminology, but in clarifying the distinctions I have identified.

Killing and Letting Die

First, then, is the distinction between actively taking life (killing) and passively allowing someone to die (not doing what would prolong living or a process of dying). As traditionally understood, it is a distinction between decisions to act to kill (for example, to give an intentionally lethal injection) and decisions not to act but simply to allow someone to die (to cease or refuse to initiate action, as in withholding or withdrawing treatment). Today multiple objections are raised to the meaningfulness and moral relevance of this distinction. To begin with, it is frequently argued that there is no real moral or even conceptual distinction to be made regarding action and inaction in this context. Decisions, for example, to withdraw treatment inevitably involve actions (as in pulling a plug or flipping a switch or removing a tube). And in either case—whether taking life or letting it go—the decision results in death.

A second objection is more serious. That is, opponents of the active/passive distinction argue that when it is used to justify not doing something (as opposed to doing something), it is specious, and used as a kind of "bad faith" attempt to escape responsibility for one's decision. A human agent is not free from responsibility of the consequences of not acting, and insofar as this distinction implies otherwise, it is simply wrong. Often an example is used wherein a person wants another person to die in order to gain something—as when one allows an uncle to drown in order to gain an early inheritance.

A variation on these objections is the argument that "intention" is involved both in deciding to take action and deciding not to take action. And in either form of decision, the intention can be precisely, or at least inclusive of, a decision about death. There are, after all, situations in which death is welcomed, sometimes in a sense even of being "planned," although it comes by the cessation, the withdrawal, of life-support systems.

Finally, objections to distinguishing between killing and letting die are often based on examples of inaction, of letting die, that are clearly immoral—as in the classic examples of inaction regarding the drowning of the uncle (if he could easily have been saved); or the man lying injured who dies because no one helps him; or the person choking to death when many are present who might have remedied the situation. These examples also tend to include morally unjustifiable *motivations* for inaction—as in my wanting my uncle to die because I want his money; or my failing to help the injured man because of my cowardice; or my letting someone choke to death because I am ashamed to be associated with this person. Examples like these are intended to discredit any claim to a moral difference between letting die and killing. Hence, if letting die can be justified, so can active killing.

Despite all of these objections to a meaningful distinction between killing and letting die, there are plausible and persuasive arguments to the contrary. For example, although pulling a plug, or removing a tube, do involve actions, they are not actions of direct killing, or at least need not be so. The way in which we describe our actions is important. Pulling a plug, for example, is an action of withholding or withdrawing treatment or systems of support; but it is an action that is necessary only to *stop doing* something, to separate an individual from some treatment or life-support system; and it is justifiable only when it can be reasonably discerned that it is no longer obligatory to actively preserve a given patient's life. Stopping CPR is really "stopping." It is not injecting or smothering or poisoning or any other form of direct intentional killing that intervenes to hasten the process of dying that is under way. Such decisions to withhold or withdraw medical treatment or life support need not involve intentions to kill; they may involve intentions to accept death and to be an occasion that allows it.

Yet pulling a plug does have some relation to a person's death. We can make all the distinctions we want—between aims and results, intended consequences and merely foreseen consequences, causing and occasioning, but our responsibility for the consequence of the death of the person whose life support we stop is real. This is why a decision to let life go requires justification. It is why letting Uncle Steve drown when we know we can easily save him is as unjustifiable as is shooting Uncle Steve. Nonintervention is not self-justifying, not an always ready alternative without moral consequences. When someone's life is let go, even if we describe this as "not prolonging dying," we need moral justification. And when examples are given of morally reprehensible failures to preserve someone's life, the only response to be made is that these failures are indeed reprehensible and hence not morally justified. To repeat: Inaction is not distinguished from action in that it needs no serious moral justification.

And yes, even though letting someone die may not be "intended" in a technical sense, the line is often blurred in this regard. On the one hand, a sign that we are not intending death is that should a patient continue to live, despite the withholding or withdrawal of treatment, we would not consider our aims frustrated; and if and when death does take place, we would attribute it to the disease that brought the patient to the brink of death in the first place. On the other hand, sometimes when we decide to stop aggressive measures of cure or even keeping alive, we can in a genuine sense wish that the person will die. How often does it happen that when the decision is made by a family member to stop life-support systems, deep in that family member's heart is the prayer to God that now this beloved one be taken quickly? This one will die, yes, of her underlying disease or injury, but we may in some real sense hope for her death, her freedom, which is why we cease aggressive measures. In anguish, we may affirm her freedom through death, though we face a terrible loss. Still, the desire for her death is not such that we move our hand to kill, but only that we remove the hand that might have prolonged life, however momentarily; we reach our hand to continue to care, but we do so in the recognition and sometimes the hope that this will allow an ending.

But more can be said about the issues surrounding the moral distinction between taking life and letting life go. They have to do with a fuller description of the elements in our decisions to act or to not act. Consider, again, the question of "intention." To let someone die need not be to intend or desire the death of that person. In the case of the rich uncle, to allow him to die in order to gain an inheritance is indeed to intend his death. But to allow him to die only because one is unable to save him, or because one cannot save him as well as oneself or others, is not to intend his death. It is to accept it. Here, of course, we risk falling into a philosophical quagmire. For as I suggested above, sometimes when a decision is made to refuse medical treatment, death is—if not intended—at least welcomed (perhaps under the terrible circumstances of otherwise prolonging dying). And almost always in such a choice, death is at least foreseen. Hence, there is a sense in which death falls within one's intention, though not one's direct intention. When a decision is made to let someone die, and the circumstance is that the patient is in the process of dying, or that the patient has no longer any possibility of conscious relationships; then it is accurate to say that what kills the person is the underlying disease or injury, not the withdrawal of treatment that can no longer help (or even comfort and respect) the patient. The decision to withdraw or withhold treatment is the "occasion" of death; it allows the death to take place. The "intention" of the decision-maker (whether the patient herself or someone who cares for her) is not the sole determinant, not even the direct and primary determinant, of death.

But why would the distinguishing features of choices to take life and choices to let life go change the moral status of one's decisions? Here disagreement runs deep. Nonetheless, those who want to maintain this distinction (including myself) argue that the two options offer two quite different *moral experiences of obligation*, and these differences in experience need not be illusory, not self-deceptive. Therefore, to accept death, to allow it and provide an occasion for it by removing unreasonable barriers, need not be experienced (and will not be experienced by many) as violating the value of human life. It is experienced, rather, as accepting the inevitable process of dying that is part of human living. The descriptive difference between active killing and passive letting die is not trivial, even though each option represents a choice whose consequence is death, and each requires morally justifying reasons. Justifying reasons for allowing someone to die emerge to an important extent in the second distinction I want to consider, the distinction between ordinary and extraordinary means of medical treatment.

Extraordinary and Ordinary Medical Treatment

The distinction between "ordinary" and "extraordinary" "means" in describing forms of medical treatments has been signaled with a variety of terms: ordinary/extraordinary, obligatory/optional, beneficial/burdensome, medically indicated/not indicated, proportionate/disproportionate. The point of the struggle for appropriate terminology is to express most clearly a concrete situational difference.[3]

---

[3] I use "ordinary/extraordinary" instead of another term simply because it has had the longest history in moral thought, and because it includes the nuances that are emphasized in most of the other terms. It also raises immediately the complexity of description needed to clarify the generally sought-for meaning.

The distinction is not one of customary or "usual" versus "unusual" treatment, nor is it one that can be captured by identifying general categories or kinds of treatments (for example, the use of antibiotics versus the use of ventilators, dialysis, organ transplantation, and so forth). Its meaning is circumstantial, situational, patient-relative, in that it refers to the proportionate benefit and burden of particular treatments relative to a particular patient. It is a matter for medical and personal discernment as to what counts morally as an "excessive" burden or what counts morally as an acceptable benefit. Relative to one patient, for example, dialysis may be "extraordinary"; relative to another it may be "ordinary."

"Extraordinary" therefore does not simply refer to rare, expensive medical interventions, and "ordinary" does not simply refer to basic medical care. What is important regarding circumstances for a particular patient may include prognosis, individual pain thresholds, multiple organ breakdowns that are irreversible, presence or lack of psychological and spiritual resources to cope with suffering, familial support, even expense: all of these and more are involved in the application of these terms. The point of the distinction, however, is that some discernment of this sort is required if one is to justify omitting (withholding or withdrawing) some form(s) of medical treatment.

Not to belabor the issue, it is nonetheless useful to reflect further on this distinction, which is finally between what in a specific case is an acceptable benefit and what is an excessive burden, and whether the proportion between benefits and burdens weighs more significantly on the side of benefit. Given varying judgments about benefit and burden, this distinction will yield different decisions in end-of-life care. What is excessive for one person may be only difficult for another. Hence, respect for the right of conscience of the individual (the patient or his designated proxy) in discerning such matters is of great importance. Yet the need has become all too frequent in American society for at least minimal commonly agreed-upon criteria for weighing benefits against burdens. Traditionally, general criteria for the assessment of burdens have included such factors as medical prognosis, expense, gravity of risks and harms, small likelihood of success of treatment, and adverse quality of life achievable through treatment. Criteria for assessment of benefits have included benefit not only for a patient's physical existence but for the person as a whole, impact on family and community, the value of prolonging life for a particular duration for a particular purpose, and so on.

The notions of both quality of life and medical futility in discerning end-of-life decisions have become more and more complex in the discernment of obligation to treat. Stark cases in point can be identified. For example, since the broadly publicized case of Theresa Schiavo in 2005, the issue of what is or is not an extraordinary means of care and treatment has been focused intensely on patients who are diagnosed medically to be in a permanently vegetative state (PVS) or in a state from which it is not possible to return to consciousness in relation to themselves or others. What differentiates these particular patients from many other cases in which the issue of extraordinary or ordinary treatment is at stake is that they are in some sense not dying, although they cannot, at least according to the best medical assessments, return to conscious awareness. They can, indeed, sometimes live an indefinite length of time (Theresa Schiavo lived for fifteen years in this state) if they are provided with needed artificial nutrition and hydration (that is, nutrition and hydration provided through medical technology). A central question at the heart of the debate in this regard is whether the provision of so-called artificial nutrition and hydration can be considered an extraordinary means (hence, not obligatory) or an ordinary one.

Artificial feeding and hydration can have clear benefits—chief among them the prolongation of life. This is especially true when these methods are used for patients who have a reasonable hope of returning to some level of health, and for whom medically provided food and hydration will be temporary, a bridge to the time when they can eat and drink without technical assistance. Yet this form of providing nutrition and hydration can also bring numerous burdens—risks of injury and infection, loss of mobility on the part of the patient (maintaining feeding tubes sometimes requires placing patients in restraints), inadequate supply of food to major organs with results such as edema, blood clotting, increased incontinence, and aspiration pneumonia. In the case of a patient for whom artificial feeding and hydration can be temporary, the benefits may clearly outweigh the burdens. For these patients, this form of treatment may be considered ordinary. For patients diagnosed as in a persistent vegetative state, it may be extraordinary.

Not many people doubt that artificial nutrition and hydration are great goods when they are needed temporarily in the care of a patient, or even when they are needed long-term for a patient who is conscious, alert, and desiring this life-saving treatment. The strongest controversy comes when the patients in question are not conscious and by all medical indications will not again become conscious.

There are those who argue that artificial nutrition/hydration in PVS cases is an ordinary (and therefore obligatory) form of care. They maintain that it is generically the same as giving drink and food in ordinary ways; that it accomplishes its proper aim of hydrating and nourishing the patient; that a diagnosis and prognosis for patients who appear to be in a persistent vegetative state may be wrong—because they may regain consciousness at some point; and that because such patients are still human beings, they must be respected as such. Finally, it is also sometimes argued that the patient will suffer from burdens of thirst and starvation if the hydration/nutrition is withdrawn.[4] It is true, they agree, that there are a few exceptional situations in which artificial nutrition/hydration may not be "ordinary"—situations in which a patient's body can no longer assimilate food and water, or in which a patient would suffer significant discomfort from the application of this technology, or simply where the technology is not available.

Alternatively, those who maintain that artificial (medically given) nutrition and hydration can be considered an extraordinary means of treatment in relation to patients in irreversible coma or a persistent vegetative state, argue that after a lengthy period of time and testing of the diagnosis, there can be moral certainty that the diagnosis and prognosis are correct; that artificial hydration/nutrition can simply be a barrier to nature running its course (since the patient would have died from the original trauma that left her or him in this state); and that artificial nutrition/hydration itself is burdensome, even though

---

[4] Empirical evidence has mounted, however, that gainsays this claim. The desire for food and drink, in fact, diminishes as death approaches, and whatever discomfort there may be when artificial nutrition/hydration is withdrawn is easily alleviated by the use of ice chips gently applied to a patient's mouth. For both sides in this particular controversy, see Richard A. McCormick, *The Critical Calling: Reflections on Moral Dilemmas since Vatican II* (Washington, DC: Georgetown University Press, 1989), 369–88; Congregation for the Doctrine of the Faith, "Responses to Certain Questions Concerning Artificial Nutrition and Hydration," *Origins* September 27, 2007; "Commentary on Responses to Questions on Nutrition and Hydration," *Origins* September 27, 2007; Gilbert Meilander, "Against the Stream," *Hastings Center Report* 14 (1984): 11–13.

the patient may not be conscious of pain or discomfort. Moreover, it is argued that a patient in a permanent vegetative state receives no benefit from this treatment. Because they lack cerebral cortical function, they also lack, irreversibly, a capacity for reflective consciousness. This means that there is, in an important sense, no longer any point to the continuing biological existence of the individual person in this world.

To understand adequately this position (of acknowledging the non-obligatory nature of artificial nutrition/hydration), however, we have to keep ourselves focused on the center of the controversy. Those on one side believe that life must be preserved if letting it go means simply not feeding someone (whatever technology is involved in providing food and fluids). Those on the other side believe that artificial feeding is not the same as ordinary feeding as such, and it along with other medical treatments can be assessed in terms of its benefit and burdens for the patient. At the heart of this second position is, as we have already begun to see, the belief that human physical life in this world is valuable, but its value is relative. It is relative to all the values that constitute possible limits to our obligation to preserve bodily life. But something more must be said. Human persons are essentially relational beings. The very purpose of human life is lodged in the possibility of relationships at a conscious level. The argument here is that there is no point to an existence that is without any possibility of conscious awareness of and affective relationships with what is knowable and lovable. It is plausible, therefore, that when physical life in this world reaches the time where there is no present capacity to relate to others, and no potential to retrieve or to grow into such a capacity, then the purpose of this physical life is gone. Without a capacity to relate to oneself, one's neighbors, creation more generally, or to God, there is no point to human life in this world.

To say that there is no "point" to continued sheer physical existence in this world, however, is not to say that the embodied person is not still unconditionally valuable. There are many persons on both sides in this debate who agree on this. In this shared view, there never comes a time when there is not an obligation to respect, care for, even love, a human person. But for those who consider artificial nutrition/hydration an extraordinary means of treatment for a patient with PVS, the nonobligation to provide this treatment may undergird a justification, and perhaps even an obligation, to allow the bodily existence of the person in this world to be let go.[5]

All of the reasons for not directly killing such a person remain in place, however.

Before considering once again the possibilities of actively ending a life, there is one more distinction to be addressed—that is, the distinction between "direct" and "indirect" action that hastens death.

Direct and Indirect Action That Takes Life

There is a third ethical distinction that has traditionally been useful in discerning medical treatments, and more generally in discerning what actions may be justified even if they lead in some way to death. The distinction is often a subtle one, and its usefulness is best understood when related narrowly to certain kinds of cases. The clearest case may be the one of giving pain medication that may have an unintended effect—hastening the death of a patient. The clinical situation is one in which a patient in serious pain can be given medication to alleviate her suffering, even if there is some reason to suppose that the medication (for example, morphine) may hasten the patient's death. If, for example, the medication that will alleviate pain will also suppress respiration to some extent, the patient may die somewhat sooner than if she were not given the medication. This decision and action, unlike some of the others we have been considering, is a decision to do something—that is, to give medication. The intention is precisely and directly to take action for the purpose of easing someone's pain. The intention of the action, therefore, is not to kill the patient. It is precisely and directly

---

[5]From some religious perspectives (a Roman Catholic view, as an example), the individual person still has a future—but not here and now in this world. Without espousing a philosophical or theological dualism, the person is affirmed to have a future that includes embodiment. Once embodiment in this world no longer provides the condition for knowing and loving, for freedom of choice, for saying yes to the life of God communicated in nature and through grace, then there is indeed no point in continuing to preserve this present form of embodiment. It is, of course, not necessary or possible to universalize religious perspectives on these matters. Nonetheless, it can be said that there are diverse but strong religious voices who espouse a position that, on religious as well as philosophical grounds, combines (1) a conviction regarding artificial nutrition/hydration as, in some circumstances and relevant to some patients, constituting an extraordinary means of treatment—with (2) a conviction that lack of any form of conscious awareness counts as a reason for letting life go.

to remedy the patient's pain. If the patient is suffering a great deal, it is ethically justifiable to treat her pain (without intending, though perhaps foreseeing the possibility of, the patient's death).

This kind of decision is also patient-relative. For some patients the risk of hastening death may not be justifiable—since the patient has a good likelihood of recovery; and/or there is little or no real risk of hastening death; and/or alternative medications will alleviate pain just as well without any attendant risk; or the patient herself requests not to be medicated, and so forth. Apart from such circumstances, however, it may be a failure of good care to leave patients in great pain just because they might die a bit sooner than otherwise. Also, adequate discernment of context, circumstances, nature of an action and its goals, must take account of the fact that patients who are not given pain medication may sometimes die sooner from the sheer gravity and stress of their pain. Moreover, broader scientific knowledge about pain relief continues to make treatment for pain more effective and more safe.

Actions in cases like these are assessed with the help of the traditional principle of "double effect"—that is, one action (giving pain medication) has two effects (the alleviation of pain and a possibly hastened dying); only the first effect is directly intended. Because of the importance of the first effect, the second effect is tolerated or relativized for the sake of the person affected. A full explanation of the principle of double effect is more complex than can be provided here, but what should be clear is that intention and action can have multiple effects or risks or consequences. How they are ordered, in terms of direct or indirect, makes all the difference to their moral status.

I will return briefly to all of the distinctions I have been describing and analyzing, but before doing this, I want to attend, however briefly, to the remaining unaddressed question of whether direct active intervention with the intention to kill can ever be justified. I consider, therefore, the possibility of a justified choice to take our own life or request that it be taken by another.

Active Taking of Life in a Medical Context

The reasons most frequently brought against taking our own life or asking another to take it for us (as well as taking the life of others even if they are unable to ask for this) are the following: (1) Our life is not our own; it belongs to God; it is God's prerogative to decide when our life should end in this world. (2) It is the law of nature to preserve our life as long as we are able; while there are limits to our power to do so and to our reasonable obligation to do so, we must not give in too quickly to the forces of death, not refuse the burdens of our whole life or cut off prematurely its possibilities. Indeed, so important to each one is her/his own life that the requirement to respect persons as persons echoes within it the prohibition, "Do not kill." (3) We are essentially social beings, and to take our life by our own decision is to injure the community (our family, our friends, and the wider communities to which we belong). Not everyone appeals to all three of these reasons, but some version of one or the other of them has leverage for many.

These reasons, or affirmations, do not just sit among us as either affirmed or rejected. Counterarguments or at least assertions are alive and well, and they can be articulated as succinctly as the positions above: (1) Our lives really are our own; it is the free agency of the one who is to die that is the morally significant feature in this choice. If God exists, it may well be that God, too, respects the very freedom that belongs to us. God may not hold, or want to hold, complete control over our dying. (2) Notions of "natural law" are not persuasive to many people, and cultural diversity calls it into question historically and culturally. (3) We are indeed social beings, but we can construe community on the model of an ecosystem where the demise of some is nature's way of making room for others. Perhaps most frequently it is argued that the suffering of the one dying overrides all other considerations that would otherwise make the active taking of human life immoral.

Here is not the place to adjudicate all of these convictions, questions, contradictions. But they set a kind of background against which the issues may be newly joined. For example (and here I repeat some phrases I used in the first of these two essays on death), for those who believe that God is their ultimate destiny—their beginning and their end, their holder in life and welcomer in death—is it conceivable that profound "acceptance" of death, acknowledgment of an ending that is indeed God's will, can be expressed through action as well as through passion, through doing as well as being done unto? For those who believe they are called to resist the forces of diminishment and death as long as they can, and to surrender in the end not to evil but to God, can this never take the form of an active decision to die? Or better, does it not always, at its most radical level, take this form? Dying holds the mystery and the hope that, as I have suggested earlier with the words of Teilhard de Chardin, our death will be truly a "communion," with God. But in communion, action and passion, giving and receiving, embracing and letting go, become two sides of the same reality.

Some years ago I stood at the bedside of a young man dying of AIDS. He had fought his disease long and hard, with extraordinary intelligence and courage. The day came, however, when it was clear that no more could be done. Aggressive treatments, even technologies for sheer life support, were finally being overwhelmed by the forces of death. As his family, friends, and physician were telling him of this dire situation, he said in what he could manage of a whisper, "You mean it's time to concede?" For him, conceding was an active surrender to God, and it entailed a decision to stop the technologies that were keeping him alive. He took no direct action (nor requested any) to end his life, though he chose to accept death and to cease prolonging his dying. Without erasing the difference between his form of letting go and a more active taking of his life, is it nonetheless possible that all the elements of religious experience could have been incorporated into one or the other?

Moreover, is it not possible, at least in exceptional circumstances, that the law of one's nature, the law of one's being, presses one to self-preservation in a manner whereby the whole of one's being must be saved? If it is possible that an individual can be in such dire straits that her very integrity as a self is threatened (by intractable pain, ravaging the spirit as well as the body), could it not be justifiable in such circumstances to end one's life, to surrender it while it is still whole?

Finally, for those who believe in the communion of saints, is there a way in which membership in community is sustained no matter how death is accepted? Is it possible that, when death becomes inevitable and surrender to God is made in the face of it, then communal bonds can be preserved and not violated in an active as well as passive dying-into-life?

I raise these questions not to suggest that it makes no moral difference if we refuse treatment or ask for a lethal dosage of medicine; for I am convinced that in most circumstances it does make a profound difference. In fact, it should be clear by now that I am prepared to argue that choices for death are more easily justified when they are choices to let a life go, under circumstances in which the burdens of preserving life outweigh the benefits for the one who is dying. I raise the questions, rather, in order to probe the possibility of exceptions to a rule. I raise them not to muffle but to intensify the deep experience of our call to cherish life and to hold back our hands from harming it. There is a time in which life and death come together for us, and our movement through death into greater life may reveal something new for us all.

I do not end without some comment on political and social struggles that continue to face us.

Social Consequences of Changes in the Law

Many persons argue against a change in policy and law in these matters not because active euthanasia or suicide are intrinsically wrong (wrong "in principle") but because they will be injurious to society. Holders of this position point to several factors: We will soon be on a very slippery slope, where what began as respect for some individuals' right of private choice becomes a violation of others' right to medical care; where we create an ethos in which individuals are pressured, socially coerced, to choose to die rather than to live as a burden to others; where the "easy way out" short-circuits the possibility of an individual and his or her family's companioning one another to the end, and only then surrendering to God. Moreover, risks of error, and pressures to expand the practice of euthanasia, are greater in a society like ours where medical care is even now (despite the progress of, for example, an Affordable Care Act) not yet equitably distributed according to factors of race, economic status, geography, and gender; and where there is already a massive breakdown in trust between patients and physicians. These are serious concerns, surely, although they are not without response. For example, potential abuses may be limited if we craft careful legislative safeguards against them. How shall we weigh these and other arguments, analyses, and concerns? I have tried to offer not so much conclusions to all of these debates, as kernels of potential insight, and in the end, only some provisional recommendations.

1. The concerns on all sides about dying point to some things that can be done that will ease our fears and remedy some situations of unfreedom. What we must do, first and foremost, with whatever terminology, is to understand the meanings of concepts like "extraordinary means," and hence to clarify the meaning and the effectiveness of refusal of treatment. If this is truly legally safeguarded, and if there is

wide and deep understanding of its medical as well as its moral and religious possibility and power, we shall learn that there is little need for direct taking of life, our own or anyone else's, although we do have decisions to make regarding our death, choices to live but choices finally to surrender to what must be and what can even be welcomed.

2. As Paul Ramsey once wrote, "If the sting of death is sin, the sting of dying is solitude. . . . Desertion is more choking than death, and more feared. The chief problem of the dying is now not to die alone."[6] To choose in the end to let go is a choice we should make with others. In the medical context, the most pressing need and the most effective safeguard against all that we fear is communication. It is to be structured by policy and nurtured by those who share our life.

3. What we must also do is to continue to press for medical progress in the management of pain. Significant strides have been made in this regard in the last decades, especially with the growing emphasis on palliative care. Along with this must come a clearer focus in the clinical setting on the goals of care (that is, to cure, maintain biological equilibrium, or to comfort) for each individual patient—goals that are appropriate to the individual's medical condition and personal values. Only so can we determine whether aggressive treatment should be continued or withheld; only so can we be clear about the requirements of care and the possibilities of alleviating suffering. If we can manage these things, the situations in which there appears no way out but through active killing—situations that are already rare—will be almost nonexistent.

4. The process of our discernment, whether in the political arena or in our own faith communities, is a process that holds a moral requirement of mutual respect. We must find the ways to secure this respect (in disagreement, in working out solutions), and through it a hope for the fruits of a discernment that will ultimately injure neither the individual or society.

I end where I began: Human life has profound value; it is even holy. It therefore deserves utter respect. Yet death may sometimes be welcomed—if it is welcomed in a way that does not ignore or violate the requirement to respect and to value each person. The questions before us are questions of what that way means and what, from all of us, it demands.

---

[6]Paul Ramsey, *The Patient as Person*, 2nd ed. (New Haven, CT: Yale University Press, 2002), 134.

CHAPTER 17

Stem Cell Research

Religious Considerations

Religious traditions have endured in large part because they help people to make sense of their lives. Major religious traditions become major because they offer some response to the large human questions of suffering and death, hope and transcendence, history and community, as well as the everyday issues of how we are to live together with some modicum of harmony and peace. Adherents to traditions of faith generally experience their shared beliefs and practices not as irrational but as part of the effort of reason to understand the actual and the possible in human life and all that is around it. Although religious sources of insight may reach beyond empirical data and logical reasoning, they need not ultimately do violence to either. When we ask profound questions such as how humans ought to reproduce themselves, or how extreme suffering can be alleviated, or whether the meaning of the human body changes when we exchange its parts, we can be helped by looking to the source and the substance of the attitudes, beliefs, and practices that animate people's lives.

Of course, when we look for guidance in the faith of believers, we do not find univocal voices—not from believers in general and not from believers within particular traditions. Roman Catholics will often not agree with spokespersons from the United Church of Christ; many Jews will not agree with many Catholics about abortion; and so

---

A version of this essay was published in *Essentials of Stem Cell Biology*, ed. Robert Lanza et al., 2nd ed. (Amsterdam: Elsevier Academic Press, 2009), 495–501. Used with permission.

on. But the division within faith traditions today is often wider than between or among them. So, there is more than one view regarding stem cell research among Roman Catholics; more than one among the different strands of Judaism; more than one among Muslims. Such disagreements do not make religious voices useless for societal and religious discernment, any more than disagreements among scientists render scientific research and the voices of scientists useless.

This essay aims to review religious perspectives on stem cell research. It is not possible here to survey every religious or theological argument for and against stem cell research. Something of an overview is presented, and then particular issues of concern articulated by representatives of some religious traditions are examined.

Mapping the Terrain

Sources for Stem Cells

The major disputed religious and ethical questions surrounding stem cell research are focused not on stem cells as such but on the sources from which stem cells are derived. Hence, debates continue to rage regarding the moral status of human embryos and the permissibility of taking stem cells from already dead fetuses. Religious thinkers who consider the human embryo sacrosanct from its inception will consistently oppose the extraction of embryonic stem cells as a form of killing (of embryos). Those who do not appraise the value of an embryo as being on a par with that of a human person are much more willing to favor embryo research in general, including the extraction of stem cells for research. Still others who emphasize the ambiguity of the moral status of embryos are more likely to weigh the advantages of embryo cell research over the possible violations of the embryo as an entity in itself. All religious traditions recognize an aborted fetus as a cadaver; hence, the derivation of stem cells from the gonadal ridge of dead fetuses may be as permissible as the harvesting of tissues or organs from any human cadavers. Nonetheless, representatives of traditions that prohibit abortion worry about complicity with and support of the moral evil of abortion when stem cells are derived from electively aborted fetuses.

Alternative sources for human stem cells are especially championed by those who are opposed to embryo stem cell and fetal stem cell research. The least objectionable sources often cited are stem cells taken from umbilical cord blood, placentas, amniotic fluid, and other forms of "adult" tissue[1] such as bone marrow and skin (given that this does not ultimately disrespect or harm the donors of the tissue). Other sources considered by the President's Council on Bioethics in 2005 included embryos that are already dead but have some remaining normal cells, blastomeres (any of the cells produced from the first division of a fertilized ovum, or zygote) biopsied from living embryos without destroying the embryos, and deliberately engineered biological artifacts that are not embryos but function like embryos minus any potential to develop into a person. A compromise source (though still controversial) is stem cell lines developed from embryonic stem cells that were harvested in the past (that is, the life of the original embryo has already been taken, and no new direct moral agency is involved in the killing of more embryos in the same lines).[2]

Problems with these sources continue, however. Research on adult stem cells is in some ways less advanced than research on embryonic cells, even though it is adult stem cells that have actually already been useful in some medical treatments. The use of embryo cadavers raises new ethical questions about in vitro fertilization and the cryopreservation of embryos (about half of which die when thawed). Removing cells from living embryos is not without risk to the embryos. The creation of biological artifacts can involve cloning (which, even when it is for research and not for reproduction, raises another set of ethical issues). Moreover, the artifacts may be "functionally equivalent" to embryos in ways that fail to settle all questions of their moral status—that is, maybe they should be respected in the same way embryos are respected, since their incapacity to become human persons may be overcome at some point in the further development of reproductive technologies. In addition, a move to "create" these artifacts crosses another moral boundary—that is, the manufacturing of human entities precisely for research, as opposed to simply using "spare" embryos—that is troubling to many people. Finally, the proposed use of already existing embryonic cell lines encounters the same objections of complicity with

---

[1]The term "adult" for the category of adult stem cells is somewhat misleading, since it includes cells that can be found in infants and children; it stands basically for stem cells that reside in already developed tissue. Scientists sometimes use the term "somatic" stem cells as more accurate.

[2]This is the route being taken by governments, including the United States, that more readily affirm the use of already existing embryonic stem cell lines when it comes to federal funding.

moral evil that is involved in the use of cells taken from aborted fetuses. For those who take seriously all of these difficulties with alternative sources for human stem cells, the alternatives do not appear as yet to resolve deep-seated scientific, philosophical, and religious concerns. In any case, some scientists argue that it is better to proceed on all fronts rather than only one. Moreover, the still undetermined (undifferentiated) nature of early embryonic cells is believed by many to be more readily suitable for the goals of research.

Other issues complicate moral assessments of the sources of stem cells and the aims of stem cell research. For example, almost all religious thinkers argue that some form of respect is due to embryos, even if not the same respect that is required for human persons. Yet there is lack of clarity about what respect can mean when it is aligned with the killing of the respected object. It is not difficult to get minimal consensus on prohibitions against buying and selling human embryos, or on safeguards like informed consent from the donors of embryos for research. For many religious believers, it makes a difference that these embryos are "spare" embryos, left over from in vitro fertilization procedures, and destined to be discarded if they are not used in research. From other religious perspectives, however, this fact in itself does not lift the prohibition against killing them.

Questions of Justice

Quite another kind of ethical issue is raised by people from almost all religious traditions. This is the issue of distributive justice. Who will be expected to be the primary donors of embryos or aborted fetuses? Will gender, race, and class discrimination characterize the whole process of research on stem cells? And will the primary goals of research in fact be skewed toward profit more than toward healing? Who will gain from the predicted marvelous therapeutic advances achieved through stem cell research—the wealthy but not the poor? The powerful but not the marginalized? What will be the overall results for respect for human persons if human embryos and stem cells are commodified, wholly instrumentalized, and in some ways trivialized?

All of these questions are questions for secular philosophical, scientific, and medical ethics as well as for religious ethics. When they are identified by religious and theological thinkers, however, they are always lodged in the larger questions with which religious traditions are concerned, and they almost always appeal to sacred texts and faith community traditions, teachings, and practices, as well as to secular sources and forms of moral reasoning.

Religious Beliefs and Ethical Questions

Anchoring religious concerns for the moral status of the human embryo, the nature of moral evil and immoral complicity, and questions of distributive justice are beliefs about the nature and destiny of human life, the meaning of bodily existence, the interaction between divine and human agency in the progress and healing of creation, the importance of consequences in moral reasoning along with the importance of religious laws and ontologically based norms, the basic equality of all human persons before God, and so forth. Even when there is no direct line between the most profound beliefs of a person and the answer to a particular moral question, such a belief makes a difference for moral discernment and conviction. There are no world religions today that oppose all human intervention in "nature," yet all religions recognize some limitations on what humans may do—either to themselves or to other created beings. All consider humility in the face of concrete reality an important antidote to arrogance or pride (and in the wake of ecological disasters, all now take account of the risks of some interventions made only for the sake of the flourishing of some human generations). No religions favor illness over health, death over life; yet each has a perspective in which health may not be an absolute value, and death may be welcomed. In the present context of stem cell research, there is no religious tradition that does not take seriously the beneficial results promised by such research.

Hence, positions of religious believers regarding stem cell research tend to be highly complex. Each tradition needs to be understood in its complexity and its diversity. This essay cannot track all of this, but it can try to show how some beliefs are coherent, whether or not they can be agreed upon by others in the same tradition or across faiths and cultures.

Particular Traditions: An Overview

A beginning understanding of positions taken by religious scholars and spokespersons in mainline traditions is, fortunately, available to some extent in the testimony and writings that have appeared in relation to the public debate on embryonic stem cell research. We have here, of course, just the proverbial tip of the iceberg. Nonetheless, these documents and essays point us to both the concrete moral positions being debated and the larger rationales behind them. In brief summaries, then, I here survey some of these positions and arguments. Following this, I focus on specific lines of argument taken by representatives of the Roman Catholic tradition. I do this not to privilege this tradition, but because its articulation of arguments is more prolific than most; it claims to be trying to be persuasive in a secular public sphere; its central positions are representative of strands of other religious as well as philosophical traditions; and it offers an ongoing critical conversation on both sides of the stem cell debate.

Hinduism and Buddhism

Representatives of the Hindu and Buddhist traditions have not been major players in the contemporary debate about stem cell research, at least not in the United States. There are historical reasons for this, no doubt, including the fact that neither are as yet majority religions in the West. Yet there is much in both of these traditions that may, for their adherents, be relevant to issues of stem cell research. Given the complexity of the traditions, it remains for their scholars and spokespersons to render accessible to outsiders the foundational beliefs and moral concerns that may shed light on such issues. Briefly, however, some elements in these faith traditions can be noted.

Both Hinduism and Buddhism incorporate beliefs in reincarnation. This complicates issues of what can be done with human embryos. According to some Hindu traditions, human life begins prior to conception; the "soul" may be present even in sperm, or it may be in some other life form before and after its human existence. Human reincarnation, however, offers a unique opportunity to influence the future of an individual. Great caution must be taken whenever actions are considered that may destroy this opportunity. On the other hand, for Hindus, a belief in reincarnation is also tied to motivation to be compassionate toward others. Good actions that will change the course of suffering for oneself and others are exhorted not only so that one can advance morally (and thereby improve one's karma), but because other people are worthy of beneficent deeds. Although the forms of compassion include nonviolence, there is in Hinduism also a broad tradition of sacrifice, wherein one human life can be taken for the sake of a higher cause. As one example of this, in 2001 the Hindu Endowments Board of Singapore expressed willingness to accept the extraction of stem cells from human embryos in their earliest stages, as long as this did not go beyond two weeks of embryonic development. It is not impossible that these convictions provide a rationale for embryonic stem cell research.

Buddhists are divided in their opinions about human embryonic stem cell research. For some, the precept against harming any living thing is determinative, ruling out the extraction of stem cells from, and the concomitant destruction of, embryos. Yet other Buddhists appeal to another element in Buddhism that offers a possible rationale for embryonic stem cell research. Buddhism's goal of self-transcendence through a process of self-forgetting undergirds a requirement for compassion, one of the Four-fold Holy Truths of Buddhism. In Mahayana Buddhism the ideal is the Bodhisattva, one who achieves self-emptying but then returns to help those in need. Again, here is a possible rationale for embryonic stem cell research. Moreover, some Buddhists believe that a soul has some choice as to where it will be incarnated. It has even been suggested that souls will not elect to embed in "spare" embryos that will only be destroyed. Hence, early embryos may not ever have a potential to become a human person and can therefore be used for some other purpose.

Whether such considerations are of overall significance in decisions to pursue embryonic or fetal stem cell research remains to be seen. At the very least it can be said that they represent large concerns for the value of human life—whether at its inception or in response to later injury and illness.

Islam

Like other world religions, there are many schools of thought among Muslims. There are also multiple sources for moral guidance, including the Qur'an and its commentaries, the *hadiths* (a second source of moral indicators supplementary to the Qur'an), Muslim philosophies that range from a form of ontological and moral realism to a version of divine command theory, Shari'a (formulations of Islamic law), and centuries of juridical literature. Testifying before the U.S. National

Bioethics Advisory Commission in 1999, the Islamic scholar Abdulaziz Sachedina attempted to provide some general insights from the tradition, taking into account the diverse interpretations of major Sunni and Shi'i schools of legal thought.[3] His analysis of various texts led him to infer guidelines for stem cell research from the rulings of the Shari'a on fetal viability and the moral status of the embryo.

Islamic traditions have given serious attention to the moral status of the "fetus and its development to a particular point when it attains human personhood with full moral and legal status."[4] The early embryo has been variously valued in different eras, depending on the information available from science. Throughout the history of legal rulings in this regard, however, a developmental view of the fetus—according to a divine plan—has been sustained. This founds the view that the moral status of personhood is not achieved at the earliest stages of embryonic life but only after sufficient biological development has taken place—the kind of development that includes a recognizable human anatomy and the possibility of "voluntary" movement. Most Sunni and some Shi'ite scholars therefore distinguish two stages in pregnancy. The first stage, "pre-ensoulment," is human biological life, but not yet human personal life. It is only after the fourth month (120 days, or the time of quickening) that the "biological human" becomes a "moral person."[5] This is to say that at this stage of development the fetus achieves the status of a moral and legal person. In the first stage, the biological entity is to be respected, yet abortion is allowed for grave reasons. In the second stage, killing the fetus is considered homicide.[6] The conclusion to be drawn is that there may be room for early embryonic stem cell extraction without violating divinely given laws or the embryo itself. In Islam, therefore, there are strong elements of the tradition that affirm embryonic stem cell research, though reasons can also be adduced against it.

---

[3] Abdulazia Sachedina, "Testimony," in *Ethical Issues in Human Stem Cell Research*, vol. 3: *Religious Perspectives* (Rockville, MD: National Bioethics Advisory Commission, 2000), G3–G6.

[4] Ibid., G3.

[5] Ibid., G4.

[6] See Valerie J. Hoffman, "Islamic Perspectives on the Human Body: Legal, Social, and Spiritual Considerations," in *Embodiment, Morality, and Medicine*, ed. Lisa Sowle Cahill and Margaret A. Farley (Boston: Kluwer Academic Publishers, 1995), 37.

Judaism

In the twenty-first century, Orthodox, Conservative, and Reform Jews take different positions on many issues of applied ethics.[7] These views are not easily specified when it comes to stem cell research. What is possible here is to present the opinions of some Jewish scholars, with the caution that not all views are represented. In the context of debates about stem cells, Reform Judaism may be the clearest supporter of this research even when it entails the derivation of stem cells from human embryos or from aborted fetuses. Jewish law does not give legal status to the fertilized ovum outside a mother's womb. When the embryo is inside a uterus, it has legal status but not that of a human person. In general, however, this strand of Judaism favors the use only of so-called "spare" embryos, those that will be otherwise discarded.[8]

Rabbi Elliott Dorff has identified theological assumptions useful for understanding a Jewish response to stem cell research.[9] These include the following: moral discernment (of what God wants of God's people) must be based on both Jewish theology and Jewish law; all human beings are created in the image of God and are to be valued as such; human bodies belong to God and are only on loan to the individuals who have them; human agency is important in responses to human illness, so that both "natural" and "artificial" means are acceptable in overcoming disease. Indeed, there is a duty to develop and use any therapies that can help in the care of the human body. Yet, because humans are not omniscient like God, humility and caution are essential, especially when human science and technology press to the edges of human knowledge.

There are grounds in Jewish law and theology for permitting the derivation of stem cells both from aborted fetuses and from human embryos. Just as abortion (though generally forbidden) can be justified for serious reasons, so also can the use of fetuses for important research.

---

[7]For Conservative Jews, laws and traditions can change; for Reform Jews, individuals can make choices regarding what traditions to affirm; for Orthodox Jews, Jewish traditions and laws constitute the predominant guides regarding moral choices.

[8]And in recent years, this has been expanded in some Jewish traditions to the use of cell lines derived from previously destroyed embryos.

[9]Elliot N. Dorff, "Stem Cell Research—A Jewish Perspective," in *The Human Embryonic Stem Cell Debate: Science, Ethics, and Public Policy*, ed. Suzanne Holland, Karen Lebacqz, and Laurie Zoloth (Cambridge, MA: MIT Press, 2001), 89–94. See also Dorff, "Testimony," in *Ethical Issues in Human Stem Cell Research*, vol. 3, C1–C5.

A fetus in utero is considered not as a human person but as the "thigh of its mother." One is not allowed to amputate a part of one's body (in this case, one's thigh) except for good reasons (for example, to remove a gangrenous limb, save the life of a mother or remove other serious risk, and perhaps to remove a fetus that is genetically malformed or diseased). When an abortion is thus justified, the abortus may be used as a source of stem cells.

Embryos can also be legitimate sources for stem cells extracted for purposes of research. During the first forty days of gestation in utero, embryos (and fetuses) are only like "water."[10] They are "non-souled," with only a liminal status. Although abortion during this time is permitted only for good reasons, the situation is different when embryos are not in the womb. Here there is no potential for embryos to develop into human persons; hence, they may be discarded, frozen, or used for promising research. Both Rabbi Dorff and Jewish scholar Laurie Zoloth argue that the duty to care for human bodies, the duty to heal, may undergird not just permission to pursue research on stem cells but an ethical duty to do so.[11]

The Jewish tradition places all of these considerations in a wider context of responsibilities to community, fairness in distribution of benefits and burdens, and caution about the connections of stem cell research to invidious programs of eugenics. Ethical norms that safeguard the common good as well as the good of individuals provide boundaries for the development and future uses of stem cell research; they focus it, perhaps obligate it, but do not forbid it.

Christianity

The diversity and pluralism to be expected in Christian responses to stem cell research mirrors to some extent the historical institutional divisions within Christianity. From the early schisms between East and West to the great Reformations in the West and the subsequent proliferations of Protestant denominations, to the Anglican and Roman Catholic Church traditions, and to the rise of new forms of Pentecostalism in the world's South, Christians have diversified in their beliefs and

---

[10]See Laurie Zoloth, "The Ethics of the Eighth Day: Jewish Bioethics and Research on Human Embryonic Stem Cells," in *The Human Embryonic Stem Cell Debate*, ed. S. Holland et al., 95–113.

[11]Ibid.

in their moral convictions and practices. There remains some important commonality in basic doctrines, largely expressed in creeds, and these are not irrelevant to issues of stem cell research. Examples include belief in divine revelation, particularly through sacred scripture; reconciliation made possible between humans and God through Jesus Christ; affirmation of the goodness of creation despite the damage sustained as the result of moral evil or sin; acceptance of the importance of human agency (in practice if not always in theology); a call to unconditional love of God and love and service of neighbor; a basic view of human equality and the obligation to promote justice. Theological anthropologies vary importantly in terms of understandings of freedom and grace, virtue and sin. Strands of Christian moral theologies diverge when it comes to the basis and force of moral norms—depending primarily either on God's command or God's will manifest in creation itself, and holding to absolute moral norms or only prima facie norms relativized according to circumstances, consequences, or priorities among aims. Law and gospel are important to each Christian tradition, though the emphasis on one or the other may vary.

Articulating an Eastern Orthodox view of embryonic stem cell research, Demetrios Demopulos begins with concern for the alleviation of suffering.[12] "Medical arts" are to be encouraged, with the proviso that they be practiced as gifts from God ordered to divine purposes. Created in the image and likeness of God, human persons are destined for participation in the life of God—hence the *telos* of the human person is referred to as *theosis* or "deification." Persons are authentic insofar as they struggle to grow into this life; they remain "potential" persons until this is achieved. But even zygotes (one-celled fertilized ova) are potential persons in this sense; that is, they, too, are in a developmental process that ends in deification. Hence, human life is sacred from the beginning and at every step along the way, entitled to protection and the opportunity to seek its destiny. "Even though not yet a person, an embryo should not be used for or sacrificed in experimentation."[13] Correlatively, practices of in vitro fertilization that yield "surplus" embryos that will be discarded cannot be condoned.

Though the development of alternative techniques and sources is

---

[12]Demetrios Demopulos, "Testimony," in *Ethical Issues in Human Stem Cell Research*, vol. 3: *Religious Perspectives*, B3–B4.
[13]Ibid., B3.

preferable, Demopulos himself does allow the use of already harvested embryonic stem cells for research. "Wishing that something had not been done will not undo it,"[14] he maintains. The compromise position, then, of continuing research on available cell lines, is accepted so long as the research does not violate other norms of justice (by maximizing profits rather than the health of persons, fostering trivial medical procedures for cosmetic purposes alone, or contributing to a questionable agenda for eugenics). The use of cadaver fetal cells is also acceptable if the abortion that provides them is spontaneous, not elected. But human life—potential human personal life—from zygote to a life beyond this world, remains sacred; what ultimately ends in God ought to be inviolable among humans.

Among Protestant denominations in the United States, some support and some oppose embryonic stem cell research. Data on these is unstable, however, as positions continue to harden or to shift. Many churches do not yet have an official policy on this issue, though spokespersons indicate a kind of majority view. For example, Southern Baptists have been, as a group, generally opposed to this research, although there is some openness to the position of using stem cell lines developed from already harvested cells. The United Methodist Church allows the extraction of stem cells from embryos that would otherwise be discarded. Presbyterians in General Assembly have likewise articulated their support of research on "left over" embryos that would otherwise be destroyed, and they have affirmed the use of federal funds to make this possible. Acknowledging the significance of concepts like "potential personhood" and the need to "respect" embryos, Presbyterians and others nonetheless have determined that whatever form this respect takes, it ought not to have priority over alleviating the suffering of actual people. The United Church of Christ has for many years been supportive of embryonic stem cell research as long as it is motivated by a clear and attainable healing benefit.

Individual ethicists from a variety of Protestant backgrounds (though seldom speaking officially for their denominations) also vary in their approaches to stem cell research. For example, Ted Peters of the Pacific Lutheran School of Theology comes down on the side of supporting embryonic stem cell research because he believes that, on balance, concern for the human dignity not of embryos but of future

---

[14]Ibid.

real persons is more compelling.[15] Ronald Cole-Turner agrees with others in the United Church of Christ by approving the extraction of stem cells from embryos, but sets conditions for research in terms of justice issues.[16] Gene Outka[17] and Gilbert Meilaender,[18] both Lutherans, share certain theological and philosophical convictions about the irreducible value of the early embryo. Both want to affirm the continuity of human life between early embryo and an actualized full person. This means that both consider the taking of the life of an embryo as a violation of the prohibition against killing. Both also want to distinguish the question of embryo stem cell extraction from the question of abortion (in a variety of ways, but primarily because in the former there is no direct conflict between a woman and a fetus).

Outka, however, finally approves of the use of some embryos for the derivation of stem cells. He does so by introducing two conditions that can exempt one from the absolute force of the prohibition.[19] The first and most distinctive is the *nothing is lost* condition. That is, it is possible to relativize the prohibition against killing when those who are to be killed will die anyway. This is precisely the condition that characterizes the situation of spare (or excess) embryos (left over from in vitro fertilization procedures) destined now to be discarded. The second condition is that *other lives will be saved* through this act of killing. Given the ultimate therapeutic aims of stem cell research, this condition is also present. It is the *nothing is lost* condition that finally allows Outka both to continue to affirm the status of the embryo as an end in itself and not a means only, and yet allow the taking of its life for purposes of research. It becomes, then, the basis of ethical acceptance of the derivation of stem cells from some human embryos, and therefore a carefully circumscribed but nonetheless positive approval of embryonic stem cell research.

Meilaender, on the other hand, in his 2001 essay remains firm

---

[15]Ted Peters, "Embryonic Stem Cells and the Theology of Dignity," in Holland et al., *Human Embryonic Stem Cell Debate*, 12–40. See also Ted Peters, Karen Lebacqz, and Gaymon Bennett, *Sacred Cells? Why Christians Should Support Stem Cell Research* (New York: Rowman and Littlefield, 2008).

[16]Ronald Cole-Turner, "Testimony," in *Ethical Issues in Human Stem Cell Research*, vol. 3, A1–A4.

[17]Gene Outka, "The Ethics of Human Stem Cell Research," *Kennedy Institute of Ethics Journal* 12, no. 2 (2002): 175–213.

[18]Gilbert C. Meilander, "Some Protestant Reflections," in Holland et al., *Human Embryonic Stem Cell Debate*, 141–48.

[19]Outka, "Ethics of Human Stem Cell Research," 193.

(though cautious and reluctant) in the conviction that embryonic stem cell research ought not to go forward; or, better, that it is not morally justifiable to use human embryos as the source for stem cells. Referencing three other Protestant theologians (Karl Barth, John Howard Yoder, and Stanley Hauerwas), Meilaender poses three arguments: (1) People should be considered persons not on the basis of potentiality or actuality, nor on the basis of their capacities, but simply on the basis that they are members of the human community. To think inclusively about the human species should lead us to honor the dignity of even the weakest of living human beings—the embryo—and thereby to "appreciate the mystery of the human person and the mystery of our own individuality."[20] (2) Immediately to opt for embryonic stem cell research is to prevent us from finding better solutions to the medical problems this research is designed to address. Given the ethical compromises involved in following this "handy" route, it would be better to "deny ourselves" this remedy and look to ones that do not denigrate the dignity of human persons however and wherever they live. (3) The church should bear witness to its beliefs by refusing to make sophistic distinctions such as those between funding embryonic stem cell research and funding the "procurement" of these cells. Meilaender is skeptical that only excess embryos or available cell lines will be used.

Along with evangelical Protestants, Roman Catholic voices have been prominent in the debates surrounding embryonic stem cell research. The position most frequently articulated in the public forum is that of opposition to the derivation of stem cells from embryos. This is the position of the Catholic hierarchy, promulgated through both Vatican and national episcopal channels. It is a position supported theologically by spokespersons (of the U.S. Catholic Bishops Conference) such as Richard Doerflinger. Yet it is not the only position espoused by Roman Catholic ethicists and moral theologians or by all Roman Catholics. The alternate position is basically the "fourteen-day theory," or the theory that an embryo in the first fourteen days of existence, prior to implantation in the uterus, is not yet even a "potential person," and hence need not be protected in the same way as human persons (or even the same as fetuses who are considered potential persons after implantation). Neither of these positions goes the route of declaring

---

[20]Meilaender, "Some Protestant Reflections," in Holland et al., *Human Embryonic Stem Cell Debate*, 143.

absolutely that the early embryo is a person, or the route of approving the exploitation of fetuses in utero in later stages of development. Since the debate between these two positions reflects similar philosophical and theological debates in other religious traditions and in the public forum,[21] it is worth looking at it in closer detail.

Roman Catholic Contributions and the Fourteen-Day Theory

Before turning to the technicalities of the fourteen-day theory, it should be noted that Roman Catholics (including the official leaders of the church) tend to worry, like people in other traditions, about issues of justice, ecology, and the well-being of the whole Earth. Apart from the moral status of the embryo, Catholic concerns are focused on questions of equity in the shared lives of persons across the world. For all the pressures to go forward with embryonic and fetal tissue stem cell research, there is little assurance anywhere that the benefits of this research will be shared in the human community among the poor as well as the wealthy, across racial and gender lines, and in countries of the world's South as well as North. Moreover, as the research goes forward (for it surely will), some safeguards will need to be in place to keep the goals of the research focused on the healing of human persons rather than on the commodification of human bodies, their tissues and cells. And the specter of human genetic engineering for enhancement purposes (and not only the treatment of diseases and injuries) is never far from the horizon. The other side of tremendous positive advances of modern technology is not to be ignored, not even if present anxieties lead desperately to seek means to lift the burdens of one generation or one group of people.

It is important to take preliminary note, also, of the shared community of discourse among Roman Catholic scholars, church leaders, and people. No matter how divided they may be among themselves regarding the moral status of the early embryo or other particular moral questions, their moral convictions are nonetheless expressed in a common language. The Catholic tradition is undivided in its affirmation of the goodness of creation, the role of human persons as agents in cooperation with ongoing divine creative activity, the importance

---

[21]See, for example, Mary Warnock, *A Question of Life: The Warnock Report on Human Fertilization and Embryology* (Oxford: Basil Blackwell, 1984).

of not only the individual but the community, the responsibilities of human persons to promote the health and well-being of one another.[22] At the same time, Catholics do disagree profoundly on some moral issues, and a key example of disagreement is the debate about the status of the embryo and the moral evil or goodness of extracting stem cells from it in a way that leads to its demise.

The reason why the debate within the Catholic community regarding stem cell research incorporates opposition over something like the fourteen-day theory is that the Roman Catholic moral tradition has consistently embraced a form of moral realism. At the heart of this tradition is the conviction that creation is itself revelatory. That is, embedded in an ultimately intelligible (though only partially so to humans) created reality lies the possibility of perceiving and discerning moral claims of respect in response to every entity, especially human persons. This is what is at stake in the Catholic tradition of natural law. Though there are historical inconsistencies, even contradictions in this long tradition, for the most part natural law has not meant that morality can simply and fully be "read off" of nature, not even with the help of the special revelation of the Bible (though this is a help). What natural law theory does is tell persons where to look—that is, to the concrete reality of the world around, to the basic needs and possibilities of human persons and to the world as a whole. "Looking" involves discernment, deliberation, structuring of insights, interpretation of meanings, taking account not only of what is similar among entities but their particular histories, contexts, relationships.

Roman Catholic thinkers engaged in discernment about human embryonic stem cell research tend, therefore, to "look" to the reality of stem cells and their sources—that is, human embryos and aborted fetuses, as well as adult tissues. Not all answers to every specific moral question are in the Bible, nor are they in official church teachings, nor in individual experiences of the sacred. Discernment incorporates all of these sources of insight, but it also requires the knowledge available from the sciences, philosophy, and whatever other secular disciplines provide some access to the reality that is being studied. The ongoing intensity of the debate about the moral status of embryos bears witness

---

[22]Margaret A. Farley, "Testimony," in *Ethical Issues in Human Stem Cell Research*, vol. 3, D1–D5. See also Farley, "Roman Catholic Views on Research Involving Human Embryonic Stem Cells," in Holland et al., *Human Embryonic Stem Cell Debate*, 113–18.

to the fact that not all inquiries can be settled by one discipline or one interpreter or within one epistemological perspective.

The argument against procuring stem cells from human embryos is primarily that it entails the death of the embryos. No one disputes this fact, but disagreement rages as to whether this death can be justified. Those who oppose its justification argue that for each human person there is a biological and ontological continuum from the single-cell stage to birth, to whatever one has of childhood and adult life, and then to death.[23] On this view, since a new and complete genetic code is present after fertilization, there is already a unique individual human person, potential in an important sense but concretely and really (inherently) already directed to full actualization. The zygote itself, as a living organism, is both the "builder and the building . . . it is self-organizing."[24] The moral status of the early embryo is, therefore, that of a human person; it does not achieve this status by degrees or at some arbitrary point in development; nor is this status simply bestowed upon it by social recognition or convention.

But if the embryo has the status of a human person, then killing it even in order to treat the illnesses of other persons cannot, from the above perspective, be justified. No human person, not even an inchoate one like an embryo, can be reduced to a pure means in relation to other ends. "Creating embryos for research purposes [or using embryos that will otherwise be discarded] is wrong because it treats this distinct human being, with his or her own inherent moral worth, as nothing more than a disposable instrument for someone else's benefit."[25] Those who oppose the extraction of stem cells from embryos on the grounds that it involves the destruction of a potential human person are not unsympathetic to the suffering that may be alleviated ultimately through research on stem cells. Part of the argument against the use of embryo sources for stem cells rests on the identification of alternative sources (particularly adult cells).[26]

On the other side of this debate are Catholic moral theologians and ethicists who do not consider the human embryo in its earliest stages

---

[23]Edmund D. Pellegrino, "Testimony," in *Ethical Issues in Human Stem Cell Research*, vol. 3, F1–F5.

[24]Benedict Ashley and A. Moraczewski, "Cloning, Aquinas, and the Embryonic Person," *National Catholic Bioethics Quarterly* 1, no. 2 (Summer 2001): 193.

[25]Richard Doerflinger, "Destructive Stem-Cell Research on Human Embryos," *Origins* 28 (1999): 771.

[26]Ibid.

(prior to the primitive streak[27] or to implantation) to be a human person, potential or actual. They hold the same meaning for "potency" as do their opponents—that is, the Aristotelian and Thomistic meaning, signifying not an extrinsic or "sheer possibility," but rather an intrinsic principle already as such actual within a being, directing it to individualized species-specific development (even though the being may not yet be developmentally fully actualized). These moral theologians argue, then, precisely *against* the view that the early embryo *has* this inherent potency to become a person. Their argument harks back to a centuries-old Catholic position that a certain degree of biological development is necessary in order for the human spirit (or soul) to be embodied.[28] The conceptus, in other words, must have a baseline organization before it can embody a human person; it must embody the potentiality as well as actuality that will lead to the formation of a human person. Although previous theories of embryological development were grounded in minimal (and to a great extent, erroneous) scientific evidence, proponents of embryonic stem cell research find in contemporary embryology insights that tend to support this developmental theory rather than defeat it.

Australian Catholic moral theologian Norman M. Ford has presented perhaps the most detailed argument in support of the view that an early embryo is not a potential human person.[29] The plausibility of "delayed personhood" is based on scientific evidence that suggests that the embryo prior to implantation is not yet a self-organizing organism. Fertilization itself does not take place in a "moment," as is

---

[27]"Primitive streak" is a term for the initial band of cells from which the *individuated* embryo begins to develop; it is present at approximately fourteen days after fertilization.

[28]Joseph Donceel, "Immediate Animation and Delayed Hominization," *Theological Studies* 31 (1970): 76–105.

[29]Norman M. Ford, *The Prenatal Person: Ethics from Conception to Birth* (Oxford: Blackwell Publishing, 2002). It should be noted that although Ford argues well for a developmental view of the embryo, he once asserted that he did not disagree with the official Catholic position of protecting embryos from the start. See Ford, "The Human Embryo as Person in Catholic Teaching," *National Catholic Bioethics Quarterly* 1 (2001): 155–60; Ford, "Are All Cells Derived from an Embryo Themselves Embryos?" in *Pluripotent Stem Cells: Therapeutic Perspectives and Ethical Issues* (Paris: John Libbey Eurotest, 2001), 81–87; Ford, *When Did I Begin? Conception of the Human Individual in History, Philosophy, and Science* (New York: Cambridge University Press, 1988). See also Thomas Shannon and A. B. Walter, "Reflections on the Moral Status of the Pre-Embryo," *Theological Studies* 51 (1990): 603–26; Richard A. McCormick, "Who or What Is the Preembryo?" in *Corrective Vision: Explorations in Moral Theology* (Kansas City, MO: Sheed and Ward, 1994), 176–88.

sometimes rhetorically claimed; it comes about through a process that takes approximately twenty-four hours, finally issuing in the one-celled zygote. When the zygote then divides, there comes to be not a definitive, singular organism, but a collection of cells, each with a complete genetic code. In other words, the first two cells, even if they interact, appear to be distinct cells, "not a two-cell ontological individual."[30] The same is true as division continues to four, eight, sixteen cells, each with its own life cycle and nutrients for sustaining its life. Cells multiply and differentiate as they are gradually specified in their potential. Some cells form membranes that will finally enclose an organized individual entity approximately fourteen days after fertilization. It is only then that a unified being can be said to be "self-organizing." Until this time, cells are "totipotential" in that they can become *any part* of what may ultimately be a human being or even a human being as a *whole*.[31] "The totipotency of the early embryo does not imply that a human individual is formed before a definitive human individual is formed with heterogeneous parts."[32]

The genotype of the zygote does not have a built-in blueprint for development, as if it were a miniature person. Only with the formation of a single primitive streak (which happens after implantation) does the totipotency of the embryo actually become a potency to develop into one human person. As Ford puts it, "If this argument is accepted, fertilization is not the beginning of the development *of* the human individual but the beginning of the formative process and development *into* one (or more human individuals)."[33] Many who find this argument plausible tend to express it more simply (though perhaps with less illumination): Since at its early stages an embryo can twin (that is, divide) and recombine, there is not here an individualized human entity with the inherent "settled potential" to become a human person. Critics of this argument respond that *if* an embryo does *not* twin or recombine, then it *may be supposed* that an individual is already existing. Ford's analysis goes further than this, however, suggesting that the very undifferentiation of cells prior to implantation disallows the identification of individuality, whether there is twinning and recombining or not.

---

[30]Ford, *Prenatal Person*, 65.
[31]Ford, "Are All Cells Derived from an Embryo Themselves Embryos?"
[32]Ford, *Prenatal Person*, 66.
[33]Ford, "Human Embryo as Person in *Catholic Teaching*," 160.

Since this articulation of the fourteen-day theory is dependent on the current state of mammalian embryological studies, Catholic moral theologians on both sides of the debate take seriously any new scientific information regarding just what is happening in the first stages of embryological development. For example, studies of the role of first cleavage (division of cells) in the development of mouse embryos suggest that an organizational process is already under way. Those who argue that the identity of the embryo is determined right after fertilization use this information to demonstrate a unitary process of self-organization. Those who support the fourteen-day theory do not deny that something is happening in the early stages of cell cleavage; they maintain, however, that the level of complexity and of organization is as yet too low to settle the individuality of a developing potential person. The embryo in its first stages must develop in order to be able to implant; only when it reaches this stage are its singularity and individuality settled.

In addition to the argument from lack of individuation prior to implantation, some theologians have noted another interesting argument in support of the lack of potential for the embryo to be a person in its early stages. That is, what is now known scientifically about the high rate of spontaneous early embryo loss (by the natural sloughing off of embryos from the uterus) undermines the credibility of the claim that human individuals begin at fertilization. In unassisted human reproduction, the development and loss of early embryos is estimated to be as high as 50 to 80 percent. From a Catholic theological point of view, it seems highly questionable that more than half of the individual human persons created by God should populate heaven without ever having seen the light of day in this world. This is a speculative argument, however, and it is generally not used today—though it remains intriguing.

There are, then, two opposing positions regarding the moral status of the early embryo articulated within the Roman Catholic tradition. This need not leave Catholics (or others) with a kind of "draw." Rather, it opens and sustains a shared significant conversation that takes account of scientific discoveries as well as of a larger set of theological and ethical insights. Moral theologians and ethicists attempt to provide reasons for their views that will be open to the scrutiny of all. Both sides acknowledge a certain amount of epistemic humility, since there are only degrees of certainty available regarding the ontological status

of the early embryo. Indeed, even official church documents acknowledge that there is no definitive answer to the question of when human
individual life begins. In 1974 the Vatican *Declaration on Procured
Abortion* stated in a footnote, "This declaration expressly leaves open
the question of the moment when the spiritual soul is infused. There
is not a unanimous tradition on this point and authors are as yet in
disagreement."[34] In 1987 a Vatican instruction titled *The Gift of Life*
admitted that its authors were "aware of the current debates concerning
the beginning of human life, concerning the individuality of the human
being and concerning the identity of the human person."[35] And Pope
John Paul II made no decision on the question of delayed ensoulment
(or "hominization") in his 1995 encyclical letter *Evangelium vitae*.

Uncertainty is dealt with in different ways by those who oppose and
those who support embryonic stem cell research. Those who oppose it
argue that even if the presence of the "personal soul" in an embryo is
only "probable," this suffices to prohibit *risking* the killing of a human
person. In other words, probability (if not certitude) warrants the safer
course. Hence, the embryo from fertilization on is to be *treated* as a
human person, with the kind of unconditional respect due to members
of the human community. This argument is reinforced by a concern
for a moral slippery slope along which human persons will cease to
be respected, no matter what their actuality or their needs.

For those who conclude, however, that embryonic stem cell research
can be permitted, uncertainty works the other way. First, the probability of an early embryo's actually representing an individualized and
self-organizing human being is much lower than is argued by opponents of embryonic stem cell research. Although there is not absolute
certitude to be gained at this point in time from scientific evidence, the
weight of the evidence *against* there being an individualized human
being (incarnated in an embryo prior to implantation) is greater and
more persuasive than any evidence for it. Moreover, the low level of
uncertainty (for those who hold this position), when placed in relation to the prospect of great benefits for human healing (and some
assurance that these benefits are not promised unrealistically) makes
it possible—without yielding to a full-blown utilitarianism—to justify

---

[34]Congregation for the Doctrine of the Faith, *Declaration on Procured Abortion (Acta apostolicae sedis;* 1974), no. 19.

[35]Congregation for the Doctrine of the Faith, *The Gift of Life (Donum vitae;* 1987), I.1.

using early (preimplantation) embryos as sources for stem cells for research. To *prohibit* all such research on the basis of a low probability of fact, or on a theological stipulation of moral status in the face of questionable accuracy of appraisal, seems itself not ethically justifiable.

Neither side in this debate wants to sacrifice the tradition's commitments to respect the dignity inherent in human life, promote human well-being, and honor the sacred in created realities. When a move forward is advocated for embryonic stem cell research it need not soften the tradition's concerns to oppose the commercialization of human life and to promote distributive justice in the provision of medical care. The ongoing Roman Catholic conversation on all of these matters can be of assistance to others in a pluralistic society as long as it remains open to wider dialogue and respect for all dialogue partners, while retaining its own integrity. This is probably a lesson for all religious and secular traditions.

One further word on these matters: It may be that the intensity of this debate regarding embryonic stem cell research will be de-escalated overall because of ongoing advances in adult stem cell research. These advances are already beyond simply the possibilities of adult stem cells for treating the tissues and organs from which they are derived. Current research that leads to de-programming of adult cells that can thereby become totipotential, *just like embryonic cells are*, opens whole new possibilities. No matter what, *thinking* about religious and ethical aspects of such issues will continue to remain important and urgent.

CHAPTER 18

Forgiveness in the Service of Justice and Love

Contemporary literature on Christian love has added exponentially to our historical understandings of love's meaning in theory and practice. On the edges of some of this literature attention is paid to the place of forgiveness in relation to love. Despite a sometime tendency to marginalize forgiveness in studies of love, at some point they must come together in both theory and practice. This is not a simple consideration, and it is often fraught with seeming contradictions or dilemmas. Yet forgiveness and love may be more essentially intertwined than we suspect. It can be said, for example, that there is no genuine Christian forgiveness without love, and love is sometimes tested in its ultimate possibility and imperative by the forgiveness it generates. Moreover, the construals of forgiveness that are central to much of Christian theology slip into caricature unless they include love in their foundation, framework, and movement. Christians believe that God's love for humans is revealed—perhaps centrally—in God's forgiveness of sinners, and that God's people (all of them sinners) are to be like God in their love and forgiveness of one another. The sin that requires divine forgiveness is the refusal of God's love; and the sins of humans against humans that require human forgiveness are the falsities and inadequacies that betray or distort our loving and being-loved. Here I will focus primarily on Christian forgiveness in terms of human forgiveness. Yet forgiveness cannot be understood Christianly apart from its relationship to divine forgiveness or apart from its context in human community and history.

In this essay I consider ways in which love and forgiveness are intertwined, and ways in which both divine and human forgiveness are themselves forms of love. I want ultimately to show how forgiveness offers a way to a form of human "decentering," better known in Christian circles as other-centered love, needed in a conflict-driven world. I do this in five steps: (1) description of the context in which new interest in forgiveness has arisen, (2) analysis of the challenges to forgiveness that are part of this new interest, (3) placement of Christian love and forgiveness in a matrix of Christian beliefs, (4) descriptive examination of the experience of forgiveness and the meanings it yields, and (5) resolution of tensions between forgiveness and justice through a proposal for "anticipatory" as well as "actual" forms of Christian forgiveness. I begin with some preliminary observations.

Forgiveness is a preoccupation not only of the Christian tradition, but of other world religions as well—in particular Judaism and Islam. The Hebrew Bible is replete with stories of God's merciful forgiveness granted to human beings (as in the promises to Noah) and in particular to the Israelites despite their infidelities (as in the provision of new tablets of the law after Moses, in response to the idolatry of the people, had destroyed the originals). The Psalmist, along with cries for God's wrath against enemies, still sings and sings again of the quality of divine forgiveness. Prophets threatened divine punishment, yet they combined lamentation with hope for forgiveness. Between and among humans, too, there are paradigmatic cases of astonishing forgiveness (as in Joseph's response to the brothers who betrayed him). Liturgically throughout the centuries, Yom Kippur, a High Holy Day for many Jews, is a day of atonement (in memory of God's merciful regiving of the law of the covenant to the Israelites). On this day divine pardon can be attained, and reconciliation among individuals may be sought.[1]

In the Qur'an, too, Allah is continually named "The Most Forgiving," or "The Most Merciful and Compassionate." Followers of Muhammed Ibn Abdallah were to believe in divine mercy, and also to imitate it.[2] The Qur'an describes believers as "those who avoid major

---

[1]Multiple interpretations and commentaries on the place of forgiveness in the Jewish tradition mark the history of rabbinical texts. For an intriguing and succinct, though not uncontroversial, overview of a pattern discernible in the Hebrew Bible, see Jonathan Sacks, *The Dignity of Difference: How to Avoid the Clash of Civilizations* (New York: Continuum, 2002), 182–88. An elegant contemporary introduction to and translation of the liturgy for Yom Kippur can be found in Rabbi Jules Harlow, ed., *Mahzor for Rosh Hashanah and Yom Kippur: A Prayer Book for the Days of Awe* (New York: Rabbinical Assembly, 1972), 325-783.

[2]For a brief but pointed English introduction to themes in Islam relevant to forgiveness,

sins and . . . when they are angry they forgive" (Al-Shura 42:37). Buddhism, on the other hand, recognizes no personal God, but in general addresses harms imposed by one human on another as requiring transcendence. The response to harm consists therefore in spiritual efforts at patience, peace, detachment, not forgiveness. Yet in a later form, Mahayana Buddhism, compassion becomes more important than psychological or spiritual equanimity. The bodhisattva offers a form of radical forgiveness precisely for the sake of the one who has caused harm.

The importance of forgiveness to various world religions notwithstanding, multiple ambiguous interpretations of its meaning and apparent inconsistencies in its practice suggest that there are many questions to be pursued, and more than proof-texts to be drawn from traditional writings. Although there is not the opportunity here to probe more fully the questions raised and insights offered from religious traditions other than Christianity, they remain on the horizon for anyone concerned about the role of forgiveness in a fractured and conflicted world.

In the last three decades, an impressive body of literature has developed regarding human forgiveness. A kind of urgency of inquiry has emerged not only among religious thinkers but among philosophers, historians, political theorists, psychologists, as well as biological and social scientists.[3] Research and analysis in these many secular fields

see Laleh Bakhtiar, "Becoming a Fair and Just Person: Sufism and Mental Health," *Park Ridge Center Bulletin* 25 (January–February 2002).

[3]Important religious writings include Miroslav Volf, *Free of Charge: Giving and Forgiving in a Culture Stripped of Grace* (Grand Rapids: Zondervan, 2005); Donald W. Shriver, *An Ethic for Enemies: Forgiveness in Politics* (New York: Oxford University Press, 1995); Desmond Mpilo Tutu, *No Future without Forgiveness* (New York: Doubleday, 1999); Raymond G. Helmick and Rodney L. Peterson, eds., *Forgiveness and Reconciliation: Religion, Public Policy, and Conflict Transformation* (Philadelphia: Templeton Foundation Press, 2001). For contributions from other fields, see, for example, Robert D. Enright and Joanna North, eds., *Exploring Forgiveness* (Madison: University of Wisconsin Press, 1998); Martha Minow, *Between Vengeance and Forgiveness: Facing History after Genocide and Mass Violence* (Boston: Beacon Press, 1998); Herbert W. Helm, Jonathan R. Cook, and John M. Berecz, "The Implications of Conjunctive and Disjunctive Forgiveness for Sexual Abuse," *Pastoral Psychology* 54 (September 2005): 23–34; Loren Toussaint and Jon R. Webb, "Gender Differences in the Relationship between Empathy and Forgiveness, *Journal of Social Psychology* 145 (2005): 673–85; Erwin Staub et al., "Healing, Reconciliation, Forgiving and the Prevention of Violence after Genocide or Mass Killing: An Intervention and Its Experimental Evaluation in Rwanda," *Journal of Social and Clinical Psychology* 24 (2005): 297–334; Steven J. Sandage, Peter C. Hill, and Henry C. Vang, "Toward a Multicultural Positive Psychology: Indigenous Forgiveness and Hmong Culture," *Counseling Psychologist* 31 (2003): 564–92; Teresa Godwin Phelps, *Scattered Voices: Language, Violence, and the Work of Truth* (Philadelphia: University of Pennsylvania Press, 2004).

have advanced particularly important issues regarding the meaning of human forgiveness, its required elements, its appropriateness in some contexts but not in others. To the forefront have come questions of the compatibility between forgiveness and justice, the conditionality of forgiveness, the potential corruption of the concept of forgiveness when it becomes primarily a therapy for victims, and the dependence of forgiveness on the expressed repentance and remorse of perpetrators of harm. Once again, it is not possible to probe here the results of these many studies or the ongoing scholarly conversations they promote, although I will endeavor not to leave them completely behind. I turn, then, to questions of Christian forgiveness by attending briefly to the contemporary context in which these and their secular counterparts arise.

Context for Forgiveness: Conflict, Injury, and Pain

What has awakened so much recent interest in questions of human forgiveness? No doubt many catalytic forces have been at work, but one of them might be described as a new and searing recognition of the lengths to which the inhumanity of humans against humans can go. The context for new interest in forgiveness, human and divine, is overall one in which poverty, oppression, exploitation, and violence seem to grow exponentially. Perhaps it has always been so. Humans have struggled throughout history for justice and for peace, for fairness and freedom, for healing of the pain in both body and spirit. Still the suffering goes on: violence begetting violence, exploitation escalating seemingly beyond remedy. New issues of race, class, and gender fuel worldwide conflicts; anger, resentment, and intractable greed fracture human relationships; religious and cultural imperialisms undergird human battles of devastating proportion—whether between or within nations, corporations, tribes, families, and even churches. Everywhere visible are both the causes and the consequences of these conflicts: destitution, war, abuses of power, systemic evils hidden behind "business as usual," and relentless but unnecessary injury and dying.

More particularly, ours is a time and a world in which "crimes against humanity" may have shaken the thick complacency that allowed toleration of unspeakable assaults on humans as human. Such crimes are perhaps not new in the twentieth and twenty-first centuries, but we are far removed from the ancients who could interpret them as a function of fate. The atrocities revealed in the Nuremberg Trials after World War II constituted a milestone in human history, one that showed to many a coming fork in the road for radical choice regarding human affairs. In experiences around the world, however, these kinds of atrocities have continued—whether in Argentina, the Balkans, Rwanda, the Democratic Republic of Congo, Iraq, or anywhere—auguring, as some maintain, the end of the history of human forgiveness or a new beginning.

The strides of contemporary globalization make it almost impossible today to isolate or ignore crimes against humanity as such. Hence, it is not surprising that as these very phenomena appear to increase, or at least become more widely visible, they have also occasioned new clarity about the rights of all humans, and they have roused on a global scale new stirrings of human concern, movements of human compassion. It would be a mistake to think in some naive way that these correlative phenomena can be identified simply as forces of evil and forces of good. We are all probably implicated in both, not the least because our opposition to perpetrators of injury and harm is an opposition more often shaped by goals of punishment than of the restoration of human relationships and societies. Western cultures in particular seem to have become more and more punitive in their response to perpetrators, ostensibly on behalf of victims. Nonetheless, it is in the midst of this complex context that new and sustained interest in forgiveness has emerged.

To some, this interest in forgiveness is dangerous, likely to mask what is "premature reconciliation" and to burden yet further the ones among us who are already most vulnerable. Others, however, find in the concept of forgiveness some inkling of the kind of decentering required of ourselves if we are ever to offset the worst forms of fear, ambition, resentment, and self-righteousness that divide us. In any case, the rise in concern for forgiveness and reconciliation may signal new energy for fashioning the "conditions of possibility" for *recognition* and *respect* of one individual for another, one group toward others, one generation for all humanity. There is some suffering that does not have to be, that can be ended in change, not in death.

Dramatic and Everyday Challenges to Forgiveness

Between and among humans the need for forgiveness is commonplace in our experience. As Hannah Arendt observed, "willed evil" may be rare, but "trespassing is an everyday occurrence," and it needs forgiveness.[4] Why else, she asks, are we enjoined to forgive not seven times but seventy times seven (Matt. 18:22)? Only through this "constant mutual release" from what we do, from the harmful consequences of actions that are otherwise irreversible, are we freed to live into the future.[5] For beings who are free, forgiveness is a necessary part of the fabric of human life. Small offenses may indeed be commonplace among us, but the fabric of relationships may be torn nonetheless.

Moreover, as we have already noted, there are uncommon offenses as well, some of which are considered so horrific that they cannot be forgiven, at least not in this world. However, it has never been easy for Christians or anyone else to identify with certainty what is meant by an "unforgivable sin." It is a sin against the Spirit, says Jesus (Mark 3:28–30; Matt. 12:30–32; Luke 12:8-10), and philosophers like Hegel have followed suit—though not necessarily with a univocal meaning for Spirit. Somehow what is at stake is an offense that blocks the movement of the Spirit, a crime against that which gives the power to forgive. But what or how could this be? On the one hand, there is some presumption that it occurs when the *agent* of the crime (the offense) chooses to refuse the forgiveness offered by the victim through the grace of the Spirit. On the other hand, it may also be that an injury so incapacitates, destroys, the *victim* that she or he is rendered incapable of forgiving the perpetrator. Such an injury would be unforgivable because the power of the Spirit could not any longer be received by the victim. These descriptions approach the question of the meaning of "unforgivable," but they seem not to settle it.

In the twentieth and into the twenty-first century, the paradigmatic case for the unforgivable sin has been the Holocaust, that unspeakable crime primarily against Jews (though others as well) under the National Socialist regime in Germany during World War II. There have been additional claims about cases comparable to this, whether on behalf of other genocidal events or even the terrifying destruction of the psychological humanity of individuals in very particular situ-

---

[4]Hannah Arendt, *The Human Condition* (Chicago: University of Chicago Press, 1958), 240. Arendt elsewhere acknowledges that the cumulative effect of "commonplace" offenses can constitute enormous evil. See her *Eichmann in Jerusalem: A Report on the Banality of Evil*, rev. ed. (New York: Penguin Books, 1965).

[5]Arendt, *Human Condition*, 240.

ations.[6] Yet the consistent probing of the possibility and the meaning of forgiveness—in the face of the "unforgivable"—that has followed the experience of the Holocaust is unparalleled, and it serves as a challenge to any other efforts at understanding human forgiveness. A close rendering of this analysis, with a stark joining of its issues, is dramatically portrayed in the writings of two French philosophers, Vladimir Jankélévitch (1903–1985) and Jacques Derrida (1930–2004), both of whom were Jewish. Jankélévitch, at one point in his writings, argues for the view that the Shoah was an *inexpiable* crime—that is, irreparable, irremediable, and on a human scale unforgivable. With this sort of crime, "One cannot punish the criminal with a punishment proportionate to his crime. . . . The penalty [therefore] becomes indifferent; what happens is literally *inexpiable.*"[7] This is why, Jankélévitch maintains, the human history of forgiveness has ended, for "forgiveness died in the death camps."[8] Jacques Derrida cautiously questions this view, but he also embraces the notion of "unforgivable" sin as central to an understanding of forgiveness.[9]

Both Jankélévitch and Derrida identify "crimes against humanity" as

---

[6]In addition to well-known claims that widespread oppression and killing are in themselves unforgivable crimes against humanity, contemporary psychological studies conclude that what counts as "unforgivable" is not only context-relative, but relative to the particular experiences of individuals—and the level of their traumatization. Practically speaking, an injury is "unforgivable" when it assaults the very worldview, fundamental belief systems, of the victim. See Beverly Flanagan, "Forgivers and the Unforgivable," in *Exploring Forgiveness*, ed. Robert D. Enright and Joanna North (Madison: University of Wisconsin Press, 1998), 95–105. For significant theological background to interpretations of such experiences, see Gene Outka, "On Harming Others," *Interpretation* 34 (October 1980): 381–93; and Jennifer Erin Beste, *God and the Victim: Traumatic Intrusions on Grace and Freedom* (Oxford: Oxford University Press, 2007).

[7]Jankélévitch, "Shall We Pardon Them?" trans. Ann Hobart, in *Critical Inquiry* 22 (Spring 1996): 558; also cited in Jacques Derrida, "To Forgive: The Unforgivable and the Imprescriptible," in John D. Caputo, Mark Dooley, and Michael Scanlon, eds., *Questioning God* (Bloomington: Indiana University Press, 2001), 30.

[8]Jankélévitch, "Shall We Pardon Them?," 567; originally in Jankélévitch, *L'imprescriptible: Pardonner? Dans l'honneur et la dignité* (Paris: Seuil, 1986). Jankélévitch offers a different view in an earlier work, *Forgiveness*, trans. Andrew Kelley (Chicago: University of Chicago Press, 2005; originally published as *Le Pardon* [Paris: Aubier-Montaigne, 1967]). As Derrida later points out, these two works are inconsistent, since *Le Pardon* does allow forgiveness of the otherwise unforgivable crimes in the Holocaust on the condition that forgiveness is at least asked for by the perpetrators and appropriate remorse is exhibited. Derrida also notes that at the end of his life Jankélévitch acknowledged that perhaps the history of forgiveness did not have to end with the Holocaust (a statement occasioned by correspondence with a young German who did, in effect, ask for forgiveness). Even then, however, Jankélévitch said of himself that it was too late for him to forgive. See Derrida, "To Forgive," 38–41.

[9]Derrida, "To Forgive," 21–51.

in some sense "unforgivable." Both consider these crimes to be not just against one's political or ideological enemies, but crimes against what makes humans "human." They are crimes so massive, so monstrous, that they cross the line of radical evil.[10] They aim at the destruction of not only the human body but the human spirit. Their motivation is the conviction that the object of their attacks has no right to be "human" or treated as human. In the Holocaust these were attacks against the very *existence* of Jews (or gypsies or homosexuals or any despised minorities) as "human." Such crimes say, "We do not want you to *be*." For Jankélévich, in the face of this kind of assault, forgiveness is impossible. For Derrida, crimes like these, precisely as "unforgivable," reveal the deepest core of the concept of forgiveness: an impossible possibility.

Derrida searches for a conceptual genealogy of forgiveness in the "heritage" of Western concepts and practices of forgiveness, based largely in the traditions of the Abrahamic religions (especially Judaism and Christianity) and in the philosophies and judicial systems they have helped to shape. He concludes that this inheritance is permeated with a view of forgiveness as something that must be earned and deserved. Although in this "heritage," forgiveness is considered a free "gift" from God, when it is exercised by humans it is nonetheless practiced and therefore continually conceptualized as "conditional." Only those can be forgiven who become worthy of forgiveness by fulfilling, at a bare minimum, certain conditions: (1) acknowledgment of fault, (2) reasonable repentance and remorse, (3) request for forgiveness, (4) expression of intent to transform their behavior, and (5) some effort at reparation.[11] Such conditionality, Derrida maintains, is in profound tension with the "unconditionality" of forgiveness that also belongs to the traditions but transcends their history. The tension between unconditionality and conditionality is analogous, he suggests, to the tension between justice and the law.

Thus, on Derrida's interpretation there is in the "heritage" a conditional imperative, proportioned to expected requirements. But there

---

[10]"Radical evil" in the sense in which Jankélévitch and Derrida intend it is not to be equated with the use of the term in, for example, Kant, for whom "radical" refers to the "root" of all moral evil, not to its "monstrosity." See Immanuel Kant, *Religion within the Limits of Reason Alone*, trans. Theodore M. Greene and Hoyt H. Hudson (New York: Harper Torchbooks, 1960), 1:15–39.

[11]These are readily recognizable as conditions incorporated in some Christian traditions of "confession," or the "Sacrament of Reconciliation." They are also visible in many Western legal and judicial processes.

is also an unconditional imperative, a "pure" concept of forgiveness that stabilizes its essential core. The latter is revealed particularly in forgiveness of the "unforgivable," forgiveness offered to the guilty as guilty—a core that must be in every act of "true" forgiveness, even though it is hidden by and within a complex web of historical conditions. The rationale of this core in human forgiveness is grounded not in the virtue of the one who forgives, nor in the offender's fulfillment of conditions, but in the sacredness at the heart of the human, even at the heart of the human wrongdoer[12]—that same sacredness that crimes against humanity aim to destroy. This dual imperative—conditional and unconditional—is not finally contradictory, though it must deal with what appear to be contradictions, or at least aporias, and ongoing tremendous tensions.[13] Yet it alone, with its two sides, can sustain both the concept of forgiveness and its power to restore human relationships in concrete historical contexts.

What makes Derrida dissatisfied with the conditional imperative is his profound suspicion that conditional forgiveness slides all too frequently into an economic exchange—corrupted by calculation, bargaining, and negotiation ("if you agree to this, I will agree to that"). When forgiveness is wholly based on the fulfillment of conditions, it is easy to "forgive," the power of forgiveness having been trivialized and dissipated. That is, the guilt of the guilty is so mitigated by agreed-upon conditions that there is little left to forgive. There is nothing that requires or even fosters conversion of heart. In the end, then, there is nothing about conditional forgiveness that is, by itself, true forgiveness.

For Derrida, the unforgivable, the inexpiable, is what really needs unconditional forgiving. Like a "gift," unconditional forgiveness is given without strings attached. It appears at the center of the meaning of forgiveness as "a force, a desire, an impetus, a movement, an appeal (call it what you will) that demands that forgiveness be granted, if it can be, even to someone who does not ask for it, who does not repent or confess or improve or redeem himself."[14] But the two imperatives, unconditional and conditional, must be held together, neither one

---

[12]Derrida, "On Forgiveness," in *On Cosmopolitanism and Forgiveness*, trans. Mark Dooley and Michael Hughes (New York: Routledge, 2001), 27–60.

[13]Very rarely does Derrida refer to the duality of these two moral imperatives as "paradoxical." He does so, though somewhat indirectly, in "To Forgive," 30.

[14]Ibid., 28.

reducible to the other nor dissociated from the other. Insofar as this can be done, the core unconditional imperative will help to anchor the conditional imperative so that forgiveness remains forgiveness all the while it is inscribing itself in the political, legal, and religious structures of human history.[15] We must see if these kinds of understandings of forgiveness have any heuristic value for understanding Christian forgiveness in the context of Christian love.

Christian Love and Forgiveness

I began this essay with a twofold claim: that there is no Christian forgiveness without love, and that the imperative to love that is central to the Christian life includes an imperative to forgive. I also averred at the start that Christian understandings of forgiveness include and depend upon insights into the relationship between human forgiveness and divine. My aim now is to place these claims within a pattern of Christian beliefs that may render them more accessible to the questions of forgiveness that have become urgent today,[16] and then to press issues particular to Christians regarding the meaning, possibility, and norms of human forgiveness. Although I use the term "pattern," and even "stages," my focus is not necessarily on temporal sequence but on the layers of meaning in the experience of Christian love and the forgiveness that can be within it.

Creative Love

The pattern I have in mind does not begin with divine or human forgiveness. It begins with God's creative love. No matter how strongly Christian theologies may emphasize the profound need of humans for "justification," for forgiveness and redemption from their sins, for rec-

---

[15]Ibid. Derrida refers to this as a "hyperbolic ethics," or "ethics beyond ethics," a concept that Jankélévitch had also introduced in his first major work on forgiveness, *Le Pardon*, but moved away from in "Shall We Pardon Them?"

[16]My articulation of this pattern needs here to be extremely brief, hence drastically elliptical. It therefore risks serious challenges not only to its details but to the pattern as such. Nonetheless, it is necessary to attempt something, however brief, that situates stages of love, command, divine forgiveness, and human forgiveness in a way that the meaning of the last is tied to and held within the meaning of the previous three. Thus will the connection between Christian love and forgiveness be relevant to my claims about forgiveness.

onciliation with God and with one another, all of this depends on and implicitly incorporates the first part of the pattern—that is, God's initial (and eternal) decision to share God's own "being" with utterly new entities that we call "creatures." As Karl Rahner suggested near the end of his theologizing and his life, "A Christian theologian is not prevented from thinking that the theme of human sinfulness and forgiveness of guilt through pure grace is, in a certain sense, somewhat secondary compared to the theme of God's radical *self*-communication."[17] It is God's giving of existence, bringing *ex nihilo* into being, and sustaining in creative love, not more Being but more beings, that constitutes the first and ongoing movement of all that follows. More specifically, among God's creatures humans receive a gift of existence that includes the possibility of knowing and being-known, loving and being-loved, by God who offers to them a direct and intimate share—a "personal" share—in God's own life and love. This in a sense holds the whole gift of God, the "pure grace" that helps us to understand the importance of all grace as it continually unfolds.

Commanded Love

Out of God's creative love comes the command to human persons to love God with their whole heart and soul and mind and strength, and to love one another as they love themselves.[18] Neighbor-love is to be universal in scope and in its unexceptionable regard for the dignity of each individual. The command to such love is an obligating imperative but also a liberating call, since it accords with and calls forth what is at the heart of the "human." The dual command to love God and neighbor is ultimately able to be experienced by humans as an imperative, a call, and an inner yearning toward "other-centered" love. This is the love whereby a human person at least wants, desires, to center her being and

---

[17]Karl Rahner, "Experiences of a Catholic Theologian," in *The Cambridge Companion to Karl Rahner*, ed. Declan Marmion and Mary E. Hines (New York: Cambridge University Press, 2005), 303.

[18]It is not possible here to clarify adequately the relationships among these loves (for God, self, and neighbor), although understanding them is crucial to discerning the moral questions they entail. Here the work of Gene Outka offers stunningly comprehensive and profound analyses and insights. See especially Outka, *Agape* (New Haven, CT: Yale University Press, 1972); and Outka, "Universal Love and Impartiality," in *The Love Commandments: Essays in Christian Ethics and Moral Philosophy*, ed. Edmund N. Santurri and William Werpehowski (Washington, DC: Georgetown University Press, 1992), 1–103.

action in relation to God above all else, and love whereby she wants to love other persons and all creation in a way that is integral with her love for God. God's own creative and inviting love awakens the possibility in humans of a responding love—not only as an intellectual affirmation of the good that the Creator *is* and the good that the created can *become*, but as an affective affirmation that is also a *unio affectus*, a union with and dwelling in what is loved, both Creator and created.

Forgiving Love

However, humans also experience within themselves resistance to God's command and appeal. Within humans, individually and together, are multiple barriers, conflicting yearnings, that prevent harmonious responses. The context of their lives and the order in their hearts appear broken in significant respects. Call it (literally or metaphorically) a catastrophic "fall" from an original set of capabilities for true and just love; or an evolutionary struggle to learn to love; or social malformations that perpetuate themselves from one generation to another; or let it be too obscure to name at all, except as the mystery of human freedom in the face of the mystery of the "human condition." Whatever characterizes the situation, humans have been estranged from God, from one another, and from their own selves. And some form of responsibility for this appears to attach to all humans, since all are both free (even if in "bondage") and estranged.

Yet God's creative and sustaining love continues. Like God's free decision to create out of love, so does this same love modulate into a love of compassionate forgiveness. On God's part, it is still infinite love, still pure grace, in presence and action, dwelling by *unio affectus* in and with humans. This eternally forgiving love is enacted and revealed in and through the life, death, and resurrection of Jesus Christ. God "has delivered us from the dominion of darkness and transformed us to the kingdom of God's beloved Son, in whom we have redemption, the forgiveness of sins" (Col. 1:13–14). The almost unbelievable good news for all humans is that "in him all the fullness of God was pleased to dwell, and through him to reconcile to himself all things, whether on earth or in heaven, making peace by the blood of his cross" (Col. 1:19–20).[19]

---

[19]I am rendering these beliefs in Christian terms, though I do not exclude ways of ar-

There is here no room for Christian theologies about a wrathful father-god exacting blood sacrifice from his son, and no room for preoccupation only with death.[20] There is only room for a story of forgiving love. Within the life, suffering, death, and resurrection of Jesus Christ, the reality and meaning of the cross are not finally suffering and death, but a relationship that holds; love and forgiving love hold. The relationship between Jesus and God forever holds; within this, the relationship between God and humanity is forever restored, and it holds. Whatever the forces of evil against him, the utter love in Jesus' heart was not plucked out, not damaged or changed—neither his love for the God he called Abba, nor the love he embodied and revealed from God for all humans, nor the love he made forever newly possible among humans. A covenant was eternally sealed, a love crucified but not destroyed. And it is this love that has lived and poured out life and love and forgiveness ever since. From here on, human struggles for just and truthful loves, and just and truthful forgiveness, continue; but the conditions for their possibility are now in place.

Missioned Forgiveness

In the Gospel attributed to John, we find the postresurrection Jesus meeting with his disciples, greeting them with peace, showing them the scars from his wounds, breathing his Spirit upon them, and giving them a mission of forgiveness (John 20:19–23). As some theologians have argued (though not necessarily commenting on this particular text), the message of forgiveness encompasses in a sense the Christian message in its entirety. It is the decisive gift of the Holy Spirit.[21] For Christians, it is what makes possible a "new heart," dying and living with Jesus Christ, partaking of God's own being and life, restoring relationships otherwise without hope. Christians are taught to ask for it every day: "Forgive us our sins, as we forgive those who sin against us." It reaches to communities as well as individuals. It is to be offered

---

ticulating a central part of their meaning in other terms, by those whose lives, situations, and traditions have been revelatory in other symbols and terms.

[20]For a telling critique and reconstruction of the Christian doctrine of atonement, see Martha Schull Gilliss, "Resurrecting the Atonement," in *Feminist and Womanist Essays in Reformed Dogmatics*, ed. Amy Plantinga Pauw and Serene Jones (Louisville, KY: Westminster John Knox Press, 2006), 125–38.

[21]See, for example, Walter Kasper, "The Church as a Place of Forgiveness," *Communio* 16 (Summer 1989): 162.

to all who desire to drink of the waters of the Spirit, to all who desire to come to the table of the Lord. The mission, then, is to forgive, and to reveal the forgiveness of God, in and through Jesus Christ.

Moreover, this is a mission not given only to a designated few but to all who share in the gift of the Spirit, all who gather to receive God's mercy along with the mission to reveal it to others. As Paul proclaims, "So if anyone is in Christ, there is a new creation. . . . All this is from God, who reconciled us to himself through Christ, and has given us the ministry of reconciliation. . . . So we are ambassadors for Christ, since God is making God's appeal through us" (2 Cor. 5:17–20).

The mission of forgiveness as Christians have understood it since Paul's ministry to the gentiles goes out to all humans—to neighbors near and far, even to neighbors who are enemies. As a reconciling mission it incorporates the call to respond to God's creative love, hear God's commandments to love, accept God's forgiving love, and make visible the new forgiveness offered by Jesus Christ. It is therefore a mission informed by a universalist love, aimed at reconciliation, forged in the hope of new relationship with God and among all human persons. Yet forgiveness is a complex concept (as we have seen), and the concept of Christian forgiveness bears further analysis. In particular, issues of context, conditionality or unconditionality, and relationship to justice are, in our efforts to understand this form of forgiveness, neither trivial nor moot. A biblical query may sharpen or intensify some of these issues and perhaps even the nature of the mission.

Forgive them: In the Fourth Gospel, the words recorded of Jesus when he gives the mission of forgiveness to his disciples are these: "As the Father has sent me, so I send you. . . . Receive the Holy Spirit. If you forgive the sins of any, they are forgiven them; if you retain the sins of any, they are retained" (John 20:21–23). This text has sometimes been interpreted, and often popularly understood by Christians, to refer to the granting of authority to judge, and out of this the power to forgive or not, to open the gates of heaven or to keep them closed. Sometimes it is put together with Matthew 16:18–20: "On this rock I will build my church. . . . I will give you the keys of the kingdom of heaven, and whatever you bind on earth will be bound in heaven, and whatever you loose on earth will be loosed in heaven." Together the texts have been thought by many to establish not only authority to judge on the part of the disciples of Jesus, but beyond this also a structure for authority in the Christian community that followed.

But what if there is another meaning to this text in the Gospel attributed to John? It is after all not like Matthew 16, where there is reference apparently to technical rabbinic procedures. And the situation is very different—with now the risen Christ commissioning his disciples to carry on his own ministry of forgiveness. What, then, if the primary meaning of the text is not that the disciples of Jesus, and the Christian community, are to sit in judgment on individuals and groups, but that they are to *forgive* and thereby to *free* people, and if they do not do so, the word of God is somehow blocked, left silent? What if the force of the mission is this: "If you forgive them, they are forgiven and freed; but if you do not forgive them, they remain bound. So then, *forgive* them, because if you do not, they will remain bound and unfree."

But can such an interpretation hold? Is this indeed the truth that Jesus said the Spirit would teach in his name, reminding his followers of all he had said? Jesus himself, after all, did make judgments; he did not offer instant forgiveness to all. Yet those he judged and challenged seem to have been only the self-righteous, those whose hearts were hardened with their own self-assurance, those who recognized no need to drink of new waters or ask for greater mercy. Others—so many great sinners—Jesus did not examine for the worthiness or perfection of their repentance; he simply forgave them when they approached him. He rejected no one—not tax collectors and not adulterers; not Peter, who had his troubles; not James and John who needed a long time to learn humility; not any of those who betrayed him; not even Judas, with whom he shared a life and a table (and who today may shine in heaven as a blazing testimony to the power of a forgiven love).

It is difficult not to hear in Matthew's Gospel the multitude of "judgment" texts.[22] Yet these have more to do with judgment as a dramatic preliminary to entering the reign of God than they do with Jesus' own mode of judging. And it is Matthew who reports Jesus' response to his critics (those who questioned his eating with tax collectors and "sinners"): "Go and learn what this means: 'I desire mercy, not sacrifice.' For I have come to call not the righteous but sinners" (Matt. 9:13). John's Gospel has little about judging, although judgment takes

---

[22]On one count, there are sixty pericopes regarding judgment in the Gospel of Matthew. See Thomas W. Buckley, *Seventy Times Seven: Sin, Judgment, and Forgiveness in Matthew* (Collegeville, MN: Liturgical Press, 1991), 17.

place in some circumstances simply because Jesus is present. Luke is clearly more concerned with forgiveness than judgment. As part of the Sermon on the Plain, Luke has Jesus listing all the ways in which God is merciful, and bidding his hearers to imitate God: "Be merciful, just as your Father is merciful" (Luke 6:36). And Jesus follows this with, "Do not judge, and you will not be judged; do not condemn, and you will not be condemned. Forgive, and you will be forgiven." (Luke 6:37–38; also Matt. 7:1–2). Beyond even this form of conditionality, and in the context of describing Jesus' mission of forgiveness, Paul proclaims, "In Christ God was reconciling the world to himself, *not counting their trespasses against them*, and entrusting the message of reconciliation to us" (1 Cor. 5:19, emphasis added).

Many texts in the Gospels and in the writings of Paul could be gathered to show either that Jesus came to forgive and not to judge, or that Jesus took the matter of judgment extremely seriously. Moreover, in many cases, one and the same text can be interpreted both ways. I am not so much interested, however, in once and for all adjudicating the importance of judgment as part of forgiveness versus the importance of forgiveness offered seemingly without judgment.[23] Clearly anyone who forgives another must have some knowledge of why forgiveness is relevant and needed—some knowledge and assessment, therefore, of the wrongdoing that is being forgiven. But just as clearly, when "judgment" becomes an overall "judgmentalism," it drains the meaning of forgiveness, obscuring the potential for the freeing of others from the burden of their offenses and dissipating the power of forgiveness for the restoration of relationships. Hence, my ultimate point here is that the mission of forgiveness—the mission given through the power of Jesus' Spirit to those who follow him—is a mission of forgiveness more than it is one of judgment.

No doubt it is the social as well as individual context that ought to determine to some extent where emphases should be placed. In a world marked by conflict and fear, by violence and hatred, the message of forgiveness will hold judgment and forgiveness together—in

---

[23]I clearly take a different view, however, from those who make blame, judgment, and condemnation essential and even central to both the secular and Christian notions of forgiveness, as, for example, Miroslav Volf appears to do. See Volf, *Free of Charge*, chap. 2. Nor do I suggest that it is only Christians who can free one another and others from guilt or fear or ignorance. I am trying both to broaden the call to forgive and to find in it a fuller meaning than the conditionality that Derrida thought so inadequate.

part prophetic against perpetrators of harm, in part offering a "new creation" because of the ministry of forgiveness. Among people oppressed and dominated, the message will refuse to "break the bruised reed" by burdening it too much with judgment. But when spoken to the powerful, if they care little for the poor and the marginalized, the message may come like lightning, striking the hearts of the agents of misery. At the same time, the message may give light to those who struggle for justice, and offer hope in forgiveness even to those who have caused the injustice.

What does all of this mean for the significance of forgiveness in our world? Can experiences of forgiveness really bear witness to a ministry of forgiveness—given by God in Jesus Christ and empowered by the Spirit? This is too large a question to be resolved here, but it suggests preliminary questions to be addressed in furthering our understanding of forgiveness. The first of these is about our experiences of forgiveness—both of being-forgiven and forgiving—and the insights they suggest. What, for example, "happens" when forgiveness is either given or received?

Meanings of Forgiveness

Human persons experience forgiveness, or the need for forgiveness, in many ways. Whether we are harmed by or we have harmed another, our interest in forgiveness depends on how much we care about the other, about our own selves, about the relationship that has been damaged or lost. It is easy to understand the necessity and the role of forgiving when treasured personal relationships are at stake. We reach out to the one we love, participating in the restoration of the bond between us, by hoping for forgiveness, by offering forgiveness. Or at the very least, we wait patiently, holding on to the love and the hope that the relationship represents. In either case, our experience is different from simply despairing of any possibility of healing the breach—worn out from our trying or our waiting, taking a realistic view of what is impossible, or walking away in anger or disgust, shame or fear, irritation and indifference. But if restoration of the relationship and loving affirmation of the beloved "other" are what we want, what do we do when we "forgive," and what happens to us and what do we do when we are "forgiven"?

When the situation is not one of person-to-person, individual-to-individual forgiveness, how do we comprehend the necessity or possibility or even strategy for forgiving? Despite many thinkers' insistence that forgiveness can take place only between singular individuals, it is possible between individuals and groups, or even between one group and another. After all, in this era of forgiveness, it is not unusual for heads of state, leaders of world religions, owners of companies, to *ask for* forgiveness from institutions and whole populations, as well as from the individuals within them. It is perhaps not so usual for individuals to *offer* forgiveness to larger entities, but it seems thinkable at least. So, when we are harmed by or we harm an institution or a group, what can forgiveness mean at all? What would we be doing in such situations if we either forgave or were ourselves forgiven? Perhaps at its core, forgiveness is the same whether offered to or received from individuals or groups.[24]

A descriptive analysis of the experience of forgiveness yields something like the following. To forgive is above all not to be passive in the face of injury, betrayal, persecution, abuse. Forgiveness may, in fact, be one of the most active responses possible in the face of whatever sort of breach occurs in human relationships. It is linguistically a "performative"—an utterance or gesture that signifies an action that accomplishes or at least aims to accomplish something. Moreover, to forgive is a complex action, for it is a choice to act in a certain way in regard to one's own self as well as in regard to the recipient of one's forgiveness. Put simply, forgiveness is a decision to "let go" of something within one's self, and to "accept" anew the one by whom we have been harmed. But what do we "let go" of? In regard to ourselves, we do not (and ought not) let go of our sense of justice, nor a sense of our own dignity as a person (I shall return to this particular issue shortly). Yet in forgiving another, we do let go (at least partially) of something *in* ourselves—perhaps anger, a desire to win in some conflict, resentment, perhaps building-blocks of stored-up pain. And we let go (at least partially) of something *of* ourselves—perhaps our self-protectedness, our selves as desiring renewed self-statement in the face of misjudgment or exploitation by another. We choose to "accept"

---

[24]Although there are a growing number of excellent theories regarding the place of forgiveness in political and social life, the one that combines Christian and secular ethics most effectively is Donald W. Shriver's *An Ethic for Enemies*. The relevance of collective forgiveness to individual forgiveness is indicated in his insistence that "our teachers have to be the victims" (67).

the other once again, to affectively sustain and renew our loving affirmation of the other, to be again in *unio affectus* with the other by whom we have been wronged and to whom we offer our forgiveness.

To fathom our experiences of forgiving—whether by gaining insight into our reasons to forgive or into the elements of the experience itself—it is useful to consider also our experiences of being-forgiven. Being-forgiven, like forgiving, involves action, in this case by the recipient of forgiveness. The action is again complex, including both "acceptance" and "letting go." If anything is actually going to "happen" in response to the offer of forgiveness, the one who can be-forgiven must choose to receive the offer and to accept the one who offers. There can be no being-forgiven without this. The form of acceptance involved is acceptance of the "word" of the one forgiving, believing in the genuineness of the intention to forgive. In the recipient it requires a "letting go" not only of shame and all that it might entail, but also of the objections and fears that may arise in the one to-be-forgiven. Since the full efficacy of forgiveness has to do with relationship, it will not "take," it cannot accomplish its purpose, unless it is actively received. When we recognize our own responsibility for injuring another, marring a relationship, losing what we treasured in the other and in our way of being with the other, we are afraid of the future that we had taken for granted and in which we had hoped. To experience being-forgiven, then, is to experience being-accepted and affectively affirmed, in spite of ourselves. To repeat: Accepting forgiveness is an action on our part—not just a passive forgetting of our offense, but a choice to accept being-forgiven. It generates relief in the recipient, but more than this, joy and gratitude that his or her failure has not finally broken the bonds of friendship, colleagueship, or family. The greater the infraction and the realization of its gravity, the greater the possibility of gratitude and a new or renewed love in response. One who has been forgiven much, as Jesus observed, loves more than one who has been forgiven only a little (Luke 7:41–47); or at least that is the possibility opened to us when we are indeed forgiven.

Although we learn what it means to be-forgiven within human relationships, the potentially paradigmatic experience for humans is the experience of being-forgiven by God. To experience the forgiveness of God is to experience one's self accepted by the incomprehensible source of one's existence and life, accepted even without becoming wholly innocent, without being completely turned around in one's ways; accepted even "while we still were sinners" (Rom. 5:8). Some human persons in history (persons like Paul, Augustine, Martin Luther) bear witness to this out of their own overwhelming experience of divine forgiveness. They testify, too, to their need to respond—in acceptance, letting go of their doubts and objections, actively surrendering to unconditional forgiveness and love. They call their responses trust, or faith, or gratitude, or love. Others whose life stories are less dramatic or well known report similar experiences of forgiveness and response. Still others hope in such grace, and if they are poets, they sometimes give us language for our own understanding. The often wry and ever-enigmatic Emily Dickinson is among the latter, speculating about another world but translating her language into this one, foreshadowing an ultimate experience of which she has only inklings—receiving and accepting eternal Acceptance:

> I think just how my shape will rise—
> When I shall be *"forgiven"*—
> Till Hair—and Eyes—and timid Head—
> Are *out of sight*—in Heaven—
>
> I think just how my lips will weigh—
> With shapeless—quivering—prayer—
> That you—*so late*—*"Consider" me*—
> The *"Sparrow" of your Care*—
>
> I mind me of that Anguish—sent—
> *Some* drifts were moved away—
> Before my simple bosom—broke—
> And why not *this*—*if they?*
>
> And so I con that thing—*"forgiven"*—
> Until—delirious—borne—
> By my long bright—and *longer*—*trust*
> I *drop* my Heart—*unshriven!*[25]

---

[25]Emily Dickinson, in *The Complete Poems of Emily Dickinson*, ed. Thomas H. Johnson (Boston: Little, Brown and Company, 1987), no. 237, italics in original text. Dickinson, of course, always found a profound ambiguity in the mystery of God, yet sustained a deep belief in the reality of God. I take this poem to express a profound trust in God, even without explicit "forgiveness." Biographers suggest that whatever "scandal" lurked

Others, like philosophers Jankélévitch and Derrida, appear to have hints not only of the need for divine forgiveness—for sins that cannot be forgiven "in this world" or offenses that are "on a human scale unforgivable." They also search for an understanding of "unconditional" forgiveness that may be possible only from God. If, for example, Derrida's concept of unconditional forgiveness (which is not unlike what can be found in Jankélévitch's writing before him) resonates anywhere, it ought to resonate here. In Dickinson's rhetorical interpretation, there is a kind of "pure" forgiveness, not a deal-maker, not one that lessens the force, desire, impetus, movement, appeal "that forgiveness be granted." It is unconditional, uncompromised by any form of negotiation, or anything else except God's desire and decision to forgive—individuals as well as whole peoples. It is, in alternate language, wholly other-centered even as it responds to human creatures God has made. The question of whether such unconditional other-centered forgiveness can be granted also by humans to humans may be lodged more fruitfully in the mysterious ways that Christians and others experience and understand, however obscurely, the willingness, decision, and desire of God to heal creation through the graced agency of God's creatures.

But when we turn back now to experiences of human forgiving and being-forgiven, it helps to ponder something like a "dropping of the heart" that is active surrender, letting go of, whatever would bind us to past injuries inflicted on us by others, or whatever would prevent our acceptance of the new life held out to us in the forgiveness of those we have injured. In both there is a letting go of our very selves, a kenosis, that alone frees us to become ourselves; and there is an acceptance, an affective affirmation and *unio affectus*, of the one to be forgiven and the one who forgives. "Dropping our hearts," surrendering our selves, in forgiveness or in trust of being-forgiven, is the beginning choice that makes renewed relationships possible. It comes full circle in the mutuality that restored relationships promise.

One more question remains to be attended to, however, in our "preliminary" questions of forgiveness. It has been framed frequently thus: What if those who injure us continue to injure us? Whether knowing or not knowing "what they do," what if there is no regret

---

in her life at some point, she did not regret her choices, but believed that she was a child, a "sparrow" of God, who loved as she could love.

or remorse, no willingness or ability to accept our forgiveness? What if the perpetrators of oppression believe their actions are justified— by whatever twisted stereotyping, judging, stigmatizing? There are, of course, countless situations like these in which injury is ongoing; abuse, violence, and exploitation do not stop. How, then, is forgiveness possible, and what would be its point? How shall we forgive in the context of the new killing fields of the century, this era's tangled webs of enslavement and new levels of destitution? In regard to *current* oppressors, must our focus be not on forgiveness, but on justice? Not on "dropping our hearts," but on a struggle against the evils that cry out to heaven for change?

The challenge in each of these questions is not to be taken lightly. I want to argue, however, that even in situations where injustices prevail, where the rights of individuals and groups continue to be violated, the disposition in the heart of the oppressed and violated (as well as those who stand in solidarity with them) ought to include (insofar as this is possible[26]) forgiveness. Or more precisely, it ought to include a "readiness" to forgive. To argue this in no way contradicts a need for resistance—against exploitation, abuse, or whatever threat there is to the human physical, relational, or moral integrity of others. If we think that forgiveness all by itself is a sufficient antidote to injustice, this is a mistake. But if we think that struggles for justice are sufficient, no matter what is in our hearts, this, too, is a mistake. The challenge and the call to forgiveness in situations of ongoing humanly inflicted evil and suffering are a call to forgive even those we must continue to resist. Forgiveness in such situations is what I call "anticipatory" forgiveness.

Anticipatory Forgiveness: The Greatest Challenge of All?

Forgiving and being-forgiven have nothing to do with tolerating grave wrongs, or (as I indicated earlier) with being passive in the face of massive (or even small) injustices. Neither the forgiveness offered by God in Jesus Christ, nor the forgiveness that can be a graced and

---

[26]"Ought" may be too strong a term here. By using it, I do not want to impose yet another burden on those who suffer under ongoing oppression of whatever kind. I simply mean that it is an appropriate disposition, one that can be freeing and strengthening, even under these circumstances. And there is the matter of the second love commandment, which I have been at least suggesting up to now can include an obligation to forgive. I do not want to back away from this. Yet I acknowledge fully that every obligation is tempered, and may even be waived, according to capacity and circumstance.

glorious human action, is to be equated with "premature reconciliation" or a covering over of exploitation and ongoing violence, large or small. Christian and even human forgiveness can include a radical "No!" to the world as a place of injurious conflict, gross injustice, and needless destruction. Indeed, forgiveness, and a Christian obligation to forgiveness, can require that we resist the forces of evil until we can do no more. Nevertheless, an attitude of forgiveness, the disposition of heart required for forgiving and being-forgiven, does entail that we not return lies for lies, violence for violence, domination as a supposed remedy for domination. In relation to such evils, a stance of forgiveness can mean "Never again!"

Anticipatory forgiveness shares the characteristics of any human forgiving. That is, it involves a letting go within one's self of whatever prevents a fundamental acceptance of the other, despite the fact that the other is the cause of one's injuries. It is grounded in a basic respect for the other as a person, for what Derrida calls the "sacredness at the heart of the human." For Christians, it can be explicitly grounded, too, in love for the other as held in being and forgiven by God. It does not mean blinding oneself to the evil that is done to oneself or to others. It does not mean passive acquiescence or silence when it comes to naming the injury that is imposed, or the perpetrator of the injury. It does not mean failing to protect victims or to struggle with all one's might to prevent the "breaking of the bruised reed." It does mean being ready to accept the injurer, yearning that he or she turn in sorrow to whoever has been injured; it means waiting until the time that the enemy may yet become a friend. It is "anticipatory" not because there is as yet no disposition for acceptance and love, but because it cannot be fulfilled until the one who is forgiven (the perpetrator) acknowledges the injury and becomes able to recognize and accept, in turn, a forgiving embrace. This is not to make anticipatory forgiveness "conditional"; on the contrary, anticipatory forgiveness comes closer to "unconditional" forgiveness than most forms of human forgiveness. It can be truly other-centered, though until it is received by the other, it cannot as forgiveness be finally fulfilled.

Perhaps nowhere is the challenge and call to anticipatory forgiveness more clearly issued to Christians than in the community of the church. It is here that the moral imperative comes forth to love one's enemies. It is here that grace should be passed from one to the other, making possible the melting of hearts and the acceptance of friend and enemy, neighbor and stranger alike. It is here that Christians are marked by the encomium, "See how they love one another." It is here where Christians can learn of the model of God's anticipatory as well as infinitely actual love and forgiveness—whether as expressed in the parable of the "Prodigal Son" (or "Merciful Father") where the son is awaited and greeted with open arms, seemingly without judgment, seemingly with only yearning desire for the son's return; or as depicted in the story of salvation historically enacted in the forgiveness of Jesus Christ, which holds out for our recognition and acceptance the forgiveness of God.

It may be that forgiveness, the very possibility of forgiveness, dies in countless human assaults on individuals and groups within countless human relationships. Yet it remains, or can remain, at least for some, a matter of hope. It could have been that forgiveness died in the death camps of Germany or on the slaughtering hills of Rwanda. But it did not, at least not for everyone—although its power for holding human lives together was shattered, crucified, in such terrible ways. Rather than the end of the history of forgiveness, contemporary crimes (great or small) against humanity may have—as Derrida suggested and Jankélévitch finally agreed might be the case—brought unprecedented urgency to its possible new beginnings.

Index